The Queen
and Her Presidents

ALSO BY SUSAN PAGE

The Rulebreaker: The Life and Times of Barbara Walters

Madam Speaker: Nancy Pelosi and the Lessons of Power

The Matriarch: Barbara Bush and the Making of an American Dynasty

The Queen
and Her Presidents

The Hidden Hand That Shaped History

SUSAN PAGE

HARPER

An Imprint of HarperCollins*Publishers*

Without limiting the exclusive rights of any author, contributor or the publisher of this publication, any unauthorized use of this publication to train generative artificial intelligence (AI) technologies is expressly prohibited. HarperCollins also exercise their rights under Article 4(3) of the Digital Single Market Directive 2019/790 and expressly reserve this publication from the text and data mining exception.

THE QUEEN AND HER PRESIDENTS. Copyright © 2026 by Susan Page. All rights reserved. No part of this book may be used or reproduced in any manner whatsoever without written permission except in the case of brief quotations embodied in critical articles and reviews. For information, address HarperCollins Publishers, 195 Broadway, New York, NY 10007. In Europe, HarperCollins Publishers, Macken House, 39/40 Mayor Street Upper, Dublin 1, D01 C9W8, Ireland.

HarperCollins books may be purchased for educational, business, or sales promotional use. For information, please email the Special Markets Department at SPsales@harpercollins.com.

hc.com

FIRST EDITION

Designed by Kyle O'Brien

Library of Congress Cataloging-in-Publication Data has been applied for.

ISBN 978-0-06-339739-2

Printed in the United States of America

26 27 28 29 30 LBC 5 4 3 2 1

To Marge and Big Bob

A sergeant major in the army air force's B-24 bomber group who served in England during World War II—as did Princess Elizabeth

Contents

Introduction | Her Father's Daughter — xi

Chapter One | "All Will Be Well" — 1

Chapter Two | Falling in Love — 15

Chapter Three | The Favorite Uncle — 34

Chapter Four | The Ambassador's Son — 59

Chapter Five | Nadir — 73

Chapter Six | Lifeline — 91

Chapter Seven | *West Wing* Meets *The Crown* — 110

Chapter Eight | The Kiss(-Off) — 124

Chapter Nine | Horses and Hollywood — 137

Chapter Ten | The Talking Hat — 164

Chapter Eleven | Hard Feelings — 181

Chapter Twelve | A Wink and a Nod — 201

Chapter Thirteen | Good Vibes — 218

Chapter Fourteen | The Favourite? — 240

Chapter Fifteen | Don't Tell His Mother	267
Chapter Sixteen | God Save the King	278
Epilogue | London's Bridge	284
Acknowledgments	291
Notes	293
Selected Bibliography	329
Index	335

The Queen
and Her Presidents

Introduction

Her Father's Daughter

The times were too precarious to worry about past grievances. The future Queen of England would never forget that lesson learned during these, the defining years of her life.

In 1939, a century and a half after General Charles Cornwallis surrendered to General George Washington at Yorktown, President Franklin D. Roosevelt and First Lady Eleanor Roosevelt invited King George VI and his wife to be the first royals to visit what the Crown had once regarded as rebel soil. The two nations needed each other as never before. The royal couple saw it as their duty to brush aside etiquette or personal danger to answer that call—a template, a model, for their beloved eldest daughter, Elizabeth, who was just thirteen years old. For the next eight decades, as she matured from a shy girl to one of the world's elder statesmen, her life would be set in place by the parents she revered and the two nations it would fall to her to help sustain—one her place of birth, the other its most important friend.

Even then, on the eve of another devastating conflagration, America's military conflicts with Great Britain were not all that distant a memory. The last American to take up arms against the British in the War of 1812, shoemaker Hiram Cronk, had died in 1905, the year Franklin and Eleanor were married. But the world had been transformed. The United States and Great Britain had fought together in World War I—the "Great War," with little thought that another would follow. Now Europe watched nervously as Adolf Hitler subverted German democracy and declared himself führer. By the time the king and queen arrived in Washington that summer, Hitler had annexed Austria and Czechoslovakia and set his sights on Poland. That invasion, British officials had made clear, would cause the United Kingdom to declare war on Germany.

Many Americans—taken by the once-and-future rallying cry of "America First"—seemed at best indifferent to Britain's struggle against the rising bellicosity of Nazi Germany. FDR hoped the youthful and engaging royals could counter those isolationist voices and win the hearts of Americans. The world had grown only more connected since the last war, Roosevelt knew, and England would soon need help from the United States again. One small irony: It was an earlier King George who had shattered the relationship between Britain and America, labeled a "tyrant" in the Declaration of Independence. Now his namesake would be called on to unite the two nations as never before.

The wartime king would help the American president and Britain's iconic prime minister, Winston Churchill, build a "special relationship" between their two nations. The term would defy definition yet somehow describe an enduring alliance. In the process, they also shaped the worldview of the future queen. After Elizabeth succeeded her father in 1952 and then outlived Churchill, she would for decades hold to the imperative to protect the two nations' ties, through times of both friction and common cause. "A living flag," said political scientist Joseph Nye.

This book is the story of that historic transformation, and the woman who would come to lead it. It began, as much of her life did, in the shadow of her father.

His Majesty, whose birth name was Albert and who was known to his family as "Bertie," was never meant to be king. A shy, awkward royal spare, as the second eldest was often called, he assumed the role after his suave older brother, Edward VIII, surrendered the throne to marry Wallis Simpson. She was an American and a double divorcée; there were those in the British establishment who weren't quite sure which attribute was worse. When George VI visited Roosevelt, he had been on the throne for less than three years. He still grappled with the perception, in the United States and at home, that he wasn't the "real" king. Americans had been particularly taken with the romance of Edward's decision to abdicate so he could wed, in his words, "the woman I love." The trip to America was part of an effort to reinforce George's reign as his own. His consort, also named Elizabeth, was warm, loyal, and blunt. From a robust Scottish noble family, she had a manner at odds with the traditionally frosty depiction of royalty. She was a fan of games, drinking, and the occasional witty riposte, as more than one president would discover. She was also brave. "What a woman!" Ambassador Joseph Kennedy would exclaim after she told him she was determined to travel to America, a potentially precarious journey on the eve of war. "Not to go would give satisfaction to the enemies," she explained.

The royal couple were honored at one formal dinner at the White House—in those days before air-conditioning, the queen said she had never been to a hotter place—and hosted the Roosevelts at another at the British embassy. Then the royal couple and their forty-person entourage traveled first to New York and then to Hyde Park. The Roosevelts' rustic home seventy miles north of the city offered a more relaxed setting and simpler fare. The images made a powerful impression around the world—not to mention on their daughter back in Buckingham Palace.

"A very extraordinary visit that had a great many facets to it because you had the feeling of what was happening over there at that time," Eleanor Roosevelt recalled in an interview published here for the first time. It was a "period of tension" for Britain and the world. The first lady caught a glimpse of the sense of unwavering commitment that defined George, a quality he would bequeath to his elder daughter. On an unseasonably blistering day, Eleanor and the king toured a Civilian Conservation Corps camp, one of FDR's New Deal programs launched during the Great Depression. "To reach the barracks we had to walk across an open field and it was just so hot!" she said. "The head of the camp said, 'Your Majesty, it is so warm. The boys have prepared their barracks and their mess hall, but they will understand if you feel it is too hot to walk across the field.' And his answer was: 'They expect us to go; of course we will go.' And we went."

Back at Hyde Park, on June 11, 1939, the picnic menu on the broad front porch of Top Cottage included hot dogs, an American delicacy unfamiliar to the royal palate, served on a silver tray. The historic visit was a smash in America, launching an enduring fascination with the British royal family. "King and Queen End US Visit After Eating Hot Dogs at Picnic" was the exuberant four-column headline stripped across the front page of *The Philadelphia Inquirer*. *The Miami News* published a front-page cartoon that showed an anthropomorphic hot dog tipping his "King Frank" crown at two royal visitors. The culinary encounter would be echoed decades later, when their daughter, slightly baffled, was served by another US president what she called "used beans." (They had been refried.)

Unknown to the public was the private bond that formed between the king and the president. Each had been tested in their roles by disability—FDR by paralysis from polio at age thirty-nine, George by a severe stutter from age eight that his father, King George V, ridiculed as a "defect." Perhaps the stress of his difficult childhood was one reason Bertie started chain-smoking when he was sixteen years old, a habit he continued until he died at age fifty-six of lung cancer.

When they left Hyde Park, the king and queen were touched by the spontaneous farewell from onlookers who had gathered at the village's small station. As the couple waved from the rear platform of the royal train, the crowd broke into "Auld Lang Syne," the affectionate farewell of old friends. "Good luck to you!" FDR shouted. "All the luck in the world!" They were headed to Canada's Maritime provinces for a brief visit before boarding the RMS *Empress of Britain* in Halifax, Nova Scotia, and sailing home to Southampton, to be reunited there with princesses Elizabeth and Margaret. The trip to America, Ambassador Kennedy would conclude, accomplished more for the legitimacy of George's reign than "ten years of faithful service in England would have done." On his return to London, the king felt so confident of American support that he contemplated launching a major peace initiative of his own, inviting Hitler, Stalin, and Mussolini to the palace to try to stave off war. But that was only a musing over lunch, soon overcome by catastrophic developments.

Three months later, Germany invaded Poland, and Great Britain declared war. The *Empress of Britain*, refitted for military duty against Germany, would be torpedoed by a U-boat in the waters off Northern Ireland. Roosevelt maneuvered to send England military aid. But the United States didn't join the fighting for more than two years after the royal visit, not until the Imperial Japanese Navy attacked Pearl Harbor on December 7, 1941.

When the Yanks finally arrived in the United Kingdom, Princess Elizabeth was fifteen years old, a monarch-in-training, watching the stalwart example of the papa she adored.

ELIZABETH ALEXANDRA MARY WOULD FOREVER APPLY THE LESSONS OF modesty, discipline, and duty that she took from him then. Her father, who had been forced to learn on the job how to be the sovereign, prepared Elizabeth for that role almost from the start—from the time she was ten years old, and her uncle's abdication transformed her future. She was included in luncheons with visiting foreign leaders as a child and delivered a wartime radio address at age fourteen. When she was eighteen, he named her a "counsellor of state," allowing her to assume some of the duties she would one day command.

"Lilibet is my pride," he once said of his proper older daughter. The mischievous Margaret "is my joy."

Queen Elizabeth II saw strengthening relations with the United States as central to her job description. Churchill, who met her when she was two years old and then became the first of fifteen prime ministers of her reign, had made sure of that. From his first encounter with the toddler, the imposing Churchill saw something special in her—"a character" from the start. "She has an air of authority & reflectiveness astonishing in an infant," he told his wife, Clementine. He relished his role as the princess's tutor. "The maintenance, and continuous improvement, of friendship between the English-speaking peoples, and more especially between these islands and the great North American Democracies, is the safeguard of the future," he wrote soon after she was crowned. He saw her as the key to the Commonwealth's survival.

"She watched America carefully," said Lord David Owen. The British foreign secretary in the 1970s now had the long perspective reached at age ninety. "She lived all through the Second World War, in which there was a transfer of leadership," Britain's former colony becoming the world's dominant power. "From the moment that Eisenhower led the coalition forces over D-Day, there was never any doubt in the Queen's mind, I'm sure—and any sensible Brit—that there could be no longer any talk of Britain being the supreme power in the world. That had passed, decisively and clearly, to America."

Stay close to the Americans, Churchill advised. That she would do, to the day she died. It was what her father would have wanted.

THE WAR YEARS DEFINED ELIZABETH'S LIFE. THEY ALSO INTRODUCED the princess to some of the future presidents she would encounter—to Eisenhower when he was an army general, to John F. Kennedy when he was the brash college-age son of the US ambassador to Britain. She gained a generational understanding of the other presidents of her era who also served in World War II. Richard Nixon, Gerald Ford, and George H. W. Bush were all young officers in naval service—as was Royal Navy Lieutenant Philip Mountbatten, a handsome (if exiled) prince and her future consort. Army Captain Ronald Reagan, stationed stateside in California because of severe nearsightedness, produced wartime training films. Two days after Pearl Harbor, Lyndon Johnson, a member of the US Naval Reserve, became one of the first members of Congress to volunteer for active duty.

Elizabeth herself became the first female member of the royal family to join the military, enlisting at age eighteen in the Auxiliary Territorial Service and being trained as a truck driver and vehicle mechanic.

Those threads gave durability and depth to the relationships between the Queen and her presidents, between her and the United States itself. By the end of her unprecedented seventy-year reign, she had conferred with thirteen sitting presidents, from Harry Truman to Joe Biden. She had met Herbert Hoover after he left the White House and Lyndon Johnson before he moved in. No other person in history, of any nationality, has ever had personal interactions with so many sitting presidents, more than a quarter of all those who to date had held the job.

This astonishing record gave her a rich reservoir. "This is now the fourth time I have had the honor of proposing a toast to the president of the United States in the very place where my father once proposed a toast to President Roosevelt," Elizabeth said at the White House in 1991, at a state dinner hosted by the first President Bush. "No wonder I cannot feel a stranger here." Sixteen years later, she delivered a fifth White House toast to his son.

As a constitutional monarch, she was the head of state, not the head of government. She didn't set economic policy or negotiate alliances or publicly opine on the issues of the day, not even such pivotal ones as Brexit. In the classic definition, essayist Walter Bagehot in the nineteenth century described the political role of the sovereign as "the right to be consulted, the right to encourage, the right to warn." Those rights were generally exercised in the privacy of her Tuesday evening sessions with whomever was then prime minister. Yet Elizabeth proved to be much more than a stoic woman in a colorful hat, giving that mockable barrel wave from a royal balcony. More than an unflappable figure in a tiara, presiding over formal occasions at gilded palaces and castles that could seem to some modern-day Americans as fantastical, to others as archaic.

"Her Majesty impressed me as someone who, but for the circumstances of her birth, might have become a successful politician or diplomat," President Bill Clinton said after being seated next to her at a banquet commemorating the fiftieth anniversary of the D-Day invasion, a seminal event that she had seen unfold from London. "As it was, she had to be both, without quite seeming to be either."

She was "this great soft-power genius," David Cameron, the twelfth prime minister of her reign, told me. He called her "one of the world's great diplomats." Joe Biden, her thirteenth sitting president, said if "you just met her, you'd think she could have been the prime minister."

She would influence presidents, and presidents would influence her.

They gave her early lessons on the reach—and the limits—of the soft power she could wield. They contributed to her confidence and helped hone her agility as she moved from being her father's daughter to a queen in command. That sure-footedness would serve her well, not only with US presidents but also with British prime ministers and Arab despots and a new generation of African leaders. She could recognize the qualities that leaders had and sometimes lacked. She would understand the nature of their drive and the costs of their ambition.

"Sometimes, one can help," she said modestly of the counsel she gave.

For more than one president, she provided a bit of credibility and a touch of glamour. She could be a wise listener, and one who could be trusted to keep private the content of their consultations. She didn't give interviews or write a memoir; the diaries she dutifully kept each day, in pencil, have not been released. "She had opinions," James A. Baker III said. By now ninety-four years old, he had served as White House chief of staff for Reagan and secretary of state for George H. W. Bush. "They were all, as far as I could tell, based upon facts. They were solid. They weren't just pie-in-the-sky stuff."

She had one of the deepest understandings in the world of the secret intelligence gathered by Great Britain and the West—more access to more information over a longer period of time than any of the leaders she encountered. Just about every day except Easter and Christmas, a government van delivered the red leather dispatch boxes holding Foreign Office cables, Cabinet papers, budget documents, and MI6 reports on international crises. She received Copy Number One of the government's weekly summary of current intelligence. During wars, she would see the highly classified daily situation accounts as well as reports on future operations.

Among other things, Elizabeth was likely the most knowledgeable person in history about secret nuclear-war contingencies, an issue on which the United States and Britain closely coordinated. For seven decades, from the 1950s until her death in 2022, she was one of only a handful of top officials regularly briefed about them.

After decades on the throne, Her Majesty had met everyone and seemed to remember everything. "You could get her to talk about meeting Neil Armstrong, Grace Kelly, Paul Newman—I mean, literally anyone who you can think of really in the post-war era who had achieved something of note, she met," George Osborne, a chancellor of the Exchequer, marveled. She once confided in Bernard Donoughue, a senior adviser at 10 Downing Street from the 1970s to the 1990s, that Harold Wilson was "just about" her favorite prime minister. "She said, 'We both love political gossip,'" said Lord Donoughue, by now age ninety. "She would say to him, 'There's this rumor in the day now; is it true?' And Harold would tell her the background and she loved all that."

Her mother had encouraged her to recognize the importance of personal relationships in world affairs. "Try and learn as much as you can from [Henry Marten] & mark how he brings the human element into all his history," Queen Elizabeth wrote her daughter when she began private tutoring lessons at age thirteen with the vice provost of Eton College. "Of course history is made by ordinary humans, & one must not forget that."

The education of Elizabeth began when she was young enough to be playing hide-and-seek on the Windsor Castle grounds and the new US ambassador to the Court of St. James's espied her. These were her roots, her introduction to power and its players. Her grounding for a life that would make her one of the most admired and consequential women in the modern world. She came of age in a time of grave peril, when the British and American partnership saved her beloved country—and set the stage for the remarkable life that would follow.

One

"All Will Be Well"

Sunday, April 3, 1938—Windsor Castle

Despite his title, the US ambassador who spotted the young Elizabeth that day was no one's idea of a diplomat.

Joseph P. Kennedy Sr. and his wife, Rose, arrived in London in March 1938, appointed by FDR and accompanied by seven of their nine children. "I am looking forward to playing with Princess Elizabeth," ten-year-old Jean told Mary Pickford, an actress and sometime newspaper columnist. "I know she will be lovely." The entire family was immediately caught up in the balls, regattas, and derbies of the upper crust. Eighteen-year-old Eunice was thrilled by the family's presentation to the king and queen at Buckingham Palace. "As I entered the Palace more excitement and joy seized me than ever before in my life," she wrote. "I had achieved the aim of every young girl—that of being presented at the Court of St. James—the world's greatest empire."

The Kennedy patriarch soon found himself thick into the rumors and gossip of the royal court. In a conversation over dinner, the Duke of Kent, one of the king's younger brothers, said he and President Roosevelt had once discussed rumors that George VI "hated Americans." Not true, the duke had assured the president. He just hated that his brothers had all had affairs with Americans, with Wallis Simpson the prime example. The story of the Duchess of Windsor—reckless, seductive, adulterous, self-involved—and her husband, the ne'er-do-well former King Edward VIII, was often discussed around Elizabeth, reinforcing it as a cautionary tale.

Soon after the Kennedys were installed, King George and Queen Elizabeth hosted the ambassador and his wife at a weekend at Windsor, the most prized invitation of all. Kennedy was a successful investor and movie producer with suspected mob ties and lofty political ambitions, filled with bitterness at the elites whose acceptance he also craved. But at this moment the royal family could hardly afford to be choosy about its associates. He was also the designated representative of what was becoming the most powerful nation on Earth. Rose Kennedy recalled the stay at Windsor "as one of the most fabulous, fascinating experiences of my life." After inspecting the luxurious rooms they were assigned—the huge bed "upholstered in red damask, and set high, so one had to use a step stool to enter it"—Joe turned to his wife and said, "Rose, this is a hell of a long way from East Boston." She had chatted at length with the queen about her children, but found it difficult to remember to call her "ma'am," as protocol required. The queen told her not to bother, putting her at ease. When Rose confided that she found it hard to sleep in London, "the queen was very much amused that I put wax in my ears" to drown out the noise of the city.

After attending Catholic mass in the village that Sunday morning, on April 3, 1938, the Kennedys encountered Princess Elizabeth while they were on a stroll through the park that surrounded the castle. The eleven-year-old was hiding in the bushes, hatless and wearing a pink coat, with a conspiratorial look that signaled she was in the midst of a game. At lunch that day, the ambassador found himself seated between Anne Chamberlain, the wife of Prime Minister Neville Chamberlain, and the princess. She was already being included in events with visiting foreign officials, honing her skills at charm and conversation.

"Princess said she liked movies, loved Seven Dwarfs, particularly the animals when Snow White talked to them, liked Silly Symphonies," Kennedy recorded in his diary. Tapping his Hollywood connections, he would send her a drawing of Snow White from the 1937 animated movie, autographed by Walt Disney, and later drawings from the 1940 Disney movie *Pinocchio*. ("I think I like the one of Pinocchio's head best, or perhaps the one of them all on the raft," she wrote in her thank-you note.) Her favorite subject in school was geography, she said, mentioning that she had just finished studying the Atlantic Coast of the United States—even then capable of a subtle diplomatic nod. She liked swimming and horseback riding, too. Indeed, the princess and the ambassador discovered they shared a riding instructor, Mr. Smith, who was teaching her to do jumps. Kennedy found young Elizabeth "very smart, well-mannered and intelligent and industrious." During a tea at Windsor Castle, when Lady Elphinstone, the queen's older sister, suffered a heart attack, Rose rushed the two princesses outdoors. The queen, thanking her afterward, remarked that she had established a bond with the girls. After all, surely no one had more experience with children than Rose, mother of nine.

Joe Kennedy was enchanted by the royal family. They were less enchanted by him.

"For Worst Ambassador, the prize must go to Joseph P. Kennedy," one of his more respected successors would decree without dispute. It was an unpromising beginning for what would become a hand-in-glove collaboration between the next generation of the Kennedy clan and the Crown.

Joe Kennedy was rich and influential, a pugnacious Irish American banker and businessman from Boston who became the first chairman of the Securities and Exchange Commission. He boosted FDR's campaign in 1932 and again in 1936, then lobbied the president for the appointment to the Court of St. James's. He harbored hopes the prestigious post might launch a political future that would lead him to the White House, the first Kennedy president in a family dynasty he envisioned. As for Roosevelt, more than one of his associates believed the president had dispatched Kennedy to England to get him out of his hair.

Even across an ocean, though, Kennedy could cause trouble. He disagreed with the British, and with his boss, about how the United States should respond to Germany's aggression. German troops had moved into Prague, effectively occupying all of Czechoslovakia. Hitler had broken his promise to Chamberlain, made just months earlier, to claim no more territory in exchange for annexing the Sudetenland, in the west. Appeasement had failed.

Amid the turbulence, John Fitzgerald Kennedy took off the spring semester of his junior year at Harvard in 1939 to visit his father in London, and beyond. In preparation for his senior honors thesis, the twenty-one-year-old student attended the coronation of Pope Pius XII at the Vatican, then traveled through Czechoslovakia, Poland, and the Soviet Union, and on to Romania, Turkey, Palestine, and Danzig. "Obviously an upstart and an ignoramus," complained George Kennan, a young State Department official at the US embassy in German-occupied Prague. Officials were "furious" at having to take time to facilitate arrangements for an ambassador's collegiate offspring during such a fraught time, he fumed.

(That said, Kennedy's thesis, "Appeasement in Munich," became a bestselling book titled *Why England Slept*, published in 1940 with the encouragement of his father. Two decades later, when JFK was running for president and Kennan was a renowned diplomat, he volunteered advice to the candidate. The newly elected president returned the favor, appointing him ambassador to Yugoslavia.)

Joe Kennedy didn't care about the sniping of career diplomats. He encouraged sons Joe Jr. and Jack to meet the "topside" people everywhere to set them up for careers in politics or government or business, for whatever would follow.

"Everyone thinks war inevitable before the year is out," JFK wrote his friend Lem Billings. "I personally don't." In any case, the prospect of another world war didn't seem to dampen his spirits. "Been having a great time," he wrote, as he handled light administrative tasks at the US embassy in London amid a heavy social calendar. "Working every day & going to dinners etc. with Dad . . . Met the King this morning at a Court Levee. It takes place in the morning and you wear tails. The king stands and you go up & bow." For going to court he had ordered "new silk breeches which are cut to my crotch tightly and in which I look mighty attractive."

Princesses Elizabeth and Margaret were among those intrigued by this sprawling American clan. They "have asked their mother many questions about the large Kennedy family and expressed a wish to meet them," a London reporter for United Press wrote in a story about Elizabeth's twelfth birthday party. The Kennedy family papers at the John F. Kennedy Library in Boston contain accounts of Elizabeth's earliest diplomatic outings. In 1939, as she was turning thirteen, she danced with Edward Kennedy at a party that featured a trick pony and a performing dog. "The first couple of times I danced with [sister] Jean, and then I bumped into Princess Elizabeth and I danced with her," the future Massachusetts senator, then seven years old, said in a diary entry he dictated to his nursemaid. "She had a very pretty blue dress with puffs in the sleeves, and a bulge out collar." She once again displayed diplomatic skills. "She was awfully easy to dance with, because she danced the steps I did, but when I danced with Jean, I had to follow her."

Elizabeth had just met Teddy's older brother, the future president.

"Met Queen Mary [the mother of King George] and was at tea with Princess Elizabeth with whom I made a great deal of time," Jack Kennedy wrote. Precisely what he meant by "made a great deal of time" with the tween-aged princess isn't entirely clear. Nor is her first reaction to him.

A FEW MONTHS LATER, SOON AFTER RETURNING FROM AMERICA, THE KING and queen invited Ambassador Kennedy back to Windsor Castle. At a luncheon he again was seated next to Princess Elizabeth, who told him she had learned the dwarves' song from the movie *Snow White* in French. She also discovered a ladybug which, with war brewing, she urged the party to pass down the table to Chamberlain "for good luck." (Perhaps a harbinger, the ladybug resisted the maneuver, as did the prime minister.) At dinner, Kennedy had a prized seat, this time between Chamberlain and the queen. She was delighted that Kennedy called the Duchess of Windsor "a tart" when they gossiped about the abdicated Edward. He recorded in his diary that the queen was astounded when he told her that the motif on the ceiling of the main ballroom at Buckingham Palace was a swastika.

But not all their conversation went so well. Kennedy remained unconvinced of the necessity for the United States to support Britain's looming battle.

"What the American people fear more than anything else is being involved in a war," Kennedy told the queen. "When they remember 1917 and how they went in to make the world safe for Democracy, and then they look now at the crop of dictatorships, quarrels and miseries arising out of that war they say to themselves, 'Never again!' And I can't say I blame them. I feel the same way."

"I feel that way, too, Mr. Kennedy . . . ," the queen replied. "But if we had the United States actively on our side, working with us—think how that would strengthen our position with the dictators."

There were omens of war that weekend. On Sunday afternoon, the king and queen, the prime minister, the ambassador, and other guests boarded a caravan of cars to inspect a nearby Royal Air Force complex of balloon barrages. The large, tethered balloons were designed to be flown over British cities and strategic facilities to force enemy bombers to higher altitudes, making targeting more difficult. The king took Kennedy aside to view what was described as "secret equipment for emergency use," kept under guard.

But the ambassador continued to insist that Britain wouldn't be able to withstand an attack from Germany and that there was no point for the United States to get involved. When Hitler's forces began bombing London, he predicted to British outrage that democracy was finished in England. Eleven days after Britain declared war on September 3, 1939, he began sending his family home to the United States—first Rose with Kathleen, Eunice, and Bobby. Then Joe Jr. and Jack. Finally Patricia, Jean, and Teddy, all gone within a week. He moved out of London to safety himself, to a sixty-room country house.

That retreat earned him the enmity of the British. For all the jocularity with the royal family and the interactions of their children, Kennedy proved himself unreliable when the stakes were raised. "I thought my daffodils were yellow until I met Joe Kennedy," Randolph Churchill, Winston's son, said sarcastically. Six days after Britain declared war, the ambassador met with the king and queen at the palace. George was incensed that Kennedy was concerned only about the financial costs of a war, not of the moral urgency to fight one. He had argued that Hitler should be permitted to occupy Eastern Europe, calling it "of little use" to Great Britain "from a monetary standpoint."

The king sent the ambassador an angry letter, one that royal secretary Alan Lascelles called "a stinker." There were only "three really free peoples in the World," George wrote—the United States, France, and the British Empire. Two of these "great democracies" were now "fighting against all that we three countries hate & detest, Hitler & the Nazi regime and all that it stands for."

A year later, in 1940, soon after Roosevelt had won an unprecedented third term in the White House, Kennedy met with him in the Oval Office to submit his resignation. He had asked to be relieved of his post. The president didn't try to dissuade him. Indeed, the ambassador already had been sidelined; the State Department hadn't allowed him to travel with the royal couple to the United States. But Roosevelt didn't want Kennedy's departure announced until he was ready to name a replacement. A few days later, the two men met again at Hyde Park, and clashed. "I never want to see that son of a bitch again as long as I live," FDR told Eleanor, leaving it to her to host him for lunch and send him on his way.

The British felt the same way. In his diary, quoted by biographer Sally Bedell Smith, the king called Kennedy "a very disappointed & rather embittered man." The Foreign Office had been debating whether and how to get Kennedy recalled for what they called his "*defaitiste*" activities. "Mr. Kennedy is a very foul specimen of double-crosser and defeatist," Sir Robert Vansittart, a Churchill ally and diplomatic adviser, wrote in hand across the cabinet minutes. "He thinks of nothing but his own pocket. I hope that this war will at least see the elimination of his type."

WHEN BRITAIN OFFICIALLY ENTERED THE WAR, SO DID MEMBERS OF THE royal family. The king's younger brother, the Duke of Kent, was an officer in the Royal Air Force. He was killed in a military plane crash in 1942, the first time since 1513 that a royal had died on active service. In the Royal Navy, Lord Louis Mountbatten, the queen's cousin, served as supreme allied commander of the South East Asia Command. A great-grandson of Queen Victoria, Louis Mountbatten was a charismatic, energetic, and ambitious naval officer who would crop up in notable roles in British military and political history over the next several decades—not least through his ultimately successful efforts to encourage a match between his nephew Philip and Princess Elizabeth. Lieutenant Philip Mountbatten, also in the Royal Navy, served with distinction in the Pacific fleet and in the Mediterranean.

In contrast to Kennedy, the king and queen did not try to escape the bombing of London, and they didn't send their daughters away to safety. Quite the contrary: They made a point of staying in the middle of it. In a show of defiance and unity, the royal couple spent most days at Buckingham Palace in London and most nights at Windsor Castle, just outside the city, where Elizabeth and Margaret had moved to live for the duration of the war.

Buckingham Palace would be struck by Nazi bombardments nine times during the Blitz. Even the small summerhouse on the grounds where the princesses and the Buckingham Palace Girl Guides troop had met was nearly demolished. At one point, George and Elizabeth were having tea and narrowly escaped injury when bombs destroyed the Royal Chapel and crashed into the Queen's Drawing Room. That prompted the queen to declare solidarity with Londoners in neighborhoods that had been harder hit. "I can finally look the East End in the face," she said. Earlier, when government officials urged that the princesses be evacuated to Canada or North America, she famously replied, "The children can't go without me. I can't leave the King, and of course the King won't go."

Even Elizabeth, at age fourteen, was deployed to enlist help from the Americans—a mission she would fill again and again as monarch in the decades to follow. In the fall of 1940, the director general of the BBC approached the king's personal secretary with a proposal to have the princess introduce a series of "Children in Wartime" programs. Two years earlier, the palace had brusquely rejected a similar request by the owner of the *New York Herald Tribune*—for Elizabeth to make a five-minute broadcast to open National Children's Week. The British ambassador had dismissed "attempts to enlist the princesses for stunts." But the situation was now more dire, and they seized the opportunity.

Elizabeth's script was purportedly directed at British children who had been evacuated to North America, but it was also designed to pull at the heartstrings of the American people and their government. "As Her Royal Highness's first broadcast, delivered at an historic moment, it would reach the minds of the millions who heard it with a singular poignancy," Frederick Ogilvie of the BBC had assured her parents. Her voice piping and her diction precise, Elizabeth addressed the children abroad who "have had to leave your homes and be separated from your father and mother." She and her sister knew how hard it could be to be away from loved ones, she said, but added, "We know, every one of us, that in the end all will be well."

The brief address made headlines in newspapers across the United States. In Washington, *The Evening Star*, which nearly every official at the White House and Congress read each afternoon, published a story and a photo of a serious-looking Elizabeth speaking into a microphone. "'All Will Be Well' in End, Princess Elizabeth Broadcasts," the headline read. The *Atlanta Journal* published the full text on its editorial page.

The British royal family became a symbol of courage and hope for a beleaguered Europe. Anne Frank, in hiding in German-occupied Amsterdam, kept a picture postcard of a smiling Elizabeth pinned to the wall of her bedroom in the Secret Annex. In her diary entry on April 21, 1944, Anne celebrated the eighteenth birthday of the princess, calling her "this beauty." The inspirational example of the queen prompted Hitler to call her "the most dangerous woman in Europe" to the Nazi cause. At one point, he reportedly contemplated a kidnapping operation in which Nazi paratroopers would land on the grounds of Buckingham Palace to abduct any royal they encountered. "Great emphasis was placed upon the hostages being captured alive," military historian Andrew Stewart wrote. As the lovely young girl who was first in line to the throne, Elizabeth would have been a particular prize.

As remarkable as the royal couple's courage was the sense of normalcy they managed to bring to their children's lives. Their family was so close that her father referred to them as "us four," an unbreakable connection, cozy and complete. They projected a resolute steadiness that reassured their nation, and presumably one another. Even Elizabeth's nickname, Lilibet, was cheerful and normal, in times that were anything but. When she was an adult, facing challenges of a different sort, the adjective repeatedly used for her would be steadfast, a characteristic that was a childhood inheritance.

In a classified operation kept secret for decades, the king and queen and their daughters were told to keep bags packed for an emergency evacuation to a private mansion in Worcestershire, in central England. The safe house had been stocked with food and weapons in case they were forced to retreat. In preparation for an expected Nazi invasion, the queen took shooting lessons with pistols and rifles in the palace gardens, sometimes targeting the rats that threatened to overwhelm London as collapsing buildings sent them into the streets. The times were terrifying, especially for a girl who kept a bag packed to flee, a girl Hitler himself had targeted.

THEN THE AMERICANS ARRIVED, AT LAST.

Army Lieutenant General Eisenhower was hailed as a hero when he took command of US forces in Britain, assigned to build cooperation among the allies for an assault on Axis forces in Europe. After three long years of war, and with no victory in sight, many in Great Britain saw the American troops as a lifeline and the Midwestern general with the genial smile as a savior.

The king and Eisenhower hadn't yet met when Ike and his deputy, Major General Mark Clark, made a quick trip to England in May 1942, a few weeks before he was to assume command. They asked if they might tour the gardens at Windsor that Sunday. There hadn't been time to arrange an official reception, but the king and queen "readily assented," and even "volunteered to stay in their quarters to avoid embarrassment to the American sightseers," an Eisenhower aide recorded. But on that sunny afternoon, the royal family was having tea on a small terrace overlooking the rose garden when they heard the distinctive raspy voice of Baron Clive Wigram, a lord-in-waiting to the king and the custodian of Windsor. The sixty-eight-year-old Wilgram was giving the tour, pointing out various flowers with his cane. "A lusty little fellow," he boasted of one. "Here's a bright little chap," he said of another.

Also sitting at the table on the terrace was Margaret Rhodes, a cousin and friend of Elizabeth, and Elizabeth Lambart, daughter of the Earl of Cavan. "Suddenly we heard male voices engaged in transatlantic chatter," Margaret recalled. "The King exclaimed, 'Oh Lord, General Eisenhower and his group are being shown round the castle. I quite forgot. We will be in full view when they turn the next corner.'" Not only would their presence intrude on the generals' visit but it would also be socially awkward. The patio was halfway up the castle wall, making it not only inevitable that the two groups would see one another but also impossible for them to converse. A royal wave didn't seem to quite suffice for these important visitors.

"Thus without another word, and acting as one, the Royal Family dived under the tablecloth," Margaret recalled decades later, astonished still. "Liz and I, our mouths gaping open, followed fast." The table was set with a silver kettle, a teapot and "all the paraphernalia," she said, but the group was hidden by a white tablecloth that swept to the ground all around them. "If he and his party had looked up towards the terrace they would have seen a table shaking from the effect of the concerted and uncontrollable giggles of those sheltering beneath it," she said. After the visitors had moved on and the coast was clear, they climbed back out, the Americans none the wiser.

When Eisenhower was formally presented to the king at Buckingham Palace on July 8, George cheerfully related the madcap moment. He described the two Americans as "one very tall"—that would be Clark, at six feet five—and the other as "simply tall." That was Eisenhower, at five feet ten. Elizabeth recalled that Eisenhower "was so staggered by the King of England hiding under his own dinner table when he had a general just walking around." The episode reflected George's wry and unpretentious persona. He often reminded Ike of it when the two men got together. "That was the sort of thing Papa enjoyed very much," Elizabeth said. As queen, she would take delight in the occasional mishap, too.

It was the beginning of a remarkable friendship between the two men, their mutual admiration forged by their alliance against the Nazis. "Even if they weren't King and Queen you would enjoy visiting with them," Eisenhower told his naval aide. The two men also shared a habit for chain-smoking. When asked by Lord Mountbatten to attend a banquet with the king, Ike quipped that he could never attend any event toasting the king's health in which smoking was forbidden. Mountbatten assured the general that wouldn't be a problem.

Eisenhower became a familiar and honored figure for many Brits. His wartime headquarters were on the north side of Grosvenor Square, a spot of green that Londoners for a time dubbed "Eisenhower Platz" because of all the US troops roaming the neighborhood. A month after the war in Europe ended, the king made Eisenhower the first American to receive the Order of Merit, the highest personal honor a monarch could give. On the day it was conferred at Buckingham Palace, Ike was also awarded the Honorary Freedom of the City of London, a rare honorary citizenship that dated to the thirteenth century. The general was driven in a horse-drawn carriage through the streets, cheered by crowds estimated in the hundreds of thousands.

"You led the Allied Expeditionary Force to an overwhelming victory; but you did more than that, for you established a tradition of trust + friendship between your people + mine which will have a lasting effect on their relations," George said in a letter to Eisenhower, written by hand on Buckingham Palace stationery. "I know well that you share my own belief that the future of civilization depends on the continuance of that spirit of co-operation between us which, from start to finish, has inspired the Allied Expeditionary Force."

The future of civilization.

High stakes indeed for the princess who just seven years later would become queen.

"MY DEAR GENERAL," THE LETTER FROM THE KING'S PRIVATE SECRETARY began, dated November 1946, a year after World War II had ended.

"The King asks me to thank you sincerely for the consignment of lemons which you have so kindly sent him," Lascelles wrote in the letter, found tucked in a box of pre-presidential papers at the Eisenhower Presidential Library in Abilene, Kansas. "The lemons were delivered to me safely this morning by the Military Air Attache at your Embassy, and they will be greatly appreciated by Their Majesties." Even in peacetime, England was still rationing food. Fresh fruit was scarce. Lascelles acknowledged that in thanking Eisenhower for the unexpected lemon airlift, and for remembering him in its bounty, too. "It was very good indeed of you to include me in this gift, and my wife will be delighted to have this generous consignment of what is now a very rare fruit in England," he said.

The lemons may have been a thank-you gift for the king's hospitality a month earlier.

By now, Eisenhower had become the US Army chief of staff, planning a postwar tour of Europe. The king invited him and his wife, Mamie, and their son John to spend the weekend at Balmoral Castle, a rare invitation to the royal family's summer retreat in Scotland. "George and Ike . . . A Kansas Yankee at Court," teased the *New York Daily News* headline over a photo that showed Eisenhower in his military uniform and the king in his kilt, made of the gray, black, and red tartan designed for Balmoral by Prince Albert, Queen Victoria's consort. Elizabeth and Margaret donned sashes with the distinctive plaid. John Eisenhower, twenty-four years old and wearing his US Army captain's uniform, danced with the princesses that evening at an after-dinner party in the castle ballroom. His father was "quite captivated" by the royal family, John said. "He had something between respect and awe of the British monarchy, almost more than any other institution."

On Sunday morning, the Eisenhowers and the royals went to Crathie Kirk, the Gothic Revival parish church nearby, for worship, hymns, and prayers.

The British king and the Kansas farm boy shared some characteristics. They were close in age, born just five years apart in the final decade of the nineteenth century. Each had taken command during difficult times—George of the Crown after his brother's abdication, Ike of Allied forces when their victory was far from assured. Neither displayed the bluster and pretense sometimes associated with monarchs and military commanders, especially triumphant ones. Both were homebodies of a sort. Eisenhower's hobbies were golf and cards; he enjoyed painting landscapes and portraits that were notable more for his signature than their artistic lift. His Majesty preferred riding horses and shooting at the country estate, Sandringham, to fancier privileges of the palace.

They also shared an affection for the king's daughter, his heir to the throne. When Elizabeth married Sir Philip Mountbatten in 1947, Ike and Mamie sent a wedding gift that underscored how they valued their relationship beyond the official. The small silver ashtray shaped in the form of a wedding ring was the present they gave "to the children of our dearest friends," he explained. "Because of our affection and admiration for Her Royal Highness," they included her "among those we hold most dear." Elizabeth was content to be a military wife—her headstrong husband intended to pursue his career in His Majesty's Navy—with the hope that decades would pass before she would be called to succeed her papa. But the king's health was declining. He was diagnosed with arteriosclerosis in 1948, a hardening of the arteries that created pains in his legs; he underwent surgery that March. For his part, Eisenhower left the army to become president of Columbia University in 1948, denying any interest in the political spotlight. Three years later, he was also appointed Supreme Allied Commander Europe, the head of the armed forces of the North Atlantic Treaty Organization (NATO).

In July 1951, he and Elizabeth met again at St. Paul's Cathedral for a service to honor the memory of US forces during the war. Churchill and Lord Mountbatten were there, too, for the presentation of an inscribed book with the names of the twenty-eight thousand Americans who died while based in Britain.

Neither the general nor the princess knew how soon their paths would intertwine again—with both in vastly different roles.

Two

Falling in Love

Wednesday, October 31, 1951—Washington National Airport

The first time Princess Elizabeth stepped foot on American soil, she was trembling. The future queen was so clearly anxious that President Harry S. Truman worried she wouldn't be able to address the crowd gathered to greet her on the tarmac.

She was twenty-five years old, lithe and determined, her posture perfect and her hair trimmed in a practical bob. Left home in London were her two young children. Prince Charles was about to turn three years old and Princess Anne was just one. Those who saw Elizabeth in person, then and later, marveled at how petite she was—standing five feet and four inches tall in the prime of her life—and at how porcelain her complexion was, a true English rose. On this trip with Prince Philip, a Washington society columnist reported the couple's entourage included "seven junketing servants," from a lady-in-waiting and a royal equerry to the princess's maid and the duke's valet. They had dozens of wardrobe trunks, deemed necessary for the endless variety of events on their five-week itinerary, from white-tie dinners to a rodeo, from reviewing troops to visiting hospitalized children. Packed as well were black mourning clothes, just in case.

Though she prayed otherwise, Elizabeth was braced to assume the crown at any moment if the father she adored took a turn for the worse. King George was desperately ill, though the doctors had been less than candid even to the patient and his family about his diagnosis. His emergency surgery on September 23, 1951, had delayed Elizabeth's departure for two weeks and prompted a heated debate behind-the-scenes about whether it was safe for her to be the first member of the royal family to cross the Atlantic in an airplane rather than by ship. (In the end, she flew.) After she arrived in Canada, the first leg of her North American journey, a prominent Italian physician who had talked with a member of the king's surgical team said in public what many suspected, that the king had lung cancer—a word that carried a stigma and was seen as a death sentence. "There are fears that the surgical operation might have been performed too late," Dr. Pietro Valdoni told the newspaper *Corriere Della Sera*.

In a framed bulletin hung on the gates, the palace had announced that the king underwent a lung resection. "Whilst anxiety must remain for some days, His Majesty's immediate post-operative condition is satisfactory." That was the truth, but not the whole truth. Only later would it be revealed that his left lung had been removed, his condition dire. So dire that during the weeks Elizabeth and Philip spent crisscrossing Canada on a special train, her royal secretary slept with a suitcase under his bed that contained a special parchment Accession Declaration, the document that would mark her immediate succession, if the worst happened. "Wherever we went, we took our black clothes, the Royal Standard, black armbands, black ties, all those things," said Michael Parker, the private secretary to Prince Philip. "I always had that box—a heavily disguised box—with me."

Elizabeth was worried about her father back home, and she faced more immediate concerns on the road. In Canada, she drew huge and friendly crowds—a million spectators in Toronto and even more in Montreal—but she wasn't comfortable in the spotlight, not yet. Newspaper columnists complained she looked wan and distracted. She lacked the open warmth and easy smile of her mother, Queen Elizabeth, who had charmed Canadians on a tour with the king a dozen years earlier.

Fortunately for her, she was about to encounter someone who would make her smile.

PRESIDENT TRUMAN, COATLESS ON AN OVERCAST AUTUMN DAY, STOOD AT the bottom of the mobile airplane stairs to welcome Princess Elizabeth when the Royal Canadian Air Force DC-4M arrived from Montreal.

Moments after she carefully walked down the steps, the plain-speaking president, whose background as a Missouri farm boy and Kansas City haberdasher was far removed from royalty, began to whisper in her ear. It was the way he might have reassured his cherished daughter, Margaret, just two years older than Elizabeth. Indeed, some thought they heard the president call the princess "daughter." Not so, he insisted to a confidant; he had called her "dear."

Regardless, his manner was paternal as he comforted a young woman nervous about her new and unaccustomed role. As Franklin Roosevelt's vice president, succeeding him less than three months after their inauguration, Truman knew something about the strains of being dropped unexpectedly into a worldwide spotlight. He told her "not to be uneasy about the situation—that everybody was friendly to her, and all she needed to do was just to tell them what she had on her mind, and she wouldn't have a bit of trouble," Truman recalled years later in a long-forgotten oral history. They climbed a rostrum draped with bunting. "After we got up on the stand, when I introduced her, I said (under my breath): Now, go ahead. Nobody's going to hurt you at all. And everybody will be happy with what you have to say," he said. "Then she didn't have any more trouble."

Elizabeth arrived in a nation enthralled with royalty, some twelve years after her parents' memorable visit. Her family's bravery against Hitler's onslaught had earned them America's esteem. Cannons boomed a twenty-one-gun salute, an honor typically reserved for visiting heads of state, not their heirs apparent. It was extended "as a courtesy and not as a right," the State Department advisory stiffly explained. The *Des Moines Register* reporter put it more casually. "The princess, officially, didn't rate that many guns," Fletcher Knebel wrote in his front-page story about her arrival, "but the US gave it to her anyway just in the name of romance."

"When I was a little boy, I read about a fairy princess," Truman declared as he welcomed her to Washington. "And there she is."

The president and the princess stood on a stand that had been erected on the tarmac outside the Military Air Transport Service terminal, flanked by Philip, First Lady Bess Truman, and the first daughter, Margaret. The group represented an occasionally awkward new reality since the end of the Second World War. The unpretentious Truman, his political career launched by the Pendergast machine in Kansas City, had risen to lead the ascendant global superpower. The patrician British couple represented a country still devastated by the long conflict and still adjusting to the decline of its empire. Each side saw the benefits of standing close to the other.

"I think your visit will improve, if that's possible, the cordial relations that exist between our two great countries, and I hope that while you are here you will have a very enjoyable time," Truman began. Then he abandoned the mimeographed prepared remarks that had been distributed to reporters in favor of a more personal ramble. "I was most happy to hear that the king had recovered so promptly so that you could make this trip," he said. He recalled his two "most pleasant" visits with George VI—once as a senator during the royal couple's 1939 visit to Washington, and again as president aboard a ship off the southern British port of Plymouth in 1945. They had met at an historic moment: Truman was returning from the post–World War II conference in Potsdam with Soviet leader Joseph Stalin and British Prime Ministers Winston Churchill and then Clement Attlee, who succeeded Churchill midway through the talks when the wartime leader's party lost the general election in Britain.

Truman also acknowledged gratefully the hospitality the royal family had shown his daughter when she had toured Europe over the summer. Margaret's engraved invitations, menu cards, printed programs, and newspaper clippings from her European tour filled four scrapbooks. Both she and Elizabeth were coming of age and dealing with the scrutiny of being the daughters of powerful men. Margaret had been invited to lunch at Buckingham Palace, where she was seated between Elizabeth and Philip. The princess had leaned over to Margaret and inquired, "Is he feeding the dogs under the table?"

"My mother . . . didn't want to get in the middle of that," said her son, Clifton Truman Daniel. "So she said, 'I don't know.' She didn't want to rat out the prince."

During her visit to London, Margaret watched from the diplomatic seats at the Horse Guards Parade in St. James's Park as the princess, riding sidesaddle, filled in for the king for the first time at the Trooping the Colour ceremony. "An endearing person," Margaret called Elizabeth.

She would also make a sharp observation: "[S]he has always struck me as unusually intelligent and absolutely aware of what the score is all the time."

In Washington, Margaret's father was captivated. "I am sincerely sorry that you can't go from one end of the country to the other as you did in Canada and let everybody in the country have a chance to get acquainted with you," the president told Elizabeth in his expansive conclusion, "because Margaret tells me that whenever anyone becomes acquainted with you, they really do fall in love. . . ."

Wearing a crimson cloak and black tricorn hat, a diamond pin in its brim and a double strand of pearls around her neck, Elizabeth already looked more at ease after Truman's whispered encouragement. When she stepped to the bank of microphones, her voice was clear and crisp, her words carried on radio nationwide and on television as far west as Omaha. Truman stood just behind, watching her with an expectant, encouraging gaze.

"Free men everywhere look towards the United States with affection and with hope," she declared, reading from her written text. "The message that has gone out from this great capital city has brought hope and courage to a troubled world."

"I thank you, dear," Truman told her when she had finished.

In England, the affectionate informality to royalty was seen as so rare, so remarkable that those four words, in quotation marks, became a banner across the front page of the London *Daily Mail*. In the *Daily Express*, the five-column headline shouted: "Mr. President Takes the Princess by the Arm and Says—I THANK YOU, DEAR." Indeed, Truman had patted the princess's arm and taken her elbow—another grace note at odds with royal protocol—as they moved to review an honor guard after a ninety-piece army band had played "God Save the King" and then "The Star-Spangled Banner."

By now, they were smiling and chatting with the comfort of old friends. Sir Oliver Franks, the British ambassador to Washington, reported to the king that the president gave "the impression of a very proud uncle presenting his favorite niece to his friends." On this trip, Elizabeth was just beginning to find her own way, to chart her own path in a role that was still unfamiliar and intimidating. Truman's warmth and encouragement helped her take those first steps.

He wasn't the only occupant of the White House, present and future, who was keeping an eye on Elizabeth during the visit.

In 1951, Jacqueline Bouvier's debonair father, "Black Jack" Bouvier, had landed her a job at the *Washington Times Herald* with his friend Frank C. Waldrop, the executive editor—but as a gofer, not as the writer she aspired to be. At that moment, when Elizabeth was making her first visit to the United States, Jackie joined the crowds on the sidewalk. She hoped to catch a glimpse of the princess and the president as they passed by in a black convertible, possibly the one now on display at the Truman Presidential Library in Independence, Missouri.

When she got back to the newsroom, she submitted a handwritten feature about how infatuated US government bureaucrats were with British royalty. "You're not a reporter!" her boss told her, but she had given him an idea. He assigned her to tag along with the paper's "Inquiring Photographer," a man-on-the-street feature. She could devise a question to ask about Elizabeth's visit, and he would decide if what she produced was worth publishing.

It was. Her first column, published in the paper two days later without a byline, had cleverly posed this query to six of the newspaper's staff photographers: "Is Princess Elizabeth as pretty as her picture?" Their assessments were mixed, by the way. "I think she is quite beautiful," Berkeley Payne said, but William H. Luers disagreed. "I do not think she can hold a candle to some of the Washington girls," he opined.

Reporters who had been covering the trip since its start in Canada instantly noticed the change in Elizabeth's demeanor after she met with Truman. Earlier, she had worn "the iron mask of royalty," a Canadian journalist said. But Truman had somehow managed to break through her reserve. British journalists told their American colleagues that he was the first official to make her appear genuinely cheerful in public. "[W]ithin a few minutes of her arrival at the airport, the Princess was engaged in laughing and animated conversation with the President," they marveled.

She told her royal secretary that she had been taken by Truman's natural manner. He was so thoroughly American, delighted by her standing but unperturbed by it. "Respectful but not overawed," his grandson told me. Truman had given her the perfect personal introduction to the freewheeling American culture—one that the proper and reserved Elizabeth seemed to enjoy, now and later. He launched what would become a string of remarkable encounters between the future queen of England and residents of the White House, ties that would have an impact on both sides of the Atlantic.

Over time, those relationships would track Elizabeth's growth from a tentative princess to a confident queen, a leader of consequence for an unprecedented reign.

THE ROYAL COUPLE HAD FIRST LANDED IN MONTREAL, THEN BOARDED A ten-car royal train to cross Canada and back again. Before stopping in the United States, Elizabeth and Philip would traverse six time zones and more than ten thousand miles in the Commonwealth nation, with events in every province, from Nova Scotia to the Yukon. The itinerary was "studded with stops like suckers on an octopus," the prince's biographer would observe.

Beyond diplomacy with the Canadians, British leaders were increasingly concerned about the strength of the bonds between the United Kingdom and the United States. Roosevelt and Churchill, with George a valorous partner, had forged historic ties during World War II. After FDR died in 1945, Truman demonstrated his trust in the British by confiding in Churchill during the Potsdam conference a grave secret: The United States had built the first atomic bomb, one that shortly would be dropped on Hiroshima. He admonished him to tell no one. Churchill, after locking the doors and windows around him and demanding total secrecy, told Lord Mountbatten. The next day, the president, after demanding the utmost discretion, told the secret to Mountbatten—who feigned shock.

But when the war was over, Truman's commitment to the special relationship didn't seem assured. A week after Japanese forces surrendered, the president abruptly canceled Lend-Lease, Roosevelt's sleight of hand that had funneled US aid to wartime Britain. Rising Conservative politician Harold Macmillan called it a "devastating blow, struck without warning" that left Britain on the edge of bankruptcy. Truman later apologized for failing to give British leaders a heads-up.

The new president also signed the Atomic Energy Act of 1946, also known as the McMahon Act, restricting access to nuclear information by other nations. Britain and Canada protested they were not only close allies but also had participated in the secret Manhattan Project that had developed America's nuclear weapons.

Most important of all, Truman was in the midst of shaping a postwar world order, one in which the United States would long hold sway. Not set was what role Britain would play in a world in which Germany and Japan would turn from enemies to allies, the Soviet Union and China would loom as rising challenges, the creation of Israel would transform the Middle East, and fresh military alliances were being created.

Within weeks of Truman being sworn into office after Roosevelt's death in April 1945, British officials began a behind-the-scenes campaign to convince the new president to make a state visit to Great Britain, a public demonstration of the primacy of the friendship between the two nations. In June, Clement Attlee sent Truman a churlish message, labeled personal and top secret. "I see reports in the papers that you propose to stop in Paris and see General de Gaulle before coming on to the Conference at Berlin," he wrote. "President Roosevelt promised me on several occasions that he would not visit France before he visited Britain. I am sure you will bear this in mind in any decision you may take."

Truman responded that same day, issuing the politicians' standard defense of blaming the press for misconstruing things. "I shall keep the promise made to you by President Roosevelt if conditions at the time make it practicable." That hedge—"If conditions at the time make it practicable"—stopped short of a commitment. Then he added a churlish message of his own: "May I express a hope that the contents of this message will not get into the papers."

A week later, King George followed up with an invitation, an effort to seal a visit. "I am glad to hear that you may have an opportunity of visiting my Country on your return from Berlin," he wrote. "The People of Great Britain will give you a very warm welcome, and I send you a cordial invitation to be the guest of The Queen and myself at Buckingham Palace." That was a plum. The only previous US president who had stayed at the palace was Woodrow Wilson, on his way to peace talks in Paris at the end of World War I.

Truman declined, but he did arrange to sit down briefly with the king on the president's ship as he was returning to the United States from the Berlin conference. It wasn't everything George wanted, but it was something. The two men would never meet again.

Five years later, after Truman had been elected to a White House term in his own right, the British were still trying to woo him to London—using his daughter, Margaret, as a go-between—and still worried about press reports that he might go to Paris first. *Quelle catastrophe!*

"I can say from personal conversations with his daughter that she is extremely keen to make precisely such a trip [to England]—(and her influence on her father is not inconsiderable)," diplomat A. R. K. Mackenzie reported to the Foreign Office in 1950. Given the potential benefits of a visit, political complications "need not prevent us from making the gesture of extending an invitation, or of sounding out the White House informally as a first step. In fact, if we do not do so, we may find we have been forestalled by the French."

Once again, the king quickly signed off on the invitation. "An excellent thing if President Truman paid a state visit here next summer," his royal secretary said. But lobbying in Washington went nowhere. Finally, in January 1951, the British ambassador to the United States admitted defeat. Sir Oliver reported he had been told there was no chance Truman would visit. This president had proven to be a homebody, making just five foreign trips during the eight years of his presidency, and none of them to Britain—or, to their relief, France.

Elizabeth's journey to Canada opened a new possibility. If the king couldn't see the president, perhaps his daughter could. She wouldn't be negotiating nuclear cooperation, the agenda of the elected government. Her father wouldn't have done that, either. But she could use her royal standing and her engaging manner to build personal relationships and reinforce the alliance that had served both countries, especially her own, so well. At a crucial moment, she could open the door for her nation's diplomats and bureaucrats in a way almost no one else could. And she could win over the American public, no small asset in a democracy.

Edward Wood, First Earl of Halifax, who had served as ambassador to Washington during Truman's first year as president, suggested helpfully that it would surely be impolite for the royal couple not to make a quick stop in the United States while they were in the neighborhood, or at least on the same continent. A "pop-over" visit, the king's private secretary called it.

All they needed was an invitation.

When the Canadian tour was announced on July 4, 1951, a Buckingham Palace official parried questions from reporters about whether the United States would be added to the itinerary. "So far the princess has not been invited," he responded, "and she has not suggested that she should be invited." That was on a Wednesday. The next day, on Thursday, the US embassy in London warned in a cable to the State Department of the potential consequences if she *wasn't* invited—presumably a message they had heard from British officials. "Were no official United States invitation forthcoming, it might be misunderstood in England," the memo said.

In Washington that morning, Truman was noncommittal, even dismissive about a possible visit. "I have no knowledge of their plans," he said when a reporter asked. "Of course, they would be welcome to come here, but I will have to find out what their plans are, before we can take formal notice of the fact."

Even that wait-and-see response was enough. His comments were immediately radioed to London, and within minutes Elizabeth had been informed of them. It was not a formal invitation, a palace official noted, but he added, "If President Truman invites them, of course they'll say 'yes.'" That message made the newspapers, too.

The princess had preemptively accepted an invitation Truman hadn't yet extended.

A week later, the president invited her. She accepted, again.

IT WAS MEANT TO BE HER INTRODUCTION OF SORTS TO A WIDER WORLD, and a test run for what was ahead for her as sovereign. When remarks were being drafted for her to deliver in Ottawa over Canadian Broadcasting Company radio, a palace aide asked about beginning with a message from the king. No, replied Lascelles, who spoke for him. "If she delivers formal message from The King, it makes her, so to speak, The King's representative and the whole idea is that she is going over on her own."

The last-minute delay in her departure because of her father's surgery threatened to disrupt her schedule in Canada, prompting a debate among top government officials over her travel plans. Churchill, now a former prime minister, wrote Attlee, the current one, to advise that "it would be, in my opinion, wrong for the Princess Elizabeth to fly the Atlantic." He knew better than almost anyone the king's dire straits. He was protective of the young woman who would soon be sovereign, a sentiment he would hold for the rest of his life. In its deliberations, though, the Cabinet decided that, "judging by the record of accidents there was nowadays no greater danger in flying the North Atlantic than in making air journeys over land," which the royals routinely did, not to mention the risks of setting a precedent "denying them the use of what was widely regarded as a normal means of travel."

A plane it would be. A double-decker Boeing Stratocruiser, to be precise, operated by the state-owned British Overseas Airways Corporation. Royal Navy warships would patrol the waters along the plane's path. The trip had an important advocate, the most important one to Elizabeth: her ailing father. It was her duty to go. So she went.

During the sixteen-hour flight, Elizabeth could not sleep. In the upstairs bar of the aircraft, Philip tried to teach her a game called Liar's Dice. Players rolled dice in a cup, concealing them from their opponents, then bid against one another on the purported value of their hands. A player could raise a bid or call a bluff with an accusatory charge of "liar!" But she couldn't concentrate on the game, and she wasn't good at bluffing, at least not yet.

"You'll never make a good liar with that Empire on your shoulders," Philip told her. The British empire on her shoulders was a significant burden indeed, one she was only beginning to figure out how to handle—even as it was slipping away. Her father would be the last British sovereign to hold the title "Emperor of India," used by British monarchs since Queen Victoria was christened "Empress." The title was retired when India, the onetime jewel in the imperial crown, achieved independence in 1947. That year, Elizabeth had traveled with her parents and sister to South Africa, where she made a poignant pledge marking her twenty-first birthday: "I declare before you all that my whole life, whether it be long or short, shall be devoted to your service and to the service of our great imperial family to which we all belong." She (and her speechwriter, journalist Dermot

Morrah) used the old word "imperial" along with "Commonwealth" in the text, a mark of the uneasy transition the nation and the Crown were making.

Now, just a few years later, Elizabeth was leading her own trip to a Commonwealth country and its neighboring key ally. At times, it seemed to be more than she was ready to handle. When the royal party reached Victoria on Canada's west coast, a city named for her great-great-grandmother, the *Windsor Star* described her as looking "tired and nervous, and jumped when the first gun of a 21-gun salute roared." A columnist for the *Vancouver Sun* said she was "obviously a bit overwhelmed by it all." His scolding headline: "Princess So Awed She Forgets to Smile." He wrote, "When she smiles, she has a beautiful smile, but some people think she doesn't smile enough at the crowds and there are reports that this information has been passed along to her by her staff."

Some people think.

That would include not only the reporter who was observing her but also her parents back home. "Are you smiling enough, dear?" her mother asked during one of their regular phone calls. They frequently talked during the trip, and her father followed the itinerary on a map with each stop marked. She was "mindful" of her mother's views and anxious for her approval, friends said. "Oh, Mother!" Elizabeth replied. "I seem to be smiling all the time." She complained to Martin Charteris, her private secretary, "My face is aching with smiling."

Philip, who had a rowdy streak, would try to lighten her spirits with practical jokes. He left a booby-trapped can, labeled as nuts, with springs inside that exploded when she opened it. He chased her down a corridor wearing novelty-store false teeth. But the prince also had an edge. He had left the Royal Navy career he loved as he adjusted to the supportive role he was now to fill, walking just behind his wife. In an argument over breakfast one morning, he was overheard calling her a "bloody fool."

"It was a long trip and it wasn't plain sailing," Charteris said. "It wasn't easy for either of them."

THAT IS, UNTIL THEY ARRIVED IN WASHINGTON FOR A STOP THAT LASTED just forty-five hours.

Truman gave the city's federal workforce the day off when she arrived. The celebratory gesture helped swell the crowds that lined the route from the airport to Blair House. The Trumans had moved into the presidential guest house across Pennsylvania Avenue while the White House was being renovated. The royal couple had been invited to stay there as well.

At the airport, the president and the princess climbed in the back seat of his armor-plated limousine, the top pulled open. Escorted by a phalanx of police officers on motorcycles, sirens blaring, they rode up Constitution Avenue through cheering crowds estimated at six hundred thousand or so, many of them waving Union Jacks. Truman held his Stetson hat on his knee as Elizabeth offered her distinctive royal half wave to the crowds with her gloved hand. "I suppose you haven't got the tradition of nuts that we've got," Truman had said with remarkably good humor, explaining the show of police force, at odds with the light security typically used for the royal family in London. Indeed, two Puerto Rican nationalists had tried to assassinate Truman a year earlier, killing a White House police officer in a fierce gun battle.

When they arrived at Blair House, Truman escorted Elizabeth and Philip to meet his mother-in-law, who lived on the fifth floor. "She'll kill me if she doesn't get to say hello to you," Truman told the princess, leading her up the stairs. Madge Gates Wallace was ninety-eight years old, notoriously cantankerous, and almost totally deaf. She was particularly disdainful toward her son-in-law, president or not.

"Mother," Truman shouted. "I've brought Princess Elizabeth to see you!" The older woman had been briefed, albeit apparently not with total clarity, about the British elections the week before. Attlee, constrained by Labour's narrow majority in Parliament, had called a snap election and lost to the Conservatives. That had restored Churchill as prime minister.

The elderly woman beamed. "I'm so glad your father's been reelected," she told the princess.

That brought a smile to Elizabeth's face. Truman burst out laughing.

In the evening, Elizabeth and Philip attended a reception in the grand ballroom of the Statler Hotel for some nine hundred journalists, an event at which she was treated more like a Hollywood starlet than a presumptive sovereign. There was no proper British deference here. "Princess!" "Liz!" photographers shouted in an effort to get her to turn their way. They urged her to pose with the bandleader, to move closer, to smile. The experience made an impression. A few days later, when the royal couple took a brief holiday near Sainte-Agathe-des-Monts in Quebec, Elizabeth mimicked the barked orders and nasal accents of the photographers. At the scenic village in the Laurentian Mountains, a visitor saw her point her home-movie camera at Philip. "Hey! You there!" she shouted in a rare public glimpse of her private sense of humor and her gift of impersonations. "Hey, Dook! Look this way a sec! Dat's it! Thanks a lot!"

THE NEXT MORNING, ELIZABETH AND PHILIP JOINED THE TRUMANS FOR breakfast at Blair House. "Nobody but our family and she and the Duke," Truman would recall years later. "She told me that that was the nicest affair that she had attended since she'd left home." Elizabeth made another friendly, almost familial gesture. At Margaret's request, she dropped by a party at Blair House, not listed on her official schedule, for the children of White House staffers and Cabinet members.

"She asked Margaret if she should wear her tiara," the president recalled, presumably not a typical wardrobe item for a daytime children's party, "and Margaret said if she didn't there'd be a terribly disappointed bunch of youngsters." So Elizabeth donned a royal tiara. She already understood the magical power of the fairy tale and the role of gowns, jewels, and glamour in the life she was to live. Just a year earlier, Disney studios had released *Cinderella*. At her own twelfth birthday party, Elizabeth had chosen *Snow White* to be shown to her friends.

The royal couple visited the Capitol, inspected the Declaration of Independence and Constitution at the National Archives, and placed flowers at the grave of George Washington in Mount Vernon and at the Tomb of the Unknown Soldier at Arlington National Cemetery. They spent two hours shaking hands at a party at the British embassy with fifteen hundred guests. It was followed by a white-tie dinner at the Canadian embassy in honor of the president, a reciprocal gesture for the white-tie dinner he had hosted in her honor the night before.

At a goodbye ceremony in the Rose Garden the final morning, Elizabeth presented Truman with an ornate eighteenth-century overmantel mirror adorned with a painting of flowers, to be hung in the refurbished

Blue Room as "a mark of our friendship as long as the White House shall stand." It was later moved to the Queens' Bedroom, named for the seven queens who had stayed there, by then including Elizabeth.

"We have many distinguished visitors here in this city, but never before have we had such a wonderful couple that so completely captured the hearts of all of us," Truman began, reading from prepared remarks he had edited in his own hand. He praised the "remarkable international friendship" between the United States and Great Britain—that is, the special relationship. "I am sure that we will do a better job for world peace because your visit here has tightened the bonds between us," he said.

He invited them to return and bring their children. Young Charles and Anne would later be joined by Prince Andrew, born in 1960, and Prince Edward, in 1964. "I don't know who the temporary occupants of the White House may be at that time," Truman said. "But you can be sure of this: No matter who they are, you and your family will always be welcome."

During the ceremony, a carpenter named Francis F. Anderson was repairing a window in the southwest corner of the State Dining Room, part of the refurbishment of the White House that had forced the Truman family to move to Blair House. He could watch the event in the Rose Garden and decided to memorialize it on a pine beam, his words hidden until they were accidentally uncovered a half century later.

"NOV. 2, 1951," Anderson wrote in pencil. "PRINCE PHILLIP & PRINCES ELIZABETH WERE HERE TODAY."

"LILIBET'S CONQUEST," *The Evening Star* HEADLINE DECLARED, USING THE princess's family nickname in its assessment of her visit.

"The simple truth is that she has conquered the heart of the Capital of the United States of America . . . ," the newspaper said. "[S]he has charmed and captivated this city." The visit was "refreshing," a respite from "big black headlines about things like the exploding A-bombs in Nevada."

The editorial also nodded at the substantive impact of her trip—the unspoken agenda that had made British officials so eager to have it happen.

She was "one of the very best ambassadors that Britain has ever sent to these shores," it said. The "friendship and unity" between the two nations, "though sometimes severely strained, constitute one of the most important and most indispensable bulwarks of the free world. And it is a bulwark that is stronger today as a result of her having come among us and shown how fine and endearing a queen-in-the-making can be."

She was already as well informed about the world as almost anyone in her government. When she turned eighteen years old, the king and the Cabinet had agreed that she should begin receiving Cabinet minutes and memoranda, albeit not the confidential annexes. The locked, leatherbound Red Box of news updates and government analyses, even intelligence reports, would be sent to her almost every day for the rest of her life. While the prime minister would be the one to press policy, she was briefed on the details and the history behind Britain's dealings with the United States. Now and later, she knew the importance of cultivating their bonds, regardless of its twists and strains.

A month later, in an annual Associated Press poll of female editors, Elizabeth was runner-up as Woman of the Year behind renowned war correspondent Marguerite Higgins. The next year, the princess was the second-most-admired woman in the annual Gallup Poll, after Eleanor Roosevelt.

The president was smitten, too. "Truman fell in love with her," Charteris, her royal secretary, said. Truman sent the king a handwritten letter, enclosing photographs of Elizabeth from American newspapers. She had a broad smile on her face, just as her mother had urged—another lesson learned. "We've just had a visit from a lovely young lady and her personable husband," he wrote. "They went to the hearts of all the citizens of the United States."

Elizabeth and Philip left Washington on November 2, 1951, a Friday. On the next Monday, Truman summoned to the White House the supreme commander of the newly formed NATO. He was General Eisenhower, who a year later would be elected to succeed Truman as president. Speculation about Ike's political ambitions had been percolating, though they didn't talk about politics on that day.

They emerged from the West Wing for the brief drive across Pennsylvania Avenue to Blair House for a private lunch to discuss military matters, including whether to call for another summit with Soviet dictator Joseph Stalin. They paused for a moment to give a cluster of news photographers a chance to take pictures. As they chatted, Eisenhower asked Truman how he had liked Elizabeth. Eisenhower had met her in London during World War II, of course, when she was a teenager and he was supreme commander in Europe.

"She was wonderful," Truman replied, and pulled out a three-page, handwritten message he had just received from her. "Here's something that will tickle you." Eisenhower put on his glasses to read it. "The memory of our visit to Washington will long remain with us, and we are so grateful to you for having invited us," she had written. "Our only sadness was that our stay with you was so short, but what we saw has only made us wish all the more that it may be possible for us to return again one day."

When she did return, six years later, she would be queen and Eisenhower would be president.

IN A LETTER TO HIS COUSIN, MARY ETHEL NOLAND, A SCHOOLTEACHER back home in Missouri, Truman called Elizabeth "a very grand person" who had "made a grand impression here." He joked, "It has been suggested that the King and I fire all our ambassadors and let Margaret and the Princess act for the two countries," but he added that Churchill would "probably object to any such procedure." The president's affection for the princess didn't extend to the prime minister, aggressively asserting his nation's interests and his own opinions. "He's going to cause me plenty of trouble," Truman predicted.

Churchill wasted no time to capitalize on the good feeling the princess had left behind. On the Monday after she departed, the British ambassador delivered a written request to the State Department from the prime minister—installed back in power just ten days earlier—asking that he be invited to Washington for a "renewal of our former comradeship."

Despite Truman's wary view of Churchill, in the afterglow of Elizabeth's visit, who could say no?

The king was relieved. "Much has happened in the world since we met in Plymouth Sound in 1945," George wrote on Sandringham stationery with the royal crest. It would be his final message to Truman. "I am so glad that you are going to renew your relations with Mr. Churchill shortly. He is a wise man & understands the problems of this troubled world. I have always felt that our two countries cannot progress one without the other, and I feel that this meeting will unite us even more closely."

When Churchill arrived in Washington in January, Truman took him on a private cruise aboard the presidential yacht, the *Williamsburg*. The prime minister held meetings with top foreign policy and military officials, and he sat in the presidential box to hear Truman's State of the Union address. He delivered his own address to a Joint Session of Congress, his third, the wartime hero sporting a cutaway coat and a blue polka-dot bow tie.

In his private sessions with the president and senior members of his administration, Churchill got some, though not all, of what he wanted. He sought reassurances about when a nuclear bomb might be used, and for what targets. He wanted, and got, promises of greater atomic energy exchanges despite the McMahon Act. He didn't get the veto he wanted for the use of American airpower from British bases, but they did agree on a diplomatically vague compromise that it would be "a matter for joint discussion."

In his speech to Congress, Churchill declared that he was in the United States "to ask not for gold but for steel"—not for financial aid but for military strength and unity. The two nations, working together, had already "altered the balances of the world," and with the leadership and growing power of the United States would "ward off the fearful catastrophe," he said. He promised to stand by the United States if the war in Korea broadened, and to back US policy in Formosa (Taiwan), China, and Southeast Asia.

Watching from the well of the House chamber were members of Truman's Cabinet, justices of the Supreme Court, ambassadors of the diplomatic corps. The first lady sat in the gallery, and the president watched most of the speech on his television in the White House.

Churchill once again had commanded the powerful audience and the grand venue he wanted. Thanks, at least in part, to Elizabeth.

ON FEBRUARY 6, 1952, THE KING DIED IN HIS SLEEP AFTER A DAY OF HUNTing hare at his Sandringham estate. Six days earlier, his face lined and worn, he had gone to London Airport to say farewell to Elizabeth and

Prince Philip as they left on an extended tour of the Commonwealth. They were in Kenya when word arrived that he had passed away at age fifty-six.

Truman sent a poignant telegram to the new Queen. "May I in this hour of sadness and renunciation assure you that Mrs. Truman, Margaret and I are thinking of you in your great loss," he wrote. The president also recorded his thoughts in his diary. "He was a grand man, worth a pair of his brother Ed," Truman wrote, a reference to the king's disreputable brother, Edward VIII, who had abdicated the throne and kept company with Hitler.

Then Truman predicted: "Elizabeth, the King's daughter, will be a good and great Queen."

Three

The Favorite Uncle

Tuesday, June 2, 1953—Westminster Abbey

Now she was Elizabeth II, by the Grace of God, of the United Kingdom of Great Britain and Northern Ireland and of Her Other Realms and Territories, Queen, Head of the Commonwealth, Defender of the Faith.

Her royal bloodline traced back more than a thousand years, to Alfred the Great and William the Conqueror. She would have the longest reign of any British monarch. Indeed, the only sovereign of any country with a longer tenure was King Louis XIV of France, who in the seventeenth century sat on the throne for two years longer than she did, starting with his father's death when he was four years old. She would preside over a world that changed in ways she could scarcely have imagined as she prepared for a ceremony suffused with the glory of a vanishing age.

The loss of her father shocked the young princess. Still, she kept a level head when she heard the news—"stoic" was a word often used to describe her, then and later—and apologized to her hosts in Kenya for having to depart so abruptly. She finally allowed herself to cry, in private, in the bathroom of her airplane on the flight home to England. In a letter to General George Marshall, whom she had met during the war, she described what she saw as her mission going forward: to make her father proud. "It seems impossible to believe that he has left us— he was so full of ideas, of plans for the future, but we shall try to carry on as he would wish," she said. Among those confident in her ability was Eleanor Roosevelt. The former first lady felt a "terrible shock" over the death of the king she had liked and respected. "He took up the burden of kingship out of a sense of duty when he had not expected to carry it. He fulfilled every duty at considerable personal sacrifice." Of the new sovereign, she wrote, "It is a heavy burden for such a young woman, but she has been trained to carry it. She has always seemed serious-minded and full of concern for the people of her country. She will be strengthened by her husband's support and the goodwill and affection of all her people."

And so she was.

On Coronation Day, Elizabeth departed Buckingham Palace for Westminster Abbey in a magnificent gold coach pulled by eight Windsor Grey horses, among them a gelding named Eisenhower—a name chosen by the royal family and a tribute traditionally reserved for chiefs of the British military services. His namesake, President Dwight David Eisenhower, had been inaugurated in Washington nearly five months earlier. He was invited to attend but instead dispatched a delegation on his behalf, including Marshall and another heroic World War II general, Omar Bradley. (US presidents traditionally haven't attended British coronations. FDR did not attend that of George VI; more recently, Joe Biden skipped Charles III's.)

The grand ceremony in London, defined by pomp and history, not only thrilled the British but also fascinated Americans. "The Coronation has given the British people an unexampled opportunity to remove their inhibitions and go haywire on a thorough jamboree," a US State Department dispatch reported the next day. "But this is, in its way, testimony to the fact that the prestige of the throne has risen, over the past forty years to remarkable heights."

Technology didn't yet exist to transmit the ceremony live across the Atlantic Ocean. Even so, on that day millions of Americans saw still photographs on television as the audio of the live radio feed was aired. After the film footage had been flown to New York, more than thirty-two million Americans watched the replay later that night. The International News Service reported that the prospect of seeing the coronation spurred sales of TV sets on both sides of the Atlantic. "For all practical purposes, today marked the birth of international television," the *New*

York Times critic declared. The stunning ratings underscored the appeal in the United States of the "radiant" young queen with a "twinkling smile," he wrote.

Among the journalists in London was a twenty-three-year-old reporter for the *Washington Times Herald*, Jacqueline Bouvier. The future first lady had gotten her start at the newspaper writing about the princess's visit to the United States two years earlier. Now she persuaded the editors to send her to London aboard the SS *United States* to cover the lighter side of Elizabeth's coronation. By then, in June 1953, Jackie was dating Jack Kennedy, the junior senator from Massachusetts and the most eligible bachelor in Washington. They would be engaged that summer and marry in the fall.

"You know what they should call this ship? The Mayflower in reverse," she quoted a passenger as remarking when the ship steamed out of New York. Those booked in first class included Louis Arpels (of luxury jeweler Van Cleef & Arpels), Walter Cronkite (of CBS), the editor of the *New York Herald Tribune*, and the ambassadors from Peru and Ceylon (now Sri Lanka). Not to mention the Duke and Duchess of Windsor, though they had not been invited to the ceremony. Edward VIII's decision to abdicate the throne had led to the coronation of first his brother and now his niece, but he and the duchess would watch the ceremony on television at their home in Paris.

Jackie filed her stories by air mail and accompanied them with clever black-and-white caricatures she sketched. "Let's lunch at Claridge's. That's where all the deposed monarchs are staying," she reported overhearing a woman say in the lobby of the Dorchester. Jackie detailed the hardships involved for the royal ladies-in-waiting, who reported they had to be in their seats for the coronation by 6:30 a.m., which meant their hairdressers would arrive at the palace at 3 a.m. "We wear tiaras, you know, and that takes a bit of arranging," one explained. The inquiring reporter investigated whether English gentlemen were still required to wear top hats and precisely what shade of pink ladies attending the races at Royal Ascot were sporting.

Standing on the sidewalk outside Buckingham Palace, she posed this question to passersby: "Do you think Elizabeth will be England's last queen?" There, she caught a glimpse of four-year-old Prince Charles, peeking out with his little sister from a palace window.

In New York City, there was another little boy watching the scene on television with his mother. Donald Trump was then six years old. One of his earliest memories was sitting with his mother and watching the ceremony across the ocean. She didn't budge for the entire day. "She was just enthralled by the pomp and circumstance, the whole idea of royalty and glamour," he said years later. Mary Anne MacLeod Trump had been born in Scotland, "serious Scotland"—in the Outer Hebrides, the remote and rugged islands off the northern coast, where people still spoke Scots Gaelic. (Years later, when he was president, Scottish officials presented him with a 1921 census record from the Isle of Lewis that listed her at age nine.) She was an ardent monarchist and a "tremendous fan" of Elizabeth. "I remember growing up with my mother where anything having to do with the Queen, she'd watch," he told me. "She just thought she was absolutely great."

He was growing up, felicitously enough, in the New York borough called Queens—named after Queen Catherine of Braganza, the wife of King Charles II, who was one of Elizabeth's predecessors and a distant uncle.

His father, real estate developer Fred Trump, born in the Bronx to German immigrant parents, felt no such fascination with the royals. He "was very brick-and-mortar," Trump recalled. But his mother "loved the ceremonial and the beauty, because no one does that like the English." He inherited his delight in gold and gilt and ceremony from her and, in a sense, from the Queen herself. As president, he would redecorate the Oval Office with a profusion of gold reminiscent of a palace.

At the state dinner she hosted in his honor, he asked her about the day of her coronation. "So she ended up in a position that she never thought was going to happen; she told me this," he said. "She was very young, but she's very smart. She figured it out incredibly, and the people were very important to her. She knew that she could only be successful and even survive as a monarchy if the people loved her."

WINSTON CHURCHILL WAS BACK LEADING THE GOVERNMENT. HE HAD fallen "madly in love" with the new Queen, her private secretary, Sir Jock Colville, would remark. Churchill's daughter agreed. "He fell under her spell," she said. As the son of an American mother, and a man who knew her nation's psyche well, his instant priority was to turn Eisenhower's affection for Elizabeth to Britain's advantage.

The aging prime minister understood the potential of the young Queen's power, setting a strategy that his successors would follow for decades. "It is natural for Parliaments to talk and for the Crown to *shine*," he declared a few days before her coronation, speaking to an audience that included her. She would serve her realm with "soft power," a phrase that American political scientist Joseph Nye would popularize years later. "She did a lot more for Britain and Britain's standing in the world than you would assume from just following the details of the law" defining the constitutional monarchy, Nye said.

Churchill wasted no time. Seventy-eight years old and recovering from a stroke, he was an old man in a hurry. He wanted Eisenhower to visit London to confer with him about world affairs, including how to deal with the rising Soviet Union. Two months after the coronation, Churchill wrote him, saying the US ambassador to Great Britain had told him "the great news that you might perhaps find it possible to come to London for a talk about things with me." The prime minister added an incentive: Elizabeth. "I told the Queen about this yesterday and Her Majesty was very pleased indeed and would return from Balmoral to welcome you at Buckingham Palace during your stay," he said. "Would some time in the last week of September or the first week of October be convenient for you and Mrs. Eisenhower?"

Eisenhower didn't bite, saying Ambassador Winthrop Aldrich had misinterpreted his "wistful thinking" about the possibility of a visit. Ike was familiar with Churchill's skills of persuasion and his gift for the grand gesture. "The fact is that I am scheduled for a number of inescapable commitments during the foreseeable future and it would be impossible for me to leave the country," he replied—a flat no.

A year later, Churchill made another attempt, once again citing Her Majesty. "When I had my last Audience with The Queen she spoke of the pleasure with which she would welcome a State visit by you to London," he wrote. "This might be combined in any way convenient with a top-level meeting." That is, a meeting with Churchill. Eisenhower declined again. "I cannot see that a top-level meeting is anything which I can inscribe on my schedule for any predictable date," he wrote. Still, he added, "I hope you will find some way of letting the Queen know how deeply I appreciate her gracious reference to the possibility of such a visit." The Anglo-American alliance remained a high priority for Churchill even as his historic tenure was coming to an end; he would step down less than a year later. In a handwritten letter when he retired, the Queen told him that none of his successors would "ever for me be able to hold the place of my first prime minister, to whom both my husband and I owe so much and for whose wise guidance during the early years of my reign I shall always be so profoundly grateful."

The failure to hold a major summit with Eisenhower during his second term as prime minister would nag at Churchill as he prepared to retire from public life. His concerns would be compounded by the eruption of the most serious diplomatic dispute between the United States and the United Kingdom in a century.

THE SUEZ COMPANY, OWNED BY THE BRITISH GOVERNMENT AND FRENCH investors, had controlled the 120-mile waterway that linked the Mediterranean and the Red Sea since it was built in the nineteenth century. The Royal Navy used the Suez Canal as a strategic route, and it was becoming an important conduit for oil tankers heading to Europe. After Egypt won independence in 1922, ending forty years as a British protectorate, the canal became to Egyptian nationalists a symbol of foreign interference.

Egyptian President Gamal Abdel Nasser, moving to establish himself as the leader of the Arab world, nationalized the Suez Canal on July 26, 1956, closing it to Israeli ships and making it an international flashpoint. British Prime Minister Anthony Eden, Churchill's successor, viewed Nasser as a dictator and a danger to the West, especially given his support from Soviet Russia. Eden publicly pursued diplomacy but privately planned military action, coordinated with France and Israel.

Their scheme: Israel would invade Egypt through the Sinai Peninsula, triggering a war that would be a ruse for British and French forces to "save" the canal from the conflict. At first, events unfolded as intended. Israel invaded on October 29. British and French paratroopers landed along the canal on November 5, which happened to be the day before

Eisenhower would win a second term in the White House. But Eden had made a costly miscalculation. He had rejected Eisenhower's counsel, then kept him in the dark.

The president had warned the prime minister that military action would risk destabilizing the region and sparking a wider war. When Britain and France went ahead anyway, Eisenhower stood behind Egypt—to the amazement of much of the world, including officials in London and Cairo. "The United States was not consulted in any way about any phase of these actions . . . ," he said in an address to the nation on October 31. "We believe these actions to have been taken in error, for we do not accept the use of force as a wise or proper instrument for the settlement of international disputes."

The United States as well as several of Britain's fellow Commonwealth nations voted in the United Nations to condemn the invasion and demand a ceasefire, a resolution that was vetoed by Britain and France. When the crisis caused a run on the pound, Eisenhower threatened in effect to bankrupt Britain if it didn't agree to an immediate cessation of hostilities.

The humiliated British government folded. On December 3, officials announced their troops would withdraw. The final British and French forces were gone by December 22, a retreat that showed the world the ebbing influence of the British Empire.

To many in the United Kingdom who remembered standing shoulder to shoulder with Eisenhower and the Americans to defeat fascism little more than a decade earlier, his support for the Soviet-backed Nasser and his hard line against London's action were seen as a betrayal. Churchill's view was more nuanced, and it was influenced by his longtime rivalry with Eden. The former prime minister wrote privately to Eisenhower, pleading for a long view. "Whatever the arguments adduced here and in the United States for or against Anthony's action in Egypt, it will now be an act of folly, on which our whole civilization may founder, to let events in the Middle East come between us . . . and it is the Soviet Union that will ride the storm . . . ," he wrote. "I know where your heart lies. You are now the only one who can so influence events both in [the United Nations] and the free world as to ensure that the great essentials are not lost in bickerings and pettiness among the nations."

Eisenhower's reply was warm, and he agreed about the overriding threat from the Soviets, suggesting that Nasser was "perhaps unwittingly" their "tool." But he was firm about the US stance on Suez. "[S]o far as Britain and France were concerned, we felt that they had deliberately excluded us from their thinking . . . ," he said. "[W]e had no recourse except to assert our readiness to support the United Nations."

The "special relationship" was in tatters, its future not guaranteed.

Restoring that closeness would rest with someone Eisenhower had adored since she was a shy teenager. He had forged a friendship with her parents and a fondness for her when he was the commander of allied forces and she was a princess. Now she was Queen and he was president. Their mutual affection had been handy when things were going well between their two nations. It would be critical now that there was trouble.

WHEN THE SUEZ CRISIS ERUPTED, THE QUESTION WAS RAISED: DID HER Majesty know?

The weekly sessions between sovereigns and prime ministers are shrouded in secrecy, ground rules that suit both sides. "We don't leak," was the injunction Margaret Rhodes, Elizabeth's friend, once spied posted on the wall above the desk of the assistant to the royal press secretary. But in the firestorm after Suez, some Brits demanded to know if their Queen knew about the invasion plans beforehand, including the collusion with Israel and France, and whether she approved of them.

Only decades later, with the release of once-secret documents, were those questions answered. Yes, she knew. And she expressed private reservations about the course her government had set.

She was reading the Red Box of briefing papers almost every day. Each week, she saw the Joint Intelligence Committee's classified summary of intelligence findings. After all, she was the formal head of the nation's armed forces, and during her reign MI6 became Her Majesty's Secret Intelligence Service. During the three weeks of greatest crisis over Suez, from November 1 to November 22, 1956, she was sometimes sent special bulletins twice a day.

Eden didn't need her approval. Indeed, it would have been a violation of her constitutional role to do anything beyond discreetly discussing her views with him in private. But her personal secretary, Martin Charteris, later said she questioned Eden's mental stability. "I think the Queen believed Eden was mad," he said. The Suez crisis "gave the Queen a great deal of concern. She was personally worried about it." There were fears that the Soviets might try to intervene militarily, risking a third world war, he said. What's more, she was troubled by "the basic dishonesty of the whole thing."

At the time, she was a relatively inexperienced monarch, thirty years old and facing the biggest foreign policy furor of her four-year reign. It was a learning experience in her role and in the subtle exercise of her power. She could "absolutely" exert influence by the way she phrased a question, said Tom Jeremy King, the Baron King of Bridgwater, who held various Cabinet posts through the years. "She might well say: 'Really?' Or: 'Why are you doing that?'" In almost a caricature of British understatement, she may have asked the prime minister a query meant to suggest the need to have second thoughts: "Are you sure you are being wise?"

AT THE BEGINNING OF THE NEW YEAR, OF 1957, ELIZABETH WAS READY TO make her first state visit to the United States, and the British were eager to arrange it. Officials from both sides had been discussing the possibility for months before the Suez conflagration. The idea "had been mooted before the Election by the American Embassy," said Harold Caccia, a veteran British diplomat posted to Washington to repair relations. But he noted the obvious. "Things have altered a great deal" since then, he said, and not in a good way.

London was skeptical that Eisenhower would be willing to invite her anytime soon. "An invitation will be regarded in some quarters in the United States as indicating that the President is determined to bury the hatchet over the Suez affair so far as the United Kingdom is concerned . . . ," a Foreign Office memo noted. Eisenhower had privately told Churchill: "I hope that this one may be washed off the slate as soon as possible." But the president wasn't ready to do that, not yet. "[A]n early invitation seems rather improbable," British officials advised—an understatement, given the diplomatic fallout. There were risks for Elizabeth, too. She might be dragged into politics instead of sailing above them, Caccia worried. "In particular, there might be a tendency for critics to say that we were trying to use The Queen's prestige to effect by sentiment what argument could not do."

Of course, that was precisely the idea. Harold Macmillan, who had become prime minister after an ailing Eden had been forced to resign, saw that as the appeal of a royal visit. To Macmillan, "this relationship was vital not only to Britain's future but also to that of Europe," said Henry Brandon, who interviewed the prime minister in London that summer. "Just as it was crucial to keep the West Germans anchored to the West, so it was essential to keep the United States anchored to Europe."

Already on the Queen's schedule for 1957 were state visits to Portugal, France, and Denmark. But anxious British officials were flagging in newspapers across the United States dismissive commentary about England's standing. "The collapse of the military thrust [in Suez] will be accepted by the Communist world and much of the West as evidence Great Britain is no longer a great power," the *Miami Herald* editorialized. Even the tiny *Council Bluffs Daily Nonpareil* in Iowa said there were fears that Britain was becoming "the tail of the US kite."

Churchill then chose the moment to deftly, discreetly intervene, in a manner befitting an elder statesman held in high regard by his royal protégé. He showed Elizabeth his private communication with Eisenhower, a letter that said the president longed for the restoration of the "old time closeness" with Britain. She was heartened, convinced that a genuine opening existed. "[I]t is most interesting to learn his appreciation of the situation," she remarked, "and I hope it means that the present feeling that this country and America are not seeing eye-to-eye will soon be speedily replaced by even stronger ties between us."

She had no authority to prevent the Suez adventure, if that was her view, but she could now play a crucial role in mending the rupture it had opened. In the spring, Macmillan suggested to Eisenhower a royal visit in the autumn. The president finally sent a formal invitation for October.

Historian Elizabeth Longford described Elizabeth's mission as biblical, likening the diplomatic devastation of Suez to Noah's flood: "Britain was fortunate to have an appealing young queen to send out like a dove from a battered ark," she said.

THE QUEEN WOULD BE IN THE UNITED STATES FOR SIX DAYS, AND SHE WAS determined to see sights that were quintessentially American. The royal staff set out to stack the itinerary with "possible events of a typically American nature which the Queen and the Duke might attend."

The packed schedule alarmed Eisenhower. It was "so crowded that it would have killed anybody but two people as young and vigorous as they," he told Macmillan, saying he would have fired any aide "who dared to set up for me a program like theirs." When Prince Philip was given a leather-bound list of the events planned for the next six days, he raised his eyebrows in mock dismay, suggesting the crush would be the death of him. "What, no memorial service at the end?" he asked.

When Elizabeth arrived at Patrick Henry Airport in Virginia on October 16, 1957, it was the first time a reigning British Queen had stepped foot on American soil. Chief of protocol Wiley Buchanan, sent to greet her, could sense her nervousness, an echo of the anxiety she had shown on her arrival as a princess. She emerged from a Royal Canadian Air Force jet clad in a coat of peacock-blue silk shantung and a hat spiked with pheasant feathers.

"For a moment I thought she looked tense and uncertain," Buchanan said. But by the time she reached the bottom of the stairs, she had composed herself. She was a more seasoned public figure than she had been six years earlier. "Her manner was formal but gracious and self-possessed," he said. "When I welcomed her to the United States on behalf of President Eisenhower, she smiled and said, 'Thank you, Ambassador Buchanan; it's a great pleasure to be here.'"

The visit began with a tour of Jamestown, which was celebrating the 350th anniversary of the founding of the first British colony in what would become the United States. (She would return a half century later to celebrate the 400th anniversary.) The royal couple visited the colonial village in Williamsburg, Virginia, and stayed overnight at the Williamsburg Inn. At a reception in the garden of the former Governor's Palace, in an exchange reported the next day by *The Virginian-Pilot*, a grande dame from an old Virginia family "swept up" to Philip "and announced that she was as well born as he." She could trace her British ancestry back a dozen generations on both sides of her family, she told him. Philip, who had less patience than his wife for pomposity, "cocked his head to one side. 'You've got it all over me, ma'am!'" he remarked dryly. "'I'm Greek!'"

That description of his lineage was true but not complete. Philip was born in Greece with both Greek and Danish royal heritage, but his family had been sent into exile when he was a toddler.

On this trip, the royal entourage with Philip and Elizabeth had multiplied since her visit to the United States as a princess, when seven traveling servants had drawn commentary.

Now they were accompanied by a staff of thirty-three, among them private secretaries and clerks, two ladies-in-waiting and four "dressers," the duke's valet and the Queen's hairdresser, four footmen and two royal equerries, two police officers and a doctor. In a safari-like procession of trunks, they brought outfits for every occasion, from a college football game to a white-tie banquet. The Queen's collection of precious jewels for the road—tiaras, earrings, necklaces, bracelets, and brooches—were priceless. As usual, the royal couple brought their own water—distilled, with no minerals, "to avoid the possibility of gastric disturbances sometimes caused by a change of drinking water."

THE NEXT MORNING, ELIZABETH AND PHILIP ARRIVED IN WASHINGTON aboard the *Columbine*, a military version of the Lockheed Super Constellation that Eisenhower used in office and had loaned them for the short trip.

"Your Majesty, you are *most* welcome; indeed you are," Eisenhower said, greeting them with "more genuine warmth and pleasure" than his protocol chief had seen before from the reserved commander in chief. He was clearly delighted to see her. There was more evidence of their pleasure at the visit: The royal couple were the first foreign dignitaries the Eisenhowers invited to stay in the White House—the Queen in the Rose Room, recently remodeled in Mamie's favorite color of pink; and the prince in the Lincoln Bedroom.

Elizabeth would have more reverence for Eisenhower than any other president, grounded in the great trial they had shared during war, and by their mutual deep regard for her father. Since those days, their lives had been transformed by an election in the United States and a coronation in the United Kingdom that had put each in a position of global authority. The affection between them was unchanged, but there was a perceptible difference. They no longer met as a favorite uncle doting on his winsome niece. This time, it was an official state visit by a sovereign to a president. Now it was a conversation between trusted allies facing momentous questions.

The trip to Washington proved to be an early lesson for the Queen, now thirty-one years old, in the considerable possibilities of her soft power.

In the aftermath of Suez, the British feared she was arriving in a position of weakness. Instead, she discovered how much her standing could shield her from controversy that would have hounded an elected or appointed official. She was the head of state with a lifetime tenure that protected her from the vicissitudes of the moment. Presidents often saw her as a sounding board above day-to-day politics—more like the pope or the Dalai Lama than a president or prime minister—and with an independent perspective worth hearing.

At this moment, the Soviets unintentionally nudged the old allies closer together. On October 4, 1957, a week before the royal couple left London, Moscow launched Sputnik. The world's first artificial satellite would orbit the Earth for three weeks, and with that seize the advantage in a new space race. The sobering news overwhelmed the sour memory of Suez. In the United States, alarm spiked over whether and how the country had lost its global edge in aerospace and engineering.

"I do hope our visit will be of value between the two countries," Elizabeth wrote the day before she left. "[T]here does seem to be a much closer feeling between the US and ourselves, especially since the Russian satellite has come to shake everyone about their views on Russian scientific progress!" She had been startled by the near-hysterical tone of the news coverage. "[T]he television is the worst of all," she said. Macmillan agreed. Sputnik's impact on the United States was "something equivalent to Pearl Harbor," he said. "The American cocksure-ness is shaken."

In the six years since she had visited the United States, she had gained confidence. She was surprised by how much confidence the Americans had lost, by how rattled Eisenhower and others seemed to be. Britain had been unnerved by the Suez debacle. Now the United States was unnerved by Sputnik's success. "It was as if they all needed a friendship shoulder to lean on," she said. When the president and the royal couple met in private, they discussed Sputnik, a sign of her engagement on substantive matters as well as less weighty ones.

During the visit, Eisenhower would celebrate his sixty-seventh birthday, on October 14. Two years earlier, he had been confronted with the realities of aging when he had suffered a serious heart attack. A month after the Queen's visit, he would have a stroke that left him unable to speak intelligibly for days.

To her surprise and pleasure, he no longer treated her as a child to be mentored but as a peer. By now, she was thoroughly up to date on bilateral relations and international developments. Macmillan throughout his tenure as prime minister would send her detailed memoranda and seek her views. During this visit with Eisenhower, so much a part of her father's generation, she discovered how he saw her as her own person, with her own power and her own voice.

"The Queen was full of delight at the impact she felt she was having—a young and energetic hereditary Monarch contrasted by some commentators with the slowed-down American elected one," said Ben Pimlott, an early and authoritative biographer. "It was the first chance in her reign to compare the two roles. She felt the Americans she met, and especially the president, displayed a surprising lack of self-confidence. When she got back, she told a friend that she had found herself having to offer—as if on Britain's behalf—a shoulder to lean on, and that she had been taken aback by the American need to be liked. . . .

"She was both flattered and a little shocked by the eagerness of the garrulous old man—a figure from her wartime adolescence, now in the middle of his second term—to unburden himself to her."

At the White House dinner, Eisenhower wore an emblem of their personal history. Around his neck hung the Order of Merit, an eight-pointed cross of red and blue enamel suspended by a small imperial crown and a ribbon of blue and crimson, an honor bestowed on him by her father. Elizabeth wore a diamond tiara that had been presented to her great-grandmother, Queen Alexandra, when she was princess of Wales in 1888, and a blue sash of the Order of the Garter, held by a diamond brooch that her grandmother, Queen Mary, had left her when she died in 1953. Her gown was embroidered with autumn leaves and berries in gold thread and pearls.

"[T]he respect we have for Britain is epitomized in the affection we have for the royal family, who have honored us so much by making this visit to our shores . . . ," the president said at the White House dinner. "I want to again say that my faith in the future of these two great countries and the whole Commonwealth of the British nations—indeed of the whole free world—is absolutely unimpeachable." He didn't mention Suez.

"I pray that the ancient ties of friendship between the people of the United States and of my peoples may long endure," Elizabeth said in her reply.

DURING THE TRIP, THERE WOULD BE SOME LESS GUARDED GLIMPSES OF the Queen. And as the royal couple had hoped, they saw glimpses of Americans who weren't wearing white tie and tails.

She had asked to see a football "match"—football of the American variety, that is. She and Philip ended up in box seats above the fifty-yard line at the University of Maryland's Byrd Stadium, joining forty-three thousand other fans to watch the Maryland Terrapins face the University of North Carolina Tar Heels. Beforehand, she walked on the field to chat with the teams' captains, wearing a $15,000 mink coat she had been presented two days earlier by the Mutation Mink Breeders Association, a trade group of US fur farmers. Collegiate marching bands, drum majorettes, and cheerleaders added to the all-American spectacle.

After the game began, watching from the stands, she sometimes seemed perplexed by the rules of the game. She asked Maryland Governor Theodore McKeldin, "How can they hit each other that hard without injury?" He replied, "Because they are in good condition and trained for it—and they wear fourteen pounds of equipment."

Maryland won, 21 to 7.

On the way to the game, their motorcade passed the Queenstown Shopping Center in West Hyattsville, Maryland. (Queenstown, Maryland, was named for the eighteenth-century Queen Anne, Elizabeth's distant cousin.) It featured a supermarket, by then commonplace for

American shoppers but a novelty in Britain. She asked to stop by when they were returning to Washington after the game, and security agents hurried back to arrange a visit—to the amazement of the shoppers and the disbelief of the Giant store manager. Called at home and assuming it was a prank, he didn't bother to come back to work. The assistant manager gave them a tour.

It was as though they were examining some exotic enclave. In England, most shoppers were still going from the baker to the butcher to the greengrocer, without the convenience and choice of a consolidated market—super, indeed. "How nice you can bring your children along," the Queen told one woman, her child perched in the seat of the shopping cart. Philip accepted a sample of cheese on a cracker. "Good for mice!" he said, hopefully not a comment on the quality of the cheese. They marveled at the range of goods available, from toiletries to Halloween costumes. Still wrapped in her new mink coat, the Queen seemed particularly taken by the potpies in the frozen-food section. By the time they left the store, word of the royal visitors had spread in the neighborhood. Children on bicycles and their elders lined up outside to wave as they left.

Not every idea the royal couple suggested for the trip worked out.

During the planning, Richard Colville, the Queen's press secretary, reported that Philip "was delighted that the suggestion of a football game being included in the Royal programme was being seriously considered," and wanted to explore other athletic endeavors. "He felt that the Duke might well be interested in the suggestion that he, and perhaps The Queen also, might visit a bowling alley one evening as an example of a pastime of the American public." Sadly, there would be no bowling on this visit, or during those that followed.

"Please come back," Eisenhower told Elizabeth as her visit was ending. "It was nice to have you." The Associated Press reporter on the scene at the North Portico called it "an easy going exchange, much in the manner of suburban couples taking leave." The royal couple invited the president to visit them, too. "Come home with us," Philip said jokingly. Elizabeth added, "I do hope you'll come."

After they left, Eisenhower walked to the Oval Office and wrote a letter to Elizabeth in longhand, addressing and sealing the envelope before his secretary could make a copy. He gave it to an aide to have it delivered to her in person in New York the next day. He cast her visit as both personal and one with global repercussions. The warmth of their visit made it clear that the special relationship had survived Suez.

"If you have had a moment in your hectic schedules to read any of our newspapers, you know that you both have captivated the people of our country by your charm and graciousness," he wrote. "I earnestly believe that your visit to this country will not only strengthen the ties that exist between our two peoples, but that it will serve to give evidence to all the free world that our nations are firmly united in the search for a just and lasting peace."

ELIZABETH AND PHILIP TOOK A SPECIAL TRAIN FROM WASHINGTON TO New York, arranged by the State Department at the then-considerable cost of $4,000—a sum lamented by protocol chief Buchanan, who accompanied the traveling party. At her request, they got off the train on Staten Island and boarded an army ferryboat so she could approach Manhattan from the water. The view of the skyscrapers was breathtaking, Buchanan said, "as if the city were standing up to greet the Queen." Fireboats pumped plumes of water in the air as army planes, navy blimps, and police helicopters flew overhead.

For the ticker-tape parade from Battery Park to City Hall, the Queen was flanked by New York Governor Averell Harriman and Mayor Robert Wagner in the back seat of a Lincoln Cosmopolitan convertible loaned by the White House and outfitted with a custom bubbletop made of plexiglass. Two hundred tons of ticker tape rained down. More than a million people lined the streets, many of them waving small British and American flags and shouting "Hi, Liz!" and "Hooray for Prince Phil!"

During her fifteen-hour stop in New York, she addressed the United Nations, attended a luncheon hosted by the mayor for fifteen hundred people—former President Herbert Hoover was seated next to her and Eleanor Roosevelt just behind—then joined an English-Speaking Union dinner for forty-five hundred at the Waldorf-Astoria. She dropped by a separate Royal Commonwealth Ball for another forty-five hundred at the Seventh Regiment Armory on Park Avenue.

At twilight, she went to the Empire State Building to take in the sights of the city from the 102nd floor.

The royal couple was running nearly an hour behind schedule when they finally left the armory for the drive to Idlewild Airport, now John F. Kennedy International Airport, to take the fourteen-hour flight back to England. "As we sped through Manhattan and out through Queens, the streets were jammed with people waiting up to see the Queen," Buchanan recalled. A jerry-rigged light on the floor of the limousine illuminated the royal couple in the plexiglass bubble, Elizabeth's tiara sparkling. "By now it was 1 o'clock in the morning, and many of the spectators seemed to have gotten out of bed. The Queen was confounded by the sight. 'Philip,' she said, 'look at all those people in their nightclothes. *I* certainly wouldn't come out in *my* nightclothes to see anyone drive by, no matter who it was!'"

It was another example of those crazy Americans, with their perplexing rules for football and their remarkable frozen potpies. When she visited the United States, then and later, she would be an avid tourist, curious and interested. As a child, she had seen the Americans as the cavalry that had rode in and saved her family, country, the world. As an adult, she liked the show tunes of Hollywood better than the operas of Europe. She was more likely to be amused by Americans' directness and informality than to be offended by their disregard for protocol.

The British press noticed, with a bit of jealousy. "Don't Put the Queen Behind Bars" demanded the seven-column headline on the front page of London's *Daily Herald* when she returned. The overline: "If it's good for the Yanks, then it should be good for us."

"The Queen is home," the story began. "Her tour has been all triumph. And everywhere people are asking: Why did she have to cross the Atlantic to become REAL? On this side of the Atlantic, there has never been such a commonsense sweeping aside of stodginess and formality. . . . We are sure that the British people would like the Queen in America better than the Queen of England."

In Great Britain, Elizabeth would always be "The Queen" and, for a steadily growing proportion of Brits, the only sovereign they had ever known. But for whatever reason—because of her early contact with Yanks during the war, because of the ebullient way Truman and Eisenhower and most presidents embraced her—she would display an ease, an openness in the United States.

By calculation or not, it was also a way to hold the affection of the American public. She understood how to play the role of queen to a US audience. She would demonstrate her grace and her self-discipline and, on occasion, her sense of humor. Part of her charm was that she didn't seem to take herself too seriously. She was also truly in tune with American popular culture. When Prince Charles was visiting Washington in 1990 to open an exhibit at Octagon House of the architecture of Christopher Wren, he spotted actor Tom Selleck in the audience. "My parents watch you every Thursday night!" he exclaimed. That would have been to see *Magnum P.I.*, aired on CBS from 1980 to 1988.

THE MORNING AFTER THE QUEEN LEFT THE UNITED STATES, THE BRITISH ambassador sent officials in London a private assessment of her trip. "A personal triumph," he called it. "During the visit there has been no suggestion that it was arranged for political purposes either to close the book on Suez or to provide for the future," Caccia told the Foreign Office. "Yet it has in a real sense done just this for Britain in America." The veteran diplomat described Elizabeth's impact, both its reach and its limits.

"Disagreements and misunderstandings will no doubt again arise between Governments in the United States and the United Kingdom," he wrote. "But in addition to our past ties, The Queen in her person has strengthened the more permanent links."

As she was flying home to London, Macmillan was taking off for Washington.

Their crisscrossed travel was juxtaposed on the front pages of some newspapers: "Queen Returns Home in Triumph" was the headline over one story and "Ike, Dulles Prepare to Meet Macmillan" on another. The trips weren't unrelated. An Associated Press story said the announcement of Macmillan's visit "caught most State Department officials and the Washington diplomatic corps by surprise." It observed: "The warm reception accorded the Queen demonstrated that basic British American relations are at a high peak of cordiality and friendship."

At the end of their meetings, Eisenhower astonished Macmillan by establishing two joint Anglo-American committees to deal with weapons and with nuclear cooperation. "The end of the McMahon Act—the great prize!" the prime minister exclaimed. (Truman had outraged London by restricting Britain's access to nuclear information.) In his memoirs, Macmillan titled this chapter "Honeymoon at Washington," a marriage revived thanks in part to Elizabeth.

THE STATE VISIT TO WASHINGTON WAS MORE THAN AN OPPORTUNITY FOR Her Majesty to build a closer relationship with the current president. It was also a chance to get to know a future one.

Richard Nixon was the junior senator from California, freshly sworn in, when he had met Elizabeth at a British embassy reception in 1951 during her first trip to the United States. Six years later, now vice president, he attended the state dinner in her honor at the Eisenhower White House. He also hosted a luncheon for the royal couple and ninety-six guests in the Old Supreme Court Chamber, on the ground floor of the Capitol. He had hoped to hold it at the more ornate National Gallery, but museum officials declined. Or beneath the soaring dome of the Capitol, but House Speaker Sam Rayburn refused to give his permission. Like his fellow Texan, Lyndon Johnson, he was not a man who swooned for royalty.

Nixon, whose constitutional role made him president of the Senate, didn't have any trouble getting permission to use the historic chamber where first the Senate and then the high court had once convened.

The room was bedecked with exotic Hawaiian flowers and the luncheon featured a complicated entrée, catered by the old-line Mayflower Hotel—breast of guinea hen with mushrooms atop Kentucky ham. Nixon offered a toast to the shared legacy of English-speaking peoples around the world; the Queen reciprocated with welcoming words in her toast. That said, the gift he sent her at the White House the next day seems, well, odd: a copy of *The Art of Readable Writing*, by Dr. Rudolf Flesch, an Austrian-born language expert who advocated short sentences and plain speaking. Chapters in the chatty 237-page volume include "The Importance of Being Trivial" and "How to Be Human Though Factual."

"Your Majesty," Nixon wrote. "I am enclosing a copy of the book which I referred to yesterday at luncheon. I thought you might find some of Mr. Flesch's rather startling ideas amusing, in view of our discussion of speaking techniques." Whether over lunch he had been offering praise or giving tips for her speaking techniques isn't clear.

A year later, Eisenhower sent Nixon to London for the dedication of the American Memorial Chapel in St. Paul's Cathedral.

The vice president arrived still reeling from what he called "one of the most depressing election nights I have ever known"—though he would face even more depressing election nights in the future. This time, in 1958, he wasn't on the ballot himself, but the Republicans he hoped to lead as their presidential nominee in two years had suffered serious setbacks in the midterm elections. Democrats had gained thirteen Senate seats and forty-seven House seats, bolstering their control of Congress, and they carried thirteen of twenty-one gubernatorial contests. It was a sign of voter weariness with the Eisenhower administration and a cautionary omen for the White House race ahead.

Nixon welcomed the opportunity to get out of town with a trip to Great Britain for the dedication of the chapel honoring the twenty-eight thousand US soldiers, sailors, and airmen stationed in Britain who had died during World War II. His itinerary included lunch with Queen Elizabeth and Prince Philip at Buckingham Palace and a high-profile address on global affairs at the Guildhall to the English-Speaking Union. The next day was Thanksgiving, when Elizabeth would join him at the US embassy to celebrate the most American of holidays.

Thanksgiving was a particular reminder of American friendship for her. In 1942, when she was sixteen years old, hundreds of thousands of US forces had been deployed to the United Kingdom to join the war against Germany. On that Thanksgiving Day, in gratitude, King George and Queen Elizabeth invited more than two hundred American servicemen and nurses to the bomb-damaged Buckingham Palace for an afternoon buffet and welcome by the royal couple and their daughters. "It is to commemorate the First Harvest Festival of the Pilgrim Fathers in New England in 1621," the king noted in his diary.

This time, the celebration started with a sartorial crisis. Nixon's dinner jacket hadn't been packed, an omission realized only when valet Dave Ball was putting out the vice president's clothes for the evening. With the Queen on her way, the men in Nixon's entourage were lined up to assess who came the closest to the president's size. The winner, or loser, turned out to be James Bassett, a veteran *Los Angeles Times* editor on leave to serve as the vice president's press adviser on the trip. "I'll never let anybody else pack Richard's clothes again," First Lady Pat Nixon vowed.

In turn, Bassett managed to borrow a suitable outfit from a Scotland Yard detective. *Punch* magazine lampooned the serial cadging of clothes with a cartoon showing a trouser-less London bobby on guard outside the embassy, hoping wistfully that it wouldn't be a long evening.

Bassett's jacket was the best fit, but that didn't mean it was a good one. "Nixon's Borrowed Tuxedo Doesn't Fit" was the blunt headline on the front page of one American newspaper the next morning. "As he welcomed the radiant Queen he tugged at his over-long sleeves and at his low-hanging coattails," the Associated Press reported. The Liverpool *Daily Post* observed that he looked "as if he had lost some weight since he last wore the dinner jacket."

Twelve years later, as president, Nixon was prepared to recall the incident when he met with the Queen at Chequers, the prime minister's country house. In the draft of his toast for the official luncheon, he made self-deprecating fun of his reputation for not being, well, debonair. "All the impeccably tailored guests were polite and didn't seem to notice my suit and made me feel perfectly at ease," he said. "And then the thought crossed my mind that perhaps they *expected* me to wear a tuxedo that didn't fit very well."

Nixon may have been uncomfortable, but Elizabeth was unconcerned, her lively manner through the evening one more example of how relaxed she seemed to be around Americans. When he explained his clothing predicament, she laughed. The menu was traditional: roast turkey with sweet potatoes, then pumpkin and mince pies for dessert. A photo shows the two of them seated side by side at the table, heads inclined together as they chatted, both with wide smiles on their faces. "Mother had never seen Elizabeth more relaxed," said Nixon's daughter, Julie.

"It was the only time that I had ever seen her in the evening without a tiara," Buchanan said—a very royal definition of more casual dress, despite her long gown. "After dinner she chatted with all of us in a most friendly and leisurely fashion, recalling in particular her drive to the airport in New York when people waited up in their pajamas to get a glimpse of her. . . . There was a very informal atmosphere, and the Queen stayed as late as she ever stays at a private function of this kind." She didn't leave until after midnight.

"A delightful dinner party," Elizabeth said in her thank-you note to Pat Nixon, handwritten on stationery with the red Buckingham Palace crest. "It was a great pleasure to be able to join you and Mr. Nixon on Thanksgiving Day." Somehow Nixon, notoriously stiff in a profession that rewards the suave, and the Queen, trained to sail gracefully through any social situation, had made a connection that would prove helpful in years to come—until it didn't.

Nixon, always defensive toward the press and about his image, didn't want anyone to think they had been wasting their time with empty fun. "The Queen takes a great interest in international problems and has a great desire to discuss them," he assured reporters at an impromptu news conference that night. "We have not been chatting about home, the family, and the pictures on the wall."

Though she could do that, too.

IN JUNE 1959, ELIZABETH AND EISENHOWER MET AGAIN TO FORMALLY open the St. Lawrence Seaway, a 370-mile waterway of locks, lakes, and channels linking the five Great Lakes to the Atlantic Ocean. Its construction enabled large ships to sail directly from the Atlantic to as far inland as Duluth, Minnesota—a boon for ports on both sides of the border. For the dedication, *Britannia* would make a five-hour cruise to the Lower Beauharnois lock, with Eisenhower on board and ships from the US Navy and the Royal Canadian Navy lining its route. It had taken decades of political debate before finally being built.

The waterway was "the culmination of the dreams of thousands of individuals" in both nations, Eisenhower said in his remarks, calling it "the latest event in a long history of peaceful parallel progress by our two peoples." In her speech, the Queen praised "the courage and persistence of those men in public life, in both countries, who brought about the political agreement essential to putting the project in hand."

Tricia Nixon, thirteen years old, attended the event with her mother and father, the vice president. "The royal yacht, *Britannia*, was delayed because there was a dense fog that engulfed the area, which made navigation very difficult," she told me. "But following the dedication ceremony at which both my father and the Queen spoke, I was presented to the Queen. And after my little curtsy and a handshake with Her Majesty, she smiled very warmly and graciously said, 'I do hope you didn't have too long a wait.'"

Elizabeth also spent a day in Chicago, feted by Mayor Richard Daley and using a limousine and driver loaned by the president. "You may be interested to know that your motor car driver in Chicago has reported independently that he had never witnessed greater enthusiasm among the crowds lining the streets," Eisenhower wrote her afterward.

Three weeks later, Ike made his final trip to England as president to confer with Macmillan before a crucial meeting with Soviet leader Nikita Khrushchev at Camp David.

Buckingham Palace had just announced the unexpected news that Elizabeth was pregnant again. Prince Andrew would be born in February 1960, nearly ten years after sister Anne. The Queen, who had been suffering from morning sickness, was on her annual holiday to Balmoral. Even so, she invited the Eisenhowers to spend two days there, the first time a sitting president had been welcomed at the royal retreat.

Elizabeth greeted Eisenhower at the gates of the estate, the Queen Mother and Princess Margaret by her side. "How nice of you to let me come," he said as he shook her hand. As a cluster of local residents applauded, he raised the fedora he was wearing. They were joined by some of the royal couple's closest chums—the Earl of Westmorland, Lord and Lady Porchester, the Salisburys, the Gloucesters, and Margaret's friend Dominic Elliot, son of the Fifth Earl of Minto. "Marvelous chap," Elliot told author Sally Bedell Smith, "and he fitted in very well."

After all, Eisenhower wasn't a newcomer to Balmoral. He had visited before, when he was a general and the guest of her father. His low-key, genial manner made his arrival seem more like the return of an old friend than the interruption of a foreign leader. From Ike's perspective, while he could find Churchill a handful, an ally who had to be managed, his affection for the Windsors would extend from King George to his daughter.

Her Majesty drove the Eisenhowers in her station wagon for an excursion through the ground's heather-covered hills. Some in the party went shooting for grouse while she and the president and others shared a picnic near Loch Muick, a sort of British crown version of an American backyard barbecue. To Ike's delight, the Queen made drop scones on a campsite griddle, a recipe she learned during the war from a cook at Windsor Castle.

"One quality of the Royal Family that has always intrigued me is the informality which prevails when its members are at home among themselves, particularly at Balmoral," Eisenhower said later. "At the afternoon picnic by the lake, the Queen acted as hostess and simple housewife, gracefully cooking the 'dropped scones' over a charcoal burner for her eight or ten guests. I tried to help as a waiter; I am quite sure that I was adjudged by Her Majesty as somewhat less than competent in this department."

When the Americans left for their next stop, to see Macmillan at Chequers, the president was given a gift of grouse from the day's shoot. The birds would be served for their dinner the next night.

Months later, Elizabeth sent the scone recipe to Eisenhower.

"Seeing a picture of you in today's newspaper standing in front of a barbeque grilling quail reminded me that I had never sent you the recipe of the drop scones, which I promised you at Balmoral," she wrote. "I now hasten to do so and I do hope you will find them successful."

The handwritten recipe card, now smudged and faded with age in the Eisenhower Presidential Library archives, lists everyday ingredients: four teacups flour, four tablespoons caster sugar, two teacups milk, two whole eggs, two teaspoons bicarbonate of soda, three teaspoons cream of tartar, two tablespoons melted butter. "Beat eggs, sugar and about half the milk together," it instructed, "add flour, and mix well together, adding remainder of milk as required, also bicarbonate and cream of tartar, fold in the melted butter."

She apologized that it was proportioned to serve a crowd of sixteen people. "When there are fewer I generally put in less flour and milk," she advised. She offered another tip, born of experience: "I think the mixture needs a great deal of beating while making and shouldn't stand around too long before cooking."

The cozy advice of old friends.

Four

The Ambassador's Son

Monday, June 5, 1961—Buckingham Palace

There was a prickly complication over the guest list.

Her Majesty invited President John Fitzgerald Kennedy and First Lady Jacqueline Bouvier Kennedy to dinner at Buckingham Palace just five months after they had moved themselves and their two young children into the White House. It wasn't a full-fledged state dinner; everyone assumed there would be time for that later in Kennedy's tenure. But it was a notable occasion, the first time an American president had dined at the palace with a British monarch since George V hosted Woodrow Wilson in 1918, a month after World War I had ended. It would turn out to be the only time the Queen and JFK met in person during his presidency, though they would become lively correspondents.

The Kennedys were in London for a happy family occasion. They were attending the christening at Westminster Cathedral of Jackie's niece, Anna Christina Radziwill, the nine-month-old daughter of her sister Lee. Rather than go to the US embassy, they decided to stay with the Radziwills in their grand five-story townhouse on Buckingham Place, around the corner from Buckingham Palace.

But the English stopover wasn't solely for family matters. Kennedy was eager to confer with Prime Minister Macmillan and David Ormsby-Gore, the British ambassador to the United States and one of JFK's closest friends, about his two-day meeting with Soviet leader Nikita Khrushchev in Vienna. The president was "completely overwhelmed by the ruthlessness and barbarity of the Russian Premier," Macmillan told the Queen. Moscow's assessment that Kennedy was in over his head would contribute to the Cuban missile crisis the next year. Two months after JFK's summit with Khrushchev, East Germany began construction of the Berlin Wall, the physical symbol of the Cold War.

Elizabeth had a rule against inviting those who had been divorced to attend royal dinners and other occasions, and with that the honor of having their names recorded in the official Court Circular. Modern realities would eventually change that practice; after all, three of her four children would divorce, including the son who succeeded her on the throne. But at the time the rule was still strictly enforced. Four decades would pass before the Church of England would allow the divorced to remarry in church. Here was the immediate problem: Lee already had been divorced once (she would eventually record two more) and her husband, Polish Prince Stanislaw Albrecht Radziwill, had been divorced twice. Even so, the presidential relatives not only lived in London but the Kennedys would be staying with them during their visit.

"I think had the Kennedys been staying at the American Embassy, I could have advised the Queen to omit the Radzinskis," Macmillan wrote in his diary, mangling the spelling of their last name. "But since the President and Mrs. K. were actually staying with the Prince and Princess, it seemed impossible to do so." American officials bristled at the idea that the first lady's sister might be barred as unacceptable. It threatened to become the sort of personal affront that could sour more substantive matters.

"After much hesitation the Queen waived her rule about divorce," Macmillan recorded, adding: "She was very unwilling to do this." Realpolitik had trumped protocol, even that grounded in religion, and by the woman whose many titles included "Defender of the Faith."

The pre-dinner jockeying set the stage for a tense evening when the Queen and first lady met.

Elizabeth was thirty-five, nine years on the throne and firmly established as one of the wealthiest and most esteemed women in the world. Jackie, three years younger and new to the global scene, was acclaimed for her beauty and charm. She and her dashing husband were being hailed as new American royalty. The 2020s Netflix series *The Crown* would exaggerate the rivalry between Jackie and Elizabeth, but the friction between them wasn't imaginary. Jackie's reception in Paris equaled the one Elizabeth had received on a state visit four years earlier. Parisians had lined the streets, waving American flags and shouting her name. President Charles de Gaulle escorted the first lady to a dinner in Versailles's famed Hall of Mirrors. At a news conference, JFK introduced himself to laughter as "the man who accompanied Jacqueline Kennedy to Paris."

When they arrived in London, too, crowds lined the streets to catch a glimpse of Jackie. "Meet the Queen of America," the *Daily Sketch* teased. The *Evening Standard* depicted her as a smiling, coiffed Statue of Liberty, one hand holding aloft the torch of freedom and the other clutching an issue of *Vogue*. The newspaper later declared: "Jacqueline Kennedy has given the American people from this day on one thing they had always lacked—Majesty."

For the actual queen, the White House couple reflected a transition to a new time. Jack Kennedy was the first US president who was close to her age, nine years older. The first two presidents she had met, Truman and Eisenhower, were members of her parents' generation and had an almost paternal attitude toward her, though this had shifted once she became head of state. But this new president was a generational peer, and one with a glamorous wife. Until now, compared to the staid Bess Truman and Mamie Eisenhower, Elizabeth had been unchallenged as the young beauty in the official photos. Now she was being upstaged. For this evening, at least, she was the dowdy one.

At Buckingham Palace that night, Jackie looked sleek in a sleeveless, silver-blue, shantung silk evening dress from Chez Ninon, a New York dressmaking salon. Her upswept hair was held by sparkling diamond pins. In contrast, the Queen's gown was ruffled blue tulle that looked fussy and dated in comparison. Jackie confided in British society photographer Cecil Beaton that she was "not impressed by the flowers, or the furnishings of the apartments at Buckingham Palace, or by the Queen's dark-blue tulle dress and shoulder straps, or her flat hairstyle." She contrasted it with the glorious French banquet that had been held in their honor at Versailles.

Even social chitchat with Elizabeth had been "pretty heavy-going," she reported to Gore Vidal, the acerbic American writer and her sort-of relative. (His mother, Nina Gore, and her mother, Janet Lee Bouvier, had each been married for a time to the blue-blooded Hugh Auchincloss.) "I think [she] resented me," she told Vidal. She called Prince Philip "nice, but nervous," and speculated about the state of their marriage. "One felt absolutely no relationship between them," she said. There was a certain irony in the observation, given the infidelities by her own husband that history would reveal.

She had complaints about the guest list, too, even though her sister and brother-in-law had reluctantly been included. "Anyway, the Queen had her revenge," she said. Jackie had wanted to meet Princess Margaret, and her husband wanted to see Princess Marina of Kent, whom he had got to know when his father was ambassador. Neither was there, to Margaret's exasperation. Jackie's, too. "No Margaret, no Marina, no one except every Commonwealth minister of agriculture that they could find," she said.

Despite all that, the dinner helped launch a partnership among JFK, Macmillan, and Ormsby-Gore, the most personal of any save that between Roosevelt and Churchill. It also began a complicated braid between the Queen and the first lady, one woven with rivalry and empathy and, finally, grief.

Jackie did see a flash of something intriguing beneath Elizabeth's stolid surface.

"The Queen was only human once," she said, in Vidal's account. "Jackie had been telling her about the Kennedy state visit to Canada and the rigors of being on view at all hours," he said. She had told the Queen, "I greeted Jack every day with a tear-stained face." For Elizabeth, that could well have been a reminder of her own early trip to Canada as a princess, when she arrived in Washington so unnerved that Truman felt the need to whisper reassurance. Elizabeth suddenly seemed to feel more sympathy for the younger woman. Both understood the price to be paid for the roles that would make each of them an icon.

"The Queen looked rather conspiratorial and said, 'One gets crafty after a while and learns how to save oneself,'" Jackie recalled. *To save oneself*—to protect your core even as the world scrutinizes you, sometimes without mercy. Then Elizabeth "marched Jackie down a long gallery," lined with dark portraits of royalty and their horses, a pastime both women treasured, and one that would become a bond. She stopped at a priceless painting by the seventeenth-century Flemish artist Anthony van Dyck. "That's a good horse," the Queen said.

THE BRITISH HAD HARBORED RESERVATIONS ABOUT THE BRASH NEW president.

Kennedy had a tough act to follow, succeeding Eisenhower, the hero of World War II. He was also the son of Joseph Kennedy Sr., who had been all but run out of London as a defeatist and a coward in the early years of the war. Macmillan, who as a rising political figure had clashed with the ambassador, described his offspring as a "young cocky Irishman"—words not meant as praise. The outgoing US ambassador, an Eisenhower-appointed Republican, had warned him that JFK was "a strange character" who was "obstinate, sensitive, ruthless and highly sexed."

"I am sure that the sooner I can meet Mr. Kennedy and discuss our affairs frankly with him, the better," Macmillan told the Queen a few days after the new president's inauguration in January 1961. But he cautioned, "I cannot hope to re-establish at once the same close personal relations as I had with President Eisenhower." Along with the long memories of the British establishment about JFK's father, Macmillan said he "had no particular reason to have any affection for the President."

But his tone brightened after Kennedy invited him to a hastily arranged session at the Key West naval base, where Kennedy was visiting. Over a hamburger lunch, they hit an instant rapport. The president had surrounded himself with "a large retinue of highly intelligent men—young and old," Macmillan wrote approvingly to Elizabeth. Later, he would say, "We seemed to be able (when alone) to talk freely and frankly to each other and to *laugh* (a vital thing) at our advisers and ourselves."

It helped that Kennedy already had made clear his disdain for the stance his father had taken as ambassador. Bernard Donoughue, later an adviser to three prime ministers, was a twenty-four-year-old graduate student studying at Harvard when he spent a day in the fall of 1958 with Senator Kennedy, then campaigning for reelection in Massachusetts. "I talked to him about his father and he disapproved strongly of his father's position," Lord Donoughue said more than a half century later, at age ninety. "He didn't like his father very much, so that was another thing to his credit."

Traversing small towns outside Boston in what he called a "small cavalcade of large Cadillacs," Donoughue watched Kennedy stump for votes outside a boot and shoe factory, reciting for workers the entirety of a favorite poem by Robert Frost, then stop by his campaign headquarters at a Boston hotel. There, the British student got a glimpse of JFK's private behavior. The senator had whispered something in the ear of the staffer who had been escorting Donoughue all day. "He indicated to me the name of the lady on the staff who he would like to have coffee with," his escort later explained. The "very, very attractive" young woman "slipped off and up the stairs and she came back about an hour-and-a-half later, looking very cheered," he recalled to me.

WHILE A GENERATION APART, KENNEDY AND MACMILLAN SHARED A DRY wit and a dark humor. During the Bay of Pigs fiasco in April 1961, Macmillan joked that his untimely death could have helped the president by providing a justification for the doomed CIA-backed invasion of Cuba. "I could really perform my ultimate service to mankind if those Cubans had only shot down my plane," Macmillan told him. "Then you could have had your little invasion!"

They also had family entanglements of a sort.

For those keeping track: The president's sister, Kathleen, had married William Cavendish, the Marquess of Hartington, who was a nephew of Macmillan's wife. (At one point, he had been mentioned as a potential suitor for the hand of Princess Elizabeth.) Kathleen, known as Kick, had been presented to King George at the annual Queen Charlotte's Ball; the British press crowned her "the debutante of 1938." But her romance with Billy Cavendish was cut short by tragedy. He was killed in combat in 1944 as he led a company of the Coldstream Guards; Kick died four years later in a plane crash in France. She was buried outside the chapel on the Chatsworth estate. The Kennedy family had suffered the grief of war, too. Joe Kennedy Jr., a navy pilot, was killed in action during a secret bombing mission over Normandy in 1944.

Jack Kennedy had suggested to Macmillan that Ormsby-Gore, a friend since they had met in London before the war, be named ambassador to Washington. The prime minister readily complied. That created more family ties all around: Ormsby-Gore was a cousin of Billy Cavendish, for one thing, and Ormsby-Gore's sister was married to Macmillan's son.

Kennedy's choice of a US ambassador to London brought with it another set of connections. He appointed David K. E. Bruce, a respected diplomat whose first wife was the sister of Paul Mellon—who happened to be a pal of Queen Elizabeth in the elite circles of horseracing.

Whew.

Macmillan had an affinity for Americans. Like Churchill, his mother was an American—an artist and socialite from Spencer, Indiana, known to everyone as Nellie. While prime minister, he would travel to Greencastle, Indiana, to deliver a nationally televised address at DePauw University. His maternal grandfather had graduated from there when it was known as Indiana Asbury Medical College.

Kennedy had an affinity for the English as well, despite his Irish heritage, with all the friction that could carry over Ireland's long and sometimes bloody resistance to British rule. A lifelong Anglophile, he would make Churchill the first honorary US citizen, putting himself squarely on the side of one of his father's fiercest critics. In *Why England Slept*, Kennedy had criticized the appeasement policy that his father had backed. Now he praised Churchill for his leadership "in the dark days and darker nights when England stood alone—and most men save Englishmen despaired of England's life." The men who doubted the survival of Great Britain's democracy included his father. JFK was hardly the first ambitious son to defy an overbearing father. In this case, the "special relationship" was the beneficiary.

Elizabeth had already proven her skill in keeping those relations strong. By now she was increasingly confident and more comfortably in command. Kennedy was the third sitting president she had encountered, and she understood more clearly what her role could require. She had compromised palace rules to placate Jackie, regardless of her own religious obligations on the matter. Now she was ready to heed her prime minister's encouragement to flatter the president with her friendly regard.

"He likes letters, he likes attention. To match this he is clearly a very effective, even ruthless, operator in the political field . . . ," Macmillan told her. "If I might venture to suggest it, Madam, I think he would welcome very much an occasional letter from You on any matter of partly international, partly political, and partly more personal interest. He is fond of writing letters and, I think, of receiving them."

Elizabeth obliged. Before the prime minister's encouragement, her letters to Kennedy mostly congratulated him on his birthday, thanked him for congratulating her on her birthday, and notified him of various ambassadorial arrivals and departures. Now she began to send more frequent and more casual missives, more like the conversational rhythm of friends. In them, she revealed more of her personality and of her humor than in the classic formulations of royal correspondence. She also invited Jackie to Buckingham Palace for lunch in March 1962, just the two of them, when the first lady was making a private visit to London at the end of her tour to India and Pakistan. The Queen followed up with a chatty handwritten letter to the president detailing what a nice time they had.

"It was a great pleasure to meet Mrs. Kennedy again when she came here to lunch in March at the end of her strenuous tour," she wrote. "I hope her Pakistani horse will be a success—please tell her that mine became very excited by jumping with the children's ponies in the holidays—so I hope hers will be calmer!" While Jackie was in Pakistan, President Ayub Khan had presented her with Sardar, a ten-year-old bay gelding. Flown aboard an air force plane to Washington, Sardar would take up residence at the Kennedy country home in Middleburg, Virginia. Jackie called the horse her favorite mount.

Elizabeth also encouraged the deepening friendship between Kennedy and Macmillan.

"I have seen my Prime Minister who has just returned from his visit to the United States and Canada and he has told me how much he enjoyed being there and particularly how much he valued the chance to talk personally with you at this present difficult stage in the affairs of the West," she wrote JFK. "It is a great comfort to me to know that you and he are so close, and that you have confidence in each other's judgement and advice; I am sure that these meetings and this personal trust and understanding are of the greatest importance to both our peoples."

In private, the prime minister had described to Her Majesty his strategy when it came to the United States. He was a pragmatist, and so adept that his nickname in Britain was "Supermac." "I have always thought about American Presidents that the great thing is to get them to do what we want," he told her. "Praise or blame we can leave to history."

"I HAVE RISKED MY QUEEN," MACMILLAN TOLD KENNEDY. "YOU MUST RISK your money."

With that challenge in a transatlantic phone call, the prime minister, the president, and the Queen executed a deft bit of Cold War choreography—one that delighted each of them with their cleverness and their success. It was just five months after their dinner at the palace.

The Cold War was global, and the West's goal was containment. The United States and the United Kingdom shared concern about Africa, including the drift of Ghana toward the Soviet bloc. Ghana had declared its independence from Britain in 1957, the first colony in sub-Saharan Africa to achieve sovereignty. It remained a member of the British Commonwealth, and Elizabeth had scheduled a state visit there in 1959, only to have it postponed for two years when she became pregnant with Prince Andrew. The new president, Kwame Nkrumah, was a founding member of the Organization of African Unity, an influential advocate of Pan-Africanism, and a person who was inclined to take offense. The Queen was so concerned about his reaction that she dispatched her private secretary, Martin Charteris, to Accra to confide something sensitive that almost no one knew—that she and Prince Philip had been trying to have another child for quite a while.

Kennedy, who during the campaign had accused Eisenhower of ignoring Africa, cultivated relationships with African leaders and supported African nationalism and independence in a way no president had done before. He invited Nkrumah to be the first foreign leader he officially met at the White House, in March 1961. When the administration launched the Peace Corps later that year, the first set of volunteers were sent to Ghana and Tanganyika.

But the Soviet Union was cultivating Nkrumah, too, even awarding him the Lenin Peace Prize. In September 1961, he returned from a trip to Russia in what Macmillan called "a dangerous mood," his commitment to democracy and Western values no longer assured. That gave the Queen's visit, rescheduled for November, a new importance and a new risk. Days before she was scheduled to arrive, Nkrumah arrested fifty members of the opposition. Bombs exploded in Ghana's capital, Accra. There was unrest on the streets.

Members of Parliament and the press raised alarms about whether she should make the trip. Churchill wrote Macmillan warning of the "widespread uneasiness both over the physical safety of the Queen and perhaps more, because the visit would seem to endorse a regime . . . which is thoroughly authoritarian." Macmillan wrote back immediately. "Her wish is to go," he said, then mentioned a side of the Queen that Churchill knew better than anyone. "This is natural with so courageous a personality." Indeed, Elizabeth was annoyed by the furor among what she called the "fainthearts."

"She is grateful for concerns about her safety, but impatient of the attitude to treat her as a *woman* . . . ," Macmillan wrote in his diary. "She does not enjoy 'society.' She likes her horses. But she loves her duty and means to be a Queen and not a puppet." He wanted her to go, too, warning that canceling the trip could be interpreted as a sign that "we did not want Ghana in the Commonwealth."

Some of Elizabeth's key events as a sovereign-to-be happened in Africa. It was in South Africa, in 1947, that she made the famous speech on her twenty-first birthday, pledging her "whole life, whether it be long or short" to the service of the Commonwealth people—or the "imperial family," as they still said then. She was there with her father, mother, and sister because the king hoped to subtly lend his support to Prime Minister Jan Smuts. His government was facing a challenge from the Nationalist Party, which aimed to introduce apartheid. The royal family was stung when their visit didn't stave off the Nationalist victory in 1948. As South Africa descended into apartheid, tensions with Britain increased until they declared themselves a republic and left the Commonwealth in March 1961. The Ghana trip was rescheduled for a few months later.

She went, of course. At a time apartheid South Africa was opening fire on Black demonstrators, she was photographed dancing with Nkrumah at a state ball, a picture plastered on front pages across the continent. "The world's greatest Socialist Monarch," Ghana's *Evening News* proclaimed. She made a silent statement of her trust in Ghana and its people, standing next to Nkrumah in the back seat of an open car, their arms braced against a supportive rail as crowds along the road cheered. She was wearing a summery dress, a feathered hat, a triple strand of pearls, and an anxious look.

"I remember being on the roadway to Achimota, waving my flags along with all the other children in Ghana," said Paul Yaw Boateng, then the son of a Ghanaian government minister and later a member of the British Parliament. His parents attended the ball in the Ambassador Hotel that night. When Elizabeth and Nkrumah danced, "it said to the people of Ghana that they were being treated and that their government, that their hero, their head of state, was treated as an absolute equal by the Queen." It was not just a social event but also a crucial political moment, Lord Boateng told me. "It was a joyful event, and it changed the terms of engagement positively and favorably, insofar as the Commonwealth and the UK and Africa were concerned—of course, Ghana in particular."

It was a milestone for Elizabeth, too. The decision to go forward with the trip was made jointly by the Queen and the prime minister, and over the objections of some government officials. It was the clearest demonstration yet that she intended to fulfill her role as a constitutional monarch to its fullest—the right to be consulted, the right to encourage, the right to warn. She had been unflappable in what could have been a difficult, even dangerous situation. She understood exactly how she was using her "soft power" and why it mattered.

"How silly I should look if I was scared to visit Ghana and then Khrushchev went and had a good reception," she had told Macmillan beforehand. She was right.

In Ghana, she had important conversations with Nkrumah about his worldview and his intentions. She wrote her friend and confidant, Henry Porchester, expressing her surprise at "how muddled his views on the world seemed to be, and how naive and vainglorious were his ambitions for himself and his country." He had a "short term perspective," refusing to look "beyond his own lifetime." In her understanding, inherited from her parents, that was the fundamental task of leaders.

She arrived in Ghana on November 9, 1961, for a weeklong visit that Macmillan called the most trying time of his life. He could talk of little else while she was there, his press secretary, Harold Evans, wrote in his diary. "She took very seriously her Commonwealth responsibilities, said the P.M., and rightly so for the responsibilities of the UK Monarchy had so shrunk that if you left it at that you might as well have had a film star."

Her visit was seen as a diplomatic triumph. Macmillan pressed the advantage by urging Kennedy to move forward with a proposal to give Ghana millions of dollars for a dam on the Volta River, a step that would demonstrate the benefits of siding with the West. Before the trip, Kennedy had warned him the financing was at risk. The American investment in a regime that was openly hostile was creating "great difficulty" with Congress, he said. "There does remain a real possibility that my decision will go to the other way," he said, though he promised to delay any public statement until Elizabeth had returned home.

When the trip was over, Kennedy and Macmillan talked again on the phone. "We must not lose it [Ghana] to that fellow Khrushchev," the prime minister said, noting that he had put even the Queen's safety on the line. "Well, I won't be ungallant," Kennedy replied. "You made the greater risk."

The next day, Macmillan relayed the good news to Elizabeth. "President Kennedy rang me up on our special trans-Atlantic telephone last night," he wrote, with news that the United States would finance the Volta Dam project. "I hope I may venture to express the opinion that this decision of the American Administration is in some considerable measure due to Your Majesty."

Kennedy's letter to Nkrumah cited his assurances "that your policy is truly one of non-alignment and independence." With that in hand, "we are prepared to go ahead with the project on a cooperative basis." The United States loaned $133 million to Ghana for the Volta Dam and an aluminum smelter project.

That wasn't the end of the story, or the conflict. In 1964, a constitutional amendment made Ghana a one-party state, with Nkrumah president for life—a dictatorship. Five years after the Queen's visit, he was ousted in a violent coup, replaced by new leaders who aligned with the West. Finally, in 2001, power in Ghana was transferred from one legitimately elected leader to another for the first time. But through it all, Ghana had remained in the Commonwealth.

KENNEDY'S FINAL FOREIGN TRIP INCLUDED SOME OF THE MOST MEMOrable public events of his presidency. In an iconic address in a divided Germany, he declared "Ich bin ein Berliner," *"I am a Berliner."* He stopped in Ireland to celebrate his family roots, and he visited Rome and Vatican City.

In the middle of it, he made a quiet side trip to England for the most private of moments.

For the first time, he visited the grave of his sister, Kathleen. In 1948, when she had been killed at age twenty-eight in a plane crash, he had been too distraught to attend her burial. Now he made an unannounced stop in Shropshire. A US Army helicopter took him to tiny Edensor, near the Cavendish family estate where Kick had been laid to rest. Standing in a steady rain, he placed a wreath of local flowers on her grave.

Five months later, he was assassinated in Dallas.

On behalf of the British government, the new prime minister, Alec Douglas-Home, offered a nationally televised tribute. "There are times in life when the mind and heart stand still, and one such is now," he said. "The loss is a deep and sad one because he was the most loyal and faithful of allies." Churchill, now eighty-eight and nearing the end of his own storied life, called Kennedy's loss "incalculable."

In addition to a note of condolence to Mrs. Kennedy, Elizabeth immediately sent a message to the new president, Lyndon Johnson, saying she was "shocked and horrified" at the news. She placed the royal court in mourning for a week and ordered the great tenor bell at Westminster Abbey to be rung every minute from 11 a.m. to noon on the day after the killing, a sign of respect usually reserved for senior members of the royal family. She held a memorial service at St. George's Chapel in Windsor, inviting nearly four hundred US service members stationed in England to attend.

Pregnant with Prince Edward, the Queen didn't attend the funeral in Washington, sending Philip in her stead. The prince, who had endured turmoil and tragedy in his own youth, was invited to the White House. Jackie found him sprawled on the floor of John-John's playroom, entertaining the little boy. The next day would be both his third birthday and his father's funeral. "Where's Daddy?" he had asked, saying plaintively that he "didn't have anybody to play with" anymore.

TWO YEARS LATER, HER MAJESTY PRESIDED OVER THE DEDICATION OF A memorial to Kennedy, built on an acre of land at Runnymede. That was democracy's sacred ground, where King John had signed the Magna Carta in 1215, establishing the principle that the monarch was not above the law. (Elizabeth was John's direct descendant, by some genealogical calculations his twenty-third great-granddaughter.) Ormsby-Gore chaired the committee that oversaw the fundraising, design, and construction of the memorial.

A path of cobblestones through the woods rose to a glade, where a seven-ton block of Portland stone had been inscribed with a quotation from JFK's inaugural address: "Let every Nation know, whether it wishes us well or ill, that we shall pay any price, bear any burden, meet any hardship, support any friend or oppose any foe, in order to assure the survival and success of liberty."

Macmillan, who had stepped down as prime minister only a month before the assassination, made a point of emphasizing in his remarks that his country and America were "allies and sister nations." So, too, Elizabeth detailed the "many ties" Kennedy and his family had with Great Britain.

"He and they lived among us in that doom-laden period which led up to the outbreak of war," she said, though she didn't mention by name the controversial father who had brought him to England in the days before World War II. She did mention his brother Joe, who died in the two nations' common combat, and his sister Kathleen, buried in an English courtyard.

The Windsors and the Kennedys were in some ways a mirror—one British royalty, the other American political royalty—and they shared the fundamental characteristic that sustained the World War II generation. In the face of challenge and loss, they soldiered on.

Attending the dedication were four of JFK's siblings—Robert F. Kennedy, recently elected as senator from New York; Edward Kennedy, Elizabeth's childhood dance partner who was in his first term as senator from Massachusetts; Patricia Kennedy Lawford, and Jean Kennedy Smith. Queen Elizabeth and Prince Philip had greeted Jackie Kennedy and her two young children, all dressed in white. Caroline, then seven years old, curtsied; John Junior, who was four, gave a small bow of his head. As they climbed the path to the memorial, Elizabeth and Ormsby-Gore led the procession.

Philip, trailing behind, held John-John's hand.

Five

Nadir

Thursday, October 17, 1957—State Dining Room, the White House

John Fitzgerald Kennedy showed Queen Elizabeth how essential her soft power could be, demonstrating that her stature and her presence could affect even the machinations of the Cold War.

Lyndon Baines Johnson showed her how limited her influence could be.

She was too discreet to say (at least in public) who was her favorite president and who was her least favorite—that is, if she even ranked such complicated relationships in that simple way. That discipline allowed more than one to assume they were at the top of the list of the best liked. But her most frustrating president was surely the bombastic Texan who deflected her invitations to London, and who never issued an invitation for her to Washington. The fact that he interrupted her historic string—the only sitting president in seven decades she failed to meet—mattered less for purposes of keeping score and more for the strains it showed between the two nations at a time of political and cultural turmoil. It was the only US administration during her reign when she found herself powerless to do much of anything to smooth what turned out to be a very rough patch. That cautionary lesson was particularly jarring after the seamless give-and-take during Kennedy's presidency.

What they had instead were the diplomatic exchanges of strangers, betraying not a hint of a personal connection. "On this celebration of Your Majesty's birthday I wish to express the best wishes of the people of the

United States and my own personal greetings, to you and to the people of Great Britain," Johnson wrote to mark her fortieth birthday, nearly three years after he had taken office. She replied, "I send to you Mr. President and to the people of the United States of America my warm thanks for your kind message on the occasion of my birthday."

LBJ was her fourth sitting president, and the toughest nut of all fourteen to crack. She was moving into middle age during his tenure—thirty-seven years old when he unexpectedly took office and forty-one when he unexpectedly announced he wasn't going to run for another term in 1968. She was no longer the young princess and not yet the venerated elder but somewhere in between, with two small children and two teenagers in the palace household. She proved willing to put up with quite a lot, including presidential rebuffs that could have been seen as insulting. The British angled almost to the end for an encounter that would never happen.

It wasn't that she needed the company. During Johnson's tenure in the White House, she formally welcomed to London seven other heads of state from four continents—Sudan and Chile, Austria and Turkey, Jordan and Pakistan and Saudi Arabia. She also made a half dozen state visits to other countries, from Ethiopia to Brazil.

But LBJ proved singularly immune to Her Majesty's considerable charms.

He had his reasons. The Vietnam War, the conflict that consumed his presidency, was one. While Great Britain formally supported the war, Prime Minister Harold Wilson refused to deploy troops there, fueling LBJ's ridicule and rage. There was also his general suspicion of elites, whom he suspected never stopped looking down their noses at a country boy like him—and who could possibly be more elite than the Queen of England?

Then there was this rub: JFK and the Brits had gotten along famously.

Kennedy reluctantly put Johnson on the Democratic ticket in 1960 because he calculated it gave him the best chance of winning the White House; the narrow win over Richard Nixon proved him right. Johnson reluctantly agreed to join the ticket because he figured it gave him his own best chance at being president. That turned out to be right, too, although not in the way he had planned, through a future election.

Despite their ostensible partnership, the distrust between the two ambitious men ran so deep that the Queen's affection for Kennedy and Kennedy's closeness to 10 Downing Street were no assets in Johnson's eyes. They were just more items on his long list of grievances with the Kennedys and how they treated him. He fumed that JFK had been more likely to listen to advice from British Ambassador David Ormsby-Gore than he was from his own vice president. During the Cuban missile crisis in 1962, Johnson complained that "the limey" was seated "front and center" at a meeting in the White House Situation Room. He found himself "down in a chair at the end, with the goddamned door banging in my back."

IN WHAT COULD BE SEEN AS AN OMEN OF THEIR ILL-FATED RELATIONSHIP, or lack of one, the only time the Queen and Johnson did meet was largely forgotten by both sides.

When Elizabeth died in 2022, news accounts reported that LBJ was the only president during her reign whom she had never met. That wasn't accurate, although the encounter was before his presidency and so brief that neither the Americans nor the British had been certain whether it had happened. Evidence settling that question was discovered by the author—not in Britain's National Archives in London or the Johnson Presidential Library in Austin but at the Eisenhower Presidential Library in Abilene.

The occasion was Eisenhower's state dinner for Elizabeth on October 17, 1957. Ike's official appointments diary included Senator and Mrs. Johnson on the list of guests, and a handwritten reference to the dinner was scrawled on LBJ's informal desktop calendar for the day. But because there was no photograph of him there or mention of his presence by him or his host, it wasn't clear whether he had attended. We now know that he did because another guest, Jacqueline Cochran, a pioneering female aviator, mentioned him as her dinner partner in an oral history at the Eisenhower library.

"Well, the only Democrat invited was Lyndon B. Johnson, then Senator Johnson, along with Mrs. Johnson . . . ," Cochran recalled. "The President and Mrs. Eisenhower and the honored guest come in, it's very impressive. And you go through the receiving line. I was down toward the end with the family and so I had no idea where I was going to sit and then Senator Johnson came over and I thought, 'oh, oh, I'm in business, I'm really going to be seated pretty high if he's taking me in to dinner' . . .

"And we were seated so tightly that you literally almost couldn't eat because there were 92 people," Cochran said. "Well, I guess they wanted as many of the family and important people as they could and I don't blame them and I sure felt important that night." A "marvelous" evening to honor the Queen, she said, calling it "the gayest, prettiest dinner that I've ever seen at the White House, and I've been to eleven."

IF JOHNSON STARTED HIS PRESIDENCY WITH A LESS-THAN-POSITIVE VIEW of the British, they also started out with a dyspeptic opinion of him.

Prime Minister Harold Macmillan, who was instantly won over by Kennedy, took an equally quick dislike of Johnson when he hosted a dinner in Washington for the vice president soon after the 1960 election. "An acute and ruthless 'politician,'" Macmillan concluded in his diary, "but not (I would judge) a man of any intellectual power." A year later, when Vice President Johnson embarked on a goodwill tour of Nordic countries in September 1963, a string of British ambassadors along the way mocked him in their private dispatches to the Foreign Office—assessments that apparently have not been previously reported.

"Predictably, the reticent Swedes were somewhat taken aback by Mr. Johnson's high-powered hand-shaking technique, by the member of his staff who followed him everywhere recording his words on a tape-recorder, by the second member of his staff who doled out entry cards to the Vice-President's office in Washington," the British ambassador to Sweden, Sir Moore Crosthwaite, reported from the first stop. He could hardly have been more dismissive of LBJ's official gifts to his hosts, describing them as "boxes with a coloured photograph of the Vice-Presidential family stuck on top."

At the next stop, the British ambassador to Norway, Sir Patrick F. Hancock, also struck a patronizing tone. "Mr Lyndon Johnson arrived at Bodo, north of the Arctic circle. The three hour programme there, which included the presentation of an American flag to the Mayor during a reception at the Town Hall, was delayed by the Vice-President's insistence on distributing personally signed admittance cards to the United States Senate."

Two days later, the British ambassador to Finland, Sir Anthony Lambert, dissected at some length what he saw as LBJ's various social missteps. "Perhaps the worst lapse from good taste was Mr. Lyndon Johnson's handling of the ceremony at the cemetery at Rovaniemi, where he loudly invited the crowd to gather round for his address and where, as on other, less solemn occasions, ball-point pens were handed out as souvenirs. My Swedish colleague, of all people, had received one of these as well as a cigarette lighter."

The American attempt to transplant Texas hospitality to the far-north latitudes did not go over any better. "No doubt, it was also a mistake to keep heads of diplomatic missions and Ministers waiting for nearly one and a half hours before appearing at the barbecue and to expect that kind of guest to queue for thirty minutes to get a portion of steak," Lambert wrote, his horror apparent. "It was difficult, too, to escape the impression that the Vice-President had all the time one eye on his own press and television at home."

At LBJ's last stop, in Denmark, British Chargé d'Affaires Cosmo Stewart recalled an earlier encounter he had during Johnson's visit to Vietnam in 1961. In his report, he managed to insult both the "electioneering" American visitor and his "slightly malicious" Danish hosts.

"Having experienced two years ago in Saigon a Vice-Presidential visit scored for full orchestra and accompaniment of 50 American journalists travelling en suite, I was somewhat apprehensive about the effect of his Texan electioneering tactics on the stolid but slightly malicious Danes . . . ," he wrote. This time, during LBJ's visit to the famed Tivoli Gardens in Copenhagen, "the Vice-President tried to shake as many of their hands as possible. Both sides had some difficulty at first, as the Danish police formed a cordon to keep back the crowd. The American 'Secret Servicemen' thereupon formed another cordon to break up the Danish police and let Mr. Johnson get at the hands he wanted to shake."

That was pretty much what Johnson would have suspected England's diplomats were saying about him behind his back. He was allergic to those born to privilege and power, certain they would look askance at his rural roots and his Texas twang. "He was always somewhat intimidated by what he called the Georgetown set, that they did look down on him because he went to Southwest [Texas Teachers] College—not an Ivy League college, not even a major Texas college," said Lloyd Hand, a Senate aide for Johnson who later became his White House chief of protocol. "He came up hardscrabble. He picked cotton when he was a young man, and he had to work his way through college and so forth. He wasn't of the manor born."

Johnson never lost the chip on his shoulder, not even after he won the White House in 1964 on his own and in a landslide.

"The British prime minister was in Washington, Harold Wilson, and he had several people with him, and Lyndon Johnson had several people on his side, and we sat down at a table," Secretary of State Dean Rusk recounted. "Lyndon Johnson looked around the table and said, 'Well, I see we have four Oxford men and three Cambridge men and four Harvard men and three Yale men—and a man from San Marcos State Teachers College.'" He was the most powerful person in the room, and in the world, but his humor was still laced with a barb and tinged with insecurity.

Lady Bird Johnson was "a little starstruck" with the Queen but her husband was not, their younger daughter recalled. Luci Baines Johnson was sitting in the apartment built for her parents' use at the LBJ Library, still filled with their furnishings years after their deaths. "Being impressed with royalty for the sake of royalty—I don't think that that was a camp that he was closely aligned with," she said.

DURING FIVE YEARS OF DIPLOMATIC EFFORT, BUCKINGHAM PALACE CAME close to arranging a meeting with LBJ just once—and then the main draw wasn't Elizabeth. It was Winston Churchill and his grand, final farewell.

Johnson was at his ranch in central Texas preparing for his inauguration as Churchill, ninety years old, neared death after suffering a stroke and slipping into a coma. The president told aides he wanted to attend the funeral, whenever it was held. Arrangements were made for a private audience with the Queen—at last—while he was in London. "Going over temporary plans for trip to Great Britain in the event of Sir Winston Churchill's death," the president's daily diary recorded on January 17, 1965, three days before the swearing-in. Then he and top aides reviewed drafts of his inaugural address before flying back to Washington that night.

It would have been his first trip to Great Britain during his presidency.

Churchill died on January 24, and his funeral was set for January 30—a magnificent celebration that would also mark the end of an era for Great Britain. It was a turning point of sorts for Elizabeth, too. When she was a child, he had been her father's wartime partner. When she was a young queen, he had been her first prime minister, one whose lessons she would forever heed. Three thousand people representing 112 countries would attend the services below the dome in St. Paul's Cathedral, among them sixteen prime ministers, six monarchs, and six presidents—at the time, the largest state funeral in history. They would even include World War II foes-turned-allies: the German chancellor, the former prime minister of Japan, and the defense minister of Italy.

But as it turned out, not the president of the United States, the biggest ally of them all.

The day before Churchill's death, Johnson had been admitted to Bethesda Naval Hospital. After his inauguration on January 20, he had stood for hours at the reviewing stand outside the White House, coatless and hatless, to salute the fifty-four bands, thirty-one floats, and fifteen thousand marchers passing by in his honor. (After a half hour, Vice President Hubert Humphrey showed the common sense to pull on an overcoat and scarf.) That night, the president and first lady made the circuit to five inaugural balls.

It wasn't surprising when the White House reported he had developed what was described, with understatement, as "a tickling in his throat." Spokesman George Reedy assured reporters that it was "not a serious matter." But three days after the inauguration, when the president's cough got worse and he complained of chest pains, he was taken to the hospital by ambulance in the middle of the night, just after 2 a.m. Chest pains made it a serious matter indeed, given that he had suffered a heart attack ten years earlier.

His heart turned out to be fine, though he would spend three and a half days in the hospital. He tried frantically to figure out if and how he could make the trip to London anyway. The White House peppered the US ambassador, David Bruce, with questions about every detail. How far was it from the airport to the hotel, to the palace, to the church? During the service at St. Paul's, could the president keep on his overcoat? Would he be conspicuous if he sat rather than stood? Could he bring his own chair? Since dress was to be white tie and tails, should he carry a black silk hat? If he brought his own humidifier—presumably to his lodgings, not into the church—would an electric-current transformer be necessary?

The Queen was willing to agree to any accommodation he wanted, even though other foreign leaders massed there weren't allowed special arrangements for their transportation, their dress, their timetable. Despite the flood of foreign dignitaries, and her own grief, she would make time to meet him in private afterward at Buckingham Palace.

"He wanted to go; he loved Churchill," Lloyd Hand recalled. "He had just come out of the hospital, so he asked me if I would go over to speak to the royal family, the prime minister's office, our ambassador, who was then Ambassador Bruce, to see if he should attend Churchill's funeral. And everybody said 'no.'" That included not only his doctors but also his wife. Even inside the church, the temperature would be freezing. He would be exposed to bitterly cold weather for hours on end.

In his diary, Ambassador Bruce said the president "has made evident his hope of attending the funeral despite medical opposition." Although Johnson had a history of bouts with pneumonia, "his will is obstinate, like Churchill's. His intimates disapprovingly predict he will make the journey."

Lady Bird and his doctors finally prevailed against the trip, but not until the last minute. Less than forty-eight hours before the service began, Rusk called Bruce—after midnight on Thursday, January 28, 1965—to say the president wouldn't be there.

After reluctantly agreeing not to go, Johnson expressed more concern about the reaction from US voters than from the Queen. A file of miscellaneous White House papers at the Johnson Library includes a typed notation on plain paper by aide Jack Valenti of what White House switchboard operators were hearing from Americans, in those days before social media. In the hours after Johnson announced that he wouldn't be going to London, a total of 166 people had called; 125 of them were listed as "Critical of decision not to go" and another seventeen called on the president to change his mind.

Six callers proposed sending the vice president instead, and four suggested former President Dwight Eisenhower, with one vote each for Lady Bird Johnson and Mrs. Douglas MacArthur. Her husband, who had died a year earlier, had been the top commander of US Army forces in the Pacific during World War II while Eisenhower had been supreme commander of the Allied Expeditionary Force in Europe.

Johnson didn't choose any of them as his representative, although Eisenhower would attend the funeral as the guest of the Churchill family. As the prime minister's coffin was carried up the Thames after the service, Ike would broadcast a tribute on the BBC. Churchill was "a great maker of history" and "a champion of freedom," the former general said. They had stood "shoulder to shoulder in global conflict against tyranny."

Humphrey was the obvious choice to lead the delegation, but Johnson had a prickly view of his vice president and an aversion to yielding him the spotlight. (In 1967, when Johnson turned down an invitation to address the annual black-tie dinner of the White House Correspondents' Association, Humphrey agreed to fill in only to have LBJ then crash the dinner and take the microphone.) Johnson never said why he didn't send Humphrey to London, but Hand noted that the president was known for getting "miffed" at some slight, real or imagined, then icing out the suspected transgressor for a time.

For the funeral, Johnson finally named Rusk to head the US delegation. At the last minute, Rusk came down with influenza and couldn't attend. The American delegation ended up being led by Chief Justice Earl Warren and Ambassador Bruce.

One more snub by LBJ, the British press concluded.

"Funeral Riddle" was the headline over a skeptical item on the front page of London's *Daily Telegraph*. The front page of the *Huddersfield Daily Examiner* called it a "blunder," made worse when Johnson offered a "lame" and rambling explanation at a White House news conference a few days later. "A shabby faux pas," sniffed the Washington columnist for the *New York Daily News*. "British correspondents to whom we have talked are most upset and they report London is too." "London" presumably included Her Majesty.

QUEEN ELIZABETH NEVER STOPPED TRYING, IN THAT STIFF-UPPER-LIP way that defined the British. But the role of spurned host was an unfamiliar one. Historians struggle to think of another case where she wanted to meet with a foreign leader—or a famous actor or star athlete or noted humanitarian, for that matter—and they just weren't interested. For it to be an American president, leader of her nation's closest ally, carried a particular sting. Some presidents had cherished meeting Her Majesty more than others—Nixon and Reagan and Trump, for instance—but all of them had been game to join her in London or Washington or both.

The Queen hadn't attended Kennedy's funeral because she was pregnant with Prince Edward, her youngest child, born in March 1964. That October, she was on the American side of the Atlantic Ocean for an eight-day tour of Canada. When Truman was in the White House, a visit to Canada by Elizabeth, then a princess, had been close enough for the British to convince the Americans to tack on a stop in Washington. But now the timing was deemed too close to the US election on November 3.

Then, Johnson would carry 61.1 percent of the popular vote against Republican Barry Goldwater, the highest percentage in US history, before or since. Harold Wilson then pulled pride of place, the first foreign leader to visit LBJ at the White House afterward. He used the opportunity to reinforce the Queen's invitation.

". . . I hope you will, Mr. President, come to Buckingham Palace to visit London," he said in his toast in the State Dining Room. He acknowledged there were strains between them. "There are always differences between friends," he said. When that happened, he vowed, "we will look you straight in the eye—and we will expect you to look us straight in the eye—and say what you would expect we can do as friends and only what we can do as friends."

In London, calculations were underway behind the scenes about how and when to draw Johnson to visit. "Please let us know when you judge the moment has arrived when he would like to receive a formal invitation from the Prime Minister," Oliver Wright, Wilson's private secretary, wrote a few weeks later to Ormsby-Gore. But the president was staying close to home, making no foreign trips during that year as he focused on enacting the most ambitious domestic agenda since FDR's New Deal. During 1965, Johnson would sign the Voting Rights Act as well as legislation establishing Medicare and Medicaid and creating key parts of his Great Society.

The next year, in 1966, the escalating war in Vietnam began to dominate his presidency. He made quick stops in Mexico and Canada, but his major overseas trip centered on Southeast Asia. During a two-week tour in the fall, he visited US troops at Vietnam's Cam Ranh Bay, attended a regional summit held in the Philippines, and made state visits to Australia, New Zealand, Thailand, Malaysia, and South Korea.

Weeks after LBJ had returned to the White House in November 1966, a Foreign Office memorandum showed alarm growing in London.

"I am not quite sure what, if anything we have yet done in any formal sense to make it clear to the President how welcome he will be if he comes to Britain," a memo to Wilson from a top aide read. "But I think that this is something we should now be looking at urgently and on which there should perhaps be a message soon to the President from yourself."

Close ties to Washington represented more than a reminder of a pleasant past. They were important to Britain's present—including its defense during a Cold War that carried the threat of nuclear annihilation—and to its future. The embrace of America helped maintain England's global influence even as its empire was disintegrating. That was crucial given the superpower standoff between Washington and Moscow, the new wall that divided East and West Berlin, the expanding war in Southeast Asia.

It was a time of cultural upheaval as well that challenged establishment institutions of all sorts, including the presidency and the monarchy. In the United States, massive protests opposed Johnson's war and opened a bitter generation gap. In the United Kingdom, the collapse of a coal-waste heap in the South Wales village of Aberfan in 1966 brought a rare public castigation of the Queen. She waited more than a week before visiting the village devastated by the deaths of 116 children and 28 adults, displaying reserve and caution when her citizens wanted a public show of comfort. The changing times were both a challenge and an opportunity for her, once she found her footing.

In American culture, there was a new British invasion. The Beatles and the Rolling Stones were reshaping popular music in the United States; designers like Mary Quant were doing the same for fashion.

But at this moment in politics, LBJ's commitment to sustaining the special relationship wasn't at all clear.

"The United Kingdom is no longer the center of an effective world system," Under Secretary of State George Ball said in a memo to Johnson. "The Commonwealth has become little more than a figure of speech; it has meager meaning in a power sense—and not much meaning in a commercial sense." The president never expressed that view quite so bluntly, but his actions signaled that he agreed.

The Queen remained at the core of British efforts to reach Johnson and with that to protect British interests. Her schedule of foreign visitors in 1967 was kept in flux amid efforts to accommodate whatever dates the White House might choose. She was already planning to host the leader of Saudi Arabia. A firm invitation to the Turkish president was delayed, then delayed again, as the Americans were wooed.

"[F]or someone as important as the President of the United States, everything would have to be done to fit in a visit, whatever the previous engagements on the Queen's very full list," Sir Paul Gore-Booth, a veteran diplomat, wrote in December 1966, though he acknowledged that canceling some other leader's plans could create "adverse" reactions. "One can only hope, therefore, that the President will not wait until the last moment."

They were prepared for the massive antiwar protests that were likely to mark a visit by LBJ. "We probably should have to cope with a small but highly vocal and active minority who can be expected to put out more flags and probably pretty uncomplementary ones for the President's passage," one memo said. "Equally, however, it would seem very undesirable that the President, on his first trip to Europe since going to the White House, should not come to Britain."

That "very undesirable" prospect was precisely what happened.

On his first presidential trip to Europe, in 1967, Johnson went not to Britain but to Bonn, to attend the funeral of Konrad Adenauer, the first chancellor of West Germany. Then, just before Christmas, LBJ left Washington for a trip to Canberra and then Melbourne, to attend the memorial service of Australian Prime Minister Harold Holt, lost and presumed drowned when swimming in the ocean. One reason the president made the trip was his gratitude that Holt had bolstered the deployment of Australian troops to Vietnam—an unspoken contrast to Wilson and the British.

While he was en route to Australia, LBJ expanded his itinerary, adding stops in Thailand and Vietnam to visit US troops and a drop-by in Pakistan. He decided to pop over to Rome and the Vatican to meet with the Italian prime minister and Pope Paul VI before finally heading home.

But not England. And not Elizabeth.

In the State Dining Room two years earlier, the prime minister had urged the president to "say what you would expect we can do as friends." As it turned out, what Johnson expected "as friends" was not something Wilson was willing to do. The British government officially supported the United States in Vietnam but rebuffed Johnson's repeated requests to back up their words with troops—not even "a platoon of Highlanders in their kilts with bagpipes," LBJ sarcastically complained.

The president and his senior aides came to view the left-leaning Wilson as a pacifist and a pest. "A little creep," LBJ called him. On a phone call in February 1965, when the prime minister pressed for a face-to-face meeting in Washington to address the deteriorating military situation in Southeast Asia, Johnson shut him down. A visit would be "a very serious mistake," he told him, saying he "did not see what was to be gained by flapping around the Atlantic with our coattails out."

Once again, he aired his ire about the absence of British troops. "The US did not have the company of many allies in Vietnam," Johnson pointedly told him. If Wilson "had any men to spare, he would be glad to have them."

Later, Johnson's rage was ignited by press reports that Wilson's government decided to cancel an order to buy fifty F-111s, a tactical fighter-bomber aircraft being built by General Dynamics, and mostly in Texas. The austerity measure came on the heels of the prime minister's announcement that all British forces stationed in Southeast Asia and the Persian Gulf would be withdrawn, a move that increased pressure on US resources in the region and underscored America's isolation.

An angry letter to Wilson from Johnson, marked "Eyes Only" and sent through a back channel, threatened the "complete cancellation" of US military contracts with British firms—and worse. He suggested England's own security could be at risk, a head-turning retreat from a precept forged in World War II and ratified by the NATO alliance. "Many in this country, including influential members of Congress, would bring the strongest pressures to bear on us to sacrifice international security interests to ease our present financial problems," he warned. "Our ability to maintain substantial forces in Europe, while fighting a difficult and costly war in Southeast Asia, would be greatly endangered."

An earlier draft of the letter, not sent, had been even blunter. In it, LBJ hadn't blamed members of Congress for "pressures" to curtail US forces in Europe. The threat came directly from him.

"Daddy, he thought that the United States had a special relationship with Great Britain," his older daughter, Lynda Bird Johnson Robb, said. That made him feel constrained about complaining in public about them. "He said, 'You don't beat up on Mother' or 'You have to understand that it's Mother,' and that there was a special relationship." In private, though, he was bitter. The British failure to deploy forces alongside the Americans in Vietnam felt like a betrayal to him, and a personal one. That's true even though in the aftermath of the costly and divisive war, which ended with a US retreat, the British reluctance would seem to many as the wiser course.

"It saddened Daddy; it really saddened him," said his younger daughter, Luci. Despite their historic connection, Britain wouldn't help him deal with the quagmire that threatened his presidency. "Just think about your girlfriend from the sixth grade who you shared so many previous memories with," she said, casting it in the most personal terms. "Now all of a sudden she didn't want to talk to you."

Actually, the Queen was all but desperate to talk to the president, a conversation she would never have, despite her best efforts.

AMID ALL THE EFFORTS BY BRITISH OFFICIALS TO ARRANGE A ROYAL VISIT in one capital or the other, the opportunity fell into their laps.

Not for Elizabeth but for her sister, Princess Margaret. She and her husband, Antony Armstrong-Jones, the Earl of Snowdon, were making plans to visit California to see Sharman Douglas, an American socialite and friend whose father had been the US ambassador to London during the Truman administration. The White House social secretary, Bess Abell, asked the president and first lady if they wanted to have the princess over for dinner.

"Princess Margaret and the Lord of Snowden are paying an unofficial visit to the United States in November," she wrote in a memo, dated July 2, 1965. "She is going to spend 20 days seeing the USA and will be wined and dined all over the country," including three days in Washington. "The State Department feels it would be a great plus for American-British relations if you would entertain her during her US visit." She added, "The size, type and glamour of the dinner could be decided closer to the date, dependent on your schedule and the world situation."

At the bottom of the cream-colored White House stationery was a small notation in blue ink: "Yes. CAJ." Those were the initials of Claudia Alta Johnson, the first lady.

The British hadn't arranged the dinner, but they did have official business to advance, given the chance. The United Kingdom faced a looming deficit and needed US support for a loan from the International Monetary Fund to avoid devaluation of the pound. There's no sign that the princess raised the topic directly, but a successful social evening with the president couldn't hurt their efforts. The White House briefing paper prepared for the president before he saw her mentioned "a series of financial crises" and England's appeals for the United States to help "meet these recurring difficulties."

Guests at the formal dinner included actors Kirk Douglas and Paul Newman and opera star Leontyne Price as well as governors and senators and a Supreme Court justice.

The evening was lively, although not nearly as lively as it was portrayed years later in Netflix's *The Crown*. The cinematic version depicted bawdy limericks, standing atop tables, even a smack on the lips. "Outrageous" and "all made up," said Hand, who was there. That said, reports of undiplomatic behavior by Margaret's entourage in Washington and at stops in Hollywood and elsewhere caused enough heartburn for the British ambassador that the Foreign Office would block the idea of Margaret making a return visit to the United States a few years later, in 1973.

But LBJ was charmed, happy to be back on the social scene a month after major surgery to remove his gallbladder.

The Queen sent her best wishes for his recovery in that diplomatic way. "I heard with great concern about your operation and am delighted that it has been successful," she wrote him. "I send my warm personal wishes for a rapid and complete recovery."

Princess Margaret celebrated the president's recovery with champagne toasts at a sparkling dinner.

"I am told by my protocol people that this visit of yours is an 'unofficial' visit," he said in his toast, his glass raised in honor of Her Majesty, as protocol demanded. "I can only wish that 'official' visits, of which

I am something of a veteran, would have such favorable results." He didn't mention the Vietnam War or the sterling crisis or other serious matters in his remarks, nor did Margaret in her brief response. She didn't leave the after-dinner party until 1:35 a.m. and the president didn't go upstairs until 2 a.m., an uncharacteristically late hour for official Washington.

Photos from the evening show a surprisingly intimate scene in the East Room. In one, the Earl of Snowdon and Lady Bird are seated at a small side table while Johnson and Margaret dance. He is in black tie; she is wearing a spectacular double-strand diamond necklace and a gauzy pink gown trimmed in sparkling beads. A picture of them gazing into each other's eyes, a small smile on LBJ's face, made the cover of *Life* magazine under the headline, "Memorable Night at the White House." The story inside called the dinner "a Radiant Interlude in History."

"Daddy was just the biggest dancer of all times," daughter Lynda Bird recalled. Then twenty-one years old and single, she attended the White House dinner escorted by actor George Hamilton. Her father "loved dancing with everybody," she said, "and so he was just dancing." The official White House diary reported that the president "had a good time, he looked well, and danced with almost every woman there."

"My father was a beautiful dancer," Luci agreed. Then eighteen, she brought as her date Patrick Nugent, the boyfriend she would marry a year later but eventually divorce. She described her father that night as though it had been a week before, not six decades. "He danced with Princess Margaret, and she looked like she was having the time of her life, and he looked like he had had the honor of a lifetime. And you just sort of felt like they were both living in the moment they had."

The president and the princess danced a foxtrot as bandleader Peter Duchin and his orchestra played "Everything's Coming Up Roses," from the musical *Gypsy*. That was a nod to Margaret's middle name of Rose.

MARGARET, NOT ELIZABETH, ENDED UP VISITING WASHINGTON DURING LBJ's tenure. And Humphrey, not Johnson, ended up visiting London.

As with Margaret's pop-in, the occasion had little to do with British efforts to cultivate the White House. Humphrey's traveling plans appeared "out of the blue," a British official noted on March 21, 1967, with his arrival scheduled for just twelve days later, on April 2. He would be traveling for two weeks in Europe "informally," not something sitting vice presidents customarily do, but even so he asked to meet with the prime minister.

And the Queen.

The White House said Humphrey wanted to make "a small presentation" to Elizabeth. Despite the late notice, she responded with an invitation to a black-tie dinner in his honor at Windsor Castle. The royal family turned out in force—the Duke of Edinburgh, eighteen-year-old Prince of Wales, who was home from his Scottish school on Easter vacation, and sixteen-year-old Princess Anne, appearing for the first time on the guest list for a state function. The meal was served on china and crystal that had been the gift of Frederick the Great.

Afterward, the Queen escorted the vice president and his wife, Muriel, into the library to view letters written to her predecessors by George Washington, John Adams, and James Madison. The Humphreys spent the night in a suite at the castle, another plum. "The British take care of things," the vice president later marveled.

Humphrey's sudden interest in sightseeing in London apparently had been sparked by a visit there weeks earlier by New York Senator Robert F. Kennedy, Johnson's nemesis and a potential challenger for the Democratic presidential nomination the next year. Kennedy was part of a congressional delegation attending a Ditchley Park Conference, hosted at an eighteenth-century country estate outside Oxford to discuss British-American relations. His request to meet with the prime minister raised concern behind the scenes about the prospect of Johnson "being miffed." They did meet, but Sir Patrick Dean, the British ambassador to the US, was tasked to "informally and discreetly" alert the White House beforehand.

By now, four years into LBJ's tenure, British officials understood exactly where they stood with this president.

"It is true that Mr. Humphrey's visit to Europe is a sign of increased interest in European questions," an internal briefing paper prepared before the visit read, one that would have been circulated to the Queen before her dinner with the vice president. "Nevertheless the fact that it is the Vice-President who has been chosen to visit Europe and the President who is going to South America for a summit meeting of Latin American presidents next month is perhaps a reminder of how foreign priorities look to President Johnson." In other words, not with Europe. Not with Britain.

After the session with Humphrey, Paul Gore-Booth, a top Foreign Office official, wrote Ambassador Dean that one reason for the vice president's sudden appearance on the scene was "to counter Robert Kennedy's recent visit" and perhaps to "spy out the land to see whether or not a later visit by himself [the president] would be advisable." He added, a voice of experience: "We doubt whether the conclusion is likely to be very positive."

He was right. There would be no foxtrot with the Queen, no invitation to visit even when she spent nine weeks next door in Canada during the summer of 1967 to celebrate the country's centennial. "As we sail through the international waters of the St. Lawrence Seaway I send you my warmest greetings on this Fourth of July," she dutifully wrote Johnson then. He dutifully wrote back, thanking her "for your thoughtful and moving message."

That was that.

On March 31, 1968, Johnson announced he wouldn't run for another term in the White House, a decision that among other things was a relief to London. The Queen never publicly expressed her exasperation with him. Those who knew her best said she was by now inclined to take things as they happened—"to go with the flow," as she put it. But it would be only human to take offense, as others did. Lord Bernard Donoughue, a political adviser for prime ministers from the 1970s to the 1990s, offered a simple reason why the thirty-sixth president never made an official visit: "I think LBJ was a bit of a bully," he said.

In November, a new president would be elected—one who saw great value in an alliance with the royal family, and in more ways than one.

Six

Lifeline

Wednesday, February 26, 1969—Buckingham Palace

Richard Milhous Nixon had a distant connection with Queen Elizabeth. He was eager to make it closer. Perhaps much closer.

His namesake was one of her distant relatives—Richard the Lionheart, the twelfth-century king and warrior of the Crusades. Hannah Milhous Nixon named one son after her husband but gave the other four the names of legendary medieval monarchs: Harold, Arthur, Edward, and Richard. "His mother was a student of history," Nixon's daughter, Tricia, said, and so competent in Latin and Greek that she could help her granddaughter with her Latin homework.

But Hannah never claimed a relation to the Crown; she had been born into a sprawling Irish Quaker family of modest circumstances near Butlerville, Indiana. She surely would have been amazed to learn that after her third son was elected president, and a year after her death, genealogists determined he was, through her father, descended from King Edward III. Who was the great-great-great nephew of Richard the Lionheart and the nineteenth great-grandfather of Elizabeth.

That common figure on their family trees would make the president and Her Majesty the most removed of cousins. It was a personal link that Nixon would seek to strengthen. They would also be close political partners, for a time. He was a relief and a fresh start after Lyndon Johnson and the cold shoulder he had given the Queen for five long years.

Nixon and Elizabeth seemed to enjoy each other's company from the start, when he was vice president and they encountered one another at a formal luncheon, a solemn chapel dedication, a lively Thanksgiving dinner. But as it turned out, if Nixon could be strategic in his relationships, so could the Queen. Put another way, he was an asset for the Crown, until he wasn't.

When Nixon won the White House in 1968, the historic alliance between the United States and Great Britain had been weakened by LBJ's disregard. Now the Queen and her government feared it might fray further given the ideological divide between the Republican president and the Labour prime minister. Harold Wilson, in office since 1964, was a man of the left while Nixon had made his political name targeting alleged Communists in the American government in the 1940s and 1950s. Wilson himself had been dogged by rumors that he was a Communist sympathizer or even a Soviet spy—accusations that were never proven, although James Jesus Angleton, head of counterintelligence at the CIA, apparently believed them to be true.

Now Her Majesty was more prepared than ever before to insert herself in matters she considered crucial. By the time Nixon was inaugurated in January 1969, she had dealt with four presidents and five prime ministers. At age forty-two, she was no longer the anxious young woman Truman once embraced. Her diplomatic skills and political judgment rivaled that of her American counterparts, and her maturity as a monarch gave her the confidence and the wherewithal to exert influence without seeming to overstep, and sometimes without even being noticed.

She was determined to renew Churchill's early advice: Stay close to the Americans. When Edward Heath, who felt differently, became prime minister in June 1970, she stepped out to forge a relationship, even a kinship, with the awkward Mr. Nixon. She was a constitutional monarch, but that didn't mean she was powerless to exert her influence when she thought it was wise.

Nixon was not a natural politician. His gestures could seem disconnected from his body; his default response to journalists' questions was defensive. Unlike many politicians, he was more comfortable in solitude than in the spotlight. She may have seen something to admire in a man who forced himself into the public eye again and again, against the inclinations of his personality. He was resilient, too—a quality that she herself would exhibit over the course of her long reign. Her country needed her diplomatic resilience at this moment in the late 1960s, after strain with the Americans over the Vietnam War and amid cultural upheaval around the globe. It wasn't clear if an ancient monarch would fit in a world where the establishments in government, education, the military, music, and more were under fire from a rising generation, transforming everything from rock music to women's rights.

Nixon gave the Queen a welcome contrast to his "more earthy predecessor," as one relieved British diplomat put it. Nixon's reflexive formality, even his stiffness, was more palatable to British tastes than his predecessor's sprawling Texas persona. What's more, Nixon moved into the Oval Office determined to end the war in Southeast Asia, a sticking point in the special relationship, and to repair ties with Europe. He planned a major trip just a month after his inauguration, built around a North Atlantic Council meeting in Brussels. The new president would also stop in Rome, Vatican City, West Berlin, and Paris. But particular attention was given to the London leg, where he would meet with Wilson and Elizabeth.

A British briefing paper, written to prepare the prime minister and the Queen, reported that Nixon was "anxious to redress President Johnson's preoccupation with Asia." The embassy in Washington also relayed a conversation with Henry Kissinger, then the White House national security adviser. Nixon "regards the British as his principal ally," Kissinger had told a British diplomat, never mind the president's efforts to also build closer relations with the French and the Germans.

Nixon was captivated by the British royal family, by the pageantry that surrounded them and the adoration they received. He yearned to emulate their grandeur and the exercise of power they had demonstrated during their days as an empire. The "imperial presidency," historian Arthur Schlesinger Jr. dubbed Nixon's administration. The executive branch had slowly been accumulating more power from other branches of government, especially since World War II. "[B]y the 1970s," Schlesinger wrote, "the American President had become on issues of war and peace the most absolute monarch (with the possible exception of Mao Tse-tung of China) among the great powers of the world."

The regal trappings were on display when Nixon arrived at Buckingham Palace on February 25, 1969. Flags of the United States and the United Kingdom fluttered from the front fenders of the black presidential limousine. A fanfare of trumpets sounded as he was escorted up the front steps. He crossed the spectacular Grand Entrance and Marble Hall, then shook hands with Queen Elizabeth and Prince Philip, waiting to greet him. As it happened, he was walking into a strange episode of royal history: A documentary film crew was on hand to record the occasion.

In 1968, Elizabeth had reluctantly agreed to allow the BBC and ITV to film her family's everyday lives—part of an effort to adjust to the public's evolving expectations of a more open sovereign. That was the case made by her press secretary, William Heseltine, and the television producer John Brabourne, a son-in-law of Lord Mountbatten. (A decade later, Brabourne would survive the IRA bombing that killed his father-in-law, his mother, and one of his sons.) It was the first time behind-the-scenes recordings of royal life, including meetings with world leaders, had been allowed. The *Royal Family* documentary didn't turn out to be high drama—no revealing confrontations à la *The Crown* decades later—but it did provide a glimpse behind palace doors that outsiders had never been allowed to see before, or since. The film was shown to mixed reviews. Some found the family interactions charming; others saw them as cringeworthy. The Queen would later refuse to allow the film to be rebroadcast. (Technology eventually triumphed: A bootleg copy surfaced on YouTube in 2021.)

Nixon's arrival is a key moment in the film. Small talk, always a difficult art, may have been even more of a challenge in front of the cameras. Known for the off-kilter comment, Nixon presented the Queen with a formal photograph of himself as a gift, which she accepted with a nod and a smile. The president seemed nervous, even apologetic, saying he would like to send her a new one that included his wife because that would be "much more pleasant to look at." The Queen smiled again and then changed the subject.

"You sound as if you're going to have a really busy few days—and the world problems are so complex now," she said, offering an opening and a life preserver.

He replied, "I was just thinking about how much more complex they are than when we last met." Since then, he noted, nervous still, "I was out, really—I mean out of power, but I traveled a bit."

When he returned to Washington, Nixon tried to transplant some regal glamour to the White House. He ordered new outfits for the uniformed Secret Service agents stationed there—double-breasted white tunics trimmed with gold braid and black-and-gold ceremonial hats. Hugh Sidey, the veteran White House columnist for *Life* magazine, attributed the tailoring to Nixon's "intense but vain search for the magic" that the royals "carried along so casually." To the president's dismay, the new uniforms were roundly ridiculed in the press, likened to those worn by ushers in old-time movie theaters. They were retired within a few years. (The US General Services Administration would sell them for $10 each to the Meriden-Cleghorn High School in rural Iowa for use by its marching band. Serendipity: The school's nickname was "Home of the Royals," with a crown as its logo.)

His first presidential trip to London had a secondary mission. During his visit, Nixon invited Prince Charles and Princess Anne to make their first trip to the United States. Charles was then twenty years old and Anne was eighteen. "I was just saying to Her Majesty, 'I've seen you on television,'" Nixon said when he met the two. Anne, smiling, said, "I don't think you've seen me on television." Nixon demurred. "Both of my daughters follow you both very closely," he told the princess and the future king. Philip responded tartly, "I'm sure one [daughter] no longer."

That was an unmistakable reference to Julie and her marriage a few months earlier to David Eisenhower—as a presidential grandson, a political catch himself—which limited any matrimonial designs Nixon might have had on the prince and his younger daughter. But there was still his older daughter, Tricia.

SUBTLETY WAS NEVER NIXON'S STRONG SUIT, AND HIS APPARENT EFFORTS to get the world's most eligible young bachelor romantically interested in his daughter were an open secret in Washington. It would have been in keeping with Nixon's penchant for strategic thinking in all things. A match between the Nixons and the Windsors, or even the suggestion of a romance, would elevate the president's stature. He saw the royal embrace as a priceless asset, one he would try to use more than once over the years.

Tricia's father wasn't her only would-be matchmaker. George H. W. Bush, then a Houston congressman and later president, had invited son George W. Bush to escort Tricia to a dinner he was hosting at a Washington club in honor of astronaut Frank Borman. After the younger Bush—then a pilot-in-training for the Texas Air National Guard and later a president himself—had spilled red wine and tried to light a cigarette, she asked for a quick return to the White House. They had no second date.

For Nixon, there would be more opportunities. Five months after he invited Charles to visit Washington, the president dispatched Tricia to Caernarvon, Wales, to attend his investiture as Prince of Wales. "America's little princess," the British press dubbed her, part of a flurry of positive publicity for the petite twenty-three-year-old. Plans for her to have tea at Buckingham Palace were canceled when the Queen fell ill. She sent an apologetic letter to Tricia, expressing concern about the rain at the investiture—"Our climate is unreliable!"—and asking her to "remember me to your father and mother." Still, Tricia was the guest of honor at a US embassy dinner-dance, attended a regatta and a garden party, and watched the tennis quarterfinals at Wimbledon. She was introduced to the prime minister's wife and to Princess Anne, though she didn't meet Charles.

When reporters pressed her on the prospect of a romantic interest, she replied diplomatically. "Let me just say, Prince Charles is my sister's age," she said. Tricia was three years older than the prince. But she acknowledged, "I suppose if you are in love with someone, things like age aren't relevant." She seconded her father's invitation to Charles and Anne to visit the White House. "Wouldn't it be great if they could come?" she said.

They would arrive the next summer, in July 1970. The Queen had seen the same value in a family visit as the president did. She sent a personal request to Nixon through the US ambassador, Walter Annenberg. Charles and Anne and their entourage customarily would have stayed at Blair House, the government guest house across Pennsylvania Avenue from the White House. But Elizabeth asked if they could stay in the White House, in the suites she and Philip had used when they visited Eisenhower in 1957, and that her parents had occupied when they visited FDR in 1939. That proximity would reinforce the closeness of the two nations and of their two families. Nixon was delighted to oblige. Anne stayed in the Queen's Room and Charles in the Lincoln Bedroom; her maid and his valet were assigned to rooms on the third floor.

But Nixon was disgruntled when the news of the visit by the prince and princess didn't generate more good publicity for him, that more of the Crown's magic wasn't rubbing off. He blamed Constance Stuart, the press secretary for Pat Nixon, with a sideswipe at the first lady herself. "He said in her (Stuart's) defense, he realizes it's an extremely difficult job dealing with Mrs. Nixon, but she just isn't getting the job done right," H. R. Haldeman, the White House chief of staff, wrote in his diary. "Some of the things like the Prince Charles party should have been major stories and weren't."

Stuart was also blamed for a behind-the-scenes runaround over who was going to foot the $35,000 bill for the party on the South Lawn—a dinner-dance for seven hundred young people that was to be the apex of the visit. "Over and over again, Connie has implied to the press that the visit is a private visit and that it is being hosted by Julie and Tricia," said Dwight Chapin, then a special assistant to the president. He would later go to prison for perjury during the Watergate investigation.

In fairness, Nixon himself promoted the idea that the visit be seen as his offspring hosting the Queen's children, casting his own family as a sort of American royalty. The White House argued that the State Department should underwrite the party "on the basis that this is an official visit since Prince Charles will at some future time be King of England." (No one knew how long it would be before that happened—more than another half century.) But the State Department protested on the grounds that "it is a private party that Julie and Tricia are giving."

As enthusiastic as he was about the royal children and his own sharing a magical evening, Nixon was unenthusiastic about financing it out of his own pocket. Like the old game of telephone, Stuart told Chapin that Pat Nixon had told her she would ask Annenberg, a businessman of considerable wealth as well as the US ambassador to the Court of St. James's. But the first lady changed her mind, saying she wouldn't ask Annenberg but somebody else should. Chapin finally sent an exasperated memo to Haldeman, who as White House chief of staff had other things to do, recounting the state of play and posing two questions: Should Annenberg be asked to pay for the party? (Check yes or no.) If so, who should do the asking? (Haldeman, Chapin, Secretary of State William Rogers, or someone else?)

Haldeman checked "yes" on asking Annenberg and "other" on whom to tap for the task, writing in "Mrs. Nixon—or Connie Stuart for Mrs. Nixon or Lucy Winchester for Mrs. Nixon." (Lucy Winchester was the White House social secretary.)

The day before the party, Annenberg sent the most diplomatic of letters to Nixon, as though the thought of paying the bill had come to him, unbidden. "That Charles and Anne might spend a few days with your young people was an exciting thought for your Ambassador," he wrote on stationery from the Madison Hotel, where he was presumably staying when the dunning call came from, well, the first lady or the press secretary or the social secretary or whomever. "It is indeed my hope that you would not regard as presumptuous if I sought the privilege of defraying the expense of the Dinner Dance tomorrow night."

Done.

The itinerary was crowded during the royals' visit, starting with lunch on the presidential yacht *Sequoia* and a cruise down the Potomac River to George Washington's estate at Mount Vernon. They ate simple cookout fare at Camp David one night—hamburgers and banana splits—and were feted at the formal dinner-dance on the South Lawn the next. When they were surveying the capital from the top of the Washington Monument, Charles challenged David Eisenhower to a dash down its 555 steps. Their race left their security details in the dust and David wincing when he walked the next day.

Perhaps the schedule was a bit *too* packed. On the final day of their tour, the prince had been taken to observe birds in a wildlife sanctuary, fitting for a man who would later design his own exquisite gardens, even acknowledge talking to his plants. But he proved not to be an instinctive fan of the national pastime. "We were told that they especially wanted to see the American sport, baseball, which we questioned," Tricia recalled. "We said, 'Do they really?'" Yes, they were assured. So they did, attending a Washington Senators game at their stadium, named for Nixon's former political rival, Robert F. Kennedy. "It was quite a warm and muggy afternoon," Tricia recalled. "I don't think we stayed for too many innings."

Next was a visit to Phillips Gallery. Charles was flagging. "'We aren't going to have a long tour here, are we?'" he asked Julie plaintively.

That may have sounded churlish, but Charles was a good sport compared to his sister.

"He was hardworking and appeared to be genuinely interested in all the people he met and the places he visited, even when, as in the case of the Phillips Gallery, I knew that his interest was perfunctory," Julie said. This was not true of his sister. The princess was having an increasingly difficult time feigning interest in the city of Washington. She jerked her arm away when House Speaker John McCormack, then seventy-nine years old, dared to touch it, a moment caught on camera, and she repeatedly rebuffed the entreaties by news photographers to smile.

Nixon scheduled a half-hour conversation about world events with Charles in the Oval Office, just the two of them. It stretched to an hour and fifteen minutes. The president gave the prince a tutorial on global challenges and made the case with another generation for the "special relationship." He later told Julie that he had been impressed by Charles's "extraordinary interest in and understanding of the entire world scene." He expressed particular interest in the problems of emerging nations in Africa, the region that so engaged his mother.

Charles sent Nixon a handwritten thank-you note on crested Palace of Holyroodhouse stationery, the official residence of the British monarch in Scotland. Their session had been "fascinating and informative," he said, offering a sympathetic view on the Vietnam War that was at odds with many young people of the day. He even referred to the new leadership in the United Kingdom—"this new government here"—with an offhand candor that his mother likely wouldn't have, at least not in writing.

"My visit to Washington gave me some sense of the close ties that do exist between the two countries, despite occasional misunderstandings + disagreements," he wrote. He commiserated about Nixon's travails in Vietnam. "I was interested to hear what you had to say about your lonely role in South East Asia. I, and I expect many people in the country sympathize with your fiendish problems, but it remains to be seen what this new government here decides to do."

At the time, the Nixon administration was slowly reducing US forces in Vietnam amid rising antiwar protests at home. Two months earlier, the

Ohio National Guard had shot and killed four unarmed college students during a protest on the campus of Kent State University, inflaming the national debate.

Throughout the trip, photos of Charles were splashed on newspaper front pages across the country, showing him sitting with or walking beside or chatting with Tricia. The heir to the British throne, accustomed to a lifetime of matchmaking by the crown heads of Europe and celebrities everywhere, later said he had no doubt about what the president was trying to do.

"I remember the first time was—we were invited to stay, my sister and I, in 1970 at the White House by President Nixon for the weekend," he recalled in an interview on CNN. "That was quite amusing, I must say. That was the time when they were trying to marry me off to Tricia Nixon." In 2005, Charles and his second wife, Camilla, visited President George W. Bush and first lady Laura Bush at the White House. (That would be a meeting of two targets for Tricia's matchmakers.) The prince gave the Bushes a mock warning: Don't try to fix up his sons William and Harry with their twin daughters the way Nixon had labored to set him up with his daughter.

Tricia, by now seventy-nine, said she had been unaware of the speculation about her father's intentions until I asked about it. "Oh, heavens no," she said, laughing. "Oh, my goodness." Since 1968, she and Edward Cox had been secretly engaged, something that would have been of no surprise to her parents and close friends, she said. During Charles's visit, Edward was attending Harvard Law School. They were married in the Rose Garden a year later.

But she didn't let Prince Charles in on the secret engagement. "Why would I have done that?" she asked. "I didn't even know him. That was personal." When the betrothal was finally announced, he sent a letter to the president—possibly sly—saying his hopes of welcoming the Nixon daughters to London sometime during the year no longer seemed feasible. "May I offer my congratulations on Tricia's engagement?" he asked. In an undated letter to Tricia, reported by Pat Nixon biographer Heath Hardage Lee, he wished her "a wonderful wedding and honeymoon."

The night of the White House party on the South Lawn, Charles had been somber as he talked with Julie about the demands and requirements for a crown prince's choice of a wife. "He seems to have made his own rules," she said later. "The head must rule the heart. Falling in love is not enough. His wife must also be his best friend. And his marriage must last forever." (That was an aspiration that proved unattainable for his first marriage, to Diana Spencer, a decade later.)

He also matter-of-factly revealed this poignant observation: "The older I get, the more alone I become."

Soon after he had returned from Washington, Charles met the woman who would be the love of his life when he was playing in a polo match in Windsor Great Park. He and Camilla Shand would date, break up, marry others, have an affair, divorce their spouses, and finally marry each other in 2005. When Charles became king in 2022, Camilla became queen.

NIXON PLANNED A JAM-PACKED FOREIGN TRIP IN THE FALL OF 1970. THERE would be official meetings in Italy, a tour of the NATO Southern Command, an audience with Pope Paul VI at the Vatican, plus state visits to Yugoslavia, Spain, and Ireland. There was time for only the briefest of stopovers in England as he flew from Madrid to Ireland.

It would be a chance to sit down with Edward Heath, who had replaced Wilson as prime minister after the Conservative Party unexpectedly won a general election in June—the "new government" Charles mentioned in his letter.

The visit with Heath was scheduled for four hours—a diplomatic blink of an eye—and one of those hours would be taken up by the helicopter ride to Chequers. "We assume the Prime Minister would wish to make the lunch comparatively small, men only and 'working,'" an aide's memo detailed. The timetable was tight: A one-on-one meeting between the president and the prime minister, the working luncheon, followed by an hour and fifteen minutes for a session with other senior officials. British aides discussed how they could exclude even Treasury Secretary David Kennedy and White House counselor Daniel Patrick Moynihan from the meeting for fear of introducing extraneous topics in the short time allowed.

"There remains the problem of Mrs Nixon," the memo went on. She would need to be entertained while the men got down to serious business. Could some member of the royal family be drafted to invite the first lady to lunch?

Then the Queen weighed in.

"I'm afraid I have a fairly weighty spanner to throw into the works," Robert Armstrong, Heath's private secretary, said in a memo a few days later. "That is that, when the Prime Minister was in Balmoral this weekend, The Queen indicated that She would be glad to come down and to meet President and Mrs Nixon during their visit; indeed, She said that it would be discourteous not to do so." Coming from the sovereign, a suggestion is closer to a command, something that Heath instantly understood. "The upshot of all this was that the Prime Minister invited the Queen to come to lunch at Chequers on October 3 to meet President and Mrs Nixon, and the Queen accepted."

She was not going there on a whim. To underestimate her interest in and knowledge of world affairs would be a serious miscalculation. Indeed, her private secretary sent a scathing memo to the Foreign Office complaining about the lack of substance in the briefing memo she had been sent before the meeting. "Inadequate and unsatisfactory," Martin Charteris called it. She found it patronizing.

"The Background Note on the United States Internal Scene would have been a useful document for a person unfamiliar with affairs," he wrote to the vice marshal of the diplomatic corps. "However for someone like The Queen who is already well informed (and in Her Majesty's case has read the reports from her Ambassadors for 17 years with care and attention) it was superficial." Worst of all, he said, the briefing didn't detail what the British hoped to achieve with Nixon's visit.

The Queen's attendance was unexpected, even unprecedented, and underscored that Nixon was not the only one keen on building bridges between the two countries. Her family time at Balmoral was sacrosanct. Only a handful of occasions were considered significant enough to interrupt it: to accept Macmillan's resignation in 1963; to welcome her son Andrew at Portsmouth when he returned from the Falklands War in 1982; to attend the funeral of Margaret "Bobo" MacDonald, her nursemaid-turned-dresser of sixty-seven years' service, in 1993. Her reluctance to leave Balmoral when Princess Diana was killed in an automobile crash in Paris in 1997 prompted a public outcry.

Nor was Elizabeth a regular visitor to Chequers, the official country estate of British prime ministers since 1921. In fact, she had never been there. She also suggested—or "suggested"—that she be seated next to the president. So did the White House advance team. "The Americans made it clear this afternoon that they would feel uncomfortable if President Nixon did not sit next to the Queen at lunch," one memo reported.

The luncheon would now be a very different sort of occasion, including the Queen and the first lady and the wives of other officials—at the time, an entirely male collection in both delegations. The addition of spouses would bump some top British officials from the main table, which could seat only eighteen people, to a secondary room and a buffet. "It would mean exiling Sir Burke Trend and Sir Denis Greenhill," a planning memo to Heath reported—that is, the Cabinet secretary and the permanent secretary at the Foreign Office. "Both of these men are resigned to their fate."

At Heath's request, the announcement from Buckingham Palace made it clear the request to attend had come from Elizabeth herself. The prime minister may have wanted to avoid accusations that he was using the Queen for political advantage. Indeed, a senior Labour member of Parliament sent a note to Elizabeth's private secretary warning that "many of our people are aroused by the political use which has been made of this"—an allegation the prime minister and the palace rebuffed.

Nixon was of course delighted to hear the Queen would be there. A White House official characterized his reaction as "inordinate pleasure." "The general atmosphere certainly seemed to be a happy and relaxed one," the Queen's secretary, Michael Adeane, told Heath the day after the luncheon. Elizabeth sent the prime minister an account of impressions from her discussions with Nixon and Secretary of State William Rogers.

It was no longer Heath's closely held working session with the president, one from which even the US Treasury secretary would be unwelcome. In a letter to Nixon afterward, Heath noted that "the time for discussion was shorter than I would have wished." It is possible to read that observation as one with an edge. Instead, the narrow negotiations on the issues he chose were replaced by something bigger and more fundamental, the freewheeling conversation of friends.

Which was, of course, her point.

Afterward, Nixon sent her a personal letter. "Your Majesty," he began.

"It was typically thoughtful of you to travel to Chequers to receive Mrs. Nixon and me during our recent visit to the United Kingdom, and I want to thank you for your signal kindness in according us this privilege. It was a special pleasure to see you again, and a unique honor to share your first visit to that beautiful house." Kissinger wrote Heath that "the generous and unprecedented gesture by the Queen" had demonstrated "to the President and all of us once again that there is indeed a 'special relationship' and that it continues to flow strong. . . ."

Heath sent the Queen a lengthy memo with his assessment of the president from their meeting.

"The first thing which struck me—and this feeling grew as our discussion went on—was that he is genuinely anxious to have a close relationship with us," Heath wrote, not mentioning that wasn't his own priority. "He said at the outset that the 'special relationship' was essentially a matter of personal relations; and these words seemed to me to be an indication of his wish to put fresh life and meaning into the concept of the 'special relationship,' which has become a little tarnished in recent years." There had been hope that the overlap in ideology between Nixon and Heath, both conservatives, would bring their two nations closer together.

But the Queen wasn't willing to trust that task to them. She was determined to get the relationship with America back on track—and she knew that Heath didn't agree. His agenda didn't start with Britain's ties with the United States. Instead, he was determined to fortify them with Europe.

Eventually, Kissinger described Heath as chilly; Nixon found him condescending. "He was the only British leader I encountered who not only failed to cultivate the 'special relationship' with the United States but actively sought to downgrade it and to give Europe pride of place in British policy," Kissinger said. "All this made for an unprecedented period of strain in Anglo-American relations." Jonathan Aitken, a British biographer of Nixon, called it "probably the most unsteady relationship of any Prime Minister and President in living memory," since Heath "was never really committed to the Special Relationship because he was dreaming of a completely new European architecture for Britain."

The relationship between Nixon and Heath ended "in mutual contempt," a top Kissinger aide said, "and once they left office, the old lions were barely civil to each other." But the Queen's intervention and Nixon's inclinations kept ties strong between the United States and Britain despite Heath.

He lasted as prime minister until 1974, through a crisis-ridden tenure that included national strikes by the miners and the dockers, the bankruptcy of the iconic Rolls-Royce company, and a global spike in oil prices. The low point came with the "Bloody Sunday" tragedy on January 30, 1972, when British paratroopers shot and killed thirteen unarmed protesters in Derry, Northern Ireland. An angry mob then burned down the chancery of the British embassy in Dublin.

Nixon would soon face fires of his own. In the summer of 1972, a break-in at the Watergate complex in Washington touched off the scandal that would grow in intensity over the next two years. Three days before Heath left office on March 4, 1974, a grand jury returned indictments for seven Nixon aides, including H. R. Haldeman and John Ehrlichman. Nixon was named an unindicted coconspirator.

AS NIXON SCRAMBLED TO KEEP HIS JOB, THE WHITE HOUSE REACHED OUT to the British about inviting him to a state visit in London—more to boost his domestic standing than for any foreign policy goal. It would show the beleaguered president in command abroad, toasted by the world's most respected monarch. The Queen's presence would be a sign of stability and respectability, attributes Nixon desperately needed as his administration sank into a political abyss.

But Elizabeth had avoided personal scandal during her own public life, although like almost every public figure she had sometimes been adjacent to it, her uncle's abdication being the most painful episode. Whatever she thought of Nixon as a person—and by all accounts she viewed him with some regard—she wouldn't risk the monarchy, or her own reputation, to save someone who was already drowning. Her views likely echoed those expressed more openly by Lord Mountbatten, who had retired as chief of the British Defense Staff in 1965 but remained an adviser and confidant to his royal relations. He had liked Nixon, Mountbatten said, and even dined with him at the White House in 1970, but felt "he turned out to be a real crook and what he did was quite unforgivable." The Queen's once-chatty letters to Nixon were still proper but less warm.

Heath's ouster in 1974 saw the return of Wilson to 10 Downing Street. The next day, Ambassador Annenberg renewed the prospect of a presidential visit. It would be "most helpful" if Nixon could visit Britain a month later, when he was scheduled to travel to Paris to sign a NATO declaration, Annenberg told him. Oh, and he hoped Wilson "would be able to persuade the Queen to offer a State Banquet for the President at Buckingham Palace."

He may have hoped that Wilson and Nixon's personal relationship—anyone was better than Heath—would smooth the way. But Wilson, in his second tour as prime minister, knew better than to get ensnared in a foreign leader's downward spiral, even an American one. He was carefully noncommittal. "He spent a lot of time getting round Nixon's persistent efforts (to) arrange a state visit to the U.K.," recalled one of Wilson's senior advisers, Bernard Donoughue. "He thought Nixon was a bit of a crook and it wouldn't be good for him, and he didn't want to embarrass the Queen." Behind the scenes, British officials began to strategize how to prevent a visit without rupturing relations. They recognized that Nixon's fortunes were increasingly precarious.

When Wilson saw Nixon in Paris a month later, in April 1974, the president again suggested a visit, a conversation the prime minister tried to deflect. "He did not relish the idea of a visit by the President for what were evidently domestic electoral purposes," a private British account of the session said. Wilson instructed the Foreign Office "to take any measures open to us to ensure that Mr. Nixon did not come to London."

It was one final odd episode with Nixon, presenting the Queen with a dilemma she was anxious to sidestep. He didn't seem to realize that, or perhaps didn't feel he had the luxury of caring. An overture to Nixon could only complicate relations with the American politicians who would take power after him. But how to say no to a president who had been an ally, even a friend? How could the Queen, who just four years earlier had wanted to align with Nixon so much that she invited herself to the prime minister's luncheon at Chequers, now keep him at arm's length?

Thomas Brimelow, a senior Foreign Office official, sent a "top secret and personal" letter to Sir Peter Ramsbotham, the British ambassador to

Washington, asking how to minimize the damage if the Queen and her government simply refused to accede to the White House request. Was Brimelow's relationship with Kissinger good enough "to work through him to deter a visit"? A year earlier, the two men had collaborated on a nuclear agreement between the United States and the Soviet Union.

Don't expect help from the secretary of state, Brimelow replied. "Kissinger cannot afford to be anything but the President's agent on such an issue," he wrote. "The President will see his political survival at stake and I doubt if he recognises any higher good." The risks were real, he warned. Nixon would feel "disappointment and disillusionment" if his old friends in London refused to receive him, "and he is a vengeful man."

He is a vengeful man.

Like it or not, Britain might have to agree to a visit, Brimelow said. "Any country, and particularly the first, which *visibly* allowed Watergate to affect its dealings with the Administration, would inevitably be the target of the President's bitterness and perhaps retribution." He added: "My impression is that, in a situation in which he feels hounded and even cornered, the President could be capable of the irrational."

They needed to drum up "a really cast-iron excuse" to prevent a visit, he suggested. If they could calculate the dates Nixon was likely to propose, for instance, the prime minister could preemptively announce plans to "undertake some visit abroad" then. Just where Wilson sought temporary sanctuary wouldn't matter as much as simply being able to plead that he was already planning to be out of the country, somewhere.

In Washington, Nixon's situation was increasingly perilous. The House Judiciary Committee began impeachment proceedings in May. But he wasn't ready to give up on the glowing optics of a state visit to London, of being received by the Queen in her palace. In July, Annenberg took Foreign Secretary James Callaghan aside "and asked what those concerned would think about a visit by President Nixon to this country in November." Callaghan, who later became prime minister, responded with a question of his own. What did Annenberg think about the prospects of the president's impeachment? The proceedings might be concluded by the end of the month, the ambassador replied with candor, or they might drag on until the end of the year.

With that, Callaghan offered an equally candid response. If the threat of impeachment were removed, "there would be no great difficulty" in hosting Nixon, he said. "If however the question of impeachment still hung over the President, a visit could cause some embarrassment to the Royal Family and others and no doubt Mr. Annenberg would want to avoid this." Annenberg "emphatically agreed."

Wilson was relieved. "J.C. cd not have put it better," the prime minister wrote in green ink across the top of the report. So was the Queen. "I am sure Her Majesty will be fascinated to read about the exchange between Mr Callaghan and Mr Annenberg," her secretary wrote back that same day, "and grateful for the way in which Mr. Callaghan has borne her interests in mind."

A month later, Nixon resigned.

NIXON'S REPUTATION WAS SULLIED, HIS POLITICAL CAREER IN RUINS. ONLY by the grace of his successor's pardon did the disgraced ex-president avoid the threat of prosecution and even possible incarceration.

From then on, he would be persona non grata in official London, including Buckingham Palace. During his first trip back in 1976, a year when he had once hoped to be hosting America's Bicentennial celebration, he had a small private dinner at the Dorchester Hotel with Wilson, then himself recently out of office. During the evening Nixon and Wilson discovered a mutual love for Gilbert & Sullivan, especially the music of *H.M.S. Pinafore*. "Although no-one was drunk," Jonathan Aitken said, "there was a certain amount of alcohol drunk by that point and suddenly Wilson taps on the table and begins the famous aria 'When I Was a Lad' and this goes on for about 12 verses. Nixon then joins in and they're absolutely word-perfect, both of them." The other diners and the waiter applauded the performance.

But Nixon was never welcomed by the Queen again. When he returned in 1978, the Foreign Office advised that "Mr Nixon now represents no-one." Peter Jay, the British ambassador to the United States, wrote: "We should be stonily proper and properly stony."

In 1992, Nixon and another former president, Ronald Reagan, were both in London to address a conference at Claridge's sponsored by the energy giant ARCO—the sort of appearances that were accompanied by big paychecks. "Old glories on the presidents roadshow," a columnist in the *Daily Express* called it, giving Nixon credit for working to rehabilitate his standing as someone worth listening to, especially on foreign policy. His address on world affairs, delivered without notes, received a standing ovation.

While the Reagans were invited to tea with Elizabeth and Philip at Buckingham Palace, Nixon was not. But one member of the royal family may have felt some lingering sympathy for him.

The Queen Mother had first met Nixon in 1954, when he was vice president and she was visiting Washington, two years after the death of her husband and her daughter's ascension to the throne. Two decades later, after he had been forced out of office, she was welcoming a group of American students to a reception in Clarence House, her residence in London. "Do you think the president was guilty, Your Majesty?" one of them asked. The Reverend Victor Stock, dean of Guildford Cathedral, described the shock among the Brits in the room at what they saw as an impossibly impudent question. "Attendant duchesses froze in horror and took several paces backwards," he recalled. "The Queen Mother fixed a gimlet eye on me and said, 'Father Stock will explain the difference between a constitutional monarchy and the presidency of the United States.'"

The student persisted, with American denseness, or disregard, when it came to royal protocol. "But do you think he did it?" he asked. Adjusting her purse and gazing into the middle distance, she acknowledged the temptation of power to take an advantage. "If I were president of the United States, I would look in the bag from time to time," she said.

No one was certain precisely what that meant, but it sounded like empathy. It was an empathy her proper and circumspect daughter didn't seem to share. Indeed, as Elizabeth matured into a power in her own right, and when the situation seemed to demand it, she could display a cold dispatch that may have surprised even herself in her younger years. She was tougher than her pleasant demeanor might indicate, tougher than this president had assumed.

Out with Nixon. On with his (unexpected) successor.

Seven

West Wing Meets *The Crown*

Tuesday, July 6, 1976—Philadelphia

When Jerry Ford became president, the sun rose for him. For Queen Elizabeth, too.

The improbable White House tenure of Gerald Rudolph Ford Jr., the only president never elected to national office, turned out to be a happy interlude for both. It was a moment of relative calm between tumultuous eras. The Vietnam War and Watergate scandal were over; the September 11 attacks and global financial meltdown and COVID-19 pandemic were years away. It was a moment when a good-natured president and a queen who didn't begrudge a bit of ballyhoo could share an exuberant celebration of the American Bicentennial.

After the unwelcome dramas and avoidances of Lyndon Johnson and Richard Nixon, the United States and the United Kingdom finally faced no cataclysmic issues and few points of friction. If the encounter between Ford and the Queen also didn't have towering consequences, it was at the least a moment to breathe a sigh of relief, to dance at a Bicentennial ball—a time when the biggest controversy would be the United States Marine Band's choice of music.

Think *West Wing* meets *The Crown*.

Well, perhaps one point of friction, even if the Americans were blissfully unaware of it.

The British considered at length the most fundamental question: Was it a good idea for the Queen of England to join celebrations of the first great loss of the empire, the first successful revolt of any European colony? The Declaration of Independence had denounced King George III as a tyrant who had "plundered our seas, ravaged our Coasts, burnt our towns, and destroyed the lives of our people." Should his great-great-great-great-granddaughter really be joining cheers for his defeat?

Their behind-palace-doors debate leaves the impression that even after two centuries, including decades of close alliance, wounds from the American Revolution had never entirely healed.

"It may be argued that it will be difficult for us to refuse an invitation to the Queen," Rowland Baring, the British ambassador to the United States, wrote in a classified message to London in 1972. "My own view, however, is that I do not think it necessarily a good idea for Her Majesty to attend these celebrations. As you know, these affairs are often organised here in a slip-shod and informal way while at the same time involving a high degree of exposure to publicity. I think that there would be a very real chance not only of embarrassment to Her Majesty, but of impairment to the dignity of monarchy."

A party hosted by these boorish Americans?

The Queen's diplomats in London were raising a red flag—or perhaps a Union Jack—even before serious Bicentennial planning was underway in Washington. In 1972, President Nixon, boosted by his forty-nine-state landslide reelection, had mused to Prime Minister Heath that he harbored "the liveliest hope" that Elizabeth would attend the Bicentennial. He planned to preside over what he envisioned as a capstone to his second term; he already was amassing commemorative gifts to present in his name. But history had other ideas. His unceremonious departure from the White House in 1974 amid Watergate slowed planning for the national festivities.

On the other hand, his forced resignation also eliminated a big hurdle for the Queen. "At least one of the complications that we faced in May, the problem of President Nixon, has been removed," a Foreign Office memo noted. There were other concerns, though, including a lack of preparation across the ocean. The Bicentennial would commemorate the US victory in breaking from Britain, but the losing side was well ahead of the winning one in considering how to mark the Declaration of Independence.

"Planning for the Bicentennial has got off to a very bad start in the United States," a British memo in 1974 clucked.

THE QUEEN HAD A THING OR TWO IN COMMON WITH THE THIRTY-EIGHTH president. Both had seen unexpected twists—an abdication, a resignation—that propelled them into historic positions. Neither had yearned for the top job before they got it. But with that the comparisons largely ended. Ford had a Midwesterner's unassuming and open manner; Elizabeth had a royal's reserve and opaqueness. Though he had been a star football player at the University of Michigan and graduated from Yale Law School, Ford had been saddled with a reputation for klutziness. In contrast, the monarch was renowned for her sure-footedness.

They had never met.

The Queen had the option of dispatching a royal alternative in her stead, and her ambassador had one in mind: the Prince of Wales, then in his twenties. "He would be more free to handle the kind of awkward situation with which he might well be confronted here and I believe that he would do an excellent job in his own inimitable style of dealing light-heartedly with the cruder and coarser features that are almost inseparable from any public junketing here," Baring said. Left unmentioned was Charles's own reputation for awkwardness. "There is no ducking the fact this will be a tough assignment," the ambassador sighed.

The whole question needed "careful consideration," Robert Armstrong, a top aide to Heath, cautioned the palace. "I think our Ambassador in Washington has some feeling that there may be a certain degree of un-inhibited zest about the American celebrations of the Declaration of Independence with which it might not be entirely desirable that the Queen should be associated; in other words, that a certain amount of ballyhoo is inseparable from this sort of celebration in America, which would conspicuously lack dignity."

The one person who appeared completely unconcerned about the purported risks was the Queen. The next day, her private secretary, Martin Charteris, wrote back with her firm response. "I do not believe we need to be over sensitive about a bit of ballyhoo if the visit is considered right in principle," he said.

Uninhibited zest? Why, yes. That there would be. Her Majesty, secure in her position at home and abroad, was ready to enjoy it. Now if only the Americans would remember to send an invitation.

BY THE FALL OF 1974, WITH NIXON IN CALIFORNIA EXILE WRITING HIS memoirs, the diplomats' calculations had shifted. The potential payoffs of the Queen's participation in the Bicentennial were increasingly seen as offsetting the potential perils.

"I am sure I need not remind you how much goodwill towards and admiration for the Royal Family there is in this country," Peter Ramsbotham, the new British ambassador, wrote in the eighth point of an exhaustive memo examining the pros and cons of her potential visit. "It is an immense asset to us at all times. But at this particular stage, when our economic situation will be difficult for at least two to three years, I think we should do our best to capitalise on it. I see every reason therefore to use Royal visits in the context of the Bicentennial both to reinforce these sentiments, and to improve our general standing."

The "economic situation" to which the ambassador delicately referred was a deepening financial crisis. A month before the American celebration, the pound would hit a new low against the dollar. The chancellor of the Exchequer was forced to ask for a bailout from the International Monetary Fund, one that would need the support of the United States. The $3.9 billion loan was the largest that had ever been requested from the IMF.

When the White House finally—finally—sent a formal invitation to the Queen in the spring of 1975, it bore the diplomatic imprint of Henry Kissinger. After Nixon's resignation, he had stayed on to serve Ford in his dual roles as secretary of state and national security adviser.

Kissinger had rejected the first draft of the president's letter to the Queen as too direct about matters better not called to mind. "In a little more than a year it will be two centuries since it became necessary for our people 'to dissolve the political bonds' which connected them to yours," it had begun. ". . . [I]t was surely inevitable that we should have evolved from the bitterest of opponents to the strongest of friends and allies." That entire page, found in Kissinger's files at the Ford Presidential Library, was marked out with a single slash of a pen. The final version was short and sweet, with no mention of dissolving bonds or once being bitter opponents or, really, anything about the messy past. "Your visit, I know, will serve to underscore the very close ties of friendship which unite our people," it read above Ford's neat signature.

Her Majesty immediately accepted. Her response, on Windsor Castle stationery, mentioned her "happy memories of previous visits to the United States." She signed it, "Your sincere friend, Elizabeth R."

Ford, whose quarter century as a Michigan congressman included few rendezvous with royalty, was jubilant. "He was very excited about the Queen's visit," recalled White House counselor Jack Marsh. In 1963, when Marsh was a freshman congressman from Virginia, he had introduced the bill that eventually created the American Revolution Bicentennial Commission. Now a senior White House aide, he would take the lead in planning the president's role during the celebrations. "The [British] Ambassador said the Queen will come, she wants to come, but we're not just sure when is the best time to come," he told Ford. "'Oh, have her come on the Fourth of July!'" the president replied.

With a nod to those at home still nervous about putting her imprimatur on the revolution, she chose to arrive in the United States on July 6, 1976, not on the Fourth itself. "July 4th was really pushing it," grumbled David Walker, first secretary of the British embassy. "Forgiveness can go so far."

That trace of British ambivalence may never have completely evaporated, even a generation later. On July 4, 2016, Prince Harry was having his second date with Meghan Markle, the American actress who would become the Duchess of Sussex. He brought her a small present in a pink box. "Cupcakes," he recalled. "Red, white and blue cupcakes, to be exact. In honor of Independence Day. I said something about the Brits having a very different view of Independence Day from the Yanks, but oh, well."

THE QUEEN AND HER CONSORT FLEW TO BERMUDA FROM LONDON AND then boarded the royal yacht *Britannia* for Philadelphia, a three-day crossing marked by heavy seas and bouts of seasickness for many of those aboard, though apparently not her. A proposal that the royal couple make a point by arriving on the Concorde, the joint UK-French supersonic passenger plane, was ruled out as politically risky. Instead, *Britannia* docked near the site where William Penn had landed his ship, the *Welcome*, in 1682. He had founded Philadelphia based on Quaker ideals of tolerance and equality, choosing its name by combining Greek words that translated roughly as "city of brotherly love." It had been the site of the Constitutional Convention, and the Queen presented the city with a six-and-a-half-ton replica of the Liberty Bell. Like the original, it had been forged by London's Whitechapel Bell Foundry.

"I speak to you as the direct descendant of King George III," she told a friendly crowd, all things forgiven on both sides. "He was the last crowned sovereign to rule in this country, and it is therefore with a particular personal interest that I view those events which took place two hundred years ago." She described the conflict not as territory lost but as a milestone that deserved celebration in Britain as well as the United States, as a "very valuable lesson" for her country.

"We lost the American colonies because we lacked that statesmanship 'to know the right time, and the manner of yielding what is impossible to keep,'" she said, quoting the eighteenth-century political philosopher Edmund Burke who, as a member of Parliament, had urged compromise with the colonists rather than war. "We learned to respect the right of others to govern themselves in their own ways." More than a century later, she said, Britain would apply those lessons when other nations in its empire demanded independence, although there had been some violent revolts then, too. "Without that great act in the cause of liberty, performed in Independence Hall two hundred years ago, we could never have transformed an empire into a commonwealth."

At the grand White House dinner the next evening, the Queen and the president toasted their joint history and current alliance. Ford began by quoting the first US ambassador to Britain, John Adams, who had spoken with Queen Charlotte, Elizabeth's great-great-great-great-grandmother. "People have come from every corner of the Earth to share in the hope, the building, and the spirit of our Republic," the future president had told her, vowing that their two nations would "share the same fundamental devotion to human dignity."

In her toast, Elizabeth mentioned Adams and his first call on King

George. "My ancestor said to him, in well-known words which are worth repeating, 'I was the last man in the Kingdom to consent to the separation, but the separation having been made, I have always said, as I say now, that I would be the first to meet the friendship of the United States as an independent power.'"

By this stage an experienced diplomat, Elizabeth was known for acknowledging past conflicts, not tiptoeing past them. She rewrote a toast drafted for a state dinner for Emperor Hirohito of Japan that somehow had managed to avoid mentioning World War II. "We cannot pretend the past did not exist," she chose to say to the head of state for one of the Axis powers. The wounds from that war were fresher and deeper than those from the American Revolution, but she made a similar point at the White House.

"Mr. President, history is not a fairy tale," she said to Ford. "Despite the good intentions, hostility soon broke out between us—and even burst into this house," a reference to British efforts to burn down the White House during the War of 1812. "But these early quarrels are long buried."

Buried, indeed. Probably unknown to her was just how apt that word was. A year earlier, when Ford was having an outdoor swimming pool constructed in a sheltered area around the corner from the Rose Garden, archeologists had unearthed a gully filled with nineteenth-century artifacts. It apparently had been used as a trash pit for debris when presidents James Madison and James Monroe oversaw the reconstruction of the White House after the fire the British had set.

Amid all the warm words, there were a few gaffes of the sort that had prompted Ambassador Baring's dire warnings of Americans' propensity for slipshod informality.

After the royal couple had arrived at the White House, the president and Betty Ford escorted them to the residence for an aperitif. When the doors of the elevator opened, son Jack Ford, age twenty-four and notorious for youthful escapades, appeared in his stocking feet and with his dress shirt undone, holding the studs. "I wanted to die," Betty Ford said. She told the Queen, "Your Majesty, I am so sorry. I'm so embarrassed." The Queen laughed and replied, "Don't worry about it. I have one just like it at home."

Her attitude was disarming, Susan Ford Bales, the president's daughter, remembered. She had come home from college for the occasion, borrowing a dress from her mother to wear. A half century later, the White House photo of their encounter was on display in the guest bedroom of her Texas home.

"I made sure that I curtsied," Susan said. "But at the same time, she was a typical mother." The Queen's unpretentious persona had put the first lady at ease, in part because she knew her reassurance was real. "They had family problems with children just like I did," Betty Ford said later.

The state dinner was being held in the Rose Garden under an enormous tent hung with Japanese lanterns, a temporary structure threatened by an afternoon rainstorm that uprooted trees on the White House grounds. Dick Cheney, then the chief of staff and later a vice president, recognizing the possibility of catastrophe, had dispatched White House staffers more accustomed to dealing with policy disputes than weather mishaps to help. "So people came out from the West Wing and we literally battened down the hatches," White House social secretary Maria Downs said.

Fortunately, the storm and its high winds had subsided by the time the guests began to arrive—among them entertainers Ella Fitzgerald, Merle Oberon, Telly Savalas, and Cary Grant; plus corporate executives J. Willard Marriott of the hotel chain and Henry Heinz II of the ketchup fortune. The White House had toned down the proposals that Downs had outlined when she was being interviewed for the social secretary job and had been asked to plan a state dinner. Using the upcoming visit of Elizabeth as her case study, she had envisioned having a demonstration of bronco busting on the front lawn and using saddles instead of flowers as table centerpieces.

"Well, you know the Queen loves horses," Betty Ford, who seemed intrigued, told her press secretary, Sheila Weidenfeld, who found the ideas flabbergasting. "Well, I know it wouldn't work," the first lady finally said. "But it *is* imaginative." Instead, the White House put more traditional baskets of flowers on the tables and presented the Queen with a gift of a bucking bronco—a bronze one—by American artist Harry Jackson. Titled *Two Champs*, the sculpture depicted legendary cowboy Clayton Danks astride Steamboat, the first nationally known bucking horse.

Comedian Bob Hope emceed the after-dinner entertainment in the East Room. Captain & Tennille, a soft-rock duo popular in the day, energetically performed their hit, "Muskrat Love." ("A cute little song," Betty Ford said later, dismissing those who were aghast.) As the title suggests, the lyrics tell the tale of a romantic encounter between two rodents named Susie and Sam.

Now he's ticklin' her fancy, rubbin' her ties
Muzzle to muzzle now, anything goes.

Or, as the British ambassador described it afterward in a tongue-in-cheek aside to London, "a vivid electronic tone-poem on muskrat courtship." Those Americans!

After that, Ford, in white tie and tails, and Elizabeth, in an organza gown of citrus yellow and a tiara, walked to the dance floor in the State Dining Room. The Marine Band launched into the next song on its playlist. Which happened to be "The Lady Is a Tramp." Ford, who typically masked his occasional temper beneath a mild demeanor, was reportedly so angry by the inadvertent juxtaposition that he was "incandescent." "Somebody made a big mistake," Susan Ford Bales said.

The Queen reportedly thought it was "hilarious." It was nearly 1 a.m. before the royal couple left the party to return to Blair House.

THE BICENTENNIAL TURNED OUT TO BE A LUMINOUS MOMENT FOR THE special relationship.

"It has been a rather abrupt transition from 'Yankee Doodle' to 'God Save the Queen,'" wrote Mary McGrory, the sharp-eyed columnist for the *Washington Star*, noting approvingly that Elizabeth "seems to be enjoying the irony of it all." She makes Americans feel better because she represents "good manners, good taste, continuity, a sense of duty and other similarly threatened values," McGrory said. In short, "the perfect Bicentennial guest" would turn out to be "the gracious representative of an old enemy who has long since become our best friend."

The celebrations captured the dynamic between the two nations, illuminating both how they were different and why they were aligned. The

Americans could be clueless about the finer points of protocol, but they had a boldness and an optimism that the British envied, one that had helped the United States supplant their empire as the globe's dominant power. In return, the Americans sometimes viewed the British as petrified by precedent, even their rules about how to address the Queen mystifying. The instructions the State Department sent the Fords before the Queen arrived included advice on everything from whether to bow (a bob of the head would be fine) to how to walk with her (on her left). But Americans found England's glorious history and gift for pageantry intoxicating, and their deftness at diplomacy at times invaluable.

Elizabeth provided a crucial connection between them. She was the embodiment of British history who also had an attitude of acceptance, an approach she showed toward emerging African leaders as well. From the start, she seemed to enjoy Americans' energy and their informality. She was an eager tourist. On this trip, she visited Bloomingdale's in New York and worshiped at Old North Church in Boston—where lanterns had once been hung to warn of the approach of British troops.

In a year, she would celebrate her Silver Jubilee, marking a quarter century on the throne, a confident monarch who had defined a significant role for herself in the two decades since she had last visited the United States. She wanted not only to attend Bicentennial celebrations but also to have a private conversation with Ford, the fifth sitting president she had met. "The ambassador indicated that he hoped the president's schedule would be such that he would be able to spend some time with the Queen other than just the official reception and the two banquets," Marsh noted in a planning memo. Soon after she arrived at the White House, the royal couple and the Fords shared a private lunch in the Yellow Oval Room, just the four of them, sitting around a small table for a conversation that was relaxed, almost familial.

Despite early concerns about the trip, their meeting was reassuring to British officials, always nervous about just where they stood in Washington and the world.

"While the Watergate storm was still blowing, I understood the reluctance to contemplate visits of a State character either to London or to Washington," Ramsbotham had written two months after Nixon's resignation in 1974. But he noted that Ford had already scheduled a trip to Asia and meetings with French President Valery Giscard d'Estaing, West German Chancellor Helmut Schmidt, and Canadian Prime Minister Pierre Trudeau. "We face a situation in which the influence of the French and the Germans with the Americans is increasing, possibly at our expense," he warned.

Now the Queen's visit and the acclaim that greeted her were reassurance that Great Britain was still being taken seriously. It was also a sign that, after two hundred years, any remaining residue of the Revolutionary War was blowing away. The genial Jerry Ford and the self-assured Queen had settled a ceasefire. Afterward, even the skeptical Ramsbotham declared the visit "a triumph."

BEYOND THE SOARING SENTIMENTS, THERE WERE SOME POLITICS, OF course.

For the Queen, a briefing paper from the Foreign Office detailed Britain's substantive concerns—securing landing rights for the Concorde; addressing differences over Northern Ireland; and opposing protectionist proposals aimed at British steel, cars, and shoes. It mentioned the American political calendar, too. "The election campaign is now in full swing," it reported, with Ford facing a Republican primary challenge from former California Governor Ronald Reagan. On the Democratic side, former Georgia Governor Jimmy Carter was winning primaries but Senator Henry Jackson of Washington state commanded "wide support" and Minnesota Senator Hubert Humphrey "is widely regarded as a likely compromise candidate."

For the president, his agenda for her trip included a boost for his election campaign.

"The Queen's visit to the White House this summer has all the markings of a Bicentennial, television extravaganza," wrote Bob Mead, a media adviser to Ford. He urged that the White House approve a request from PBS to broadcast live not only the arrival ceremony but also the state dinner, from the receiving line beforehand to the dancing afterward. "Candidly, this being an election year, it would give the President and Mrs. Ford some lovely exposure," he said. "It's a free bonus."

It was a deal: PBS televised a three-hour program that followed the royal party through the evening—a "coup" for the network, *The New York Times* declared, not to mention for the president.

By then, the GOP primaries were ending with neither Ford nor Reagan having clinched the presidential nomination. That explains why Clarke Reed, the founder of an agricultural-equipment company who was Mississippi's Republican chairman, found himself invited to a White House dinner for the Queen of England. Oh, by the way, his state's convention delegation was still uncommitted. "I was hustling delegates at that time," James A. Baker III recalled a half century later. "We used invitations to that dinner to make a big impression." Baker was then the chief delegate counter for Ford; he would later be a White House chief of staff and Cabinet member for Reagan and for George H. W. Bush. He was ninety-four years old when we talked, and still delighted by his stratagem.

"I was furious," Nancy Reagan fumed in her memoir. "The White House stands for something more important than partisan politics and uncommitted delegates—or at least it should." (Her outrage seems a bit overblown, given the string of presidents who had used White House social events for political advantage. The Reagans would do that themselves once they moved in five years later.)

A few weeks later, Reed threw his support behind Ford, a step that helped him claim the nomination at the Republican National Convention in Kansas City in August. Amid conservative outrage, Reed soon stepped down as chairman of the Mississippi GOP and expressed regret for his action.

On the other hand, he did get to have dinner with the Queen.

THE BRITISH WERE BIPARTISAN. HER MAJESTY WAS INTERESTED IN MEETING Jimmy Carter while she was in Washington—hedging her bets, just in case he won the White House in November.

By now, he was the presumptive Democratic presidential nominee. But before the Queen invited him to her reciprocal banquet, a white-tie affair at the British embassy the night after the White House dinner, Ambassador Ramsbotham checked with Vice President Nelson Rockefeller about whether that would cause any heartburn for the White House. Rockefeller asked Ford. The president's response, relayed to the Queen's deputy private secretary: Don't do it. Rockefeller "was given a clear indication that President Ford would not wish Governor Carter to be present at any official function," a memo from the embassy said. Period.

Carter was crossed off the guest list.

Later, Ford raised no objection to the idea of Carter being invited to a different meal with the Queen during her visit, something without the publicity and attention given the formal dinner. "The President was squared and an invitation extended," the ambassador reported, "only to be regretfully declined because of Carter's desire not to lose his 'outsider' image before the Democratic convention." Carter was not above political calculations of his own.

The embassy dinner was notable for other reasons, too, including the encounter between Her Majesty and Muhammad Ali. The heavyweight boxing champion was limping from a bout two weeks earlier in Tokyo with professional Japanese wrestler Antonio Inoki, billed as the "War of the Worlds." (The judges had ruled the fight a draw.) "How are you feeling?" the Queen inquired—as always, thoroughly briefed. "Which leg was hurt the worst?"

Then there was the blind date the British ambassador arranged for the evening when one of the guests—that would be actress Elizabeth Taylor—needed an escort after being divorced for the second time from actor Richard Burton. Navy Secretary and man-about-town John Warner, later a US senator, was drafted. Before the year was over, Taylor and Warner were married—her seventh husband, counting Burton twice, and his second wife. By the time the Queen would be back in the United States on her next official visit, though, they had split.

AFTER WASHINGTON, THE QUEEN WENT TO NEW YORK CITY FOR A LUNcheon at the Waldorf-Astoria, flew to Virginia to see Thomas Jefferson's Monticello, then traveled on to Newport, Rhode Island, where she hosted a final dinner with the Fords, this time aboard the royal yacht.

To greet him, Elizabeth overruled Royal Navy protocol so he would be piped aboard *Britannia*. The boatswain's call, which dates to the Crusades, was an honor generally reserved for specific members of the royal family and flag-rank officers. This evening, like the rest of her Bicentennial tour, was as informal as royal visits can be—just twenty people gathered for dinner, including the Fords and Kissinger and Rhode Island Governor Philip Noel.

During after-dinner drinks in a stateroom, Ford and Noel were discussing their careers as college football stars—Ford at the University of Michigan, Noel at Georgetown University and then Brown—and the impact that might still be felt on their middle-aged bodies. "Ford could see through my pants that I was wearing knee braces—which I was," Noel said. "They were state of the art and just introduced. So Ford said, 'Can I see them?' So I lifted up my pants leg to show him."

The Queen, sitting nearby, turned and spotted Noel's unexpected display of leg. "Governor Noel," she queried, unfazed. "Is that your knee?"

Her final stop in the United States was in Boston, where the American Revolution had been sparked—where "it all began," she said in a speech at the Old State House. The first reigning British monarch ever to visit the city, she would leave aboard *Britannia* for Halifax, Nova Scotia, to open the Montreal Olympics and watch Princess Anne compete as a member of the British equestrian team. As the ship sailed out of Boston Harbor, there was an echo of the tribute from the Americans who had gathered at the small station in Hyde Park, New York, to watch King George VI and Queen Elizabeth depart nearly four decades earlier. Their royal visit had helped seal the two nations' crucial alliance in World War II.

Now, as the Queen waved from the ship's deck, the Royal Marine Band on board played the same music that the well-wishers had sung spontaneously to her parents as their train pulled out of the station: "Auld Lang Syne."

Eight

The Kiss(-Off)

Saturday, May 7, 1977—Buckingham Palace

Sometimes a kiss isn't just a kiss.

The one-term governor of Georgia, a graduate of the United States Naval Academy who had served aboard a navy submarine and then returned home to Plains to operate his family's peanut farm, had been elected president in the wake of Watergate. James Earl Carter, known for his toothy smile and his promise never to lie, had the least diplomatic experience of any president in modern times. His tenure would eventually see the towering achievement of the Camp David accords between Israel and Egypt. But as he took office, the contrast in experience with Richard Nixon, who considered foreign policy his forte, and even Ford, who had served in federal office for decades, was striking. But when Carter made his first trip abroad as president, to Great Britain for an economic summit and NATO meeting, he was riding a honeymoon high in job-approval ratings—welcomed at home and abroad as an unpretentious fresh face.

When he had visited London four years earlier, as the governor leading a Georgia Industrial Development tour, Carter had only been able to gaze at Buckingham Palace through an iron fence with the other tourists. This time, he was greeted inside for a black-tie dinner honoring the G7 leaders of the world's wealthiest democracies, the first among equals. Indeed, the palace had planned to host the dinner three days later, but the White House said the president wanted to leave London by then to return to Washington. His absence would create "a bad impression," the Foreign Office privately cautioned, and the banquet was moved to suit his schedule.

Elizabeth was greeting her sixth sitting president. Carter was greeting his first queen.

She was dressed in a glittering citrus-yellow gown and spectacular jewels, diamonds flashing in her necklace, her earrings, and the bracelets atop her long white gloves. As photographers took pictures of her welcoming the visiting foreign leaders, she stood chatting easily first with Carter to her left, then with French President Valery Giscard D'Estaing to her right.

Carter, arriving alone in a limousine with the presidential seal on the door, had been escorted into the palace by Prince Philip. The president looked eager, nervous, and a bit out of place. The black bow tie of his tuxedo was clownishly large even for the style of the 1970s, twice the size of those of other male guests. He seemed nearly overwhelmed by the spectacular surroundings, "one of the most beautiful places I've ever seen," he would later say. "A bit wide eyed about the pomp and color," *The New York Times* reporter observed.

The *Chicago Tribune* correspondent called him "openly awed" as the dinner began. "When a pair of tall double doors swung open, and Queen Elizabeth II entered, resplendent in a bejeweled formal gown, the President's famous smile was that of any mere peanut farmer in the presence of a royal woman. He approached her hesitantly, and sat in awe by her side." Another reporter said he "acted almost like a child who had made the big time."

Afterward, the president stopped to speak to a few journalists gathered in the rain outside the American ambassador's residence in Regent's Park. "I had a good place to sit," he told them. "I was between the Queen and Princess Margaret, and across the table was Prince Charles and Prince Philip, and the Queen Mother was there, too, so the whole family was very gracious to us tonight."

Over a dinner of salmon fillet St Germain and mousse de volaille à la crème, their conversation had ranged from expanding waistlines to world peace. "One of the things I told Queen Elizabeth was how much the American people appreciated her coming over last year to celebrate our 200th birthday. And she said that it was one of the warmest welcomes she'd ever received," Carter said. "But we just talked about the need for world peace, and how much it meant to the other countries when she came in to visit, and how close our own nation is to England because of our common historical background and heritage."

On matters more prosaic, the Queen had "complained about having seven different uniforms she had to wear on annual occasions and how difficult it was to fit into them when her weight tended to increase," he disclosed decades later. "We decided it might be good to shift to centimeters on everything except the waistlines, which would continue to be measured in inches."

She was the most practiced of conversationalists. "She could chat with the Sphinx, such is her training," an American columnist once admired. The White House delegation told British officials they were struck by "the absence of the pomp and stuffiness which they had expected to find." Carter found the warmth welcoming, possibly beyond what was intended.

His first offense was meant as a compliment. The fifty-two-year-old president told the Queen Mother, in a sparkling ecru lace gown, that she reminded him of his mother. (Then seventy-six, she was just two years younger than Miss Lillian and had a similar directness, although their life stories could hardly have been more different.) This was something that people often told the Queen Mother, a confidence that she didn't want to hear. "One of the banes of my life" was that she tended to remind middle-aged men of their mothers, she complained. "I recognize the glazed look that comes over their faces . . . a sort of glazed look of memory" just before they announced this insight.

Carter's second offense, also unintentional, was worse.

He leaned in and kissed her on the lips.

"I took a sharp step backwards," the Queen Mother recalled. "Not quite far enough."

"It was not his intention," Evan Dobelle told me a half century later. An early backer of Carter, he had been tapped as the administration's chief of protocol, although as the mayor of Pittsfield, Massachusetts, he had even less international experience than the president did. Standing near Carter that night, he saw the episode unfold. "He leaned forward and went to kiss her on the cheek, and she turned her head—and right on the lips." The Queen Mother looked "sort of shocked," he said.

Elizabeth's outspoken mother would surely have relived the moment with her—presumably unhappily—after the guests had gone.

Perhaps it was just another example of people, especially Americans, becoming unnerved in royal settings. Walter Annenberg, the business executive and philanthropist appointed by Nixon as ambassador to the Court of St. James's, was mocked in the British press for dissolving into babble when the Queen had asked how he was finding his new residence, not really a trick question. "We are in the embassy residence, subject of course to some of the discomfiture as a result of a need for elements of refurbishment and rehabilitation," he replied as he seemed to struggle to find a way to stop talking. "Even the president of the United States can be so in awe of the presence of these people that they . . . [do] something silly," Adam Jogee, a member of Parliament and a fan of Carter, suggested to me as a possible explanation for behavior the Queen Mother saw as wildly inappropriate.

For six years, Carter's kiss remained a royal secret. Then it became a British sensation. A London gossip columnist quoted an "anti-toast" the Queen Mother had given at a private dinner at Clarence House, her London residence. She apparently had the practice of delivering "anti-toasts." That is, "she raises her glass and utters the names of people she does not particularly like." On this occasion, she was quoted as "anti-toasting" Tony Benn, a Labour member of Parliament and leading anti-royalist who had accused the hereditary monarchy of corrupting British society. Idi Amin, the brutal ruler of Uganda, then in exile in Saudi Arabia. And Jimmy Carter.

Why? "Because he is the only man, since my dear husband died, to have had the effrontery to kiss me on the lips."

THE PRESIDENT HAD BEEN BRIEFED BEFORE THE TRIP ON ROYAL PROTOCOL, including the injunction not to touch the Queen, not even to extend a hand until she had extended one, much less plant a kiss. "He wasn't over-concerned about that," Dobelle said. Monarchs? "I don't think that particularly impressed him." Like his fellow Southern Democrat, Lyndon Johnson, Carter held no particular truck with the elites and the establishment, the folks who never imagined he could win the White House. Nicholas Henderson, the British ambassador to the United States, described Carter as "a southerner with a chip [on his shoulder] the size and shape of a cathedral."

What's more, Carter seemed to have a propensity to greet with a kiss, even with women he didn't particularly know. A kiss he had once aimed for the cheek of Jacqueline Kennedy Onassis had also landed on her lips when she unexpectedly turned her head. "Carter's first act on British soil was to kiss a lady—Phyllis Lady Stedman, a 60-year-old baroness," The Associated Press reported on his arrival. Lady Stedman, a Labour member of the House of Lords, was representing the Queen in the greeting party that was standing at the foot of the steps of *Air Force One* after it had landed at Heathrow Airport. The president shook hands with Prime Minister James Callaghan, then also shook hands with a saluting police officer, who appeared perplexed by the egalitarian gesture.

It was raining—not unusual in springtime London—but Carter was unprepared for the weather. Unlike nearly everyone else on the tarmac, he wasn't wearing an overcoat, nor did he have an umbrella overhead as he delivered his arrival speech in the drizzle. In his remarks, he praised the two nations' "special mutual commitment to world peace, toward addressing in a courageous fashion the special problems that afflict human beings in the need for better health care and better education and jobs so that we won't be robbed by inflation." He paid tribute to their "special and very precious relationship."

The lack of ceremony at the airport might have been a good fit with Carter's general determination to reduce presidential pomp and circumstance. It was also appropriate for Britain's current economic straits. In January, the Labour government had been bailed out by a record $3.9 billion loan from the International Monetary Fund, conditioned on an austerity program. "There were no blaring trumpets, no gun salutes, no rolling drums," a columnist for a North Carolina newspaper wrote. "There was no shelter," only "a damp red carpet" that stretched to the steps of *Air Force One*.

Even so, Carter and Callaghan were greeted by big and enthusiastic crowds when they visited an industrial region of Britain the next day. "Jim Callaghan asked Carter to come on a visit to Britain, and he said, 'If you come, I'd like you to come up to the Northeast of Britain, to Newcastle,' and I'll be there to meet you and take you around a different part of UK," David Owen, then the British foreign secretary, recalled. "And Jimmy Carter accepted that, and he became a 'Geordie,' which is what we call people in the Northeast. And he took a slogan that Callaghan had given, got the pronunciation completely right, and the Geordies loved him."

The private Foreign Office assessment of the side trip took a snarkier tone.

"The warmth of the reception at Newcastle obviously impressed the Americans, but this sort of reception was not really unexpected," the report said, considering "the fact that Newcastle does not receive many such distinguished visitors." Still, the memorandum acknowledged that the president's visit to Great Britain had addressed the public's reservations about him. He had come across in news coverage as "a genuine, effective and impressive leader."

But downbeat times were ahead for the United States and the United Kingdom. The world's major market economies would suffer inflation and stagnant growth, an economically and politically toxic combination dubbed "stagflation." The Iranian revolution would prompt the second oil shock of the decade. Then, in 1979, fifty-three Americans were taken hostage at the US embassy in Tehran, a crisis that would persist for the rest of Carter's presidency.

"During these awkward middle years of the late 1960s and 1970s, the Anglo-American dance card was not well arranged," said Raymond Seitz, a Foreign Service officer who was then the first secretary at the US embassy in London; he would return as ambassador for presidents George H. W. Bush and Bill Clinton. "Both countries were preoccupied and frustrated." Great Britain was increasingly looking to Europe; the United States was putting a priority on partnerships with West Germany and Israel and others. Queen Elizabeth was otherwise occupied, too, with the celebration of her Silver Jubilee and the relief that her son and heir had finally chosen a bride—a relief that would turn to concern and, finally, full-scale alarm.

Callaghan was fond of Carter, a senior aide said, calling him "a very nice, decent man" if not a great president.

Still, British officials had reservations about Carter and his team. Some depicted his approach to foreign policy as naive and his advisers as uninformed in the ways of diplomacy—just the sort of combination that might lead to a social misstep like an unwelcome kiss on the

Queen Mother. "My mind had grown accustomed to the usual adjectives used for the President's staff—young, inexperienced, arrogant, etc., but I still found it a shock to see for myself how true this all was," one wrote. "The first dawn of realisation came for me when the new Chief of Protocol mentioned that he had never been out of the United States before."

At the Buckingham Palace dinner, Prince Charles told Carter he planned to visit the United States later in the year, including a stop in Georgia, the president's home state and one that had been named for royal ancestor King George II. Carter said he hoped it would be possible for them to meet, but afterward the White House didn't seem interested. "I spoke twice to the Chief of Protocol, Ambassador Dobelle, about the Prince of Wales's itinerary in case the President wished to invite him to Washington or to join him in Georgia," Peter Jay, the British ambassador to Washington, wrote Lord Owen. "There was no follow-up from the American side."

As it turns out, Carter had created complications on another front with the Queen, an affront not previously reported.

Soon after the state banquet had ended, Carter called Dobelle and told him to cancel the tea he was scheduled to have with Elizabeth the next day. Syrian President Hafez al-Assad had called National Security Adviser Zbigniew Brzezinski and asked that Carter meet with him in Geneva to discuss Carter's hope of forging a groundbreaking peace in the Middle East. Carter had agreed. It would be the only in-person meeting between the two men during Carter's presidency.

About 11 p.m., Dobelle reached the royal protocol chief at home to say that the president wouldn't be showing up for tea. "Really?" he replied frostily, not quite believing that Carter was canceling on Her Majesty. He warned: "The Queen will be quite steamed about this."

Steamed in private, though she would never publicly express annoyance with Carter, or with any other US president. She was usually eager to engage with them. She had multiple encounters with Carter's two predecessors and the six presidents who would follow him.

In this case and others, her actions may speak louder than her words. After such a star-crossed first encounter, is it simply a coincidence that she would never see Carter again?

SHE WAS KEEPING BUSY ELSEWHERE DURING THE TWENTY-FIFTH YEAR OF her reign.

There was more royal travel, for one thing. During three months in early 1977, she and Prince Philip visited more of the United Kingdom than any previous monarch had done in such a short period of time—to a total of thirty-six counties in Scotland, England, Wales, and Northern Ireland. During the summer, they launched a globe-circling tour of the Commonwealth—to Tonga and Fiji, New Zealand and Australia, Papua New Guinea and the West Indies and, finally, Canada. She was also becoming increasingly accessible to the public—a reality of a changing world, like it or not. That scrutiny would catch her sister Margaret's affair with a much-younger lover and the end of her unhappy marriage. The tabloids would chronicle the pressure on Prince Charles to wed, an endeavor complicated by rumors of his affair with Camilla Parker Bowles. It was in 1977, when he was dating Sarah Spencer, that he first met her sixteen-year-old sister, Diana. They would be engaged and marry in 1981.

But this moment would also show the Queen in her element, expanding her approach to her role and laying the groundwork for a modern monarchy for the rest of her reign and that of her son. Her Silver Jubilee was a triumphant celebration of all that. After a national service of Thanksgiving at St. Paul's Cathedral, the procession down the Mall (pronounced to rhyme with "pal") to Buckingham Palace drew an estimated one million people to watch and cheer as she passed in a royal carriage, wearing a petal-pink dress and a wide smile.

Carter sent his son, Chip, and daughter-in-law, Caron, to represent the United States at the celebration in June. They hadn't yet met the Queen when they were among a crowd watching the fireworks on the twenty-fourth floor of the Shell Centre, on the south bank of the Thames. As she walked by, she recognized him and walked over. "You're Chip Carter," she said, mentioning his appearance on a late-night British talk show. "I watched you on the telly last night, and you were really funny." The next day, the young Carters had a private audience with her at Buckingham Palace, and Chip presented a gift from the president: A set of six gold-rimmed commemorative plates decorated with reproductions of paintings by American artist Winslow Homer. The Queen's assistant private secretary, Robert Fellowes, sent a letter on palace stationery the next day thanking the president for "the splendid gift" and saying the plates would be "treasured" as "a token of a friendship which is among Her Majesty's chief pleasures in this her Silver Jubilee year."

The gift was one more sign of Carter's lack of bedazzlement with the monarchy, not to mention his famed frugality. "He wasn't big on buying new gifts for people with taxpayers' money," Dobelle said. In a White House vault, Dobelle and his wife, Kit, had found a collection of official gifts that Nixon had planned to present during the Bicentennial, if only he hadn't been forcibly retired in California by then. They included three dozen sets of the commemorative plates in mahogany boxes with a plaque on the front with the names of President and Mrs. Nixon. A year earlier, the Ford White House had considered giving a set of the plates to the Queen as a gift when she visited during the Bicentennial but decided against it.

"We had little tiny plaques made and put adhesive on it that they promised me would never come off for a century," Dobelle said. The new plaques, with Carter's name, were glued on in place of Nixon's imprint. The engraving on the monarch's gift would read: "Presented to Her Majesty Queen Elizabeth II by President Jimmy Carter June 1977."

In other words, to celebrate the Queen's twenty-fifth year on the throne, Carter regifted a present left behind in storage by his disgraced predecessor. Her Majesty was presumably unaware of its provenance.

FOR THE REST OF HIS WHITE HOUSE TENURE, CARTER'S RELATIONSHIP with the Queen was generally limited to the occasional obligatory birthday greetings and expressions of best wishes. "I was delighted to learn of the birth of a son to Princess Anne and Capt. Phillips," Carter wrote her in November 1977. "Rosalynn and I enjoyed seeing them here at the White House this summer."

Anne had been four months pregnant when she made her first solo visit to the United States, soon after the president's visit to London. She met with Carter and with First Lady Rosalynn Carter at the White House, then toured the Smithsonian's Museum of History and Technology. The exhibits included a reproduction of a log cabin, the storied humble beginnings of more than one American president. "They have to be born in a log cabin," S. Dillon Ripley, secretary of the Smithsonian, told her with a smile—an exaggeration, since no American president had been born in an actual log cabin since James Garfield, elected in 1880. Still, the British royal family might have thought it explained the sometimes-perplexing behavior of presidents.

"Even now?" the princess asked.

"It helps," Ripley replied.

THERE WAS ONE EVENT, AGONIZING FOR THE ROYAL FAMILY, THAT DEmanded more than an obligatory message.

On August 27, 1979, Lord Mountbatten boarded the *Shadow V*, a fishing boat he kept near his summer home in County Sligo, Ireland. He was joined by family members along with a small crew. After they had set out to sea, a bomb planted by the Provisional IRA detonated, killing Mountbatten; his fourteen-year-old grandson, Nicholas Knatchbull; and a teenage Irish crew mate, Paul Maxwell. Lady Brabourne, the mother-in-law of Mountbatten's daughter Patricia, died the following day from injuries sustained in the bombing. The attack on Mountbatten, a great-grandson of Queen Victoria who had served in the Royal Navy for much of the twentieth century, was the most brazen assassination of a relative of the royal family since the Romanovs were killed during the Russian Revolution. Mountbatten had been warned for years that he was one of the IRA's top targets, but he refused to change his annual summer plans.

Prince Charles, vacationing in Iceland, was distraught when he heard the news of the murder of a man whom he called his "honorary grandfather" and who had been a surrogate father figure. "[A] mixture of desperate emotions swept over me—agony, disbelief, a kind of wretched numbness," he wrote in his diary that evening. "Life will never be the same now." Philip was in a fury. "What makes it so bitter is that it was deliberately perpetrated by some people who probably consider themselves to be civilized human beings," he wrote in a letter to a friend.

The Queen was devastated by the tragedy, and outraged. Mountbatten had helped bring her together with the husband she loved. She and Philip spent the first part of their honeymoon at his home, Broadlands. He had doted on the couple and their children. She felt "bitter anger of such senseless waste of life," she said in an anguished letter to Annenberg, the former US ambassador to Britain. "We must not be intimidated by such horrible people."

Prime Minister Margaret Thatcher—who would herself come close to being assassinated by the Provisional IRA a few years later—denounced the attack, vowed retaliation, and extolled Mountbatten as "a legend in his lifetime." Philip and Charles met the coffin containing his remains when it was flown back to Britain, and Charles read the lesson at the funeral in Westminster Abbey. It was taken from Psalm 107, fitting for a naval officer: "They that go down to the sea in ships, that do business in great waters; These see the works of the Lord, and his wonders in the deep."

President Carter sent condolences. But he underestimated the gravity of the moment. The statements he released in public and sent in private, just four or five sentences long, were judged in London as inadequate and maddening. "It is with a profound sadness that Rosalynn and I learned of the tragic death of Earl Mountbatten," read his telegram to Thatcher, which echoed his public statement. "He was an extraordinarily wise and courageous statesman and soldier."

Mountbatten, aside from being a treasured member of the royal family, had served as the last viceroy of India, playing an important part in talks that led to an independent India and Pakistan. As first sea lord and then chief of the defense staff, he had cultivated relationships with American political and military figures on NATO and other strategic issues. He had known every president from FDR to Nixon. As chair of the Military Committee of NATO, he had discussed with Kennedy and senior American generals the options in case of a confrontation with the Soviets in Berlin. Even Lyndon Johnson had called him "an old friend." Carter and his staff were either unaware or uninterested in paying tribute to the role Mountbatten had played in keeping the special relationship strong—indeed, in protecting the security of the United States as well as of the United Kingdom.

The Foreign Office memo complained about Carter's "deficiency." "Like you, we have been struck by the lack of reference in the message to the circumstances of Lord Mountbatten's death: no mention of murder or terrorism, no condemnation," it said. In her letter to the president, Thatcher made a point of citing all that. It was "a brutal and senseless murder," she said in her letter to Carter, calling on the US government to urge Americans "to refrain from supporting organisations involved in violence." Fundraising for the IRA among Irish Americans was a point of controversy throughout the "Troubles."

For the Queen, he would not be the last American president who didn't seem to fully understand or acknowledge her family's very personal and painful tragedy.

AFTER HE LEFT THE WHITE HOUSE, CARTER BUILT A REPUTATION AS THE most admirable of former presidents. But the story of the errant kiss nagged. In his thirtieth book, published to mark his ninetieth birthday, he disputed the Queen Mother's account of their long-ago encounter, though he blamed unnamed reporters for its propagation. "When we said good night, I kissed her lightly on the cheek and she thanked me for coming to visit," he said. "More than two years later, there were reporters in the British papers that grossly distorted this event, stating that I had deeply embarrassed her with excessive familiarity. I was distressed by these reports but couldn't change what had happened—nor did I regret it." (The firsthand account by Dobelle, his protocol chief, disputes Carter's version.)

Carter never returned to Buckingham Palace after the 1977 dinner. Elizabeth never visited the United States during his term. After Carter left the White House in 1981, British officials expressed no regrets about the lack of a closer relationship. "There is a deliberate conspiracy on almost everyone's part to try to forget Jimmy Carter," British ambassador Robin Renwick reported a decade later. When Carter died in 2024 at age one hundred, Prince Edward was sent to his state funeral—a step down from the royal representation for most other modern presidents. Charles, Elizabeth's heir, had been dispatched to the funerals of Ronald Reagan and George H. W. Bush. Prince Philip, her consort, had attended John F. Kennedy's funeral.

The Royal Visits Committee in 1977 began considering whether to invite Carter for a state visit, a return for the Queen's state visit to the Ford White House during the Bicentennial. A year later, it was still "no more than an aide Memoire," one report noted, just a suggestion that hadn't been pursued. They decided to wait—that is, wait to see if he managed to win a second term. By 1979, the idea of a visit would come with an important addition, mentioning "PRESIDENT CARTER OF USA (or successor)."

"It was pretty clear that Jimmy Carter would not get a second term," Lord Owen said. British diplomats were skeptical that Carter would be reelected well before that became the conventional wisdom in Washington. In 1980, Carter would face a damaging primary challenge from the left by Massachusetts Senator Edward M. Kennedy. By then, Labour's Callaghan, who was friendly with Carter, had been ousted as prime minister, replaced by the Conservative Margaret Thatcher, who was less impressed with him. He held on to the Democratic nomination but lost the general election to Reagan in a landslide.

Her Majesty didn't spend any time lamenting Carter's departure. When Reagan was inaugurated, one of the first messages he received was what he called "a very nice message of congratulations" from the Queen, who also praised him for the end of the Iranian hostage crisis that had plagued the Carter presidency until its final hours. Reagan thanked Thatcher for the kind words. "We appreciate that very much even though that wasn't our problem to deal with during these past several months," he said. "I will tell her how pleased you were," the prime minister replied.

Now it was not Carter but his successor who would get a state visit to the palace. Not to mention a horseback ride with the Queen.

Nine

Horses and Hollywood

Friday, April 2, 1982—The Falkland Islands

Before dawn on a blustery spring morning, Argentinian troops began landing on the Falkland Islands—first with naval special forces in small boats, followed by landing craft with infantry and armored vehicles. Within hours, they had seized control of the British colony from the small garrison of Royal Marines and raised the blue-and-white Argentine flag, claiming sovereignty of the islands based on a decree from 1493 by Pope Alexander VI dividing the New World between Spain and Portugal. What transpired after that quick victory would test Britain's resolve and its relationship with the United States and a new president.

And the influence of Her Majesty.

Margaret Thatcher, Britain's hard-charging prime minister, dispatched a naval armada to the South Atlantic, 127 ships in all, in a deployment that included Prince Andrew, then a helicopter pilot on the HMS *Invincible*. The White House was publicly neutral as Secretary of State Alexander Haig shuttled between London and Buenos Aires, trying to mediate. On the eve of the invasion, a phone call from Reagan to the Argentine leader, General Leopoldo Galtieri, had fallen on deaf ears as war loomed. Behind the scenes, UN Ambassador Jeane Kirkpatrick argued that the United States needed to protect its ties to Argentina, seen as a bulwark against communism in Latin America.

The British were watching the administration's debate with some concern. The White House position seemed to be in flux. On April 5, the same day the British task force set sail, Reagan equivocated, telling reporters that it was "a very difficult situation for the United States, because we're friends with both of the countries engaged in this dispute." He called once again for "a peaceful resolution of this with no forceful action or no bloodshed." Six days later, appearing on CBS's *Face the Nation*, Kirkpatrick expressed sympathy for the Argentine position. "If the Argentines own the islands, then moving troops into them is not armed aggression," she said.

While the president's senior advisers were divided about what to do, White House Chief of Staff James Baker said he believed from the start that Reagan would stand with the British eventually, when it mattered. But the slow and uncertain pace of decision-making worried British leaders at 10 Downing Street and in Buckingham Palace, where not only the Queen's sovereign territory but also the safety of her twenty-two-year-old son were at stake.

In Congress, the junior senator from Delaware, Joe Biden, sponsored a Senate resolution siding with the British. It passed seventy-nine to one. Over the next several weeks, royal sea and air forces engaged the Argentine military from the waters off the Falklands, and commandos conducted daring raids. Royal Navy ships were lost to bombs and missiles. The first landing of British troops in force took place on May 21. By May 29, the British had scored their first major victory: More than a thousand Argentines surrendered after the Battle of Goose Green.

Even as the Queen's forces pushed toward Port Stanley, Washington hoped for a diplomatic solution. On May 31, Reagan delivered a Memorial Day speech at Arlington Cemetery, quoting Winston Churchill and praising the valor of those who died to defend democracy. But then he phoned Thatcher to convince her to stop the advance, to be open to a compromise. He congratulated her on the British successes so far, then implored, "I think an effort to show that we're all still willing to seek a settlement, consistent with our principles would undercut the efforts of some of the leftists in South America who are actively seeking to exploit the crisis."

Thatcher would have none of it. "This is democracy and our island, and the very worst thing for democracy would be if we failed now . . . ," she said. "I have to retake them now. I didn't lose some of my finest ships and some of my finest lives, to leave quietly under a cease fire without the Argentinians withdrawing."

Five days later, on Haig's orders, Kirkpatrick reluctantly sided with Great Britain, voting to veto a United Nations resolution calling for an immediate ceasefire. But moments later she announced her instructions had changed and the United States wanted to abstain, a switch UN rules didn't permit. That was a diplomatic embarrassment for the Americans and another red flag for the British.

Just four days away was an event that had been months in the planning, set to take place thousands of miles from the windswept Falklands battlefields: Reagan's first meeting with the Queen, part of his first presidential trip to Europe. The tour's capstone, at least for the White House, was something uniquely Reagan. He and the Queen, both keen equestrians, were scheduled to ride horses together at Windsor Castle.

The Falklands crisis loomed as a complication. The Argentines seemed "incapable of reasonable compromise," James Rentschler, director of Western European affairs on the National Security Council, had written in a memo to his boss. "Assuming that a miracle rabbit or two will not pop out of our hat . . . all of this argues for the earliest possible expression of support for the Brits in ways that are politically unambiguous for them." With undiplomatic candor, he detailed the personal stakes for the president. "Unless such practical expression is soon forthcoming—and absent the kind of Argentine give which now seems unlikely—I can't imagine that the President would have a comfortable stay in Windsor Castle come June. Even less can I picture him happily riding with the Queen through Windsor's woods on that occasion."

"Even less can I picture him happily riding with the Queen through Windsor's woods."

Ronald Wilson Reagan was poised to be the first US president to stay at Windsor Castle, and the first to go horseback riding with the Queen. They would be at Windsor Home Park, the countryside where William the Conqueror once rode. It had been the strongest draw England could offer for the presidential itinerary on a crucial trip that was already packed with a G7 summit in France, a NATO meeting in West Germany, and an audience with Pope John Paul II at the Vatican.

"This is proper royal polity because we're at war and there's the head of the armed forces of the U.K. taking our greatest, most important ally out for a ride," royal biographer Robert Hardman said, seeing echoes of World War II in the moment. "Reagan obviously had a very good and strong relationship with Margaret Thatcher, but I think it was given extra heft and extra gravitas and extra strength, really, by the royal connection."

By the Queen, and her horse.

THOUGH HIS FAMILY ROOTS WERE IRISH, REAGAN'S ADMIRATION FOR ALL things British dated to 1932, when he was a senior at Eureka College in Illinois and his girlfriend's parents took them to see a British theatrical company perform *Journey's End*. The drama by English playwright R. C. Sherriff depicted the lives of British officers in the trenches during World War I. Reagan identified with Captain Stanhope, the war-weary hero, and the performance fueled his determination to become an actor.

"I was drawn to the stage that night as if it were a magnet," Reagan wrote in his memoir, *An American Life*. Early in the acting career that followed, in 1948, he would make his first trip to London to film a movie called *The Hasty Heart*, a war drama in which Reagan played the lone Yank at a makeshift British military hospital in the jungles of Burma during World War II. He had a brush with the royal family then. While attending the performance of another play, he and the rest of his cast were presented to Elizabeth's mother, then the queen, and Elizabeth's husband, the Duke of Edinburgh. Elizabeth didn't join them because she was recuperating from the birth of Prince Charles two weeks earlier.

Reagan would remember London's winter weather as miserable and the war-damaged city as dreary, but the British themselves as "wonderfully cheerful, warmly humorous people."

Elizabeth, then twenty-two years old, had been an avid moviegoer since she was a girl. She would recall having seen some films starring Reagan. "People around her had told me this, that she had known Ronald Reagan as an actor, and she'd seen him in movies," Reagan aide Frederick Ryan Jr. said. As an adult, the Queen saw every film in the James Bond series; sometimes visited film sets; and regularly attended black-tie royal premieres of movies at the Odeon Theatre in Leicester Square, her arrival heralded by royal trumpeters.

In 1956, she created a sensation when she appeared at London's Empire Theatre to meet some of the biggest stars of the day, including Marilyn Monroe, then in London to perform in *The Sleeping Prince*. The actress stood between stars Victor Mature and Anthony Quayle; Brigitte Bardot and Joan Crawford were lined up onstage as well for a moment's welcome from the monarch. A photograph of the evening shows Marilyn and the Queen shaking hands and sharing a look of delight. Elizabeth is wearing a black evening gown and jeweled crown, Marilyn a form-fitting gold lamé dress with a dangerously deep décolleté.

Hollywood, like horses, was a passion Elizabeth and Reagan shared.

When he was governor of California, Reagan and Nancy had met Prince Charles, then a twenty-five-year-old lieutenant in the Royal Navy. While HMS *Jupiter* was docked at San Diego, he spent the weekend visiting Sunnylands, the lavish Palm Springs estate of Walter Annenberg—the businessman and philanthropist who was then the US ambassador to Great Britain, appointed by President Nixon. A photo in *The New York Times* shows Charles in a safari suit and brown sandals, energetically gesturing at something out of sight as the Reagans and the Annenbergs stand alongside. That night, Charles was feted at a dinner that included Bob Hope, Frank Sinatra, and other Hollywood celebrities.

"I so enjoyed meeting the Reagans," the prince wrote the Annenbergs afterward. "They were full of charm and great warmth, and it was great fun to listen to Mr. Reagan, whether he was being serious or funny."

Nancy and Charles would develop a particular affection. In May 1981, as President Reagan was recovering from an assassination attempt, she hosted a dinner for the prince at the White House. Cary Grant, Audrey Hepburn, the Annenbergs, and others attended. Dessert was an elaborate "Crown of Sorbet Prince of Wales," with brown-sugar "feathers" fashioned atop a royal "crown." "Mrs Reagan and the Prince hit it off perfectly," British ambassador Nicholas Henderson, seated to the first lady's left, observed. She would join Charles in New York in June and attend his wedding in London in July.

Knowing how much the wedding invitation meant to her, Reagan had encouraged Nancy to go even though he would stay in Washington, still recuperating. In his diary, he sounded a bit forlorn. "Saw 'Mommie' off for London & the Royal Wedding," he wrote on July 23, 1981, using his family nickname for Nancy. "I worry when she's out of sight 6 minutes. How am I going to hold out for 6 days. The lights don't seem as warm & bright without her." When she arrived in London, the British press was less enamored. "The one-time starlet of such B-films as 'The Next Voice You Hear' (1950) and 'Hellcats of the Navy' (1957) flew into Heathrow yesterday with 12 secret servicemen, five hat boxes and six dresses," *The Guardian* sniped. Attending a polo match featuring Charles, she arrived in a lengthy motorcade, sirens blaring; she was wearing an Adolfo suit and sporting high heels that sank into the muddy ground.

After the wedding, she was included in the family party—seated at the Queen's table, along with Princess Grace of Monaco, another American actress who now found herself in a new role. Elizabeth asked Nancy to mention to her husband the prospect of a visit to the United Kingdom. It would be the first royal invitation for a state visit to a president since Woodrow Wilson in 1918.

Elizabeth and Ronald Reagan would have an instant affinity. Despite their considerable differences, those who watched the Queen and the president up close saw similarities. Both were sure-footed in their public roles, and both understood how essential the performative aspects of their jobs were. Elizabeth had been in the public eye from the day British newspapers reported her birth. Reagan had developed that skill on the movie set, a presence that served him well in politics. He was the modern president most comfortable in a spotlight; the authoritative biography of him is subtitled *The Role of a Lifetime*. As leaders, both understood the importance of looking and acting their parts, and of displaying a kinship with their citizens that could feel personal. But they also shared a reserve, protecting a private core. Reagan, who had few confidants beyond his wife, was "like one of those one-way see-through mirrors: he could look at us, but there was no way in which we could peer back at him," Henderson observed. Those words were strikingly similar to author Craig Brown's description of Elizabeth. "With her interior world screened from public view, and her conversation restricted by protocol to questions not answers, she became a human looking-glass: the light cast by fame bounced off her, and back on to those she faced," he wrote.

"They both understood their unique positions in the world," said Mark Weinberg, a White House aide who was with Reagan at Windsor Castle and later encounters between the two leaders at the president's ranch and aboard the Queen's yacht. "They understood they were symbols. They understood that they acted on the world stage." That was reflected in their dress and demeanor, always proper. But they also managed to be grounded, to display "a commonality." During her private time in Scotland, Elizabeth would pitch in to cook and clean up at family barbecues. At his California ranch, Reagan would clear brush. Both felt most centered when riding horses, at heart a solitary enterprise though one that carries a bond between rider and mount.

Indeed, Elizabeth had a greater personal ease with Reagan than she did with Thatcher. The first woman prime minister of Great Britain was a devoted royalist; the depth of her curtsies was the stuff of palace legend. But she also had a tendency to lecture just about everyone, even if they happened to be a queen or a president. There was particular heat between her and Elizabeth on policy toward South Africa's apartheid regime. In a notorious episode of indiscretion, an anonymous source who turned out to be the royal press secretary told a *Sunday Times* reporter in 1986 that the Queen saw Thatcher's approach to governing as "uncaring, confrontational and divisive."

In contrast, the Queen's connection with Reagan was immediate and enduring and uncomplicated. He was born to modest circumstances in small-town Illinois; she was an heir to the British throne. But as adults, they had a better understanding than most of the roles each filled, of what they required. For the British, it would mean something for them to have such a rapport, especially at a time of war.

REAGAN'S FIRST OFFICIAL TRIP TO EUROPE WAS IN MANY WAYS A DISASTER. The jet-lagged seventy-one-year-old president dozed off while meeting with the pope, a Vatican catnap caught live on television. At an economic summit in Versailles, his entreaties failed to dissuade European allies from proceeding with plans to help construct a $10 billion Soviet pipeline that would bring natural gas to Western Europe and deliver hard currency to Moscow, something the Soviets desperately needed. Violent protests erupted on the streets of Paris and West Berlin depicting Reagan as a warmonger or a stumblebum, or both.

On the other hand, the horseback ride went well.

"The trip was coming up and [Deputy Chief of Staff Michael] Deaver and I said, 'We've got to do something special to make this trip special,'" Baker recalled. "'What are we going to do?' And we came up with the idea that we would have them ride horseback on the grounds of Windsor Castle." Reagan was instantly taken with the idea.

Because it mattered to the president, it mattered to the Queen as well, Baker said. "She was very conscious of the 'special relationship,' and she wanted to nurture it."

Afterward, no occasion from the tour would be recalled by Reagan with such fondness, and to the end of his life. All that for what was, basically, a photo op, a cinematographic one. The president and the Queen rode well-behaved horses on a carefully arranged route that bristled with security. They were trailed for a time by Prince Philip and Nancy Reagan in an open carriage drawn by four bays. The first lady's affection for horseback riding—closer to tolerance than love—was grounded in her devotion not to horses but to Ronnie. Two royal equerries and two Secret Service agents followed on horseback, along with a Range Rover carrying security forces as law-enforcement personnel from both countries guarded the woods on foot.

Not everyone was taken by the photogenic images. Reagan was a suspect figure among many in Europe, seen as risking a nuclear confrontation with the Soviet Union. Although he was a prodigious writer and reader, he never overcame his reputation among his critics as a sunny dunderhead. "Reagan is just a movie star acting the part of a king, and the Queen is like a movie star in a film about Britain," Tony Benn, a Labour member of Parliament and no fan of the monarchy, grumbled in his diary. "I find it embarrassing to live in Britain at the moment."

For the president, though, the moment was a confluence of things he adored. He called it a "fairy-tale experience" to meet the Queen. Their mutual love of horses became a bond. He kept horses at his mountain ranch near Santa Barbara and relished riding more than almost any other pastime; one of his often-repeated aphorisms was that "there is something about the outside of a horse that is good for the inside of a man." Elizabeth, who took her first riding lesson at age three and was given her first pony at four, not only rode but also kept a stable of racing horses. She was respected on her own merits in the British racing community for her expertise in horseflesh. Some close to them observed that both the president and the Queen related to horses better than they did to most people, possibly including their own children.

The British, whose diplomatic skills had been honed through centuries of managing an empire, grasped the importance of the horseback ride for the Americans. It would have been hard to miss, given the focus by the White House, especially Deaver, the president's imagemaker and the senior aide closest to Nancy.

Before Reagan arrived, the Foreign Office prepared a series of exhaustive briefing papers for the Queen and the prime minister. They listed every previous presidential trip to England since Woodrow Wilson in 1918, ran through the biographies of the president and first lady, and analyzed Reagan's political standing back home. "The press is already predicting" that a poor showing in the November midterm elections, combined with Reagan's age and "uncertain command of government could see him written off as a lame duck president," the British ambassador wrote—an analysis that failed to foresee Reagan's landslide reelection in 1984.

Eager to start the trip on a good note, the Queen dispatched Prince Philip to receive the Reagans at Heathrow Airport. Despite tensions over the Falklands, or perhaps because of them, she also wanted Thatcher to be present at the arrival—coming from the Crown, this was the definition of a command performance—and even specified what she should wear. A curt note from the Lord Chamberlain's office to Downing Street instructed, "The Queen wishes you, as Prime Minister, to be present on this occasion and to arrive at the special waiting room at Heathrow Airport." She should be there by 5:40 p.m., it specified, adding, "Day dress with a Hat will be worn." It closed with one more demand: "I shall be grateful for an early acknowledgement of this letter."

The prime minister's office responded the next day, confirming that she would be at the designated waiting room on time and properly clothed. "I note that day dress with a hat will be worn," it said.

The public greeting at Heathrow was prescribed by protocol, down to the prime minister's hat. But the private welcome that followed at Windsor—

between two leaders who had never met before—was remarkably casual and warm. Dress was black tie, in that royal way, but the conversation was all but familial. Just seven people sat around the table—the Queen and the duke; the president and the first lady; Princess Anne; and Deaver and his wife, Carolyn. "The corgis were at everybody's feet and chasing cats around the dining-room table," Deaver recalled.

The president was charmed. So was the Queen.

Both were members of the Greatest Generation, born fifteen years apart, with compatible interests. During his presidential tenure, he would make three trips to London; she would visit him in California. They would share the closest personal ties she had with any president, and ones that would last for years after he had left the White House. "They just kind of hit it off as friends," Weinberg said. "I don't know if there's any great mystery or complication to it. They just enjoyed each other's company."

"She had an obvious rapport with Ronald Reagan, because they both knew and loved horses," agreed Lord Boateng, then a Greater London councillor and later a member of Parliament. "These are not unimportant things."

The canter through the park turned out to be more than a photo op. It sealed what might be called a very special relationship. In middle age and mid-reign—fifty-six years old and thirty years on the throne—Elizabeth was confident in her role as monarch and her influence in global affairs. With Thatcher's rise to power, the Reagan administration also had the closest ideological fit with Downing Street of any US administration since Jack Kennedy and Harold Macmillan.

THE HORSEBACK RIDE WAS SET FOR THE NEXT MORNING. FROM THE start, British officials had identified it as the immutable element of the trip. "I need hardly to say that the only absolutely stable and central item in any discussion of the President's visit is this riding event," Henderson had written in February, four months earlier. There were disputes and deliberations over issues from the president's accommodations—including the demand to install the castle's first shower—to a clash over the venue for his speech to Parliament. But there was never a question about the horseback ride.

"In the frequent exchanges with Deaver about the visit I had found that however doubtful he was concerning this or that proposal his eye invariably lit up at the prospect of the President's riding with the Queen," Henderson recalled. At one White House meeting, Deaver had declared, "'Carter couldn't have done a thing like that,'" adding with delight: "Think of the photo opportunity."

The Queen did draw the line at one White House idea—that several senior Reagan officials join them on horseback. National security adviser William Clark, for one, told the British ambassador that if others would be riding, he'd like to be one of them. That was not to happen. She did not intend to "ride in a posse," *The Times* of London reported.

The drumbeat of excitement grew loud enough to alarm Elizabeth, anxious about the glare of publicity for what was clearly not going to be a private ride. She asked Michael Palliser, the top civil servant at the Foreign Office who was making a farewell visit to Washington, to find out more about the president's riding preferences, and his prowess. What kind of saddle? What sort of horse? "Clearly, too, the Queen was beginning to get anxious about the glare of publicity in which this private ride was destined to take place . . . ," Henderson said. "This ride was going to be a worldwide box-office draw." When White House aides weren't responsive, Henderson deployed what he called "unusual channels." He fed queries to his wife, Mary, who would raise them with her friend Nancy Reagan, who in turn would ask her husband and then report back.

The ambassador advised the Crown equerry, Sir John Miller, to choose for Reagan a mount that looked impressive but was guaranteed not to cause any trouble. "One that was accustomed to the razzmatazz of the Trooping of the Colour, looked and was powerful, but behaved like a lamb," as he put it.

That would describe Centennial. The president was beaming when he came in view of the news photographers astride the eight-year-old black stallion, a gift to the Queen by the Royal Canadian Mounted Police in her Silver Jubilee year. The Queen was riding alongside on her favorite horse, a twenty-year-old black mare named Burmese.

Reagan wore an open-collared shirt, a tweed jacket, and tall riding boots. The Queen sported tan jodhpurs and a checked wool jacket with a scarf wrapped around her hair. After all the back-and-forth beforehand, he was using an English saddle. "Does it ride well?" shouted a reporter in the press pool, the small group of journalists allowed to witness the moment. "Yes," the president replied, jokingly offering to jump over the clustered press corps. "If you stand still I'll take it over the top."

The Queen was "tidy, restrained, and proper," *The Times* of London said, in contrast to Reagan, who "plumped for the Tom Mix school of equestrian discipline and jogged around in his unfamiliar English saddle with a rolling freedom more usual in Wyoming than Windsor." The scene was something out of the movies, the columnist wrote—in other words, precisely the image Deaver had wanted. "The retreating figures on horseback might have been the closing shot of a John Ford Western were it not for the distraction of the ensuing train of security men . . . and the dimly visible figures with walkie-talkies hiding in surrounding bushes." *The Daily Telegraph* said: "Hollywood itself could hardly have bettered the scene."

Reagan was ready to tarry but the Queen was ready to go. She began to move her horse away, looking back to see if Reagan got the hint. He finally did, then caught up with her. They would ride for an hour, at one point greeting farmers in a field and at another waving to onlookers along a canal. At least, he waved. Concerned that he wasn't watching where Centennial was headed, she briefly took the reins and pulled his horse away from the water. At the end, at the top of the Long Walk, reporters were close enough to shout questions again. Reagan called the Queen "charming" and "down-to-earth." He admired her riding style. "It's called the forward seat," he explained, "the modern riding, and you know she was in charge of that animal!"

A FEW HOURS AFTER THEIR RIDE, AT HIS ADDRESS IN THE ROYAL GALLERY of Westminster Palace, Reagan delivered a full-throated backing of Britain in the Falklands, leaving no doubt—finally—of where the United States stood.

"On distant islands in the South Atlantic young men are fighting for Britain," he declared. "And, yes, voices have been raised protesting their sacrifice for lumps of rock and earth so far away. But those young men aren't fighting for mere real estate. They fight for a cause—for the belief that armed aggression must not be allowed to succeed, and the people must participate in the decisions of government, the decisions of government under the rule of law. If there had been firmer support for that principle some 45 years ago, perhaps our generation wouldn't have suffered the bloodletting of World War II."

Britain's goal for Reagan's visit: achieved.

The three US television networks broadcast the speech live, and in time it would be seen as one of the most significant of his presidency. Standing in front of portraits of British monarchs and murals of the battles of Trafalgar and Waterloo, flanked by ceremonial Beefeater guards in scarlet, Reagan predicted the end of the Cold War. "The march of freedom and democracy . . . will leave Marxism-Leninism on the ash-heap of history," he declared, not the conventional view of the moment, but one that would turn out to be prescient.

He told a favorite anecdote about an elderly London woman who was pulled from the wreckage during the Blitz, a tribute to British resilience, although possibly an apocryphal tale. The rescuers "found a bottle of brandy she'd stored behind the staircase, which was all that was left standing," he said. "And since she was barely conscious one of the workers pulled the cork to give her a taste of it. She came around immediately and said, 'Here now, there now, put it back. That's for emergencies.'"

At a white-tie banquet that night, the first dinner at Windsor Castle honoring a US president, the Queen thanked him.

"I greatly enjoyed our ride together this morning, and I was much impressed by the way in which you coped so professionally with a strange horse and a saddle that must have seemed even stranger," she said in her toast, to laughter. Then her tone turned serious. Britain was facing "naked aggression" in the Falklands, she said, her first major public comment on the crisis. She noted their nations' long alliance in the battle for freedom. "The friendship must never be taken for granted," she said, "and your visit gives me the opportunity to reaffirm and restate it."

Three days later, the final British assault on Port Stanley to reclaim the Falklands began. By June 14, all Argentine forces had surrendered. The war was over.

DURING THEIR RIDE, REAGAN HAD EXTOLLED TO THE QUEEN THE VIRTUES of Rancho del Cielo, the ranch in the Santa Ynez mountains that he had bought eight years before. Would she like to visit? She would. "The Queen was dying to go riding with Ronnie," Nancy said.

Elizabeth had wanted to see the West Coast during her first visit to the United States as Queen, in 1957, but time and protocol had made that impossible. When Henderson met with the Queen before he was dispatched to Washington as the British ambassador in 1979, she mentioned again her desire to go to California. Three years later, as he was preparing to return to London, the Reagans hosted a private dinner for him and the prospect of a royal visit to the West Coast came up. The ambassador mentioned the idea of *Britannia* perhaps docking in Santa Barbara. Nancy told him she had never seen the royal yacht but longed to do so. "There was a gleam in her eye," he said.

Finally, the trip was set for early 1983. The itinerary would include stops at the Reagans' ranch, the Annenbergs' estate, and Silicon Valley, as well as events in Los Angeles, San Francisco, and Seattle. At Philip's request, they also scheduled a weekend to view the wildlife at Yosemite National Park in California. The ten-day trip was tagged at the end of one the royal couple already was scheduled to take, with state visits to Jamaica, the Cayman Islands, and Mexico aboard *Britannia*.

The US leg of the journey was designated a "royal visit," not a "state visit," but the preparations were no less exhaustive. The briefing paper prepared for the Queen was a tome, divided into three sections, US "Domestic Affairs," "The United States and the World," and "Britain's Relationship with the United States." "Although our interests have tended to change since the UK joined the European community, we are still on closer terms with the US than with any other major country," it said. That was not news to Her Majesty.

The briefing on Reagan detailed everything from his father's occupation ("a shoe salesman") to his preferences for breakfast ("fresh orange juice, fruit and cereal, sometimes a boiled egg, and decaffeinated coffee") to his record on delivering on his campaign promises ("a mixed one"). His mother was of Scottish stock, it noted, with a grandfather born in Peckham, in London, and great-grandparents from Tipperary, in Ireland.

"The Reagans also like to escape to their ranch near Santa Barbara in California where Mr Reagan spends his days riding, chopping wood, clearing brush and in other outdoor pursuits," it reported. "He has a spaniel named 'Victory,' that was given to him during the Presidential election campaign. The President loves riding and has a number of horses including a particularly fine stallion presented to him by President Portillo of Mexico and a black thoroughbred called 'Little Man.'"

It was the first time Reagan had invited a foreign leader to his ranch, a privilege that would later be extended only to those with whom he had the deepest relationships—Thatcher, Canadian Prime Minister Brian Mulroney, and Soviet leader Mikhail Gorbachev. It was the only time the Queen would visit an American president at his own home, not at the White House, a personal touch that echoed her parents' visit to FDR's Hyde Park before World War II.

The trip was also notable for a less salutary reason: the catastrophic weather.

The royal yacht docked in San Diego on Saturday, February 26, 1983, amid historic rains. The flooded roads made it treacherous even to drive out of the dockyard. The only way to plow through the rising waters was in a commandeered US Navy bus. To the astonishment of the British press trailing her, Her Majesty donned knee-high galoshes and climbed in. "But she's *never* been on a bus," protested a reporter for the *Daily Mail*. She and Prince Philip perched on the first two seats, "like two kids on an adventure," said Selwa "Lucky" Roosevelt, Reagan's chief of protocol.

"The Queen is in a very jolly mood," her press secretary, Michael Shea, later told reporters. "So much of the Queen's life is planned that she finds it quite enjoyable when things go astray." Astray indeed, rare for figures whose travel schedules were typically set months and years in advance, their every movement scripted.

This time, there would be boats and borrowed buses, jeeps and loaned presidential planes.

On Sunday, the royal couple was supposed to sail up the California coast on *Britannia*. But a tornado over Los Angeles made that impossible; Reagan gave them use of an air force plane to fly instead to Palm Springs for lunch with Walter and Lee Annenberg at their Sunnylands estate. Then Hollywood for dinner, on Sound Stage 9 at 20th Century Fox, recently vacated by the hit TV series *M*A*S*H*. The five hundred guests included former President Ford as well as Hollywood stars—Frank Sinatra, Dionne Warwick, Bob Hope, Perry Como, even an aging George Burns.

So far, so good.

Then the rains worsened. The drive to Reagan's ranch Tuesday would be treacherous. "We were sure the Queen wouldn't come, because it was terrible to get up the roads, and once you got there, it was all foggy," Nancy said. "You couldn't see your hand in front of your face. But she was determined to come." The limousines were ditched as useless. Four-wheel-drive vehicles were substituted instead for a seven-mile drive of hairpin turns. Some of the roads were submerged; downed tree limbs were everywhere.

"They made it up the mountain, but when they got to our home, it was so foggy no one could see more than a few feet," the president recalled. "I tried to explain how beautiful the place really was and apologized for the weather, but the Queen said, 'Yes, if it was *just* dreary, but this is an *adventure*.'" The Reagans were disappointed; she bucked them up. A photo shows the Queen in high boots and a blue felt hat, smiling gamely as water dripped off her Burberry raincoat. Nancy is wearing a red raincoat and a tight smile; Reagan, in jeans and a denim jacket, looks unperturbed. The Queen described the trip to the ranch as "delightful and terribly exciting."

A horseback ride was clearly impossible. They went inside the modest house, where a fire was burning in the fireplace, and shared a Tex-Mex lunch of tacos, enchiladas, chiles rellenos, guacamole, and refried beans—another echo of her parents' visit to Hyde Park, when Eleanor Roosevelt served Elizabeth's parents hot dogs, something they had never seen before. "Mr. Deaver, that was so enjoyable," the Queen said afterward. "Especially the used beans."

Not on the menu: substance.

She hoped to discuss what was going on around the globe. The Cold War was at its height; a week later the president would label the USSR an "Evil Empire" in a landmark speech. "Here she was having tete-a-tete with the leader of the Western world," Sir Brian Fall, a senior Foreign Service officer, told royal biographer Robert Hardman. "And yet he refused to talk politics. It was all about being on the farm and chopping wood! I think she'd have enjoyed some serious politics." If that was to Elizabeth's disappointment, it was to Nancy Reagan's delight. The lunch at the ranch was "wonderful," the first lady said afterward. "No one talked politics."

Her Majesty liked spending time with Reagan, but she found the stage direction he received from his White House staff amusing. "A member of her staff recalls, 'People kept coming up to the president and saying things like, "Mr. President, your thinking on Nicaragua this morning is as follows. And if you're asked about the Middle East, Mr. President, this is what you should say. And, Mr. President, if you're asked about the Federal Reserve Bank's policy, this is your thinking on that,"'" author William Shawcross related. "Somebody who was standing near the Queen heard her say, 'And they call *me* a constitutional monarch?'"

She could have a mischievous view of Nancy Reagan, too. On the sidelines of her California trip, she was spotted doing an impression of the first lady, whose look of rapt adoration at her Ronnie was often mocked.

Nancy left the ranch with them to go to Long Beach for dinner on *Britannia*. The first lady would stay overnight on the royal yacht. "I spent that evening with the Queen, sitting on a sofa in the large living room, talking about our children like old friends," she said. Their offspring were the subject of some heartburn to each of them. The Reagans were estranged from Michael, his son from his earlier marriage to Jane Wyman. Nancy's dealings with stepdaughter Maureen were sometimes strained, and her relationship with her daughter, Patti Davis, then thirty, had been fraught for years, though it would ultimately warm. The first lady fretted even about the child with whom she was closest, twenty-five-year-old Ron Jr., dismayed about the older woman he had married and the career he had dropped out of Yale to pursue, in the ballet.

For her part, Elizabeth confided her nascent concerns about Princess Diana, struggling in her new royal role in ways that would later become disastrously clear. She had married Prince Charles two years earlier in St. Paul's Cathedral, becoming the Princess of Wales to the adoration of the British public and much of the world. Their son William had been born a year earlier; Harry would follow a year later. But the fissures in their fairy-tale romance were already beginning to show, and the tabloids were taking notes. The Queen didn't know every detail, not yet, but she could see that the princess, and the marriage to her son and heir, was in trouble. Not that she was entirely sympathetic. The war, and her father, had taught her that there were things more important than one's personal feelings. She had a make-the-best-of-it attitude about life and had little patience for those—including her eldest son and daughter-in-law—who didn't.

Britannia was scheduled to sail to San Francisco Wednesday, but because of the foul weather the royal couple used a presidential plane to fly instead. With the yacht not yet docked, the White House hurriedly booked dozens of rooms at the posh St. Francis Hotel for the British entourage, including the presidential suite for the royal couple. "That caused me a terrible problem because it gave us a whole night that I hadn't planned for," recalled Deaver, who was handling the trip. "I went up to the Queen and said: 'We have a free evening tomorrow in San Francisco, and I have called Trader Vic's and they're going to give us a special room and I just thought it would be fun.'

"And she said, 'Oh, a restaurant! That's wonderful!' And the Queen turns to the Duke of Edinburgh . . . and says to him: 'Philip, Mr. Deaver has this wonderful idea about going to a restaurant!' And he turned around and said: 'A restaurant? Surely you are kidding? A restaurant?'" It was the first time she had eaten in a restaurant in seventeen years. She sampled Trader Vic's trademark rum punch and cracked open her fortune cookie, reading the message and tucking it in the purse she always carried.

The next night, on Thursday, she was the guest of honor at a black-tie dinner hosted by Reagan at the M. H. de Young Memorial Museum in Golden Gate Park. Her visit had been "spectacular and has fulfilled a long-standing ambition on my part to visit California and the West Coast," the Queen said as she began her toast. "What better time than when the president is a Californian?" Her outfit was almost a parody of royalty—a wedding cake of a dress, constructed of champagne-colored taffeta with ecru-and-gold sleeves festooned with oversized bows on the shoulders. She wore a pearl-and-diamond tiara and jeweled earrings and necklace.

"I knew before we came that we had exported many of our traditions to the United States," she went on, her delivery deadpan. "I had not realized before that weather was one of them." Seated beside her, Reagan erupted in a gale of laughter.

On Friday, Elizabeth hosted a dinner for the Reagans on *Britannia*, by now safely docked in San Francisco, on a date that happened to fall on their thirty-first wedding anniversary. The engraved silver box she gave them as a gift is in a place of honor in the Reagans' apartment at his presidential library.

For his gift to her, Reagan had arranged for the Queen to be presented during her Silicon Valley visit with her first computer, a $24,000 Hewlett-Packard 250 Model 25. "It was very early on in computers," said James Rosebush, a senior White House staffer who was accompanying the Queen. At the reception that evening, she came over with a question. "Do you think we can use that at Buckingham Palace?" she asked him. The answer turned out to be yes. She would install it there and use it to track her horse breeding, training, and racing operations.

DURING THE TRIP, SECURITY WAS A CONCERN, AND A POINT OF FRICTION.

Four decades later, the FBI revealed that there had been an assassination threat against Elizabeth during her West Coast visit. A police officer in San Francisco frequented an Irish pub known as a gathering place for sympathizers of the IRA. About a month before the Queen was scheduled to arrive, he reported that he had been called by a man who said his daughter had been killed in Northern Ireland by a rubber bullet. The ammunition was developed by the British Ministry of Defense to use for riot control during the sectarian "Troubles." Though designed to cause only pain, the bullets were blamed for the deaths of seventeen people—including a twelve-year-old girl and a fourteen-year-old girl who had been killed two years earlier in Belfast.

"He was going to attempt to harm Queen Elizabeth and would do this either by dropping some object off the Golden Gate Bridge onto the Royal Yacht Britannia when it sails underneath, or would attempt to kill Queen Elizabeth when she visited Yosemite National Park," the FBI report, declassified in 2023, said.

There was no sign he tried to deliver on his threat, but the Secret Service arrangements to protect the royal couple were stringent.

The Duke of Edinburgh often bristled at their strictures as overreach. His anger boiled over during a ride in the limousine heading back to *Britannia*, docked in San Diego. He had turned on the light inside the limousine, and the agent in the front seat asked him to turn it off, saying it could made him a target for someone on the street. "I'll be damned if

I'll turn off the lights," he retorted. "These people have come out to see me." Only the intervention of Lucky Roosevelt, who was also in the car, convinced him to accede. "I said, 'Sir, if you don't turn off the lights, these men will lose their jobs.'"

Later in the trip, Reagan was running a few minutes late, delaying the start of a motorcade that also included the royal couple. "Get this car moving," Philip demanded; the agent in the driver's seat demurred. The prince picked up a magazine from the seat pocket, rolled it up, and smacked the driver across the back of his head. "Move this fucking car, and move it now!" he shouted. The agent didn't respond. Neither did the Queen, sitting next to her husband, staring silently ahead.

After they arrived at their hotel, she sent an aide to invite the agent to join the prince and her for a nightcap—an apologetic gesture. He refused. A White House official was in the room; the British messenger appealed to him. Declining Her Majesty's invitation could cost him his job, he pleaded. The agent finally agreed. "I want to make it clear that I'm doing this for you, not for them," he said.

"Prince Philip was very irritated, *constantly*, about the security—how unnecessary all the security was," Deaver said. "Every time they moved, we treated it as if it were a presidential motorcade. And it drove him crazy. I don't know what it was about the American security that was so overdone. He made his comments in no uncertain terms on what he thought about it."

"He's very attractive," Roosevelt said of Philip, "but he has a bit of a temper."

The prince could also be more cynical about Reagan than his wife. After a small luncheon the president had hosted, Philip told Gyles Brandreth he noticed a card tucked next to Reagan's place that identified the guests around the table, complete with arrows indicating where they were seated. "He was much amused to see an arrow pointing that direction saying, 'Elizabeth Queen of England, call her such-and-such.'"

REAGAN'S AFFECTION FOR THE QUEEN WAS APPARENT, LUCKY ROOSEVELT said. She often found herself waiting with the president for one foreign leader or another to arrive, but she said his eagerness to greet the Queen was distinct. "He had the greatest affection for her," she said. Roosevelt, who was married to a grandson of President Theodore Roosevelt, had accompanied the royal couple throughout their West Coast tour. Four decades later, by then ninety-five years old, she flipped through a three-ring binder of photographs and memorabilia from the trip, kept on a bookshelf in her Washington apartment. She pointed at pictures of Elizabeth and the president together. "The Queen looks very happy," she observed.

After Elizabeth and Philip returned to England, British Ambassador Oliver Wright sent his private assessment of their trip to Foreign Secretary Francis Pym. Even the dreadful weather had proved to be an asset, he reported, showing Americans what a trouper the Queen was. "Nor could the Head of State of any other ally command the attention and enthusiasm of the President and government of the United States as the Queen did," he went on, noting her unprecedented invitation to Reagan's ranch.

"As the Queen put it in her own farewell message," he said, "she hoped that the visit would serve 'to remind the world that we are allies for always.'"

ALLIES FOR ALWAYS? SEVEN MONTHS LATER, THERE WAS TROUBLE.

Even before his presidency, Reagan was worried about the spread of communism in Latin America. In Grenada, a year before he was elected to the White House, a Marxist dictator had taken power after a bloodless coup. The first Marxist-Leninist nation in the British Commonwealth continued to recognize Elizabeth as its queen. But the tiny Caribbean island began to build an international airport with a nine-thousand-foot runway—long enough to accommodate the largest Soviet aircraft, planes that could be loaded with weapons for leftist insurgencies in Central America. That got the Reagan administration's attention.

So did this: In October 1983, a radical faction in Grenada executed the prime minister, formed a military council to rule the country, and put the Crown's representative, Sir Paul Scoon, under house arrest. The Organization of Eastern Caribbean States asked the United States for help, and Scoon made a secret appeal.

Two weeks later, at dawn on October 25, 1983, the United States invaded Grenada in Operation Urgent Fury, deploying a joint force of six thousand troops that included army Rangers, navy SEALs, air force tactical units, US Marines, and the 82nd Airborne Division. Despite glitches in communications and an absence of up-to-date maps, the world's greatest military power unsurprisingly managed to prevail within days. Several hundred American students attending medical school on the island were evacuated; protecting those US citizens was one reason cited to justify the invasion. An interim government was appointed, elections were held in December, and the date of the invasion, on October 25, would become a national holiday.

Not everyone was on board, though. In the United Nations, the General Assembly by a lopsided 108 to 9 adopted a resolution that "deeply deplores the armed intervention in Grenada, which constitutes a flagrant violation of international law and of the independence, sovereignty and territorial integrity of that State." Reagan shrugged that off. "It didn't upset my breakfast at all," he told reporters the next day.

More problematic was the rage of his closest global ally.

Thatcher had been told the United States was considering military action but not that it had decided to move ahead. As US forces began reconnaissance missions, hours before the invasion would be launched, she called Reagan. "She was livid," Robert (Bud) McFarlane, the White House national security adviser, said. She demanded that the operation be called off. Grenada was a member of the British Commonwealth, she reminded Reagan. What was the United States doing launching a military operation there? Why hadn't she been informed? He was obligated to ask the consent of the British Crown and prime minister before invading, she declared. "They're the Queen's islands!"

Theoretically, Grenada's Marxist leaders could have appealed to the Queen to help repel the invaders—that is, to battle the US forces—although that seemed an unlikely course.

Reagan listened to her outburst, "occasionally holding the receiver a couple of inches from his ear" to protect his hearing, McFarlane said. But the president didn't relent, asking instead for her "understanding and support" of the course he had set. The Marines and army Rangers landed on Grenada a few hours later. Reagan was "deeply disappointed" at Thatcher's outrage, Secretary of State George Shultz said. "He had supported her in the Falklands. He felt he was absolutely right about Grenada."

This wasn't known at the time: The failure to keep the British informed was an accident, a snafu. "There were a lot of things going on right at that time," said Raymond Seitz, then an executive assistant to Shultz. For one thing, on that Saturday, October 22, an armed gunman had taken seven hostages at a golf course where the president was playing; the hostages were eventually freed. On Sunday, a bombing in Beirut had killed 241 Marines and sailors in their barracks, one of the deadliest terrorist attacks on Americans in history. Hours later, on Monday, the reconnaissance missions on Grenada were launched, and the invasion began Tuesday morning.

"We just dropped the ball on it, not consulting or informing or whatever the British," said Seitz, who would later serve as the US ambassador to Great Britain. The diplomatic oversight may be hard to believe, but he insisted it was true. "And I think the Queen was offended by that."

Actually, reports on the strength of the Queen's offense varied.

"I think the Queen has made it clear she's immensely displeased by the attempt of President Reagan to use her representative as a cat's paw," to cite Sir Paul Scoon's plight as one of the justifications, Labour Party spokesman Denis Healey huffed. But Sir William Heseltine, then her private secretary, would later use less heated language. "I wouldn't get unduly fussed about Grenada," he said. "I think the Queen was a bit peeved that the Americans had launched themselves into one of her dominions without warning." She took her role as sovereign of the Commonwealth seriously, deserving of consultation in advance by both the president and the prime minister.

"A bit peeved," perhaps. But she signaled privately that she was pleased with the outcome, given that a stable and democratic government had been restored in the Commonwealth.

When Reagan was in London the next spring for the G7 summit and the commemoration of the fortieth anniversary of D-Day, the Queen hosted a black-tie dinner at Buckingham Palace for the visiting world leaders. There seemed to be no hard feelings. The president had the best seat in the hall, between herself and the Queen Mother. Elizabeth hosted the Reagans for lunch, too, in her apartment. "It was a warm & pleasant visit," Reagan wrote in his diary. "They are both nice & she is an outstanding human being."

A year later, on the sidelines at his first summit with Soviet leader Mikhail Gorbachev, in Geneva in November 1985, Reagan confided in senior aides a private conversation he had with the Queen. "At some point and for some reason, he starts to talk about the Queen," Kenneth Adelman, then director of the US Arms Control and Disarmament Agency, told me. She had confided to Reagan that she was "inclined" toward the liberation of Grenada, even though the United States had launched an invasion without giving her a heads-up. "She said she really didn't mind on Grenada, but no one should ever know that and she couldn't take a view on it."

That put her at odds with her prime minister, and telling Reagan about it was the expression of a personal opinion on foreign policy—something she almost never did, considering her role as a constitutional monarch. Of course, it also delighted her friend Ronald Reagan. He had crossed Thatcher, to be sure, but on this the Queen was in his corner.

When Elizabeth was visiting Canada and Reagan was campaigning in Michigan for reelection in 1984, the two spoke. She told him she was sure there will never be a wider divide between the United States and Great Britain "than the river that currently divides us." Soon afterward, when he was talking to Thatcher, he mentioned the comment with appreciation.

The role being played by the United States and the United Kingdom as leaders of the free world also had its naysayers. During an interview on CNN in 1987, Thatcher was asked about criticism from "a prominent real estate developer in the United States," one Donald Trump, about US expenditures on Europe's defense. Thatcher responded, "It is vital that we all defend the frontier of freedom. It is vital that we stick together, because if we do not, we could be picked off one by one and it is as important to the United States as to Western Europe."

That didn't settle the issue for Trump. Three decades later, when he was president himself, he would be in a stronger position to press the question.

REAGAN WOULD DEVELOP A PARTICULAR AFFECTION FOR THE QUEEN Mother.

At the Buckingham Palace dinner that concluded the G7 summit in London on June 9, 1984, he was seated between Elizabeth and the Queen Mother. Nancy Reagan was across the imposing Spanish mahogany table between the Duke of Edinburgh and Prince Charles, with a view through the windows in the State Dining Room of the palace's broad lawn and gardens. The table was set with turquoise-bordered Minton china that had been made for Queen Victoria and English cut-crystal glasses—five at each place—that had been made for Elizabeth's coronation. "E II R" was hand-engraved on each of them.

Canadian Prime Minister Pierre Trudeau, seated on the other side of the Queen Mother, spoke up with a challenge. He said he had "read somewhere" that Reagan could recite by heart "The Shooting of Dan McGrew," by Robert W. Service, a popular Canadian poet who had been born in England of Scottish descent. "I'm not sure he really believed I could do it," Reagan said later. "[M]aybe he just wanted to put me on the spot and see how I'd handle it." The two men rubbed one another the wrong way; Reagan had bristled at the summit earlier that day over what he saw as Trudeau's condescension toward him and Thatcher.

The Queen Mother was seated between the two leaders. As it happened, she was also a fan of the poem and of one of its main characters, a lady named Lou. "Oh, do you know 'The Shooting of Dan McGrew'?" she asked Reagan. Why, yes, he did, Reagan allowed. She urged him to recite it. What happened next was not an embarrassment for Reagan but a demonstration of his narrative powers, his ability to command the room, his memory. He had learned the poem as a boy in Dixon.

Back of the bar, in a solo game, sat Dangerous Dan McGrew,
And watching his luck was his light-o'love, the lady that's known as Lou.

Through ten stanzas detailing a deadly barroom brawl, the Queen Mother chimed in each time on the refrain, "the lady that's known as Lou," through to the dramatic conclusion.

"When we were through," the president said with satisfaction, "everybody at the table applauded."

Princess Diana wasn't there. She was curtailing her public engagements because of her pregnancy; Prince Harry would be born three months later, in September. Not that she minded missing the dinner. She didn't share the Queen Mother's delight in Reagan. She privately called him a "Horlicks"—that is, a boring old man—and said Nancy had come to London only to get her picture taken with members of the royal family. She was determined not to cooperate with that goal.

That didn't stop Diana, no stranger to staging photographs herself, from attending a dinner in her honor on November 9, 1985, at the White

House, hosted by Nancy. The first lady engineered Princess Di's dance with actor John Travolta. That photo would be iconic—for the glamour of the Reagan White House, the beauty of the princess, the heartbreak that was down the road.

AFTER REAGAN LEFT THE WHITE HOUSE IN 1989, HE AND ELIZABETH REmained friends and correspondents. In 1990, he wrote her an emotional condolence letter. His distinctive cramped handwriting filled the front and back of his formal stationery, the eagle from the presidential seal engraved at the crest.

"Your Majesty," he began.

"I have just learned of the death of your favorite horse and know what a painful loss that can be," he said. Burmese, the gift of the Royal Canadian Mounted Police, had died at age twenty-eight. She was the Queen's favorite mount, the one she had chosen for their ride in Windsor Park. "We have something in common," Reagan went on. "I first had to have my black thoroughbred Kelley put down because of an injury. Like yours he was a gift to me from the Northwest Mounted Police in Canada and I miss him very much. So far I have not found a replacement."

For eighteen years, she had ridden Burmese in the annual Trooping the Colour ceremony. In 1981, when a teenage gunman in the crowd fired six shots at the Queen—blanks, as it turned out—the mare had startled but then steadied. They completed the ride as if nothing was amiss, burnishing the reputation of both horse and rider for being imperturbable. When Burmese was put out to pasture in 1987, Elizabeth decided to ride in a horse-drawn carriage and review the troops from a dais rather than train a new horse.

"Well please know that Nancy and I are thinking of you and offer you our deepest sympathy and every good wish," Reagan said. "We hope a replacement for your loss can soon take his place. I'm still hoping the same for myself.

"Warmest regard—Ronald Reagan"

A few days later, the Queen's reply was equally heartfelt.

"Dear Mr. Reagan," she wrote in her loopy hand on cream-colored stationery with the red emblem of Windsor Castle. "How very kind of you to write me that note of sympathy after the loss of poor old Burmese.

"I returned from Canada on the Monday and twice saw her playing happily in her field with her young companions as I walked my dogs that evening. The groom found her unable to get up the next morning and the vet said she'd had a heart attack. She was 28 so she had a long life for a horse." She commiserated with the former president over his loss, too. "I'm sorry to hear you also have lost your R.C.M.P. [Royal Canadian Mounted Police]. I have still got the one you rode when you were here! A very good Troop horse too.

"All good wishes to you and Mrs. Reagan.

"Elizabeth R"

Reagan's home was filled with memorabilia from their visits. After the Reagan Presidential Library was opened in Simi Valley, the apartment built for the Reagans' use would feature more silver-framed photographs of the royal family than it did of Reagan's four children.

Ten

The Talking Hat

Saturday, May 11, 1991—The Oval Office

Queen Elizabeth hadn't made a formal state visit to Washington since the Bicentennial celebration in 1976, though in 1983 she had dined with Ronald Reagan at a Hollywood version of a state dinner during her trip up the West Coast aboard *Britannia*. His successor, George H. W. Bush, had been instantly enthusiastic when the British broached the idea of her return. Joseph Verner Reed, the president's chief of protocol, told him she was amenable to making a state visit. "Absolutely," Bush said. "Make her the star for May."

By then, both would be riding high in the wake of the latest wartime alliance between the United States and the United Kingdom. The president was basking in worldwide praise and record approval ratings after leading a short and successful campaign to expel Iraqi forces from Kuwait. By now, the Queen was in such command of her soft power that even Soviet leader Mikhail Gorbachev was willing to bend to her rules if it meant an invitation to her castle. But both Bush and the Queen would welcome a boost. For her, trouble was brewing with the behavior and misbehavior of the next generation of royals, and his glide to reelection would soon encounter disastrous turbulence.

In London, there was hope that seeing the Queen engaged in the pomp and pageantry of an official visit—squired by a polite, patrician, and popular president—would remind her people of what majesty could mean. The acerbic British American author Christopher Hitchens called her US visit "a holiday from the cares and trials that increasingly beset her court in London, where each week brings rumors of marital stress, of tension over the succession, even of abdication." The Windsors "are beginning to fray," he said. A *Washington Post* story welcomed Elizabeth to town with a bit of rude doggerel: "The Queen's a frump, Chuck's a chump, Fergie's plump and her Dad's a cad," the story began. Perhaps the tour and its hoopla would push her family's dysfunction from the spotlight in favor of her own undiminished appeal to Americans.

In Washington, three days before her arrival, Bush was struggling unhappily with remarks White House speechwriters had drafted for him. "The tree speech and the arrival are fine," he tapped out on his typewriter, his message laced with typos and creative punctuation. ("The tree speech" referred to the comments he would make when Elizabeth planted a new small-leaved linden to replace one Franklin Roosevelt had put on the South Lawn in 1937 to commemorate the coronation of her father, King George VI; it had been blown down in a storm a year earlier.) Bush had never been an orator, especially compared to his charismatic predecessor, who after all had gotten his start as an actor. That Saturday morning, Bush was worried that the words written for him to deliver at a White House luncheon and two formal dinners were, well, boring.

"Is there any way to get something more anecdotal or personal in the toast at the White House. Any humor"? he asked. "[A]nything she likes to do. I know she loves thoroughbred horses." Then he posed a more fundamental question. "Does she like humor?" Bush wasn't sure about that, and some of his aides seemed determined to wring out every light touch from the royal occasion. "I'd like the WH toast to be a little more relaxed and personal," he pleaded, signing the note "gb."

The debate over the potential perils of mixing humor and the Crown wasn't new to him. Two years earlier, preparing for his only previous encounter with the Queen, the draft of his toast for a luncheon at Buckingham Palace included a joke, one that seemed unlikely to offend. "May it please Your Majesty: Although today marks our first meeting, the papers have been reporting that we are, in fact, related. My children got all excited. I had to explain that we are actually '13th cousins twice removed.' Apparently, that's like being related through Adam and Eve."

But those lines had been circled in red ink and marked "delete." White House adviser James Pinkerton cautioned about the dire consequences of using such familiar language, however innocent the intent. "The reference to any blood relation between the Queen and the President is more apt to offend than to charm—not only the Royal family, but many British and Americans," he wrote. "The merest suggestion of such a relation, even in the context of self-denigrating humor, is likely to be misconstrued as self-inflation and American pretense to aristocracy. The British, needless to add, take the credentials of the Royal family very seriously."

"I objected to that?" Pinkerton asked when I interviewed him for this book three decades later. "I admit, I've forgotten all that, but that sort of sounds like me."

Thirteenth cousins twice removed? The reference was out. But the connection wasn't hard to believe. George Herbert Walker Bush—of the Greenwich (Connecticut) Bushes; son of a US senator and investment banker; graduate of Greenwich Country Day School and Phillips Academy—was the bluest-blood president since FDR. That distinction was one he did more to hide than highlight. It was only partially obscured by his decision as a young man to transplant to Texas and transform into an oilman who favored country music, pork rinds, and the game of horseshoes. Perhaps that's why he sometimes came across as uncomfortable in his own skin and awkward in his speeches. As Texas Governor Ann Richards memorably cracked in the keynote address at the 1988 Democratic National Convention: "Poor George, he can't help it. He was born with a silver foot in his mouth."

Bush's luncheon toast in 1989 also had this: "The last time we broke bread with Prince Philip was at a Texas cook-out at the Vice Presidential residence, a meal that surely had been outdone this afternoon." Bush had written in the margin: "Does one 'break bread' with Royalty?"

"Break bread?" Apparently, royalty does break bread; the comment stayed in.

Now, with Her Majesty on her way to Washington, Bush still worried about inadvertently causing an affront, of seeming presumptuous. An early version of his toast for the reciprocal dinner at the British embassy included this: "The past four decades have been salad days both for you and the friendship of our Nations." Bush had circled the words "salad days" with a note, "too colloquial + informal?"

"Salad days"? Perhaps a step too far. It was out.

In the final version of his White House dinner toast, a few lighter words managed to survive and a reference to her love of horses was added, as he had suggested to his speechwriters. "The relationship between America and Great Britain . . . has perhaps never been more special," he began. "We've got a lot of things in common. Americans share the Queen's love of horses. And I often wonder if I'd be standing here today if it weren't for a horse fancier named Paul Revere." That got polite chuckles. He praised the Queen's resilience, on the throne and in daily life. "Rain or shine, your long walks have left even the Secret Service agents panting away," he said, then mentioned his diagnosis, ten days earlier, of atrial fibrillation. "I'm glad that my fibrillating heart was not taxed by a competitive walk-off today."

The president had asked: Does the Queen like humor?

As it turned out, she could handle humor, even the accidental sort—which Bush found out the hard way, in the Incident of the Talking Hat.

THEY GREETED ONE ANOTHER AS FRIENDS WHEN SHE ARRIVED AT THE White House on May 14, 1991. On a brilliant hot day, he introduced her to officials lined up on the South Lawn, among them Vice President Dan Quayle and Army General Colin Powell, then the chair of the Joint Chiefs of Staff and later secretary of state. Hundreds of White House staffers and well-wishers gathered behind ropes, applauding and snapping photos. Among them were the president's daughter Doro and a clutch of his grandchildren.

The program proceeded as planned—at first. The Old Guard, a US Army fife-and-drum corps in uniforms patterned after the American Revolution, played "The British Grenadiers." Howitzers fired a twenty-one-gun salute on the Ellipse. The Marine Band performed "God Save the Queen" and then "The Star-Spangled Banner." Sig Rogich, a former Las Vegas impresario and political ad maker now working with the White House to help stage events, had reversed the traditional position of the podium, to show the Mall and the Washington Monument in the background. The standard view of the White House was "too mundane," he had decided.

The problem with the podium would turn out to have nothing to do with its placement, though. When Bush, who was six feet two, finished delivering his welcoming remarks, he stepped away for Elizabeth. Who was five feet four. The podium had been set for his height, not hers, and the small step tucked under the podium wasn't pulled out—an oversight that would become the subject of a White House blame game. "Of course, one forgets that the president's quite tall," the Queen's lady-in-waiting said later. The Queen agreed. "Well, he's huge, really," she said, speaking from personal experience.

"She's gone!" NBC reporter Jim Miklaszewski shouted from the press stand. "All I got is a talking hat!" That was all any of the photographers could capture. A striped purple-and-white hat with a broad brim, to be precise, perched just above the set of microphones as the sound of the Queen's voice could be heard from the loudspeakers. "The British press were horrified and were like, 'This is going to be a really big deal,'" recalled *New York Times* photographer Doug Mills. Rogich briefly considered rushing the stage to pull out the step, but it was already too late. Bush, standing just behind the Queen on the dais, seemed unaware that anything was awry, but Barbara Bush could see how it looked to the rest of the world. "You literally could not see her face as she spoke, just the hat bobbing up and down," she recorded in her diary that night.

The first lady thought it was funny. The president did not.

"Presidential Gaffe Turns Queen into Talking Hat" was the headline in *The Times* of London. A *Washington Post* columnist asked, "Couldn't they have found a phone book for her to stand on?" One newspaper dubbed her "the Hat of State."

The hilarity over protocol-gone-wrong overshadowed the humor in her opening remarks, a reference to the revolution that had wrested control of the colonies from her ancestor, King George III. "It is fifteen years since our last visit to Washington," she said, "when, with a gallant disregard for history, we shared wholeheartedly in the celebrations of the 200th anniversary of the founding of this great nation."

Bush was embarrassed and angry about the misstep over the missed step. Afterward, he confronted Reed. "You were supposed to pull it out," Bush told the protocol chief. Reed retorted, "You were supposed to pull it out." That was an impolitic response to the president, to be sure, but two

White House aides told me it was an accurate one. "I don't know who missed it in the protocol briefing, but he forgot to pull it out and nobody told her it existed," Bobbie Kilberg, a senior White House aide, said.

Bush wasn't ready to accept responsibility. "You better go and explain to Her Majesty that it was your fault," he ordered Reed. The staffer hurried across Pennsylvania Avenue to Blair House, the government guest house where the royal couple was staying. "She was very understanding, dismissing the incident and deeming it all quite funny," said White House aide Roman Popadiuk, who talked to Reed afterward. "Her husband, the Duke of Edinburgh, however, was more taciturn and proper and was not amused."

The next day, the president was still fuming.

"How come you didn't take out the step for the Queen, Mr. President?" a reporter asked him.

"That's what we hired Joseph Reed for," he replied.

Reed eventually crafted a rejoinder. He said he wanted the world to see the Queen's "beautiful" hat.

Perhaps it was never a good idea to assign this task to the president, who would have other things on his mind. From then on, in his administration and future ones, someone else would be assigned the pull-out-the-step responsibility. What's more, Bush was under the weather. The discovery of his abnormal heartbeat had been followed a few days later by a diagnosis of Graves' disease, a thyroid disorder. Always lean, he had lost thirty pounds, and his legendary energy was flagging.

His son, George W. Bush, who had flown to Washington from Texas to attend the state dinner, was struck by the change in his father's appearance. He told author Mark Updegrove that he had never seen his father look old before. It was an early warning sign of a weariness, physical and political, that would undermine the elder Bush's bid for a second term a year later.

Behind the scenes, the younger Bush witnessed the president's consternation. "It was one of the greatest faux pas in the US history of protocol," George W. Bush pronounced with what might have been a bit of hyperbole. "I remember my dad being furious. He just couldn't believe it. The good thing was it was not a slight on Her Majesty. It was a slight on the protocol. And she handled it well." The president took her to see the horseshoe pit he had installed in a nook of the South Lawn. When she tried throwing a horseshoe under his direction, she made a joke about her hat. "She had quite a sense of humor," said Kilberg, who was there. "She realized that she looked like an idiot. But he was mortified by that." In the space of ten minutes, she said, "he must have apologized forty-five times."

The Queen presented Bush with four silver horseshoes marked E II R, for Elizabeth Regina the Second. Bush judged them too precious to throw and instead demonstrated his horseshoes expertise with one of his own. He missed the stake by a mile.

Two days later, she would become the first British monarch to address a Joint Session of Congress. Her script had long been written, edited, and vetted by the prime minister's office. But aide Robert Fellowes and British ambassador Antony Acland had an idea. "Her Private Secretary and I said it would be excellent if she could start her speech with a very simple joke," Acland said. "She was somewhat reluctant to do this. She said she wasn't in the habit of making jokes in her speeches." Whether to say that new first line was the subject of discussion for at least three hours—"The whole morning," US Ambassador Raymond Seitz said. "'Should I do it? Shouldn't I do it?' The last thing she wanted was to say something that would be a lead balloon, not a joke."

The thrust of her speech was serious business, and the House chamber was full, although Massachusetts Representative Joseph P. Kennedy II and some others boycotted to protest the British presence in Northern Ireland.

But she set a light tone with her new opening line. "I do hope you can see me today from where you are," she had begun, her delivery deadpan. That prompted a roar of laughter and a standing ovation, just twelve words into her speech.

Does she like humor?

Why, yes. Even if she only occasionally showed it in public.

BUSH AND THE QUEEN WERE IN SOME WAYS A MATCHED SET. THEY WERE close in age; he was just two years her senior. (Among presidents, only Carter was closer, by four months.) Like Prince Philip, Bush fought for his nation's navy during World War II. Both Bush and Elizabeth had raised big families; she had four children and he had six. The Bushes came from backgrounds of privilege; his father was a US senator and Barbara's ancestors had arrived on the *Mayflower*.

But Bush never had the ease with the Queen that marked Reagan's relationship with her, the closest of any president. And with his proper nature, Bush never had the teasing exchanges that she had later with his puckish son, George W. Bush, who didn't fret about the prospect of a little humor.

The Windsors and the Bushes did share a love of dogs. Elizabeth was devoted to her collection of corgis, Barbara Bush to her English springer spaniel named Millie.

At the 1989 luncheon at Buckingham Palace, Barbara Bush had been chatting with the Queen, who had just returned from a private visit with Will and Sarah Farish at their horse farm in Kentucky. Farish was a friend of both the Queen and the Bushes; George W. Bush would appoint him as the US ambassador to the Court of St. James's. In March, Millie had given birth to a litter of six, and Barbara had given the second pup, named Pickles, to the Farishes. "I asked her if she had seen my little puppy," Barbara wrote in her diary. "She said rather cooly that we'd talk about that later, and I thought, 'Oh my, you are not supposed to ask the Queen a direct question or something.'" Chagrined, she let the moment pass. After lunch, Elizabeth took the Bushes to a table of gifts, presenting them with formal photographs of her and of Philip in silver frames—the standard royal remembrance.

Then she gave Barbara another photo, this one in a leather frame and inscribed. It showed Her Majesty with Pickles. "I was so thrilled that I almost cried," the first lady said. "There was our sweet little puppy. She looked so big. Nothing could have made me happier."

The more consequential connection came a year later, forged by war.

The Queen had paid close attention to Operation Desert Storm. Prime Minister Margaret Thatcher had been a driving force for international action after Iraq invaded Kuwait in August 1990. "This is no time to go wobbly," she had memorably urged Bush. So was John Major when he succeeded her in December. Elizabeth requested a series of briefings from the military, in addition to the written updates she received as a matter of course every day. Through her private secretary, she kept in touch with the prime ministers and the foreign secretary.

On the day the ground campaign by coalition forces began, on February 24, 1991, she delivered the first special televised address of her thirty-nine-year reign.

"As a nation, we are rightly proud of our armed forces," she began, a solemn figure in a green silk dress, seated behind a desk in Buckingham Palace. "That pride has been fully justified by their conduct in the Gulf War so far. As they with our allies face a fresh and sterner challenge, I hope we can unite in prayer that their success will be as swift as it is certain, and that it may be achieved with as small a cost in human life and suffering as possible. Then may the true reward of their courage be granted: A just and lasting peace."

In just one hundred hours, Iraqi forces retreated. The war was won.

That summer, at the G7 summit in London, the Queen hosted foreign leaders at Buckingham Palace. A rare video of the event showed the royals out in force—Princess Diana chatting with Norma Major, the wife of the prime minister, while Prince Charles bragged that he had sold lithographs he had made to fund a summer school program he supported. "So at least I feel I've earned it," he said. The Queen chatted in French with French President François Mitterrand, then discussed the Gulf War in English with former Prime Minister Edward Heath and US Secretary of State James Baker. Heath noted that he'd gone to Baghdad and warned Iraqi leaders against going to war. Now he heard they wished they had taken his advice. "Well, [Baker] couldn't go to Baghdad like you," she declared. "You're expendable!"

THREE MONTHS LATER, SHE ARRIVED IN WASHINGTON.

The trip had been in the works before Saddam had ordered his troops to invade Kuwait, of course, but the quick allied victory provided a fresh energy and an historic framework for her visit. In the capital, she spoke not only to a Joint Session of Congress but also to the Metropolitan Police Boys and Girls Club. She hosted a sprawling garden party at the British embassy for eighteen hundred people—"most of them straining for just one glimpse," as British broadcaster ITV later reported. There were plans for her to visit a resident of a new public-housing project. When the British and American advance teams toured the site, they cautioned Alice Frazier,

President Franklin D. Roosevelt, at right, with King George VI and Queen Elizabeth, the parents of Queen Elizabeth II, at Hyde Park in 1939. Eleanor Roosevelt is at left and Sara Roosevelt in the center.

Courtesy of Franklin D. Roosevelt Presidential Library

Above: President Harry Truman and Princess Elizabeth in a presidential limousine in 1951, leaving Washington National Airport for Blair House.

Arthur Marasco, US Army Signal Corps; Harry S. Truman Library & Museum

Right: The motorcade taking Queen Elizabeth II up Pennsylvania Avenue to the White House in 1957.

Photo by Popperfoto via Getty Images

President Dwight Eisenhower and Queen Elizabeth at Balmoral Castle in 1959. They are flanked by Princess Anne and Prince Charles.
AP Photo, File

President John F. Kennedy and Jackie Kennedy with Queen Elizabeth and Prince Philip at Buckingham Palace in 1961.
Bettmann via Getty Images

President Lyndon Johnson and Princess Margaret at the White House in 1965.

Photo by Mark Kauffman via Getty Images

Above: Queen Elizabeth and Prince Philip with Jackie Kennedy and her children, John Jr. and Caroline, at the dedication of Britain's Kennedy Memorial at Runnymede in 1965. British Ambassador David Ormsby-Gore is next to the Queen.

Photo by Hulton Archive via Getty Images

Right: Then–Vice President Richard Nixon and Queen Elizabeth at Thanksgiving dinner in the US embassy residence in London in 1958.

Richard Nixon Presidential Library & Museum

President Gerald Ford and Queen Elizabeth at the White House in 1976.
Gerald R. Ford Presidential Library

President Jimmy Carter with Queen Elizabeth, Prince Philip, and the Queen Mother at Buckingham Palace in 1977. Italian Prime Minister Giulio Andreotti is to the right.
Press Association via AP Images

President Ronald Reagan and Queen Elizabeth at Windsor Castle in 1982.
Courtesy Ronald Reagan Presidential Library

President Reagan and Queen Elizabeth at a dinner at the M. H. de Young Memorial Museum in San Francisco in 1983. They are flanked by Secretary of State George Shultz and Helena Shultz.
Courtesy Ronald Reagan Presidential Library

Above: President George H. W. Bush and Queen Elizabeth on the South Lawn of the White House in 1991, an arrival ceremony that became known as the Talking Hat.

Arnie Sachs/CNP via Getty Images

Left: President Bill Clinton and Hillary Clinton with Queen Elizabeth at Buckingham Palace in 2000.

PA Wire, Press Association via AP Images

President George W. Bush and Queen Elizabeth at an arrival ceremony on the South Lawn of the White House in 2007.

Martin H. Simon/ picture-alliance/dpa/AP Images

President Barack Obama and Michelle Obama with Queen Elizabeth and Prince Phillip at Windsor Castle in 2016.

AP Photo/Alastair Grant Pool

Prince William, Michelle Obama, and President Obama with Prince George at Kensington Palace in 2016.

Pete Souza/The White House via Getty Images

President Donald Trump and Queen Elizabeth at Windsor Castle in 2018.

Richard Pohle/Pool Photo via AP

Above: President Donald Trump and Queen Elizabeth at Buckingham Palace in 2019.

Dominic Lipinski/PA Wire, Press Association via AP Images

Right: President Joe Biden and Jill Biden with Queen Elizabeth at Windsor Castle in 2021.

Steve Parsons/Pool via AP

whose three-bedroom apartment the Queen would see, that she was under no circumstances to touch Her Majesty. The instructions were received as "smooth as silk," Anna Perez, Barbara Bush's press secretary, recalled. "Mrs. Frazier did not say a word."

But when the official entourage arrived, the sixty-seven-year-old great-grandmother engulfed the Queen in the sort of bear hug that is strictly forbidden with monarchs. Elizabeth gave a game smile, though she didn't hug back. "She was a little startled," Perez said, "but she reacted fine."

"They said I wasn't supposed to do it but I just couldn't stop myself," Frazier told reporters after the officials had left. "She has her palace, but I have my palace right here, and I'm proud of it." She felt a certain kinship with Her Majesty. "Shoot, she's a woman just like I am. If she didn't have that crown on, she'd be just like me." (For the record, the monarch wasn't actually wearing a crown for the visit; she was sporting a maize-colored hat that matched her patterned suit. Barbara Bush had no headwear at all. "All the Brits had on their hats and gloves," she said afterward. "I didn't own a hat, but I did wear my gloves.")

The British ambassador insisted there was no royal offense at the breach in protocol. "One didn't want to make a fuss about it," Acland insisted. But the US ambassador to the United Kingdom noted how rare such an embrace was, and how thoroughly American. "In the US, this was great; it was warm, it was nice, there was nothing phoney about it at all," Seitz said. "In Britain one just does not *do* that!"

Elizabeth also attended her first Major League Baseball game—a "baseball match," as she put it. "The Queen and The Duke of Edinburgh have received a copy of the rules of the game," Sig Rogich reported beforehand. She was accompanied by Bush, first baseman and captain of his team at Yale. They sat in the owner's box at the fading Baltimore Memorial Stadium as the Orioles hosted the Oakland Athletics. (The A's won, 6–3, not that the royal couple was there to see it; they left after the second inning.) Behind the scenes, FBI officials had raised concerns about potential protests by Irish groups. A letter had been published in a Philadelphia Irish newspaper alerting readers that she was going to attend, and one group had reserved a sizable block of seats. Video footage of the event showed a few protesters in the bleachers holding signs with messages like "England Out of Ireland." But the situation was deemed safe enough for the Queen to go out on the field to greet the players, albeit with a bulletproof shield erected beside the dugouts. More than thirty thousand fans gave her a standing ovation.

In three days, she made eighteen appearances, from the sporting to the serious. She took in a performance of *King Lear* at the Folger Shakespeare Theatre. At Blair House, where she was staying, Benedicte Valentiner, the general manager of the government guest quarters, got a behind-the-scenes glimpse of how the Queen readied herself. "She sometimes came down before anyone else, and I would find myself alone with her," Valentiner remembered. "She would stand in the front hall quietly, completely at ease with herself, I think looking inward." She didn't invite conversation. Valentiner said she would "jump out of the way, so to speak, looking like a palm tree," so as not to intrude on a moment as Her Majesty silently prepared for the day.

After Washington, she would become the first British monarch to visit Texas, including a stop at the LBJ Library. Lyndon Johnson was the only president during her reign she didn't meet while he was in office, but now she sat down for martinis in the Johnsons' private apartment with his widow, Lady Bird. They were joined by her daughters, Lynda Bird Robb and Luci Baines Johnson, as well as Governor Richards. "Prince Phillip was over here on this sofa; the Queen was over here," Luci said, pointing around the room and describing a visit she said had put the entire state of Texas "on a high."

Elizabeth had already made a stop in Florida, her first visit to that state. The royal yacht had sailed to meet her in Miami, where she was hosting a formal dinner for former Presidents Reagan and Ford. The White House had to intervene to keep the dinner on track. While docked in Miami, *Britannia*'s crew had flushed the ship's lavatories—a violation of Miami Port Authority rules that brought a protest from the authority's chief. "He said we had polluted his harbour, that we were fined ten thousand dollars and that we had to leave in two hours," the ship's captain, Rear Admiral Robert Woodard, said. Only after a call from the White House were they permitted to stay.

While in Florida, she made a special stop to pay tribute to the military alliance between the two nations. Visiting the US Central Command headquarters at MacDill Air Force Base, she met with General Norman

Schwarzkopf, commander of the coalition forces in the Gulf War, and presented him the badge of a Knight Commander of the Order of the Bath. He was the ninth American military officer to receive an honorary knighthood from a British sovereign.

In Miami, Elizabeth also stopped by the Coconut Grove Elementary School. "The boys were told to bow, the girls were told to curtsy, and we were told not to speak to her," Uriah Goldfinger, then twelve years old, recalled three decades later. But in that cheeky American way, like Alice Frazier in Baltimore, he couldn't let the opportunity pass. "How long have you been queen?" he asked. "Too long," she replied. "Wait and read about it in your history books."

The quip prompted speculation that the sixty-five-year-old monarch might be signaling she was ready to retire. "Probably not but, well, you never know," the *Evening Standard* correspondent covering the trip wrote in a column headlined, "The Pathos of Being Queen." The palace had to put out reassurances. No, they said. She was staying. She had been making a joke.

PRESIDENT BUSH AND QUEEN ELIZABETH WERE MEETING AT A TIME OF global transformation: The Soviet Union was collapsing, the Cold War over. Both would play a part in that.

When Bush won the White House in 1988, his victory was seen by some as a sort of third term for Reagan. Not since Franklin Roosevelt's long grip on American politics, then Harry Truman's election, had a party managed to hold the White House for as many as three elections in a row, but Reagan's popularity was soaring amid economic contentment and relief over the end of the Cold War. It would fall to his former vice president to manage the aftermath, including seven meetings with Gorbachev as they negotiated landmark limits on nuclear weapons.

The British had played a crucial role in winning the Cold War, too. Thatcher—dubbed "the Iron Lady" by the Soviets—had been among the first to identify Gorbachev as a reformer the West could do business with, as she put it. Now, as part of her efforts to help forge and manage a new era, Thatcher prepared to greet Gorbachev in London in April 1989.

Her Majesty made an important addition to the geopolitical equation, conferring legitimacy on the Soviet leader at a crucial moment. She did that by inviting him to lunch.

A problem of apparently global proportions erupted, though, one that demonstrated how much the Queen's "soft power" could be worth. A foreign policy aide to Thatcher, Charles David Powell, reported that "people in Moscow were alarmed to hear that the lunch with the Queen would be at Windsor Castle rather than Buckingham Palace," as had originally been agreed. "This was seen in some quarters as a down-grading of the visit" because Moscow TV viewers were more familiar with images of the palace.

Considering the enormous size and fabled history of Windsor Castle, one of the Queen's favorite residences, Powell dismissed the concerns as absurd. "I urged [the Russians] not to make an issue of this," he said, pointing out to them that Reagan and Nikita Khrushchev had been happily welcomed to the castle in the past. The Russians continued to bring it up anyway, making "very heavy weather" about it—British parlance for making something more difficult and complicated than it needs to be. Since the days of Lenin and Stalin, the Soviet Empire was centered on a projection of power and influence. Gorbachev's emissaries worried how the Soviet public would respond to their leader being received by the most famous woman in the world in what a Russian official referred to as "a suburban castle." The Soviets equated having the luncheon at Windsor with Gorbachev receiving the Queen at a dacha rather than the Kremlin. (They were, however, delighted by the suggestion that Princess Margaret offer Raisa Gorbachev a private tour of the Royal Dress Collection at Kensington Palace.) The British called the Soviet protests "crude bullying tactics." But they had threats of their own. They informed Moscow that continued persistence on this matter would be "ill-received." There was no need to say by whom.

The "unfortunate Windsor castle complication," as one British official diplomatically described it, threatened to unravel the entire visit. In a flurry of confidential communications, the Queen made it clear she would not be moving from her castle to her palace to accommodate the Soviets. It was Gorbachev who caved—one more sign of how powerful her imprimatur could be.

WHAT DIFFERENCE DID THE QUEEN'S TRIP TO THE UNITED STATES MAKE?

In his report to London, Ambassador Acland detailed the photos that had been published in newspapers, the crowds that gathered along the way, the gifts that had been presented, the personal relationships that had been burnished. It was a wide-ranging essay by the veteran diplomat on the value of sending Elizabeth to America, this time and all the others.

"It would be wrong... to pretend that many more Sterling motor cars, or holidays in Britain, or contracts at Lloyds of London will immediately be sold as a result, although I would guess that some will be," he wrote, describing the value as broader and more subtle. "For me, the success of the visit can be simply put: it reminded millions of people in both the United States and Britain that our two countries are, and remain, the best of friends."

Under "problems," he wrote: "We were lucky that there were no major disasters during the visit, and, although occasionally we seemed to be skating on thin ice, somehow we always managed to reach the side in time." The ambassador addressed one of those close calls. "Some of the mistakes, such as the President forgetting to pull out the step for The Queen to stand on during the White House Arrival Ceremony, probably could not reasonably have been foreseen or prevented."

Translation: The Talking Hat was not his fault.

BY THE FOLLOWING YEAR, BUSH HAD HIS PROBLEMS. ONCE CONSIDERED A sure bet for a second term, he found himself trailing both Democrat Bill Clinton and third-party hopeful H. Ross Perot. The citizenry that had hailed him as a foreign policy hero was now more interested in a president who promised to focus "like a laser" on the economy and their kitchen-table issues.

The Queen had her problems, too.

In March, son Andrew announced his separation from Sarah Ferguson; before the end of summer Fergie was caught by a paparazzo as she sunbathed topless in St. Tropez while American financial adviser John Bryan sucked her toes. In April, Princess Anne was divorced from Mark Phillips. In June, the bombshell *Diana: Her True Story* was published, with its insider account of royal family dysfunction; Prince Charles and

Princess Diana would announce their separation six months later. As his marriage was disintegrating, Charles turned to Nancy Reagan for consolation, telling the former first lady that his marriage was "a Greek tragedy." "One day, I'll tell you the whole story . . . ," he promised her. "It's so awful. Very few people would believe it."

And in November, a devastating fire broke out in Windsor Castle, destroying one hundred and fifteen rooms, including Queen Victoria's Private Chapel and St. George's Hall. (The oldest and largest inhabited castle in the world, it has more than a thousand rooms in all.) The restoration would take five years and cost 36.5 million pounds, more than 42 million dollars.

The costs for the Queen from the year were more than financial. The "Squidgygate Tapes" and "Camillagate"—leaked phone conversations between Diana and Charles to their lovers—became tabloid fodder that overshadowed whatever royal good works were underway to mark her fortieth year on the throne. The scandalous headlines raised questions about just how good a mother she had been, raising children so entitled, so prone to misbehavior. For some British taxpayers, it eroded support for the monarchy itself.

"Nineteen ninety-two is not a year on which I shall look back with undiluted pleasure," Elizabeth said with British understatement four days after the fire, in a speech at the Guildhall marking her Ruby Jubilee. "In the words of one of my more sympathetic correspondents, it has turned out to be an *annus horribilis*."

It was not a year George Bush would look back on with undiluted pleasure, either.

JOHN MAJOR HAD A STORE OF RESPECT AND AFFECTION FOR BUSH, WHO had helped bring the Cold War to a peaceful conclusion, then marshaled an international coalition to expel Iraqi forces from Kuwait. They overlapped in power for about two years, from Major's election in November 1990 to Bush's departure from the White House in January 1993. Both succeeded more charismatic figures from their own parties, Margaret Thatcher and Ronald Reagan. They shared an instinct for moderation, though each was willing to wage the most hard-fought of campaigns.

As Bush battled for reelection in 1992, Major and some other allied leaders harbored a certain suspicion toward Clinton, the baby boomer governor of Arkansas who had dodged the Vietnam-era draft and faced allegations of extramarital affairs. His experience in foreign affairs was limited, and on the issue of conflict in Northern Ireland, of central import to the British, Clinton's stance seemed to them uncertain, even unmoored.

While Clinton's foreign policy advisers assured British officials he would be "extremely cautious" about intervening in Northern Ireland, a step that influential Irish American political leaders were urging, the Foreign Office wasn't convinced. The candidate's public comments left the door open to what they saw as American meddling in home affairs. "[I]t is extremely irritating that Clinton has felt it necessary to pander in this way to Irish American voters despite our efforts to lobby him towards a more sensible course," Jonathan Powell, the British diplomat assigned to track the Clinton campaign, grumbled in a private memo a month before the election.

That helps explain why British officials were interested in doing what they could to boost Bush's reelection bid, despite the stated tradition of staying out of the other side's domestic politics. In early 1992, Bush had privately assured Major he would avoid doing anything that might complicate Major's campaign; his Conservative Party would come from behind to win a fourth consecutive election that April. "Obviously we're rooting for you, and it's very important that you win," Bush told Major in the campaign's final weeks. Major sent a similar private message to Bush a few months later, when the president was campaigning for his own reelection. In August, when James Baker reluctantly left the State Department to become White House chief of staff, an effort to revive Bush's lagging campaign, the prime minister wrote an encouraging note that left no doubt where he stood. "If you think you are swapping international preoccupations for domestic, you are in one important sense mistaken: a great deal rides on your success for all of us," Major told Baker.

Some of the help from across the Atlantic was less discreet. Eight weeks before Election Day, the Bush campaign invited two strategists from Major's campaign to bring their blueprint for victory in a campaign by an embattled incumbent at a time of economic weakness, facing an electorate that was hungry for change. Brandishing charts and surveys, they advised obliterating the opponent with personal attacks—that is, obliterating Clinton.

Worst of all, the Home Office in October had rifled through its files in search of embarrassing disclosures on Clinton. There were rumors, never backed up by evidence, that as a Rhodes Scholar at Oxford in the 1960s Clinton had inquired about obtaining British citizenship to avoid being drafted. In Washington, State Department officials wanted to search Clinton's passport records on a parallel mission, to see whether he had ever explored renouncing his American citizenship. Their actions, when exposed, would prompt a special counsel's investigation that lasted three years before concluding that the Bush administration officials had been "stupid, dumb and partisan" but not criminal.

British officials told reporters that their "comprehensive" check of their files was conducted out of "sheer helpfulness" to the news media. At the embassy in Washington, Peter Westmacott called it "a misunderstanding," which in diplomatese wasn't exactly a denial. "But the impression was given to some in the Clinton campaign that the Conservative government had been more helpful than necessary to those seeking to dig dirt," he acknowledged.

More helpful than necessary.

Indeed, "some" in the Clinton campaign included the candidate.

On the day before Clinton's inauguration, Major had sent the new president an appropriate congratulatory message, offering him "heartfelt good wishes." The letter Major sent Bush that day was considerably more effusive, saying the outgoing president "embodied all that is best in human and political values." With his departure from the White House, he said, "I am sure there will be pain in your hearts, as there certainly will be in ours."

Bush had not survived the transition from Cold War commander to an evolving era with a new generation of leaders—notably Clinton in the United States and Tony Blair in the United Kingdom. While the Queen wasn't subject to the vagaries of election campaigns, there would be challenges for her in the changing world as well.

Princess Di would be one of those challenges, and her tragic death one that the Queen stumbled on before she recovered her footing. Bill Clinton in the White House would be a challenge, too.

Eleven

Hard Feelings

Tuesday, November 30, 1993—Buckingham Palace

B ill Clinton was the new president, but it was George H. W. Bush who was being greeted by the Queen.

It was just the latest in a string of ticklish moments as the Anglo-American alliance adjusted to the Clinton years. He was preparing to make his first presidential trip to Europe while the predecessor he had ousted was being knighted. The timing was "not ideal," a Foreign Office memo acknowledged. "But there is little we can do about it now." They would have to "make certain that the White House are kept informed of plans for former president George H.W. Bush well in advance so they are not unpleasantly surprised nearer the time on the juxtaposition" with Clinton's own visit.

Bush was in London at the invitation of the ARCO Corporation, delivering one of those private speeches that contribute to the prosperity of former presidents. Her Majesty invited him to lunch at Buckingham Palace to recognize his leadership in the first Gulf War. She made him an Honorary Knight Grand Cross of the Order of the Bath, the highest order of chivalry the United Kingdom government can award.* During her long

---

* The imposing ornate medal—a Maltese cross on top of an eight-pointed star, with three crowns in the center flanked by laurel branches—would be displayed at the George Bush Presidential Library and Museum, then being planned on the campus of Texas A&M University.

reign, Elizabeth would present the honor to only one other US president, Ronald Reagan. Why the Queen gave such a singular honor to Reagan was clear enough—he was her closest friend among all the presidents as well as an important ally. But Bush was a favorite of her prime minister, John Major, and the Queen herself seemed puzzled by his resounding election defeat to a small-state governor enmeshed in a string of scandals. She thought Bush was a good man who tried hard, and despite his occasional awkwardness, she had grown to like him, too.

Clinton would come around to a similar view about the elder Bush, but in 1993 the relationship between the forty-first and forty-second presidents was frosty at best. During the 1992 campaign, Clinton had depicted Bush as an elitist who was indifferent to the struggles of the middle class; Bush had labeled Clinton a "bozo," attacked his character, and questioned, darkly, his youthful trip to Moscow. On leaving office, Bush had promised not to criticize his successor for a year, but he then joined critiques of Clinton's actions in Somalia, Bosnia, and Haiti. A briefing paper for the Queen sent the day before the palace luncheon detailed those controversies and also mentioned the next Bush generation. "Other members of President Bush's family are hoping to enter politics," it noted without assessing their prospects. "His eldest son, George W. Bush, announced on 8 November that he would run for Governor of Texas next year and Jed Bush, his second son, also announced his candidature for Governor of Florida." The name of Jeb Bush was misspelled, perhaps a sign of how attention already had turned from the former president to the current one.

The Queen had good reason to be anxious about spotlighting their ties to a president who was no longer in power. "We will need to be braced for a resurgence of the 'Brits back Bush' story during his visit to the UK, given the high level at which he will be feted," Westmacott warned.

Clinton himself needed no reminder. He had never forgotten that the British government had tried to help reelect his opponent.

THE NEW PRESIDENT INSISTED THAT THE BRITISH MEDDLING IN THE 1992 campaign didn't affect his actions in office, although the coolness toward Prime Minister John Major would linger. In 1995, when Major was visiting the United States and invited the president to a dinner at the British ambassador's residence—an invitation a president would have customarily accepted—he declined. "Billy has regretted the invitation to POTUS for dinner wioth [sic] Major at the British Ambassador's," National Security Council staffer Andrew D. Sens wrote in an email, found tucked in a file at the Clinton Presidential Library in Little Rock. Then he asked: "Who tells the British?"

When I interviewed Clinton three decades later, he professed to have long forgiven the election intrusion.

"I was actually happy he [Major] did it because I knew it meant the campaign was wasting time on something where there was no there, there," he recalled with a dispassionate tone he likely didn't have at the time. But he also hadn't been dismayed that the British were concerned whether there might be repercussions. "After the election, the British press fretted that the special relationship between our two countries had been damaged by this unusual British involvement in American politics," he wrote in his memoir. "I was determined that there would be no damage, but I wanted the Tories to worry about it for a while."

After their first meeting at the White House, in February 1993, Clinton and Major were scheduled to hold a joint news conference. Clinton's briefing paper beforehand, listing suggested responses to likely questions, included one about the British search of its files: "Doesn't the Prime Minister owe you an apology?" The two suggested responses didn't answer the question, which was probably the point. "The campaign is over and I am looking toward the future, not the past" was the first. The second: "It has been a matter of interest to the press, not to me. I consider the matter closed."

As it turned out, the first questioner did ask Clinton how he was feeling with the campaign behind him. Ron Fournier of the Associated Press, who had covered Clinton at the Arkansas statehouse before becoming a White House correspondent, didn't mention the British search of Clinton's files. It was the president who raised it, unbidden, in his reply—an unmistakable message to Major, who was standing by his side. "You are a good one to answer that question since you know that, compared to previous campaigns I have been in, this was just sort of another day at the office, and once you achieve the responsibilities of office, that's what you have to do," Clinton said to Fournier. Then he joked: "I told the prime minister today that I was just grateful that I got through this whole campaign with most of my time in England still classified." The reporters in the East Room laughed. So did the prime minister, a bit uncomfortably.

Forgive? Perhaps. Forget? Neither Bill Clinton nor Hillary Clinton would do that.

"John Major had literally rifled through the British Foreign Office looking for anything that could be used against Bill during his time as a Rhodes Scholar in Oxford," Hillary Clinton told me, still indignant. "That was deeply difficult for us to understand, so it took a while to repair the relationship" between the two men.

That's where the Queen stepped in, doing what she had always done to smooth Anglo-American tensions. She had been inviting Clinton to visit her since before his inauguration, sending a telegram on January 18, 1993, congratulating him on taking office and saying she hoped he could visit Britain "in due course." The British floated the idea of a state visit to England a year later, just before the commemoration of the fiftieth anniversary of D-Day. It would have been a clear and public demonstration of how strong the two nations' ties remained. But Clinton told British Ambassador Robin Renwick that he would prefer a shorter first visit to London, something with less ceremony. That may have been a subtle way of letting the Tories fret about the impact of their intrusion in the election. Great Britain wouldn't be the first foreign country the new president visited. It would be the twelfth, after he had traveled to Japan and South Korea and the Czech Republic and Ukraine and Belarus and elsewhere.

The early chill between the Clinton administration and the British government would get colder before it was warmed by the election of a new prime minister more in step with Clinton. The Queen would try to help, too, though she would have some hard feelings of her own.

BILL CLINTON WAS NOT THE SORT OF AMERICAN LEADER FAMILIAR TO THE Queen. He was the leading edge of a new political generation, one that shared less history with Elizabeth than his recent predecessors. When they finally met at the D-Day commemoration on June 4, 1994, he was forty-seven years old and the eighth sitting president she had met as sovereign. But he was the first who hadn't served in uniform during World War II—her most formative experience—or for that matter in any other war. While a bit of an Anglophile from his days at Oxford, he didn't share the sense of enchantment with the royal family that Richard Nixon and Ronald Reagan did. He also was the first president who was younger than she was, by twenty years. Clinton was bright, energetic, and deeply immersed in domestic policy. But during the bitter 1992 campaign, Republicans had portrayed him as a philanderer, a draft dodger, and a general reprobate—a rogue with buttery charm and the sobriquet "Slick Willie." Clinton publicly confessed to causing pain in his marriage, an indirect confirmation of infidelity. These were not characteristics that the ever-proper Elizabeth might easily overlook, even as rumors of her husband's own wandering eye persisted for decades. Clinton also had a reputation for being informal, even sloppy, and routinely late for appointments. Those were traits she would not abide. He also could be a bit of a rambler. Years later, a senior aide to the Queen recalled a meeting between Clinton and Prince Charles. Clinton talked on for so long, according to the account, that Charles pressed a secret button to summon an aide to end the session.

The British weren't impressed by Clinton's opening months in office, according to reports that would typically have been sent to the Foreign Office and the monarch.

"Clinton spent the year struggling to come to grips with his new job," Jonathan Powell, the British diplomat who had tracked Clinton's campaign, wrote in a memo sent on the last day of 1993, Clinton's first year in office. (Powell would later serve as Prime Minister Tony Blair's chief of staff and Prime Minister Keir Starmer's national security adviser.) "It is a big jump from the Arkansas State House to the White House." He credited the president with formidable political skills but little discipline, and a tendency to court disaster. "Clinton's first law of politics still seems to hold: as soon as the President is up in the polls, the White House does something stupid to bring him down again."

On global affairs, he wrote, Clinton had failed at leadership, calling his attempt to come up with a foreign policy doctrine "a damp squib." The president and European leaders had clashed over the response to ethnic violence in Bosnia in the wake of the breakup of Yugoslavia. Then a conflict of deep personal importance to the Queen as well as her government erupted. For the British, it would be the most damaging divide between the two nations since the Suez crisis nearly four decades earlier.

GERRY ADAMS WAS THE LONGTIME LEADER OF SINN FÉIN, THE POLITICAL arm of the Provisional Irish Republican Army, labeled a terrorist organization by Great Britain. In 1994, he was invited to speak at a conference in New York on Northern Ireland sponsored by the National Committee on American Foreign Policy. He needed a US visa to attend.

The United States had set two conditions for allowing his visit, and Adams hadn't met either of them—that he renounce violence and commit to the peace process outlined in the Downing Street Declaration, an agreement reached in December 1993 by Major and Albert Reynolds, leader of the Republic of Ireland. Officials at the State Department, the FBI, and the Justice Department all opposed granting Adams a visa. Raymond Seitz, then the US ambassador to Britain, vigorously opposed it, too. Admiral William J. Crowe, a former chair of the Joint Chiefs of Staff whom Clinton would appoint to succeed Seitz, "thought I was wrong," Clinton said. So did Secretary of State Warren Christopher. "The only real support I had was basically in the White House," from Anthony Lake, Sandy Berger, and Nancy Soderberg on the National Security Council staff.

Massachusetts Senators Edward M. Kennedy and John Kerry, New York Senator Daniel Patrick Moynihan, and other powerful Democrats of Irish descent were pushing for the visa. In a letter to the president, they called it an opportunity to support moderate forces in the IRA at what could be a pivotal point. Delaware Senator Joe Biden also was among those who infuriated Prime Minister Major by lobbying Clinton to approve the visa. Real estate developer Donald Trump attended a $200-a-plate fundraiser at the Essex House hotel for the Friends of Sinn Féin. Clinton recognized the risks of defying London. He posed this question: "Would it do irreparable damage to our relationship with Great Britain?" Damage, to be sure. Would it be irreparable? Would it be worth it?

The president had other considerations in mind, too. "Clinton wanted to do things that were historic," said Leon Panetta, then the White House chief of staff. Forging a peace in Northern Ireland, after a quarter century of violence between Protestants and Catholics known as "The Troubles," would be the stuff of legacy. In his drive to reach a Northern Ireland agreement, Clinton was constantly measuring "how much can be tolerated in which directions," one of his senior national security staffers said. Four years later, with the signing of the Good Friday Agreement that restored self-government to Northern Ireland, Clinton would claim vindication. "A good gamble," he called it then.

But at this moment—when he approved a two-day visa and Adams attended the conference—it wasn't clear whether the gamble would pay off. Outraged British officials warned that the damage to the bilateral relationship would be lasting. *The Sunday Times* in London called it a "shameful decision." The decision was "naive or opportunistic, or both," Seitz said. It "disheartened" the British and got him summoned to 10 Downing Street for a diplomatic dressing-down. "This little debacle also demonstrated that British interests—on a matter of deep importance to Her Majesty's Government and minor importance to the United States—did not weigh heavily in the political scales of the Clinton White House," he said.

Major was so furious that he would refuse to return Clinton's phone call for almost a week—an unprecedented British snub of a US president. For a time, the British government stopped sharing sensitive intelligence information about Northern Ireland with the White House for fear it would find its way to the IRA.

For the Queen, the offense was deeply personal.

That the Americans would do business with the IRA, which had assassinated Lord Mountbatten, the man she called "Uncle Dickie," the one who had orchestrated the crucial meeting with Philip when she was thirteen years old, was difficult for her to bear. Though more than a decade had passed since the murder, the wound was still painful, the loss deeply felt. It didn't help matters that Adams was unapologetic. "What the I.R.A. did to him is what Mountbatten had been doing all his life to other people," Adams, then Sinn Féin's vice president, told *Time* magazine, "and with his war record I don't think he could have objected to dying in what was clearly a war situation." An official IRA statement called the "execution" of Mountbatten "a discriminate act to bring to the attention of the English people the continuing occupation of our country." Those were words Elizabeth would remember.

Three decades later, Hillary Clinton got a glimpse of the depth of the royal family's enduring grief. As secretary of state during the Obama administration, she recalled being seated next to the Duke of Edinburgh at a luncheon during Barack Obama's state visit in 2011. A few days earlier, the royal couple had returned from a groundbreaking trip to Ireland, the first by a reigning British monarch in a century. "Well, that looked like quite a successful visit," Hillary Clinton said to him. "It was a nightmare for me," Philip replied. "I was shaking hands and breaking bread with people who had killed my uncle."

SIX MONTHS AFTER CLINTON APPROVED THE CONTROVERSIAL VISA FOR Adams, he met Her Majesty for the first time. The fiftieth anniversary of D-Day was a poignant reminder of how close ties between their two nations had been, and how much they had mattered.

Clinton arrived at the Royal Air Force Mildenhall base in Suffolk from Rome, where he had met with Italian Prime Minister Silvio Berlusconi and had an audience with Pope John Paul II. He visited the Cambridge American Cemetery and Memorial, where 3,811 American war dead were buried. Major hosted him for lunch at Chequers, the prime minister's country retreat, to discuss Bosnia. Then the Queen convened a grand banquet at the Guildhall in Portsmouth, where many of the Allied troops had sailed from for the invasion.

Whatever her misgivings about Clinton, or perhaps because of them, she went all out for him. It was the largest state dinner of her reign, with fourteen heads of state and another five hundred guests. She made it her business to be close to him on that visit, literally.

"The Queen had been placed next to two European royals," between the King of Norway and Prince Bernhard of the Netherlands, Major recalled. "And President Clinton and President Mitterrand had been placed well below the salt at the other end of the table." The prime minister objected to the seating plan, but the protocol office was unmoved. "The fairly frosty response from an official was that elected presidents were lower in protocol than monarchs!" he said. Finally, Major's private secretary reached out to the Queen's private secretary, who talked to the Queen. She changed the seating, protocol or not.

"Of course, people will expect President Clinton and President Mitterrand to sit beside me," she replied, "and, in any event, I see my cousins all the time." That night, Clinton was seated to her right and the French president, François Mitterrand, to her left. Hillary Clinton, across the table between Philip and Major, watched as Elizabeth charmed her husband. "They had an amazing, lively conversation, with her laughing, him telling stories," Hillary said. The Queen wore a diamond tiara that sparkled in the candlelight.

Bill Clinton recognized both the Queen's range and her restraints. "She wasn't just a bystander," he told me. "She knew what the heck she was doing, and she knew her briefs, and she was very familiar with the complexities of these issues." But while she probed for his views, she never ventured far in expressing her own. At the dinner, he complimented her on her deftness. "Adroit," he called her. She seemed to find the comment patronizing, replying with a crispness that made him laugh at the memory. "Of course I keep my opinions private," she replied. "That's my job. That's what I'm supposed to do." There were a few times when she broke that taboo with American presidents—with Reagan on Grenada and later with Obama on Brexit. And with Clinton when it came to his determined efforts to push for a breakthrough in Northern Ireland.

"She wanted to make sure that I understood, when we were at Portsmouth, I think, how hard this was going to be for them to do what it would take in Northern Ireland," Clinton said. She understood the compromises that would have to be made, the legitimate grievances of the past that would never be fully addressed, including the one closest to her heart. "It was clear to me, without her saying it, that whatever personal feelings she still harbored about the IRA . . . that she wanted to stay with the government" through the peace process. "When she talked, I could tell she got it. Not that she agreed with me, but that she understood completely what was going on."

His message to her: "The only thing I ever said was we all had to take risks for peace. And if we do, it might not work, but if it does, it'll be worth it."

Clinton's itinerary on that trip didn't include a visit to Buckingham

Palace, but the Queen offered another royal reward. The leaders of the other Allied nations would board the royal yacht *Britannia* at Portsmouth for the reenactment of the invasion, reviewing a fleet of international warships and then sailing toward France. The flotilla would include ocean liners carrying World War II veterans.

Only the American president would be invited to stay overnight on *Britannia*.

"Bill's major role in the Northern Ireland peace process, starting with his giving a visa to Gerry Adams—that was explosive, and it was explosive in the British government," Hillary Clinton said. She believed it had "disturbed" the Queen, despite her discipline in diplomatic affairs. "Part of the reason I believe that we were invited for such a special experience to stay on the *Britannia* was in part to smooth over some of the challenges."

Behind the scenes, that sleepover was the subject of months of calculation and diplomatic back-and-forth. Clinton presumably would want to cross the channel on a US ship; the British worried it would be "awkward" if all the other heads of state were aboard *Britannia* and the American president wasn't. The overnight stay could finesse that concern. In December, Renwick queried London, "Would the President be welcome to spend the night of 4 June in Britannia?" Yes, the answer quickly came back from Foreign Secretary Douglas Hurd, an invitation that required the Queen's assent. The next day, Renwick mentioned the possibility to White House counselor David Gergen.

Two months later, a handwritten note on top of the latest British planning document, dated February 7, 1994, said, "Pres. Clinton will now stay overnight on Britannia." But given the general disorder of the Clinton White House, London wasn't confident that was the final word. "The Americans are leaning towards Britannia," a March 8 memo advised. Finally, six weeks before the commemoration, Westmacott reported that the schedule was "firm" and they would be on board.

The Clintons were assigned suites nine and eleven, the best accommodations on the yacht besides the Queen's own. Once again, Elizabeth was reminded of the divide, generational and otherwise, between her and the leader of the free world. In the morning, Clinton went for a run around the dockyard wearing what *Britannia*'s captain disdainfully described as

"DayGlo neoprene things." "He stopped to talk to every dock worker, every crane driver," Sir Robert Woodard sniffed. On his return, the president paused on the gangway to stretch as the ship's company stood at attention. He would be "politely late for breakfast."

Both the president and first lady were struck by Elizabeth's hospitality. "We were in close quarters," Hillary Clinton said. "It was just like being with a family that was having a good time together despite the solemnity of the occasion." She saw "a more playful and somewhat, you know, funny and very incredibly warm side of her as well."

"It was comfortable. It was easy, and there was a lot of kind of relaxed banter," Bill Clinton said. They talked about the historic alliance between the United States and Britain, from the Blitz to the current day. "I loved it. I thought it was a kind thing for her to do, something she didn't have to do, to ask us to stay there that night. And I'm sure it was done in larger measure for symbolic reasons, because of what D-Day meant to both of our countries and how we did it together. But it meant a lot to me, both as president and as a person."

Which, of course, was the point.

PRESIDENT CLINTON'S FIRST ROYAL VISIT ENDED WITH POSITIVE FEELINGS, but they weren't going to last long. The Queen's relationship with the kinetic Arkansan would never be smooth.

In May 1997, Clinton was scheduled to go to Paris for the signing of the NATO-Russia Founding Act, establishing a framework for cooperation with Boris Yeltsin's government, and then to The Hague for an EU summit that commemorated the fiftieth anniversary of the Marshall Plan. More than fifty current and former heads of state would attend. The White House added a stop in London to meet with the new prime minister, Tony Blair, a fresh start after the friction that marked the president's relationship with Major. Clinton and Blair already were close. Both were young, smart, and smooth pols who were charting more centrist courses for their parties. Blair had modeled some of his mottos—"New Labour," for one—on Clinton's political nomenclature. Both had attended Oxford and, by the way, were married to lawyers who had careers in their own right. Both were less in awe of the monarch than their conservative predecessors, and they didn't seem to mind if others knew that.

Elizabeth invited the Clintons to tea while they were in London. The Clintons declined.

To be clear, the Queen was not accustomed to having invitations turned down, no more than presidents were. "The Americans said that the President and Mrs. Clinton were very grateful for HM The Queen's invitation to tea at the Palace, but would wish to decline politely," Philip Barton, Blair's private secretary, reported. Clinton's team had "no clear idea" what the president planned to do instead, but they advised that he "wanted to be a tourist," walking through gardens and visiting shops, then having Indian food with Blair.

The thanks-but-no-thanks response was considered appalling enough that when the files were released by the National Archives in Britain nearly a quarter century later, in 2021, it sparked headlines. The Americans also declined a follow-up suggestion that just Hillary Clinton and Cherie Blair join the Queen for tea. The two women instead spent the afternoon at the Globe Theatre for a performance of William Shakespeare's *Henry V*, the story of an undisciplined young prince who would mature to defeat the French at Agincourt during the Hundred Years' War.

In the end, President Clinton didn't do much sightseeing. At Downing Street, he addressed the British Cabinet, and he and Blair took a few questions from reporters there. They had dinner together with their spouses, but not the Indian food London was famed for, the cuisine the White House had anticipated. Instead, they ate at a fancy French restaurant, Le Pont de la Tour, spending the equivalent of $360 on a meal that included halibut, salmon, sole, and rabbit. The restaurant sent a complimentary bottle of champagne to the table. As they left, other diners in the restaurant clapped and cheered.

The picture of the president and the prime minister dining at a restaurant, not a palace, reinforced the point that they represented a new, younger, less hidebound sort of political leader—part of a world that had less reverence for the monarchy, the epitome of historic and hidebound. At age seventy-one and after forty-five years on the throne, Elizabeth to some seemed a bit old hat.

At the same time, Blair was irritating the Queen by urging the Crown to modernize, including in its finances. At the end of the year, his government followed through on his predecessor's suggestion to decommission *Britannia*, to Elizabeth's open regret. There was a coolness between her and Blair that may well have spread to his new chum, Bill Clinton. In a story allegedly told by a senior French diplomat to a former Commonwealth prime minister and then passed on to a British journalist—that is, not firsthand—the French diplomat asked the Queen who had been her favorite prime minister. "That's not the right question," she reportedly responded. "What you should ask me is who has been my least favourite." The answer: "Mr. Blair, of course."

Soon after the Clintons returned from London in 1997, having turned down the Queen's invitation, they made things worse. They hosted a White House dinner for Diana, Princess of Wales, then viewed by the Queen as a difficult, even disastrous former daughter-in-law who was portraying herself as a victim of the royal family. Clinton found Princess Di charming and attractive, though, and she returned the compliment. After visiting the White House, the thirty-five-year-old princess was chatting with billionaire Warren Buffett at a party hosted by *Washington Post* publisher Katharine Graham. "She had been at the White House that day and she had said that Bill Clinton was the sexiest man alive," Buffett said later. He joked, "And I didn't ask her who the least sexy guy in the world alive was. I was afraid I might get my play in there."

Two months later, on August 31, 1997, Diana died in a car crash in Paris while being hounded by paparazzi. The shocking loss of the young, beautiful princess immediately gripped the world's attention. When he heard of her death, Clinton interrupted his vacation at Martha's Vineyard in Massachusetts to make a comment, one that might be interpreted as a tweak of the royal family. Diana had made it clear that she thought her former in-laws created a stifling environment for her and her children, William and Harry. "For myself, I will always be glad that I knew the Princess and always think of her in very strong and positive terms, as will Hillary," Clinton told reporters. He said he hoped that "everyone who can will support her two fine sons and help them have the life and future that she would want."

Later, in a private telephone call with Blair, Clinton confided, "I worry a lot about those kids now." The prime minister agreed. "She was such a rock of stability in the sense she connected them with the outside world," he said. Even aides loyal to the Queen said Diana had been the only family the boys had, in any real sense of the word. The royals were not normal humans, as one senior aide put it. They were raised more by the palace staff than by their parents. Diana had been the exception.

The Queen did not care much for parental advice from anyone. A member of a more stoic generation, she found it hard to come to terms with the broad and deep reactions Diana's death had generated. She would routinely remove words hinting at emotion from her speeches, finding them unseemly. The decision to add a single line of humor at the beginning of her speech to Congress in 1991 was preceded by three hours of deliberations with her inner circle. She was slow to acknowledge her nation's grief, remaining in Balmoral Castle with Prince William and Prince Harry, then fifteen and twelve years old. She was still struggling to adjust to a new era that Diana had represented, one in which the public expected to witness the emotions and vulnerabilities of even the royal family. In London, mourners were piling flowers, notes, balloons, and stuffed animals along the railings at Buckingham Palace and Kensington Palace. But the Queen had rejected suggestions that she should make a more public demonstration of her own feelings. Facing rising criticism, she finally returned to Buckingham five days after Diana's death, emerging from her Rolls-Royce to look at the tributes and speak with those gathered there. The next day, she gave the second special televised address of her reign, speaking "from my heart" about a princess she said she admired and respected. "I share in your determination to cherish her memory," she said.

Not everyone at the palace felt that way. Hillary Clinton attended Diana's funeral, an appearance that created concern among British officials about what she might say. Diplomats at the US embassy cautioned her to avoid saying much of anything "to avoid entanglement" in the "increasingly 'nasty' Palace politics" surrounding Diana's death. The first lady heeded that advice, making brief comments—"We grieve for her children, her family and her country"—but not taking questions.

Though far closer to Prince Charles, Nancy Reagan remembered Diana as "a beautiful young princess who seemed to have all the world before her." Former President George H. W. Bush also offered a gracious comment. "We will always remember our many family contacts and her vivacious spirit with great warmth and fondness," he said. Others were less gracious. On Howard Stern's radio show a few months later, the shock jock asked Donald Trump, then a frequent guest, "You could've gotten her, right? You could've nailed her?" Trump replied, "I think I could have." The two men joked that before dating her, Trump might have demanded she get an HIV test first. Actually, Trump so aggressively tried to court Diana with flowers and attention after her divorce from Prince Charles that she reportedly complained the real estate developer gave her "the creeps."

QUEEN ELIZABETH DIDN'T MAKE AN OFFICIAL VISIT TO THE UNITED STATES during Clinton's eight-year tenure, a trip she had made during the presidency that preceded him, of the elder Bush, and during the presidency that followed him, of the younger Bush. She never celebrated Clinton at a state dinner in her palace or her castle, as she did his successors, the younger Bush, Obama, and Donald Trump.

Hillary Clinton told friends that omission was a disappointment. But it wasn't all the Queen's doing. The stars never seemed to align. Bill Clinton had turned down the opportunity early in his first term when the British suggested a state visit in 1994, then 1995. Later in his tenure, when the White House *was* interested, the Monica Lewinsky affair had exploded, raising concerns and second thoughts in London. As with all things related to America, Elizabeth followed the evolving scandal. It was impossible to avoid it.

So did her government. Blair happened to be scheduled to visit Washington two weeks after the scandal broke in the mainstream press. While the Queen was often the one dispatched to protect relations with the United States during times of trouble, that task now fell to Blair. It made sense; he was closer to Clinton than she ever was.

"The president ends the week in better shape than he began it, but his political future remains hostage to possible further disclosures from the Lewinsky/Jones cases," British Ambassador Christopher Meyer wrote to the foreign office a few days before Blair's arrival. Clinton was "a natural born Houdini" who was being helped in public opinion by a strong economy, Meyer said. But he added that the situation was "not stable," comparing it to Nixon and Watergate. "Nixon was finally done for when his taped profanity lost him the support of Middle America," he said. "The Lewinsky-Jones cases could still do something similar to Clinton."

Blair disregarded that cautionary note, giving the embattled Clinton the warmest possible endorsement at the White House dinner in his honor. "Bill, I am pleased to call you a good colleague and I'm proud to call you a good friend . . . ," he said. "I know I'm not alone in supporting you. I know the American people support you, too." That got extended applause from the formally dressed crowd in the East Room. He paid tribute to Hillary Clinton for her "dignity and grace, and within the past few days the whole world has seen those qualities of dignity and grace again."

"Great statement; bless you," Clinton said to him in a quiet aside as glasses clinked, a private comment picked up by a C-SPAN microphone. Blair replied, "My pleasure."

The toast paid off. "Your prime minister didn't have to say what he said at the press conference," James Steinberg, the deputy national security adviser, told the British ambassador. "We owe you big time." In his report to London, Meyer added this: "The task will be to call in the debt at the right moment."

A month later, the ambassador wrote a memo to John Holmes, Blair's principal private secretary, titled "Prime Minister's Visit to Washington: Cashing the Cheque." The Clinton administration appreciated the "generosity" of Blair's remarks, he said. "In good American style, they have pointed out that we have a very large cheque to cash and ask what we are going to spend it on." The answer was Northern Ireland, a paramount issue to both Clinton and Elizabeth, albeit for very different reasons. The British would encourage the president to "withstand pressure from the Irish lobby" and to press Gerry Adams to accept a compromise settlement. That was the price they asked Bill Clinton to pay for Blair's public embrace at a dark moment.

Even so, the Queen's advisers were wary about proceeding with planning for a state visit, just in case. "We decided to go slow on the issue of the invitation to Clinton, for 1999, until the scandal-scene clarified," said

John Kerr, just back from two years as ambassador to Washington. Meyer, who had succeeded him, replied, "The only rational judgement to make at the moment is that, as you say, scandal will not bring his Presidency to a premature end." But he noted, "We should, however, always have at the back of our minds that [special counsel Kenneth] Starr might dig up something really damning."

With some reassurance about Clinton's stance on Northern Ireland, Her Majesty gave her approval to extend an invitation for a state visit. "The Queen is very relaxed about what form the visit should take and what events might be included," a Blair aide wrote. She was accustomed to dealing with men who had behaved badly—in her family, her government, the world. "She was not prudish," a senior British official said, though he added dryly, "She would have regarded it as not impressive to sleep with the intern." The British already had discussed whether Blair would formally invite Clinton when they saw one another at the G8 Summit in Birmingham, England, in May 1998.

But Blair didn't raise the issue then, and the British got cold feet again as the first presidential impeachment since Andrew Johnson loomed.

"I do not see how we could invite Clinton, with the shadow of impeachment over him," Meyer wrote on December 8, 1998. "If the House does not impeach him, my enthusiasm for this project would still remain pretty dimmed. He will be tarnished by the Lewinsky business. We hardly need a state visit to improve the situation. We now need to raise our eyes to the successor, whoever that is."

Eleven days later, the House of Representatives voted to impeach the president; the Senate trial that followed would end in acquittal. The impeachment threat was over but the taint on his presidency remained. During the Watergate scandal, Nixon had pressed the British for an invitation for a state visit, a notion the Queen had carefully sidestepped. Now the White House told London that Clinton was "keen" on making a state visit before he left office. The Queen apparently was not.

"We had previously thought the Clintons would rather not have the pomp and ceremony of a State Visit, preferring instead a more flexible arrangement," John Sawers, one of Blair's top aides, wrote after having a "friendly half hour talk" with Sandy Berger, the White House national security adviser. "But I was struck that Berger himself raised the idea." It was already too late. "It would be much better to save a full State visit until the new President is in office in 2001," a Foreign Office memo advised. In September, the US embassy raised the idea again. But Steinberg told Meyer that the White House wouldn't press it if the British didn't want it to happen. Their response, diplomatically delivered: They didn't.

"So there are no free rides in life," Clinton told me years later. He was referring to the historic calculations and miscalculations of other foreign leaders, but the comment was also apt for his own. "You have to live with the consequences of what you do. And very often in politics, they're a mixture of good and bad." He would never be the president being feted at one of those white-tie dinners at Buckingham Palace, with dinner served on King George IV's Grand Service and entertainment afterward by Scottish bagpipers. With Queen Elizabeth to his left, charming and bejeweled.

DURING CLINTON'S FINAL WEEKS IN OFFICE, HE RETURNED TO THE UNITED Kingdom, mostly to celebrate and fortify the Good Friday Agreement. In Dublin, Bertie Ahern, Ireland's taoiseach, equivalent to a prime minister, praised Clinton as "the best American president Ireland has ever had." In Belfast, Clinton and Blair visited Stormont, the stately home of the Northern Ireland Assembly. The fragile power-sharing government had been set up two years earlier by the accords. There, the United States, Britain, and Ireland agreed to do more to implement agreements on police reform and the disarmament of terrorist groups.

By now, Clinton's gamble had paid off. The American role in Northern Ireland that had caused so much friction was now seen as invaluable. "Early on, there was a great deal of disquiet in the British government about what the Clinton administration was doing over Northern Ireland," said Sir David Manning, a British diplomat who advised Blair and later served as ambassador to Washington. "Later, they acknowledged that actually what the Clinton people did was very helpful." Indeed, he said, "Without them, securing the Good Friday Agreement would have been much more difficult, perhaps impossible."

This time, the Clintons accepted the Queen's invitation to tea.

After spending the night at Chequers with Blair, the president and first lady flew on the *Marine One* helicopter into Hyde Park in central London.

With the president's armored limousine trailing behind, the Clintons took a stroll, occasionally stopping to shake hands with surprised passersby on their way to work. Clinton had been up until 4 that morning, watching Vice President Al Gore concede the 2000 presidential election to George W. Bush in the wake of a decision by a divided Supreme Court on the counting of ballots in Florida. In his first presidential visit to London and his last, Clinton found himself shadowed by the Presidents Bush.

At Buckingham Palace on December 14, 2000, they joined Elizabeth for a half hour in the Queen's Audience Room, the chamber where she met privately each week with the prime minister. While her parents had tea and coffee with the Queen, daughter Chelsea was given a private tour of the palace's state rooms by Christopher Lloyd, the surveyor of the Queen's pictures, an art historian in charge of the royal collection. When their tea ended, the Queen took what Clinton called an unusual step. "She got her proper little purse and came down the elevator with us, walked us out to the street, to our car," he said, leaving the palace through a side entrance. "There was no big crowd or anything; it was a personal gesture. And I'll never forget looking at her, holding her purse, waving good-bye to us as we drove away." The complicated connection between the Clintons and the Windsors was finally eased.

On *Air Force One* as he flew back to Washington, reporters asked Clinton what he had talked about with the Queen. He had told her that he enjoyed playing a round of golf with her son, Prince Andrew, one summer at Martha's Vineyard. "He beat the living daylights out of me," he said. (Years later, the two men would share a more explosive connection over Andrew's close ties, and Clinton's more distant ones, to the convicted sexual predator Jeffrey Epstein.)

They also discussed the situation in Zimbabwe, the Commonwealth country where she had taken a behind-the-scenes role in ending white minority rule in what was then known as Rhodesia. She expressed concern to Clinton about growing violence around the parliamentary elections in June, the first national election in which the ruling party had faced real opposition.

"She's very careful, you know. She observes strictly the British tradition of not making policy statements," Clinton said. "But she's a highly intelligent woman who knows a lot about the world. She has traveled a lot.

She has fulfilled her responsibilities, I think, enormously well, and I always marvel, when we meet, at what a keen judge she is of human events."

Clinton, a pol to the core, mused about her influence. "Elizabeth had a particular ability to say things to other leaders and to her own government, in private, that kept the show on the road. And there's something to be said . . . for keeping the show on the road," he said. When we talked, the former president, at age seventy-eight and a quarter century out of office, was reflective. Without hard power to exercise, the Queen knew that her ability to forge relationships could make a difference, usually on the edges and occasionally at the center of things. "She knew that how people felt had something to do with how they could think," Clinton said.

Even when there were hard feelings.

Twelve

A Wink and a Nod

Tuesday, May 14, 1991—The White House residence

Their relationship may have been so relaxed from the start because when they met he wasn't yet the president of the United States, with all the weight that carried. He was the forty-four-year-old wisecracking managing partner of the Texas Rangers baseball team whose father happened to be president. George Bush the elder, whose heed to protocol had been honed during his service as ambassador to the United Nations and envoy to China, was hosting Queen Elizabeth for a state dinner that night. George Bush the younger was invited to a welcoming lunch in the White House residence. He arrived wearing what even he acknowledged were "rather gaudy" cowboy boots.

"Mother said, 'You're not going to wear those boots, are you?'" he recalled. "I said, 'I'm sure Her Majesty would like them.'" With that, he hiked up his pants to show off their tooled-leather glory. Barbara Bush turned to the Queen with mock horror, a response she routinely used with her oldest son, the one given to impertinence. "Your Majesty, I just want you to know I'm going to move George as far away from you as possible during the luncheon!" Elizabeth, then sixty-five years old, replied with a question that sounded more like a mother than a monarch. "Are you the black sheep?" she asked him. He replied, "I guess you can say that, Your Majesty." She made a diplomatic observation. "All families have them," she said. Which prompted him to pose a provocative question of his own: "Who's yours?"

Barbara interjected, "Don't answer that!"

The Queen asked why she saw her son as such a dangerous luncheon partner. "I told her that he said what he felt and besides that, he threatened to wear cowboy boots in the evening to the State Dinner." One potential pair featured an outline of Texas; the other declared "God Bless America."

Which one was he planning to wear that night?

"Neither," he replied. "Tonight's pair will say 'God Save the Queen.'"

Afterward, Bush recalled their instant rapport, one that would continue for years. At that first meeting, he saw her not only as "a regal person" but also "as a mom." What's more, the "twinkle in her eye" jibed with his own family's dynamics. "My mother and I, we like to tease, and she fit right in," he said. It seems unlikely the Queen came away from that encounter thinking she had just met a future president of the United States. But she did find him amusing, then and later.

That evening, when George W. and his wife, Laura, came through the receiving line before the dinner, the Queen gave an inquiring glance at his feet. Without a word, he lifted the edge of his formal black pants to show off his footwear. As promised, or threatened, he was sporting cowboy boots, the "God Bless America" version, festooned with US flags.

ELIZABETH'S RELATIONSHIP WITH EACH US PRESIDENT WAS DISTINCTIVE—shaped by who they were, where she was during her reign, and what issues of the moment united and divided their two countries. With a few presidents, her feelings were clearly more personal. Dwight Eisenhower was a friend of her father and her childhood hero during the dark days of World War II. Ronald Reagan was a member of her generation who shared her passion for horseback riding. Her relationship with the gentlemanly George H. W. Bush was fond. The one with his puckish namesake? Downright cozy.

The younger Bush was in many ways the opposite of his father—mischievous when he was proper, down-to-earth when he was patrician, more conservative, more Texan. Nicknamed "W," he teased her in a way no other president and only a handful of other foreign leaders ever dared, and she teased him back. "In public, she's very demure," yet still capable of putting out "a zinger," he said. He was close in age to her eldest, born two years before Prince Charles, though Bush and Charles had very different personalities. She shared some characteristics with Bush's mother, the formidable Barbara Bush, in her command, her sharp eye, and the wit she would sometimes unsheathe. "She thought Mother was funny," Bush said. So did he.

In one way, the Queen had a unique kinship with the new president. She, too, had assumed a demanding job that the father she revered had held.

George Walker Bush would be the first US president Queen Elizabeth invited to London for the most formal of occasions, a state visit. At the end of her long reign, he would be the only president ever to both be honored by her at a state visit in London and return the honor to her with a state visit in Washington. During his White House tenure, they would meet during five separate visits to one country or another, the most encounters of any sitting president.

His presidency and his enduring legacy would be defined by the September 11 terror attacks in 2001, then by the wars he would launch in response in Afghanistan and Iraq. Great Britain would join those battles, at considerable cost and controversy. Their partnership would underscore the "special relationship" and then cast a shadow over it. It was a reminder to some in England of the downsides of an alliance in which the United States took the lead in charting the course—sometimes wisely, in history's judgment, and sometimes not.

In time there would be massive demonstrations against the Iraq War on the streets of both Washington and London. Antiwar sentiment would contribute to Prime Minister Tony Blair's resignation in 2007 and help Democrats regain control of first the Congress in 2006 and then the White House in 2008. The divisive debate would be one more example of Elizabeth's steadying hand—her ability to maintain bilateral ties when they were strained, to focus on the values that bound the United States and Great Britain even when the politics of the day risked pulling them apart.

JUST TWO MONTHS BEFORE HIJACKED PLANES STRUCK THE WORLD TRADE Center in New York and the Pentagon in Washington, Bush met with Elizabeth for the first time as president, visiting Buckingham Palace with Laura Bush for lunch on July 19, 2001. He had stopped in England to see the Queen and to meet with Blair before heading to the G8 summit in Italy.

Protesters were gathered outside the palace, albeit just a few hundred of them, and focused mostly on the environment. "Wanted for crimes against the planet—the outlaw known as the Toxic Texan," one banner said. A thirty-one-year-old PETA activist from West Lafayette, Indiana, stripped and streaked outside the palace, wearing only socks, tennis shoes, and a motto written across his back that read "GoVeg.com." A bigger problem was the London weather. Bush and the Duke of Edinburgh were drenched by a sudden rain shower as they were reviewing the troops, the Guard of Honor of the First Battalion of the Devonshire and Dorset Regiment. Prince Charles jokingly blotted the president's suit when they returned to the protection of the palace entrance. The Queen apologized for the weather. "Perfect day!" Bush insisted. "We really appreciate your hospitality." The luncheon that followed featured "perfectly pressed linens and china emblazoned with the royal coat of arms," Laura recalled.

That would soon seem to be an innocent time.

The 9/11 attacks in the United States struck close to home in the United Kingdom. On that morning, Prince Andrew was aboard a British Airways flight headed to New York; the plane turned around and returned to London. Andrew's ex-wife, Sarah Ferguson, the mother of two of the Queen's grandchildren, was in New York. She was running a few minutes late for a meeting scheduled for 8:45 a.m. in the offices of her Chances for Children charity, in the World Trade Center. The first plane struck at 8:46 a.m. as a handful of the group's staffers were gathered to greet her in the lobby of the North Tower. Everyone who was on the 101st floor, where the charity's office was located, would die that morning.

In all, sixty-seven Britons would be among the nearly three thousand people killed in the Twin Towers. It was the highest number for any country except the United States, and the deadliest toll in history among British citizens in a terror attack.

That day, Elizabeth was on vacation at Balmoral Castle. She quickly sent a message to Bush expressing "growing disbelief and total shock" at the attack and offering her sympathy, then talked on the phone to the Lord Chamberlain's office about what else the palace could do to express solidarity and grief. Under the summer schedule, the next Changing of the Guard was thirty-six hours away, on Thursday morning. They agreed that the Band of the Coldstream Guards would play "The Star-Spangled Banner," observe two minutes of silence, then play "God Save the Queen." The band had never performed the US national anthem; they hurriedly rehearsed it. As they marched down the Mall toward the palace in their distinctive scarlet tunics and high black bearskin hats, they also played a medley of marches by John Philip Sousa, the American composer and conductor.

A crowd of about six thousand people, many of them Americans and some clutching miniature US flags, were standing along the fence and at the entrance to watch. US ambassador William Farish and Prince Andrew attended, too. Many of the Americans sang along to their national anthem. Some sobbed.

The next day, "The Star-Spangled Banner" would be played for the first time at St. Paul's Cathedral, at a memorial service for the lives that had been lost. The Queen, who was usually loath to upend her time at Balmoral, flew in from Scotland to attend. The Duke of Edinburgh read St. Paul's Letter to the Romans: "If God be for us, who can be against us?" Nearly three thousand Americans and Britons filled the pews, and thousands more gathered outside to listen to the service through oversized speakers. The congregation sang the "Battle Hymn of the Republic," the defiant song by abolitionist Julia Ward Howe on the triumph of justice over evil. The moment clearly moved the stoic Elizabeth, who had spent so much of her life working to solidify her bond with America. When she left the church, she had tears in her eyes.

In New York a week later, a prayer service was held at Saint Thomas Church to remember the British victims. Prime Minister Blair and former President Bill Clinton were seated in the front pew. The British ambassador, Sir Christopher Meyer, read aloud a letter from the Queen. It closed with some of the most memorable words of her reign, a phrase that Clinton would call "so wise and so true," so perfect for the moment.

"These are dark and harrowing times for families and friends of those who are missing or who suffered in the attack—many of you here today," she wrote. "Grief is the price we pay for love." Her open expression of emotion was especially striking because it was so rare.

The outpouring from Blair and the Queen cemented the Anglo-American alliance with an emotional closeness not seen since World War II. In a special address to Congress eight days after the attacks, Bush recalled the playing of the national anthem at Buckingham Palace. "America has no truer friend than Great Britain," he said.

A YEAR AFTER BUSH MOVED INTO THE WHITE HOUSE, THE QUEEN WAS STILL curious about how he had gotten there. So she asked an expert: Bill Clinton. She of course knew that he had defeated the elder Bush in 1992, only to watch his vice president lose the disputed 2000 race to Bush's son. Her Majesty and Clinton were meeting one last time—a coincidence, really—in Australia.

Clinton had been out of office for just over a year, his travels no longer the subject of much interest by the news media. Elizabeth was on her Golden Jubilee tour and getting more news coverage than she wanted. She landed in Adelaide to protests and demands that she fire Governor-General Peter Hollingworth, the Crown's representative in Australia. (Facing allegations of covering up child abuse when he was the Archbishop of Brisbane in the 1990s, he eventually resigned, but not until a year later.) The next day, she made a side trip to the Barossa Valley vineyards and met with fellow corgi breeders, the dogs she had adored since childhood—as always, a source of respite and pleasure.

The former president was on a speaking tour of Australia, with stops in a half dozen cities. He and the Queen both happened to be staying at the Stamford Plaza Hotel in Brisbane on March 1, 2002. "She was kind enough to invite me to tea," Clinton said. An Australian security agent assigned to his protective detail described the meeting years later on his blog. "Away from the media, away from politicians and away from formal meeting expectations," Anthony Manning recalled. Clinton arrived accompanied by Manning and a Secret Service agent. The president, who was habitually tardy, arrived on time, but the Queen, who was meticulously prompt, was running late. Clinton and Manning had soft drinks in a separate suite and waited.

"He commented that he genuinely thought the Queen was an amazing person and that only she could keep him waiting and he did not mind," Manning said. "Just a show of pecking order!" Clinton joked, a reflection of his recent change in employment. When she was ready, he went in.

He and the royal couple talked, naturally, about politics.

Prince Philip "was free, then, to be somewhat more outspoken with me because I was out of office," Clinton said. Blunt as always, Philip bemoaned some of Blair's policies. At the time, the prime minister was hinting at higher taxes and more spending on social services. "He clearly was skeptical of some of the more liberal initiatives being undertaken," Clinton said.

The Queen, in contrast, was focused on Washington.

"She was more interested in asking questions about what was really going on in America," Clinton recalled. "She wanted to understand why we [Democrats] had lost the White House when we had a sixty-something percent approval rating for the administration and what happened." Al Gore had won the popular vote but lost the Electoral College count to Bush in an election ultimately decided by the Supreme Court. The pointed question was a sign of Elizabeth's serious and sophisticated interest in American politics.

It was a puzzle that Democrats in the United States were wrestling with, too, as the Anglo-American alliance was put to a new test.

TWO YEARS LATER, WHEN BUSH ARRIVED IN LONDON FOR A STATE VISIT ON November 18, 2003, there were massive demonstrations against the Iraq War, which had been launched in March. But the day's first security crisis would be inside the palace, and almost comic.

"INTRUDER" was stamped in red on the front page of the *Daily Mirror* the morning after the Bushes had arrived and been ensconced in the Belgian Suite, the finest guest apartment at Buckingham Palace. The intruder who had managed to infiltrate the inner sanctums of the palace was, it turned out, a reporter named Ryan Parry. For two months, he had been working as a footman, a job he landed after giving false references. The revelations in his story included the detail that Tupperware boxes of cereal had to be lined up just so on the crisp white linen tablecloth of the royal breakfast table each morning, and the news that the Queen spread her toast lightly with marmalade, then fed much of it under the table to her dogs. Prince Edward swore at a footman, it was reported, and Princess Anne sometimes dropped the F-bomb.

The faux footman had been working in the palace to welcome Bush the previous evening and would have been around to help serve him breakfast except that the headlines on that morning's front page meant he was no longer employed by the Crown. "Had I been a terrorist intent on assassinating the Queen or American President George Bush, I could have done so with absolute ease," he wrote.

For years, the Secret Service had seen British security as too lax while the royal family had viewed US security as intrusive and overblown. It had been a regular source of friction. The Americans would insist on sending long motorcades through London streets; members of the royal family would sometimes just drive themselves. With these headlines, the Americans might have felt vindicated, but the Bushes didn't move out of the palace, instead finishing their stay in the elegant two-bedroom apartment. The president reported that the Queen was "unruffled," even by the huge protests outside. "She had seen a lot during her life," he said, "and it didn't seem to faze her."

How Her Majesty viewed the war in Iraq, increasingly controversial as no weapons of mass destruction were found, was left unasked and unanswered. She had delivered an address to the nation approving of the elder Bush's quick ejection of Iraqi forces from Kuwait in 1991. "Fully justified," she called it. But this was a much longer and more ambiguous conflict—one that demanded the deployment of American and British troops in the Middle East for the foreseeable future. There was speculation about whether she had asked her classic pointed questions of Blair during their private weekly sessions—questions of the "Are you sure you are being wise?" variety—or even pressed him to justify the invasion. That was a storyline added to a British play, *The Audience*, when it was staged on Broadway in 2015. But it would not have been her style, or the role she saw for herself, to express a public view or to discuss the issue head-on with the visiting president. "No," a senior palace adviser said flatly when I asked if it might have come up between them, adding for emphasis, "No, no, no, no."

Even in her private conversations with Blair, who was unalterably linked with Bush on the war, "she wouldn't have lectured anyone," British biographer and personality Gyles Brandreth said. But there were issues she might well have raised. "Her real concern with any war was the armed forces," about their safety and well-being. That was the concern Prince Charles raised in a private letter to Blair a year after Bush's visit. Expressing concern about the capabilities of the Lynx aircraft, he wrote, "I fear that this is just one more example of where our Armed Forces are being asked to do an extremely challenging job (particularly in Iraq) without the necessary resources." In 2005, the *Daily Express* splashed an exclusive on the front page: "Queen's Fury at Snub to War Heroes," reporting her outrage at the failure of Blair and his Cabinet to do more to help veterans returning home with grievous injuries.

Her Majesty, a careful reader of *The Daily Telegraph*, knew opposition to the Iraq war was rising. In February, more than a million people had joined an antiwar march in London, the biggest street protest in the history of the United Kingdom. Even the Queen's own role in the war had come under scrutiny—with some speculating that the sovereign, who had the power to declare war, could intervene in decisions on Iraq. (In 1999, when the Clinton administration had been contemplating tougher action against the regime of Saddam Hussein in Baghdad, she had quietly vetoed a proposed law that would have moved the power to declare war in Iraq from the monarch to the government.) In June 2003, Vladimir Putin arrived for the first state visit to Britain by a Russian leader since Czar Alexander II in 1874. In her welcoming speech, the Queen acknowledged that their two nations initially had disagreed on the conflict but urged him to support the war now that it was underway. The visit would be remembered more for the fourteen minutes the notoriously tardy Russian leader made her wait before he arrived at the palace. When Home Secretary David Blunkett later apologized that his dog had "barked very loudly" at Putin when he finally showed up, she replied, "Dogs have interesting instincts, don't they?"

During Bush's visit in November, one hundred thousand protesters demonstrated in London, toppling a seventeen-foot papier-mâché effigy of the president in Trafalgar Square, an echo of the triumphant destruction of Saddam's statue in Baghdad in the war's early days. In a poll in *The Guardian*, just 43 percent of the Britons surveyed welcomed Bush's visit, while 36 percent wished he had stayed home, and 21 percent didn't care one way or the other.

Blair remained supportive of the war, but divisions in his Labour Party and other factions in the Parliament meant Bush didn't receive an invitation to deliver an address to a joint session, something both President Reagan and President Clinton had done. Instead, Bush spoke at the Banqueting House, a historic setting from the seventeenth century. King Charles I had been beheaded on a black scaffold built in front of it. Still, it lacked the emotional resonance of the Palace of Westminster, where Parliament meets. He acknowledged the controversy over his appearance, mentioning a stunt by American illusionist David Blaine, who had recently spent forty-four days in a transparent box suspended in midair. "It was pointed out to me that the last noted American to visit London stayed in a glass box dangling over the Thames," he said. "A few might have been happy to provide similar arrangements for me." That got a laugh.

Then he delivered a defense of the Iraq War, which had been launched in March. "In some cases, the measured use of force is all that protects us from a chaotic world ruled by force," he said. "We will use force, when necessary, in the defense of freedom. And we will raise up an ideal of democracy in every part of the world."

The Queen noted their nations' long history in her dinner toast that night, as well as an acknowledgment that they didn't always see eye to eye. "Like all special friends, we can talk frankly and we can disagree from time to time."

Neither mentioned his cowboy boots, the topic of lighter times. "I probably didn't want to bring it up because I had gone from slightly wisecracking son to President," Bush said. The dinner was white tie and tails, an outfit he didn't own and had to rent. This evening, he was wearing the prescribed black shoes. Thirteen members of the royal family were in attendance, and the menu, as always, was printed in French. (*Delice de flétan rôti aux herbes* was the main course.) "Our places were set with ten pieces of silverware and seven crystal wine goblets," Bush said later, joking, "Evidently, word hadn't reached the royal pantry that I had quit drinking."

The next evening the Bushes hosted a reciprocal dinner at Winfield

House, the US ambassador's residence. The menu and the vibe—a Tex-Mex theme—could hardly have been more different. It started with a corn and avocado soup topped with fried tortillas; the main course was lamb, and the side dish was described as a "medley of beans and bacon." Dessert was fudge brownie pudding. It was one more of those deliberately casual American evenings, or as casual as a black-tie dinner with the British monarch can be. It was squarely in the tradition of FDR serving King George hot dogs, and Reagan offering Elizabeth refried beans for lunch at his ranch.

During this visit, Bush said his conversations with the Queen were mostly social and personal, not about policy. "I'm fond of her," he said. "And, the more I've learned about her, the fonder I've become." At tea, he asked to meet her corgis; she pressed a button and they tumbled into the room behind "a well-dressed fellow." Bush approved of that, too: "I always believe you can get an insight from whether or not a person can relate to animals."

A DECADE AFTER RONALD REAGAN ANNOUNCED HE HAD ALZHEIMER'S disease and withdrew from public life, he died during the younger Bush's tenure, on June 5, 2004, at his Bel Air home in California. He was ninety-three years old.

The Queen mourned the loss of her old friend, a kindred spirit. The two had stayed in touch since he moved out of the White House in 1989. That year, the Queen had awarded him an honorary knighthood and presented him with the insignia of an honorary Knight Grand Cross of the Most Honourable Order of the Bath, the first president to receive the highest orders of chivalry. Two years later, she hosted him and former President Gerald Ford at a black-tie dinner aboard *Britannia* in Miami. Her almost comic attempts to provide the decaffeinated coffee Reagan had requested were caught by cameras recording a documentary, *Elizabeth R: A Year in the Life of the Queen*. "It's coming," she assured him. "We try our best."

The recording also gave a rare glimpse of their substantive conversations, beyond scripted toasts and social chitchat. In this case, the topic was government spending. "Now, if you've got two-thirds of the fund paying for the bureaucrats and give only one-third to the needy people, something's wrong there," Reagan said.

The Queen, in words that might have been uttered by any member of the Conservative Party, replied, "But you see, all the democracies are bankrupt now, because of the way the services have been planned for people to grab." That sort of candid political comment was one she almost never made in public, particularly one that could be seen as criticizing her own government. It seems Prince Philip wasn't the only one in the royal family concerned by Blair's liberalism.

"I know, we tried to get some of these things changed and reduce them," Reagan said. "For example, we have a rule to this day that a supervisor's salary is based on the number of people he supervises. Well, now, you have a group of people that have no interest in reducing the payroll, even if they can, because it will reduce their salary."

"Obviously, yes," she replied. "It's extraordinary, isn't it? I think the next generation is going to have a very difficult time." Reagan nodded in agreement.

They had exchanged letters, marking birthdays and mourning the death of the Queen Mother. Elizabeth often ended them as "Your Sincere Friend." Their fondest passages were, of course, about horses. In 1994, Elizabeth reported that she had injured her wrist when she was riding Centennial. "I'm sorry to say that I was riding the horse you rode at Windsor and wasn't paying enough attention! He just tripped and fell and I had my hand on his neck which luckily then pushed me away from him as he rolled over on his side! So in one way I was lucky but it is very frustrating to be in a plaster, unable to use my hand."

When Reagan died, Elizabeth penned a handwritten letter to Nancy and gave it to Prince Charles to deliver in person to her at the funeral. The former first lady kept it in the first of four three-ring binders that she filled with sympathy notes from foreign leaders, US officials, Hollywood stars, and others.

"I shall remember the many times I met President Reagan and the happy times we had," the Queen wrote, mentioning in particular their ride at Windsor. While Reagan was the first American president the Queen seemed to consider a true friend, another would unexpectedly come along down the road.

A HALF CENTURY AFTER HER FIRST VISIT TO THE UNITED STATES AS QUEEN, Elizabeth wanted to return one more time.

"It was designed to coincide with the fiftieth anniversary of her first state visit," said Sir David Manning, then the British ambassador to the United States. "And it was understood, privately, that she might well not come again." In 2007, in "book-ended symmetry," she would begin her American tour with a stop in Jamestown, Virginia, where she had begun her visit in 1957. Then she was celebrating the 350th anniversary of the founding of the first English settlement in the New World; now she was celebrating the 400th. At the Williamsburg Inn, where she again stayed overnight, the hotel displayed black-and-white photographs of her as a stylish young woman during her first visit. By this point, she was eighty-one years old and an icon—a status reached by virtue of her record-setting tenure, her steadiness, her cautious adaptability. She had long been the best-known woman on the globe, and the most widely beloved. After a lifetime of travel around the world, she would make just one more trip outside Europe after this one.

The tour was scheduled to include this bonus: The devoted horsewoman, who maintained racing stables of her own, timed it so she could finally attend the Kentucky Derby.

"At the start of 2007, we received word that Queen Elizabeth of England wanted to make another visit to the United States, and the White House immediately sprang into action to host a state dinner in her honor," Laura Bush said. The timing was serendipitous for President Bush, whose approval rating was sinking to record lows over Iraq. The visit by Her Majesty would be a welcome moment for both of them—despite, or even because of, the occasional glitch.

"I've seen her amused when things went wrong," recalled Manning, who was waiting to greet her plane at Richmond International Airport. "I remember that they rolled the red carpet out as the plane stopped, but they missed the door. So it had to be rolled up and rolled out again. And you could see little faces at the aircraft windows watching as the carpet was repositioned. I suspect there would have been a slightly mischievous smile on her face." She displayed a broad smile as she walked down the mobile stairs in a lilac coat and a salmon-colored hat festooned with silk flowers. She was greeted by Tim Kaine, then the governor of Virginia and later a US senator and the 2016 Democratic vice presidential nominee.

Since her previous visit, archeologists at Jamestown had found remains of the original fort. She viewed with interest and amusement a display of medical instruments, including a long iron spatula labeled as a treatment "for severe constipation." "David!" she called out to Commander David Swain, a Royal Navy doctor traveling with her. "You ought to have some things like that!" Later, she addressed the Virginia General Assembly and expressed her condolences for the victims of a mass shooting on the Virginia Tech campus the previous week. A lone gunman had murdered thirty-two students and teachers before committing suicide.

At her next stop, she attended the 133rd running of the Kentucky Derby at Churchill Downs in Louisville. She watched from a balcony in a private suite, easy to spot in a lime-green dress and hat with fuchsia trim, as Street Sense, the 9–2 favorite, came from nineteenth place to win. She spent the weekend with William Farish, the former US ambassador to Great Britain whose farm in the Kentucky bluegrass was famed in horse-racing circles.

It was her fifth visit to stay with Farish and his wife, Sarah. She greeted the Queen with a kiss on both cheeks—"A rare sign of familiarity never seen in Britain," one British author noted. In the late afternoon, at Lane's End Farm, Elizabeth sipped a martini and worried about the performance of granddaughter Zara Phillips, Princess Anne's daughter, at the Badminton Horse Trial. "Nobody pays any attention to what Granny thinks," she complained.

Finally, she arrived in Washington and had one more teasing exchange with George W. Bush.

On the South Lawn, the twenty-one-gun salute sounded and the Old Guard Fife and Drum Corps marched and played. The White House was determined to avoid the "talking hat" incident that had marked her last state visit, with this president's father. Behind a podium with the presidential seal, Bush read prepared remarks saluting Britain and the Queen for their steadfast support in recent conflicts, and for her long reign. They had been together three years earlier, in 2004, to commemorate one of those alliances, gathering with other leaders on the beaches of Normandy to mark the sixtieth anniversary of D-Day. That event had uncomfortably underscored the divisions in the World War II alliance over the war in Iraq. France and Germany had declined to join the multinational coalition that launched the invasion.

In the Rose Garden, Bush began: "You helped our nation celebrate its bicentennial in 17—" He caught himself before he finished the year, 1776. "In 1976!" he corrected himself. He looked over at her with a smile and winked, then turned back to the assembled dignitaries. "She gave me a look only a mother could give a child," he told them to laughter. The next night, when she hosted a reciprocal dinner at the British embassy, she began with a smile. "I wondered whether I should start this toast saying, 'When I was here in 1776 . . .'"

"Your Majesty, I can't top that one," he replied.

THE PRESIDENT INVITED A LAST-MINUTE GUEST TO THE WHITE HOUSE, one more sign of his intimate relationship with the Queen.

On Saturday, Laura Bush watched the running of the Kentucky Derby on TV, with cutaway shots of Elizabeth at the racetrack. The first lady called Amy Zantzinger, the White House social secretary, with an idea: Invite the winning jockey to the State Dinner. That prospect had already been in the mix. His name was Calvin Borel, a Cajun famed for his instinctive connection with horses. Once Zantzinger reached him—and convinced him that her call wasn't a prank—they sorted out the logistics. But the dinner was on Monday, and his fiancée, Lisa Funk, was understandably concerned that she didn't have anything appropriate to wear. Amy arranged for a store in Louisville to open on Sunday so Lisa could find a dress. For Calvin, a white-tie-and-tails outfit was rented from the same store that was providing the president's garb.

The jockey would create what George Bush would affectionately remember as "another classic moment" with Her Majesty, a sign of how relaxed the mood could sometimes be even in the most formal of settings. "So Calvin Borel comes in, and he says something like, 'Hey, Queen!'" Apparently unaware of the rule never to touch the monarch, a beaming Calvin wrapped his arms around both Elizabeth and Laura for the official photograph in the receiving line. "It was awkward for the protocol people," the president said, "but it damned sure wasn't for the Queen and me."

The sense of informality extended to the seating plan. Laura and Secretary of State Condoleezza Rice had insisted that the dress code be white tie for the only time during Bush's eight years in office. But the president insisted on arranging the seating, putting personality above protocol. "I wanted to put some friends of mine there so they could say they'd had dinner with the Queen," he said. "And I put some notables, too." She sat between him and Chief Justice John Roberts. Also at their table were Nancy Reagan, legendary sports broadcaster Jim Nantz, and professional golfer Arnold Palmer. "It was not a very stuffed-shirt table, let me put it to you that way."

After dinner, violinist virtuoso Itzhak Perlman performed in the East Room, and the Army Chorus ended the evening with "The Battle Hymn of the Republic." That was the song the Queen and the congregation had sung at the memorial service in St. Paul's just after 9/11, six years earlier.

Elizabeth and the president would meet one more time, in June 2008, for a low-key visit at Windsor Castle the day after the official commemoration of her eighty-second birthday. The purpose of the stop, Bush's briefing papers said, was simply "to demonstrate respect for a close friend of the United States and the world's third longest reigning monarch." The memo suggested the Bushes chat about having seen the Lipizzaner horses in Slovenia and congratulate the royal couple on the first marriage of a grandchild—by Peter Phillips, the son of Princess Anne.

The 2007 dinner in Washington had a more serious tone and a valedictory air.

Bush noted that it was the fourth state dinner that had been held in her honor at the White House. "On previous such occasions, you've been welcomed by President Eisenhower, President Ford, and another President named Bush," he said in his toast. "Over your long reign, America and Britain have deepened our friendship and strengthened our alliance."

Her toast was aimed not only at this president but to the United States itself, and not just about this moment but her entire life. She began by recognizing the "steadfast commitment" of the country "in support of a Europe whole and free." She mentioned the wartime alliance forged by Winston Churchill and FDR during her childhood, and she recalled the warm welcome she had received from President Truman when she was a young and nervous princess on her first visit to the United States. There was a "simple truth" behind the two nations' enduring ties, she said.

"Divided, all alone, we can be vulnerable. But if the Atlantic unites, not divides us, ours is a partnership always to be reckoned with in the defense of freedom and the spread of prosperity," she said. "That is the lesson of my lifetime."

Her Majesty was in regal wear, including a jeweled tiara that her grandmother, Queen Mary, had given her as a wedding present. She wore a three-strand diamond necklace and the blue sash of the Order of the Garter. She was making her final visit to the United States and delivering her final words in the White House. Now eighty-one years old, she had legacy on her mind—her legacy, forged in part in this foreign land.

THE NEXT DAY—ON THE LAST DAY OF HER FINAL VISIT TO THE UNITED STATES—Elizabeth saw for the first time the World War II Memorial, which had opened on the National Mall just three years earlier. President Bush had asked his parents, whose lives were shaped by that conflict, to accompany the royal couple. Elizabeth, Prince Philip, and George H. W. Bush had all served in uniform in the war that had started the special friendship for her family and her country with America.

"We are happy to have you here," said Marjorie Gallun, eighty-five, one of the American veterans gathered at the memorial. Two Union Jacks were draped over a picket fence nearby. Elizabeth replied, "We are happy to be here."

A National Park Service ranger escorted the Queen along the edge of the fountain at the memorial's center, the Lincoln Memorial looming behind them. They crossed in front of the Wall of Stars, adorned with 4,048 stars, one for each hundred American military personnel who had died in the war. Chiseled in stone: "Here we mark the price of freedom."

Thirteen

Good Vibes

Wednesday, April 1, 2009—Buckingham Palace

At the start, neither side was certain whether the new president and the Queen would hit it off. For one thing, his family had been jailed by hers.

Barack Obama was making the first stop of the first overseas trip of his presidency—the leader of a new generation, forty-seven years old and America's first Black president. He was meeting Queen Elizabeth, the epitome of the world's old guard, at age eighty-three poised to greet her eleventh sitting president. When he was born, in 1961, she had already been on the throne for nine years and met five of his predecessors. The only intersection between their two families was a problematic one, nothing like the joint service in World War II that had been a bond between her and most other recent presidents. Quite the opposite: Obama's Kenyan grandfather, who had worked as a cook for a British captain, had been arrested by her father's colonial government on false charges of subversion. After being imprisoned for six months, he was released, filthy and frail and suddenly aged, a story told and retold by the Obama family in Kenya with bitterness and sorrow.

The dismissive British colonial attitude toward Kenyans was also directed at Obama's father, one of eighty-one Kenyan students chosen to attend US universities through a pioneering scholarship program. While studying at the University of Hawaii, Barack Obama Sr. would meet

Obama's American mother, Ann Dunham. Files in Britain's National Archives from 1959 and 1960 show colonial officials raising objections to the program, describing the students as second-rate and warning they could pose "a considerable menace" when they returned home after being exposed to African "extreme nationalism" on American campuses.

It was an unpromising landscape for British hopes of maintaining the "special relationship," that amorphous concept that had claimed no particular allegiance from Obama. "You wouldn't necessarily think that a Democrat president . . . with his heritage and everything else would be particularly, necessarily a soulmate of the Queen—of this long, historic line of monarchs stretched back in history," David Cameron, then the leader of the Conservative opposition and later prime minister, told me. For whatever reasons, perhaps because of her conservative temperament, the Queen's relationships with most Democratic presidents prior to Obama were trickier than those with their Republican counterparts—nonexistent with Lyndon Johnson, weird with Jimmy Carter, wary with Bill Clinton. The exception was John F. Kennedy, but in his case their ties went back to their youths.

In London, officials who advised Her Majesty worried that Obama would view Britain as nothing more than a faded colonial power. There was friction over the long Afghanistan war, a cautionary tale of the consequences from the alliance of George W. Bush and Tony Blair. The prime minister's support of the Iraq War had cost him politically, and the two countries had taken divergent responses to the global recession. The White House was also aware of an "undercurrent of unease" about the new president, not from the royal family but from the British establishment. "I think they genuinely thought he might harbor some anti-colonial attitudes from his Kenyan background," said Ben Rhodes, Obama's deputy national security adviser.

When Obama arrived in the Oval Office, he returned to the British embassy the bronze bust of Winston Churchill that Bush had borrowed, replacing it with one of the Rev. Dr. Martin Luther King Jr. Still in place was a bust of Churchill that had long been displayed in the White House residence, outside the Treaty Room. Even so, in a diplomatic world accustomed to reading tea leaves, the move from the Oval Office was seen as a worrisome sign. "Some said it was a snub to Britain," Boris Johnson, then the mayor of London and a future prime minister, wrote in an op-ed in the *Sun* designed to be provocative. "Some said it was a symbol of the part-Kenyan President's ancestral dislike of the British empire." Obama also didn't invite British Prime Minister Gordon Brown to be the first foreign leader he welcomed to the White House. That hat tip went to Prime Minister Tarō Asō of Japan, a sign of the Pacific priorities of the new president, who had grown up in Hawaii and Indonesia. It was a signal that Elizabeth would not have missed.

Two months later, in April 2009, the G20 summit was being held in London. The Queen invited all twenty world leaders to a reception at Buckingham Palace; she asked only Barack and Michelle Obama to a private audience beforehand. The president teased his wife about what she should wear. "You should wear one of those little hats," he said. "And carry a little handbag." She didn't take his fashion advice. When they were escorted into the royal apartments, she was wearing a simple white top and black skirt and a black cardigan, a double strand of pearls around her neck. Neither she nor the Queen sported a hat, but Elizabeth, in a petal-pink dress and a triple strand of pearls, did have a small black handbag looped over her left arm, as usual.

"Everything was such a whirlwind back then," Michelle Obama recalled. "We had just begun adjusting to life as President and First Lady with two young daughters. And just like that, we were heading to London for our first official international trip." She quipped: "Growing up on the South Side of Chicago, you don't get many chances to meet a Queen."

The briefings on protocol didn't make her feel more relaxed. "Before meeting Her Majesty, I remember being given a lot of instructions. There were rules about where we were to stand and how I was supposed to curtsy. I had never met a royal before, and to be quite honest, I really wasn't sure what to expect. But upon meeting the Queen, any nervousness or uncertainty I had quickly disappeared. Her Majesty had such a power to her, but not simply because of her station. She was, of course, polished and poised. But she was also warm and personable, inviting and inquisitive."

They started with small talk about jet lag.

"We're still trying to stay awake," Michelle said as the two couples lined up for a photograph, their chitchat caught by television cameras. The president added, "I had breakfast with the prime minister; I had meetings with the Chinese, the Russians and David Cameron, and I'm proud to say I did not nod off in any of the meetings."

"Can you tell the difference between them?" joked Prince Philip.

"It's all a blur," Obama replied with a smile.

The royal couple presented the Obamas with their standard gifts, signed photographs of themselves in silver frames, and the Obamas gave the Queen a gift that was anything but standard: an iPod loaded with forty Broadway show tunes, plus footage of her visits to the United States in 1957 and 2007. It also included Obama's speech to the 2004 Democratic National Convention, which had ignited his national political prospects, and his 2009 inaugural address.

That gift, with its self-promotional overtones, made some Obama aides cringe and late-night comics laugh. "Now she can listen to Lil Wayne on the treadmill without anyone bothering her," comedian Jimmy Kimmel said. Rhodes acknowledged, "I guess the gifts weren't seen as sufficiently regal."

At the reception that followed, there would be a bigger kerfuffle.

"You're so tall," Elizabeth had remarked to Michelle as the two women chatted. She replied, "Well, the shoes give me a couple of inches. But yes, I'm tall." The first lady was an inch under six feet; the Queen stood a full head shorter at five feet four. She eyed Michelle's black Jimmy Choos and shook her head. "These shoes are unpleasant, are they not?" she said, admitting that her feet hurt, too. The two women looked at each other and laughed, then compared the height of their heels. Michelle put her hand across the Queen's shoulder, as though to stand on one leg and display her shoe. The Queen put her arm around Michelle's waist for just a moment.

That casual encounter, caught on camera, ricocheted through the British papers and social media. It was ridiculed as one more example of those presumptive Americans and their violations of the rules about royals, which hold that you never touch the monarch. "The unthinkable: she gave the Queen a hug," the *Guardian* correspondent huffed. "The monarch, for her part, responded with equally flagrant disregard for convention by returning the gesture." It's not clear which move—Michelle's "faux pas" or the unexpected display of the Queen's "touchy-feely side"—shocked the writer more. The story chronicled previous instances, just four of them, when someone had "initiated physical contact with Elizabeth without ending up in the Tower." Two were Australian prime ministers, one a Canadian cyclist, and Alice Frazier of Baltimore, who engulfed Elizabeth in a bear hug when she was touring a housing project during her 1991 visit to the United States.

"No-one—including the ladies-in-waiting standing nearby—could believe their eyes," a British columnist wrote. "In 57 years, the Queen has never been seen to make that kind of gesture and it's certainly against all protocol to touch her."

Michelle worried she had revived "campaign-era speculation" that she was "generally uncouth and lacked the standard elegance of a First Lady," and that she might have distracted from her husband's debut on the world stage. The controversy gained so much steam that a palace spokeswoman felt the need to push back, calling it a "mutual and spontaneous display of affection and appreciation between the Queen and Michelle Obama."

Gyles Brandreth saw the Queen soon afterward when someone asked her about what had become an incident of international debate. The British author and celebrity relayed the conversation he had overheard. "Oh, well, that was—," the man had said, his face and body language the aristocratic personification of outrage. Elizabeth dismissed the idea of offense. "'Oh, no, no,'" she demurred. "Lovely, they were a lovely couple, lovely people, really."

It was the start of their friendship. Before the tea, in the teasing exchange with his wife, Obama seemed to view Elizabeth as a caricature who carried small purses and wore elaborate hats. At their meeting, each found the other intriguing. Maybe his attitude, respectful but not awed, helped. He was surprised at how normal she acted; she may have been surprised that he did the same. "My suspicion is that for someone that iconic, who has been that iconic for that long, having people who behave reasonably normally was probably a nice change of pace," Obama said. It also reflected the ease the Queen often seemed to feel with Americans. Since her first visit to the United States, royal correspondents had remarked about glimpses of a spontaneous side she rarely showed at home.

"Now we have met," the Queen told the Obamas as they were leaving the palace. "Would you please keep in touch?"

KEEP IN TOUCH THEY DID.

During his White House tenure, Obama would meet with the Queen during four visits, matching the number by Ronald Reagan, the president with whom Elizabeth was closest. Obama and Elizabeth would spend time together three times in England and once in France. (On the seventieth anniversary of D-Day, in 2014, they were seated together at a luncheon hosted by French President François Hollande.) Their relationship represented what Rhodes called "a powerful form of validation" for Obama back home. Some of his opponents, including Donald Trump, never stopped questioning Obama's birthplace, his legitimacy for the office. But from their first meeting, the Queen of England did everything she could to make it clear she harbored no such doubts, that the first Black president had her respect and acceptance.

Obama recorded a video message of standard diplomatese marking the Queen's Diamond Jubilee in 2012—"A steadfast ally, loyal friend, and tireless leader"—but the two also engaged in a more humorous exchange, uncommon in a world generally governed by the traditions of centuries. Prince Harry, at the time thirty years old and still a member in good standing of the royal family, engineered a promotional spot for the Invictus Games, his charitable enterprise for wounded warriors, which in 2016 would be held in Orlando. Seated side by side on a floral loveseat, Harry is showing the Queen a program for the games when his cell phone begins to play "Hail to the Chief." Purportedly on FaceTime were the Obamas, talking smack over which country would bring home more gold medals. "Hey, Prince Harry, remember when you told us to bring it at the Invictus Games?" Michelle says in a challenging voice. Obama adds: "Careful what you wish for" as a military officer behind him mimes a mic drop and says "boom."

The Queen's royal dismissal: "Boom? Really? Please."

In 2009, two months after their first presidential visit to London, Michelle Obama returned on a private visit with her two daughters, Malia and Sasha, and her mother, Marian Robinson. The Queen invited them to the palace and arranged for a ride in her gilded carriage around the royal grounds for the girls, then ten and seven years old. They were thrilled, as just about any girl of any age from any place would have been.

The hospitality went both ways, and with the next generations of royals.

Prince William visited the Oval Office for the first time in December 2014 for a fifteen-minute conversation with Obama. British diplomats said it was focused on wildlife protection and was intended "in preparation for his own role one day." Charles made efforts to build a relationship with Obama, especially over the environmental issues the prince championed. In March 2015, the Prince of Wales and Camilla, Duchess of Cornwall (they had married in 2005) met with Obama and Vice President Joe Biden in the Oval Office during a four-day trip to Washington by the royal couple that also included a ceremony marking the eight hundredth anniversary of the Magna Carta.

"I think it's fair to say that the American people are quite fond of the royal family," Obama told Charles amid the clatter of news photographers' cameras as they sat under a portrait of George Washington.

"That's awfully nice to know," he replied.

Leaning in, as though to impart a secret despite the microphones swaying on poles above their heads, Obama added *sotto voce*, "They like them much better than their own politicians."

WHEN THE OBAMAS ARRIVED AT BUCKINGHAM PALACE FOR A STATE VISIT on May 24, 2011, the Queen gave the president a tour of memorabilia from the Royal Archive, items that had been selected and displayed for their resonance with Americans in general and this president in particular.

There was a note in King George III's handwriting from around 1780, as the tide was turning for the rebels in the American Revolution. "America is lost!" the king bemoaned. "Must we fall beneath the blow?" But he went on to speculate about a better relationship after the war, of trade with his former colonies and the importance of "a future friendship and connection." There were books and relics from early Hawaii, where Obama was born, and records from a visit in 1860 by the then–Prince of Wales to Obama's home city of Chicago. A handwritten note by the Queen Mother to Elizabeth, then a princess, told her about the 1939 picnic at President Roosevelt's home at Hyde Park. They ate under the trees "and all our food on one plate," she said, her amazement apparent. "Some ham, lettuce, beans and HOT DOGS TOO!"

Also on display were letters from Abraham Lincoln, who was one of

Obama's heroes, and a sympathy note from Queen Victoria to Lincoln's widow. Victoria's diary was opened to entries that conveyed her sympathy for Black slaves—"To what can human nature descend," she lamented—and her excitement about meeting a former enslaved person. Josiah Henson had "endured great suffering and cruelty" before escaping to British Canada, she wrote.

The world's long struggle for racial equality was an unexpected connection between Obama and the Queen, a source of shared feeling and regard. While she represented a staid institution and had a conservative temperament, she had long stood on the right side of history, aligning herself against white minority rule in Rhodesia (now called Zimbabwe) and the apartheid system in South Africa, even when that created friction within her own government. It was a common cause that linked them across race and generation.

Kenya, the land of Obama's father, proved to be a bond, not a division.

"Remember, she was in Kenya when her father died," Hillary Clinton, who served as Obama's secretary of state, said. "She became queen-in-waiting while she was in Africa at a former colony. And to be in the presence of someone whose paternal line dates from Kenya—I just think there's a lot about that which the Queen found very fascinating." In 2008, Uhuru Kenyatta, the son of Jomo Kenyatta, Kenya's first president, had become a deputy prime minister. Five years later, the younger Kenyatta would be elected president himself. Elizabeth had known both father and son. Obama was interested in how that history helped explain what was happening in his father's homeland.

Elizabeth had deeper relationships than anyone else in the British government with African leaders in countries that had been part of the British empire, many of them now in the Commonwealth. She knew them as well as any Western leader and frequently referenced the Commonwealth "family." When the white government in Rhodesia unilaterally declared independence from Britain in 1965 while maintaining its allegiance to the Queen—the first unilateral break by a British colony since the American Revolution—she made a symbolic but unmistakable statement about where she stood. She awarded Humphrey Gibbs, the British governor, a personal knighthood, known as a KCVO, Knight Commander of the Royal Victorian Order. "That was one of the few borderline examples of her interfering" in substantive issues, royal biographer Kenneth Rose said. "She was taking the side of the governor against her prime minister"—that is, against Rhodesian Prime Minister Ian Smith. Gibbs had formally dismissed Smith and his government, though they had simply ignored him.

There was particular interest in that conflict within Obama's inner circle. The emergence of Zimbabwe as a biracial democracy had been the topic of the thesis written at Oxford by Susan Rice, Obama's national security adviser. She had concluded that the Queen's role and her stature was crucial in reaching a peaceful transition that recognized Black rights. "The five contingents' allegiance to Queen and Commonwealth was a remarkably valuable asset in dealing both with white and black Rhodesians," Rice wrote in the thesis, now on file at Oxford.

"I think without her hand it's questionable if it would've happened when it happened," Rice told me. "The Queen worked behind the scenes to bring pressure to bear on Thatcher to begin a process to negotiate the transition of Rhodesia to Zimbabwe," from white minority rule to Black majority rule, ratified in the Lancaster House agreement. In the peacekeeping and election monitoring that followed, she had "the legitimacy to have a voice and play a role."

The Queen asserted her opposition to white minority rule in South Africa as well. Though it had been a founding member of the Commonwealth before leaving in 1961, she refused to visit while apartheid was in place. Her stance put her at odds with Prime Minister Margaret Thatcher, who opposed sanctions on Pretoria. When the brutal system of racial divide was finally being dismantled, African National Congress president Nelson Mandela was released from prison and South Africa rejoined the Commonwealth. He and the Queen forged a friendship of mutual admiration and warmth. Mandela, a personal hero to Obama, was African royalty himself, born into the royal family of the Thembu people. He had an easy manner with the Queen. He would tease her in ways few others dared, even calling her Elizabeth to her face.

"Elizabeth, you've lost weight!" he exclaimed loudly and mischievously at one arrival at Buckingham Palace, prompting her to break into laughter. She adored Mandela; no one would call her "Elizabeth" more than once unless she allowed it. She enjoyed the company of the Obamas, too, and admired them. She brought out a warmth in the aloof president that he was known to lack in some other private settings.

FOR A STATE VISIT TO LONDON, A FOREIGN HEAD OF STATE IS TYPICALLY greeted on Horse Guards Parade, then travels down the Mall in a horse-drawn coach with the Queen. But the Secret Service found that arrangement too exposed, too vulnerable for a president. Instead, when the Obamas arrived, they were driven onto the palace grounds in the presidential limousine—eight tons of armor nicknamed "The Beast"—for a welcome ceremony on the lawn.

The Queen and the Duke of Edinburgh, Prince Charles and the Duchess of Cornwall stood with the American couple on the West Terrace as the Band of the Scots Guards played "God Save the Queen" and "The Star-Spangled Banner." From nearby Green Park, a forty-one-gun salute sounded—twenty-one rounds for a head of state, and another twenty rounds because the salute came from a royal park. Then Obama and Philip inspected the troops.

Elizabeth herself escorted the Obamas to the Belgian Suite, the most elegant guest accommodations in the palace. Newlyweds Prince William and Kate Middleton had been the most recent occupants, on their wedding night just a month earlier. In 2003, George W. Bush and Laura Bush stayed there. So had King Edward VIII before he abdicated the throne in 1936. The six-room garden apartment was decorated with priceless artwork. Paintings by eighteenth-century artists Canaletto and Thomas Gainsborough hung on the walls. A portrait by Johan Joseph Zoffany of George III, the king who sparked the American Revolution, showed him almost iridescent in a gold cape. The windows had been bomb-proofed at the insistence of the Secret Service before Bush's visit. But that updated touch wasn't matched by the two bathrooms in the suite, both off a hallway, neither connected to a bedroom. Adjacent to the main bedroom was what the British call an Edwardian toilet, or a "thunder box"—a closet-like enclosure, paneled in mahogany, with a toilet tucked inside. Obama was just the second American president, after the younger Bush, to make a formal state visit to England during Elizabeth's reign. (Later, Donald Trump would be the third.)

In her toast that night, the Queen celebrated "the tried, tested, and, yes, special relationship between our two countries." In his response,

Obama praised "this great country . . . and this special relationship," and he thanked her for the hospitality she had shown his daughters. Her Majesty had seen a dozen presidents and prime ministers, he noted, which "makes you both a living witness to the power of our alliance and a chief source of its resilience."

But there was another of the protocol stumbles that seemed to bedevil American visitors. In short, Obama inadvertently cued the band too early, prompting a muddle of music and words. The template of toasts ends with the words, "To Her Majesty the Queen," the signal to the Scots Guard band to launch into "God Save the Queen." But the president uttered those key words in what turned out to be the middle of his remarks. The band began to play, the guests stood, and Obama kept talking. Elizabeth gazed straight ahead. When he finally finished and raised his glass, the music was still mid-anthem. "That's very kind," she said quietly, not moving to raise her own glass until the band had finished.

The Queen, who had surely presided over more formal dinners than anyone else, ever, anywhere, was unperturbed. With all that experience, she was also known for running a tight ship. "She and I shared a love of an efficient receiving line," Michelle Obama confided, "sometimes sharing a look when our husbands indulged in long conversations late into the night."

Indeed, that's precisely what happened after this dinner was over and the guests were standing and chatting, drinks in hand. Elizabeth was ready to call it a night; Obama gave no sign he was ready to go. About midnight, she enlisted the chancellor of the Exchequer to help. "The Queen came up to me," George Osborne said, "and she said, 'Will you tell the President it's time to go to bed? Because I can't go to bed until he goes to bed.'" He said yes, of course, but was unsure precisely how he should proceed. Obama "was in a white tie looking pretty dashing, and he was having a vodka martini or something," Osborne recalled. "And I was thinking, what am I supposed to do?" He was rescued by the Queen's private secretary, Christopher Geidt. "He said, 'Don't worry, Chancellor; I heard what the Queen said to you; you don't have to do it. We're sorting it out.'" Geidt had a word with one of Obama's aides, and the evening finally ended.

Afterward, Obama and two advisers, Jon Favreau and Rhodes, retired to the Belgian Suite—in part to prepare for his speech to Parliament the next day, in part to dish on the royal dinner they had just shared. "Did you see the bling on the Queen?" Obama marveled. He had been struck by her discussion, and dissection, of the leaders she had encountered over decades. He had asked her about every president she had known: "'What about Eisenhower?' 'What about Kennedy?'" While she didn't rank them, Rhodes said it was clear she liked some more than others. She was astute and pithy in assessing the foreign leaders she had met. At the time, the Arab Spring was convulsing the Middle East, and the Obama administration had found itself struggling to deal with Israeli Prime Minister Benjamin Netanyahu. The Queen's perfunctory comment: "Bibi. Difficult." Very few people impressed the cerebral, confident Obama as much as she did.

"She had this wonderful, matter-of-fact, deadpan wit and insight," Obama told me. "I mean, she had seen a lot. She'd been there since Churchill, and she had gone through pretty much every world leader and would have opinions about the Shah of Iran or Kwame Nkrumah. I mean, [she's] just got a lot of unique perspective on world affairs." That said, she was "fairly circumspect and restrained," especially in discussing those who were still alive, and especially in discussing other presidents. "She was very careful not to want to ever make herself an issue with respect to day-to-day politics or bilateral relations."

The Queen offered another connection for Obama, one that was personal. She reminded him of his grandmother, Madelyn Payne Dunham, nicknamed "Toot," who had helped raise him in Hawaii. The two women were born four years apart but into circumstances that were entirely different—Madelyn in rural Kansas and Elizabeth into British royalty. But both had aged to be stoic, solid women who shared some characteristics— the important ones, Obama said after sitting next to the Queen at the dinner. "Courteous," he recalled. "Straightforward. All about what she thinks. She doesn't suffer fools."

The next day, speaking in historic Westminster Hall, Obama began with humor.

"I am told that the last three speakers here have been the Pope, Her Majesty the Queen and Nelson Mandela," he said. "Which is either a very high bar or the beginning of a very funny joke." What followed was a defense of democracy in challenging times, and a closing that returned to the threads of colonialism and race.

"In a world which will only grow smaller and more interconnected," he said, "the example of our two nations says it is possible for people to be united by their ideals instead of divided by their differences; that it's possible for hearts to change and old hatreds to pass; that it's possible for the sons and daughters of former colonies to sit here as members of this great Parliament, and for the grandson of a Kenyan who served as a cook in the British Army to stand before you as president of the United States."

THEIR UNEXPECTED FRIENDSHIP WAS SEALED BY A BROOCH.

They had exchanged gifts when they arrived at the palace. The Obamas presented the Queen with a leather-bound album with memorabilia and photographs of her parents' visit to the United States in 1939—no iPod this time. Philip, a competitive carriage driver, received custom gear for his horses. The royal couple's gifts to the Obamas included facsimiles of letters from several US presidents to Queen Victoria, Elizabeth's great-great-grandmother.

Michelle Obama also gave Her Majesty a vintage, American-made pin from 1950 featuring 14-karat yellow gold, diamonds, and moss agate. She had found it at the Tiny Jewel Box, a posh store a few blocks north of the White House. The pin was pretty, but it wasn't big or flashy or fabulously expensive—and jewelry might seem to be a risky gift for the Queen of England.

"I think it's fair to say that she's got a pretty big jewelry box, meaning, literally, the crown jewels," Barack Obama laughed. "The whole expression, 'crown jewels,' comes from her jewelry box." He had seen evidence of that up close at the white-tie dinner. She entered wearing a diamond-and-pearl tiara, a diamond necklace, pearl drop earrings, and a pin at the top of her blue sash that was dripping with diamonds and pearls. "The Queen's got this dress—it glitters. It looks like a rhinestone, shimmery dress. And we're sitting there eating, and I realized, 'You know what? That's not glitter or rhinestones. They're diamonds all up and down this dress.' And so between the little crown she's wearing and the dress, she's probably got, I don't know, $20 million worth of stuff that she's walking around in." (For the record, the bodice of the Queen's white silk crepe gown was embroidered with Swarovski crystals—not diamonds, though still spectacular.) Afterward, he teased his wife. "You got out-gifted here."

The next night, the Obamas hosted a reciprocal black-tie dinner at Winfield House, the US ambassador's residence.

"The Queen steps out of the car, and she's got that little brooch on," he said. "That's all. She's got her little suit with her little purse and the hat, and her only adornment is this little brooch on her suit." She was wearing earrings and a necklace, but the lone pin on her shoulder was impossible to miss, a bit of gold and green on her white dress. Michelle said to her, "Oh, Your Majesty, you're wearing the pin." The Queen replied, "Oh, yes, I think it's quite nice." Her no-fuss thoughtfulness was a "nice touch, smart diplomacy, the reason why she was beloved," he said.

Nice, smart, beloved—and, perhaps, sometimes sly. She would wear the brooch in public just one more time, at a memorable moment.

BY THE TIME OBAMA WAS PRESIDENT, ELIZABETH HAD BECOME AN INcreasingly venerated figure—for her age, her time on the throne, her steady grace, her global standing—and with that came a greater willingness to reveal herself. Through the decades, after all, she had adjusted in subtle ways to suit the times. She had grown in the job, and her encounters with presidents contributed to that, from Eisenhower, who was old enough to be her father, to Obama, who was young enough to be her son.

Matthew Barzun, the US ambassador to the Court of St. James's during Obama's second term, came from a family that had its own historic lineage. A media entrepreneur who helped start the CNET Networks in the 1990s, Barzun was also a descendant of John Winthrop, a renowned English Puritan lawyer who had helped found the Massachusetts Bay Colony in the seventeenth century. The family of Barzun's wife, Brooke Brown Barzun, had a notable past, too: owners of the distilling empire founded in the nineteenth century that included Jack Daniel's.

One of his father-in-law's favorite stories about that iconic Tennessee whiskey had parallels to Her Majesty, Barzun said. "He said, 'One thing that people love about Jack Daniel's is that the bottle never changes, and the key to the perception that the bottle never changes is that the bottle always changes.'" That is, the design was repeatedly but subtly updated to stay aligned with public tastes—the goal being to never look either dated or trendy. Elizabeth was like that, he said. "Steadfast," he called her.

For decades, her clothing was classic in design and typically bright and monochromatic in color, from her fanciful hats to her sensible shoes, the better to be spotted in a crowd from a distance. Early on, she had settled on a short symmetrical coif that suited her (and her tiaras) and stuck with it, forever. But over time she would show more of her humor and her feelings, including after the British public demanded that with the death of Princess Diana.

For the opening ceremonies of the 2012 London Olympics, the Queen and her corgis were filmed in a James Bond–inspired video that started at Buckingham Palace and ended, to all appearances, with the eighty-six-year-old monarch parachuting into the Olympic arena in a sparkly salmon-colored dress before being introduced up in the stands. (Full disclosure: There was a stunt double involved.) The jaw-dropping gag would have been hard to imagine early in her reign.

She would, however, rue the advent of smartphones. To present his diplomatic credentials to her, Barzun and his wife arrived at Buckingham Palace carried in a horse-drawn carriage, a top hat on his head. They could hear the buzz from the tourists massed near the gates. "You could hear them say, 'Who are they? Do you think they're royal?'" When he met the Queen, he asked her how she dealt with such crowds as a matter of routine. "They always had cameras and they picked them up, took a picture and put them down," she told him. But now they hold up their smartphones to record the scene. "They keep them up and they never take them down—and I miss seeing their eyes." Even after decades, she missed the small human connection of the moment.

THE RAPPORT BETWEEN THE QUEEN AND THE PRESIDENT WAS ALWAYS helpful, and always more crucial when there were strains between the two nations.

Obama had a better relationship with Cameron than he had with Gordon Brown, whose Labour Party suffered setbacks and was ousted from power in 2010. But the United States expressed outrage when the Lockerbie bomber, convicted of the attack on Pan Am Flight 103, was given an early compassionate release from a Scottish prison. The British were annoyed when Obama blamed the Gulf of Mexico oil spill on "British Petroleum." The British and the French pushed the United States to do more to boost the Arab Spring, especially the uprising in Libya. There were concerns about the war in Afghanistan, where both the United States and the United Kingdom had troops deployed in harm's way.

The president's visit with the Queen didn't resolve any of those issues, but it did calm the climate in which they were considered. Cameron would be a leading beneficiary of that warmth. As soon as the state visit in London was over, planning began for him to visit Washington.

"We spent quite a lot of time talking about incoming state visits or her outgoing state visits and how to make the best of it—what was really important and how we could maximize the benefit for the UK," Cameron said, saying that her skill and "diplomatic heft" enabled Great Britain to "punch above our weight" in the world. "She brought it to bear with the American president in all sorts of ways because she knew how important it was for the U.K."

While he was in Washington, Cameron was given the easy access of old friends. For one thing, he was the first foreign leader Obama invited to ride on *Air Force One*.

The two men went together to Dayton, Ohio, to attend an early round of the NCAA men's basketball tournament—Cameron's first basketball game, a sport that was Obama's passion. Sitting courtside, Obama explained the rules of the game; one news photo showed the two simultaneously devouring hot dogs. On the flight back to Washington, Obama noticed that Cameron was struggling with jet lag. "He said, 'David, why don't you use my bed and put your feet up,'" Cameron said later. So he did.

"I bet Roosevelt never did this for Churchill," Obama said to him.

DONALD TRUMP WAS THREE YEARS FROM ANNOUNCING HIS FIRST POLITIcal bid—aiming for the top, running for the White House, and to nearly everyone's surprise, winning it.

He continued to be outspoken about his views of all things royal, the family he followed so closely. He chastised Catherine, then the Duchess of Cambridge, after a paparazzo used long-distance lenses to shoot photos as she sunbathed topless at a private chateau in the south of France in 2012. (The British royal couple would be awarded monetary damages by a French court for invasion of privacy.) "Kate Middleton is great—but she shouldn't be sunbathing in the nude—only herself to blame," Trump had tweeted when the photos were published in the French magazine *Closer*. Who could fault the photographers, just trying to make a buck? "Come on, Kate!"

At the time, he was surely unaware that she would be among those greeting him at a royal dinner in his honor seven years later.

THE OBAMA WHITE HOUSE REACHED OUT IN 2015 TO INVITE THE QUEEN for a state visit in the United States, but they had waited too long. There was "so much back-and-forth" trying to arrange it, Ambassador Barzun said. But palace officials demurred. "She really can't do the trip," they told the Americans. "She would if she possibly could." By now she was eighty-nine years old, in the sixty-third year of her reign. She had visited one hundred and sixteen countries. Her final state visit would be to Germany that June.

Instead, the Obamas dropped in to see her, one last time. Not as leaders of allied nations. As friends.

There were other stops on the president's foreign itinerary, of course, starting with a US-Gulf Cooperation Council summit in Saudi Arabia beforehand and ending with a meeting of four European leaders in Germany afterward. But Obama's schedule was arranged so he would be in London to have lunch with the Queen on the day after her ninetieth birthday, just in time to celebrate that milestone.

She was, Obama said, "truly one of my favorite people." That was not a description the famously cool Obama offered casually. She was reserved, too, but those close to her said she felt the same way about him. At their first meeting, during his first overseas trip as president, he had acknowledged to her his realization of the absurdity of his new job, about bringing not only his own plane but his own helicopter and his own bulletproof car. She knew as much as anyone in the world about the occasional absurdity of their roles. As a documentary crew was filming massive candelabras being placed in the center of a 160-foot mahogany table before a state dinner, she had noted, straight-faced, "We don't actually live like this all the time." After decades in the spotlight, she had seen it all, and survived, and remembered.

"I sometimes imagined just the shock and frustrations that Michelle and I had moving into the White House, and I would think about, 'Well, what was this like if you're seventeen, eighteen, nineteen, and you're doing this for seventy years?'" he said. "I think in an unspoken way, she maybe understood that I understood both her constraints, but that underneath all the pomp and circumstance, she's still a person."

"They're similar people," Susan Rice said. How so? "Smart, dry-witted, poker face in public, but with dry comment to make privately." And they liked each other. "I just got her and I think she got me," Obama said. At bottom, perhaps it wasn't more complicated than that.

The Obamas spent the night at the US ambassador's residence, then flew on *Marine One* to the Home Park helipad on April 22, 2016. It was three days after Hillary Clinton and Donald Trump had won the New York primaries on their way to claiming their parties' presidential nominations. Her Majesty wanted to pick up the president and first lady for the short drive to Windsor Castle in her black Land Rover, with the Duke of Edinburgh in the driver's seat. There was a rub: For eight years, Obama had only ridden in vehicles driven by Secret Service agents, a safeguard considered necessary for his protection. The Queen wasn't persuaded. These were her guests, on her turf. It was one of the very few occasions in which the security argument didn't prevail; the personal one did. The West Wing finally overruled the Secret Service because it was clearly important to the royal couple. Philip, age ninety-four, would drive.

After the protocol disputes of previous visits—when the first lady had touched the Queen's shoulder, and when the president had muffed the timing of his toast at the state dinner—the Obamas had been thoroughly briefed on proper royal choreography. He was to get in the back seat next to the Queen: Check. She was to get in the front seat next to the prince: Check.

"I was given specific instructions beforehand that I was to sit next to Prince Philip," Michelle said. "Our teams had litigated this endlessly—and I wanted to ensure everything went as planned. I remember approaching the car and seeing Her Majesty. We said our hellos, and then she waved me over to sit down next to her in the back. I hesitated for a moment. And she looked at me and asked if I was trying to follow some rule they gave me."

Why, yes, she was. "That's rubbish," the Queen said. "Sit wherever you want."

"And that was that," Michelle said. "So I sat next to her. Royal protocol was broken—and Her Royal Highness couldn't have cared less. But that's just who she was. Beneath all of the trappings was a kind-hearted, no-nonsense woman who was just trying to go about her life. . . . For all the protocol and regulations that were always surrounding her, she wasn't afraid to shake things up every once in a while, to remind people that she was both a queen and a human."

They drank wine with lunch; Philip had a few beers. They reminisced about the previous eight years and considered the political future. She was curious about Trump, who had taken the GOP primaries by storm. "Why is this person so close to running your country?" she asked Obama. That was a question the president and nearly every other pol in America was trying to figure out.

They also discussed the biggest current controversy in Great Britain, over Brexit. Her view on whether to leave the European Union was the subject of endless speculation during her reign and after her death. "QUEEN BACKS BREXIT," the front-page headline in *The Sun* breathlessly announced during the debate, drawing the palace's denial. She was "politically neutral," they said. A 2025 book by royal correspondent Valentine Low declared the opposite: "The Queen was a Remainer," that is, against Brexit.

In fact, at the fiercest time of the furor, she had expressed her real views to Obama. It was a sign of the affinity and the trust she felt for him. At their luncheon, she was not only wary of Brexit but also dismayed by how Cameron was handling it—a very rare royal critique of a prime minister, in public or private. In a calculation that turned out to be disastrously wrong, Cameron had called a referendum for June, two months away. "She said, effectively, 'It's hard to understand why a prime minister, who presumably understands politics, would put a public referendum forward that he didn't know what the answer would be of such importance,'" Obama told me. He was surprised by her candor. It was the only time she commented directly on British politics to him. "Clearly, there was an assessment on her part that, regardless of the details of policy, having as big a decision as the

UK pulling out of the EU was not one that, from her perspective, should have been decided by plebiscite."

She never took a public position on Brexit, but in this conversation, she worried that the referendum just might pass. It did, 52 percent to 48 percent. During the campaign, she had told a senior Cameron aide that she thought their PR strategy was a miscalculation. "Instead of focusing on the economic risk of leaving, she said the argument we should be making was, 'Better the devil you know,'" a senior British official said. That is, focus on the benefits and the stability of staying in the European Union.

Obama's visit was an opportunity to try to boost Cameron in his battle against Brexit. After the president's lunch with the royal couple, the president met with the prime minister, and then they spoke with reporters. If Britain left the European Union, Obama warned, it would find itself "in the back of the queue" for a trade deal with the United States. Brexit backers were hoping for a bilateral accord that might help ameliorate the economic consequences of leaving the EU.

That evening, the Obamas visited Prince William and Catherine at Kensington Palace for drinks and dinner. Prince Harry was there, too. Prince George, then two years old and third in line for the throne, was allowed to stay up past his bedtime to meet his first American president. Wearing a monogrammed white robe and wooly slippers, he demonstrated how to ride the wooden rocking horse the Obamas had sent as a baby present.

A few weeks later, at the annual White House Correspondents Association dinner in Washington, Obama made a self-deprecating joke about their encounter as one more sign of his waning stature as a lame duck, his exit from power approaching. "It's not just Congress," he said. "Even some foreign leaders, they've been looking ahead, anticipating my departure. Last week, Prince George showed up to our meeting in his bathrobe. That was a slap in the face," he said with mock distress. "A clear breach of protocol."

The photograph was projected on oversized screens in the Washington Hilton ballroom. It showed the president sitting on his haunches, face-to-face with George. They seem to be deep in conversation, a serious expression on the toddler's face.

NEITHER OBAMA NOR THE QUEEN WERE GIVEN TO HYPERBOLE, EVEN when politics might have made that a useful trait. Neither swooned to flattery themselves. Elizabeth was reserved by nature and training; Obama could seem detached even with members of Congress whose support he was supposed to cultivate.

Yet in a conversation with Gyles Brandreth, the Queen put Obama in very high company. "She told me she was grateful to have had the opportunity to meet 'so many remarkable people' during her lifetime," Brandreth relayed, "from Mother Teresa to Barack Obama."

Obama would make a similar point about her. When Rhodes wrote a draft of Obama's eulogy for the memorial service for former Israeli Prime Minister Shimon Peres in 2016, the President told him he wanted to make a point about three people who to him represented the twentieth century. Peres was one of them, a peacemaker and a link to repercussions of World War II. Mandela was another, a revolutionary. The third was the Queen, a symbol of the established order.

"I think each of them in their own way were a bridge, that they were there at the creation of, and the fight for, this new order, but still had a foot in the old," Obama explained. "Each of them had survived and come out on the other side and made their own transition in terms of how they viewed the world and adapted to it, rather than insisting on going backward. In that sense, I think they embodied the transition that took place in the twentieth century into the twenty-first, into a more enlightened world, and they were a part of that."

In his speech, he described them as "leaders who have seen so much, whose lives span such momentous epochs, that they find no need to posture or traffic in what's popular in the moment; people who speak with depth and knowledge, not in sound bites." They were "giants of the twentieth century that I've had the honor to meet."

At the start, neither side was certain whether the president and the Queen would get along. As it turned out, they did, and more.

THEN THERE WAS DONALD TRUMP.

The Queen's interest already had turned toward the man who just might be the next president. A month before the 2016 election, Prince

Harry introduced girlfriend Meghan Markle to his grandmother at a casual encounter in Royal Lodge, where Sarah Ferguson then lived. "It was all very pleasant," Harry wrote in his memoir, *Spare*. "Granny even asked Meg what she thought of Donald Trump." Meghan dodged. (Her theory that politics was a no-win game with prospective in-laws could have applied even if they didn't happen to be royalty.) Markle tried to change the subject to Canada.

"Granny squinted. I thought you were an American," Harry recounted. "I am, but I've been living in Canada for seven years for work." That is, for the filming of her USA Network TV series, *Suits*. "Granny looked pleased. Commonwealth. Good. Fine."

Her interactions with the most controversial president of her reign would start soon enough.

Fourteen

The Favourite?

Monday, June 3, 2019—Windsor Castle

Queen Elizabeth was not smiling as she watched the whirlwind of the helicopters' blades flatten her flowers. "It ruined the garden," a senior palace aide said. "She was furious about that." The annoyance lingered to the point that she reportedly complained about it to Australian Prime Minister Scott Morrison when he arrived later. "Come and look at my lawn," she told him. "It's ruined."

But nothing could spoil this moment for President Donald Trump.

He had wanted a state visit, and being toasted by Her Majesty, since his inauguration. Whatever else his presidency might bring, he saw a state visit to England as a highlight, a personal milestone with a meaning beyond politics. He was "slightly awestruck" when he talked about her, National Security Council staffer Fiona Hill said, and his voice and face would soften. "A meeting with the Queen of England was the ultimate sign that he, Trump, had made it in life." The monarch's personal charm and storied history were just one side of the appeal. The other was the mirror she would provide, reflecting the stature he had long sought.

Finally, he was arriving. But it had taken two years of effort to overcome British alarm about this unexpected new American president. Kim Darroch, the British ambassador to Washington, had written his private assessment of the Trump White House at the five-month mark of the administration, in June 2017.

"The starting point is that this is our single most important bilateral relationship," he said. "As seen from here, we really don't believe this administration is going to become substantially more normal; less dysfunctional; less unpredictable; less faction riven; less diplomatically clumsy and inept." His take on the president himself was damning. "For a man who has risen to the highest office on the planet, President Trump radiates insecurity," he wrote, with consequences not yet clear. He could be "at the beginning of a downward spiral, rather than just a rollercoaster; something could emerge that leads to disgrace and downfall." But Darroch cautioned that Trump had a history of surviving scandals, likening him to the inextinguishable cinematic cyborg portrayed by Arnold Schwarzenegger when he was an actor, not a governor. "Trump may emerge from the flames, battered but intact, like Schwarzenegger in the final scenes of The Terminator."

Darroch warned: "Do not write him off."

Two years later, Darroch would be ousted for writing those words while Trump would still be standing—and standing just where he wanted to be. He was climbing out of the *Marine One* helicopter and walking across the Buckingham Palace lawn toward the Queen for the start of his state visit.

"They gave me a tremendously, the five-star dinner, and it was really incredible," Trump told me. "I sat with her for hours, and Camilla was on my right and she was on my left, and we talked for a long time." They had "a great chemistry together," he said with satisfaction.

"There was a great honor for me to know her, then ultimately get to know her well."

AFTER TRUMP WAS INAUGURATED, THE FIRST FOREIGN LEADER HE WELcomed to the Oval Office was the British prime minister, Theresa May. It was a month after Darroch had filed his disquieting assessment, though the cable hadn't yet leaked to the White House and the world. May's own observations of the new president in action would quickly make their way to a curious Queen Elizabeth. She had already asked his predecessor, Barack Obama, to explain Trump's political rise.

The invitation was a sign of the affection Trump held for Great Britain.

So was his choice of Oval Office decor, reviving a ruckus from the opening days of Obama's tenure. President George W. Bush had borrowed a bust of Winston Churchill from the British embassy to display. Obama returned it, putting instead in pride of place a bust of Martin Luther King Jr. Republican critics saw that as a slight to a heroic ally.

Candidate Trump had promised to bring Churchill back. Hours after the new president was sworn in at noon on January 20, 2017, Darroch had the bust, which had been on display for eight years in the residence's library, secured in the trunk of one of the embassy's Land Rovers. He drove it to the White House, where it was unloaded and carried in. "No fuss, no hassle," as he put it. When the prime minister arrived, Churchill's resolute visage was back on display in the Oval Office.

Despite the friendly landscape, the president and the prime minister had some discomfiting exchanges during their private session. They disagreed on the competence of German Chancellor Angela Merkel, the need for sanctions against Russian President Vladimir Putin, even the standing of May herself. "Why isn't Boris Johnson the prime minister?" Trump asked her. "Didn't he want the job?" Johnson, sometimes described as a rumpled British version of Trump, was then her foreign minister. Two years later, he would succeed her at 10 Downing Street.

When they emerged from the Oval Office and walked along the Colonnade, heading toward the residence for an official luncheon, there was another uncomfortable moment, this one in full view of TV cameras. Trump reached out and held May's hand for almost ten seconds—an inexplicable interlude, and an eternity when it was shown and reshown on social media. It "took Theresa by surprise," a top aide acknowledged. May later described Trump in general as unsettling, a view she surely shared with the Queen.

At their joint news conference, though, all was bonhomie—with a plum.

"The special relationship between our two countries has been one of the great forces in history for justice and for peace and, by the way, my mother was born in Scotland—Stornoway, which is serious Scotland," Trump said, veering from his scripted remarks for a familial side note. Then he got back on track: "We pledge our lasting support to this most special relationship."

May called their session a sign of the "strength and importance" of their nations' bonds. "And in a further sign of importance in that relationship, I have today been able to convey Her Majesty, the Queen's hope that President Trump and the first lady would pay a state visit to the United Kingdom later this year," she said, "and I'm delighted that the President has accepted that invitation."

Behind the scenes, British officials had debated the wisdom of the invitation, or at least the timing. Darroch was among those who argued it was too soon, especially for a disruptive figure whom foreign leaders were still nervously appraising. "[H]aving secured the first White House visit, we could afford to wait and see how the Trump presidency panned out," the ambassador urged. He noted that Trump's two immediate predecessors, the younger Bush and Obama, hadn't made state visits until the third years of their presidencies.

But the British, like governments around the globe, were anxious to develop a working relationship with Trump. The Queen was eager to see him, face-to-face. "According to one former member of staff, she was intrigued to meet a head of state who, like her, had a Scottish mother and who, like her, happens to own a large area of Scottish countryside," royal biographer Robert Hardman said. Elizabeth owned the Balmoral Estate; Trump had upscale golf courses in Turnberry and Aberdeenshire.

For Trump, there was no need for deliberations about Her Majesty's invitation. He accepted on the spot.

When May was flying back to London, though, Trump signed a controversial executive order barring travel to the United States by citizens from seven predominantly Muslim countries. Protests erupted in England to the Muslim ban and to Trump's derisive comments about immigrants. The Liberal Democratic leader, Sir Vince Cable, protested that a state visit would "embarrass" the Queen and the country. The mayor of London, Sadiq Khan, declared Trump "not welcome" in the city. An online petition demanded the British government block a state visit by the president. "Donald Trump's well documented misogyny and vulgarity disqualifies him from being received by Her Majesty or the Prince of Wales," it read, commanding enough signatures—more than 1.8 million of them—to trigger an automatic debate in the House of Commons, one that lasted more than three hours.

"It would have been far wiser to wait to see what sort of president he would turn out to be before advising the Queen to invite him," said Lord Ricketts, who had been Prime Minister David Cameron's national security adviser. "Now the Queen is put in a very difficult position."

FOR DECADES, THE WORLD HAD BEEN WATCHING THE SOAP OPERA THAT was the British royal family.

The Queen's children had been involved in one mishap after another. In the 1990s, there had been front-page headlines about the slow collapse of the marriage of Prince Charles and Princess Diana; about the recently separated husband of Princess Anne being served with a paternity suit in New Zealand; and about the general disorder that was Fergie, the Duchess of York and the wife of Prince Andrew. (Her shenanigans would later pale in comparison with much more serious revelations about his association with Jeffrey Epstein.)

Trump, who inherited his mother's fascination with the British royal family, was among the Americans tracking every twist. To his delight, his path would occasionally cross with the royals.

Prince Philip gained his respect with a rebuke to the press during a visit to New York when the real estate mogul was by his side. "I was a celebrity, and they had celebrities invited, and he was there representing something," Trump told me. "The press was going crazy. I was standing next to him and they said, 'Please move back.' They wanted more room. And he looked at these hundreds of photographers and he said, 'No, no, *you* move back.'" The prince didn't budge; the journalists did. It was, perhaps, an early lesson to Trump on the possibilities of confrontation with the news media.

Diana was the featured guest at a $1,000-a-ticket charity gala at the Brooklyn Academy of Music that Trump and his first wife, Ivana, attended. At the 1989 dinner, Trump recalled that they had entertained Prince Charles a year earlier at his Mar-a-Lago club in Florida. "We played polo," he said, though the "we"—a royal we?—presumably didn't include Trump on a horse. He said they had seen the Princess of Wales at a Red Cross Ball in Palm Beach—actually, probably a reference to a

United World College Ball in 1985 at The Breakers hotel that Charles and Diana attended. His enchantment with Diana was clear in *The Art of the Comeback*, published in 1997. By then, he was in the process of separating from his second wife, Marla Maples. "I only have one regret in the women department—that I never had the opportunity to court Lady Diana Spencer," he wrote. He called her "a genuine princess—a dream lady."

He stoked rumors that Diana might buy an apartment in Trump Tower, and he announced that Charles and Diana had joined Mar-a-Lago. "Charles and Di join, but separately," an Associated Press story credulously reported. "Complete nonsense," a Buckingham Palace spokesman replied. Pressed to explain, Trump "clarified" that he had offered the prince and princess honorary free memberships, but that they hadn't responded.

NOW THAT TRUMP WAS PRESIDENT OF THE UNITED STATES, IT BECAME more difficult for the royal family, or anybody else, to ignore him. That said, his determination to visit Her Majesty slammed headlong into Britain's newfound desire to delay it.

"It was an impressive display in exquisitely polite obfuscation," said Fiona Hill, who during her opening weeks at the National Security Council was assigned to work on the trip, promised but not yet scheduled. One complication was the lack of standard diplomatic notetaking during the meeting between Trump and May. In those chaotic early days of his first term, there was only a "bare-bones account," subject to interpretation and misinterpretation. What exactly had the prime minister offered? The British hedged, but Trump did not. "The president, for his part, was very clear that he had been invited for a State Visit to the United Kingdom with all the bells and whistles," Hill said.

On this, he was right. "A state visit," May had specified at the White House news conference, and one to be held "later this year." That is, in 2017.

Every time Trump encountered May and other British officials, he would drop not-so-subtle hints about scheduling the visit. In the middle of a meeting, apropos of nothing, he would mention his desire to play golf once more at Turnberry. But the British had experience with keeping a certain diplomatic distance from controversial presidents. During Watergate, Richard Nixon had angled for an official visit as respite or rescue—an invitation that was never ruled out but also never arrived. During the Monica Lewinsky scandal, Bill Clinton's desire for a state visit before he left the White House was discreetly sidestepped.

Other European capitals were all too willing to welcome the new president. Trump attended his first NATO summit in Belgium in May, adding a stop in Italy. Before his first G20 summit in Germany in July, he visited Poland. A week later, he traveled to France, where President Emmanuel Macron hosted a dinner at the Eiffel Tower. "Relationship with #France stronger than ever," Trump posted on social media with a photo of the two leaders and their wives, a breathtaking view of Paris behind them.

But no London.

Woody Johnson, a billionaire businessman and co-owner of the New York Jets, had been appointed ambassador to the Court of St. James's by Trump. He worked on scheduling a presidential visit to open the new US embassy in London in February 2018. The George W. Bush administration had begun building on a site more resistant to terrorist attack than the iconic building in Grosvenor Square. For one thing, the new cube-like complex on the South Bank of the Thames sported an eight-foot-deep moat along the river. Trump rejected the idea. Opening an embassy, not to mention one no longer in the center of the city, didn't offer the sizzle he sought.

"He liked Grosvenor Square . . . and didn't see a need to build a new embassy across the Thames way far away from the center of London," Woody Johnson recalled. "I don't necessarily agree with that, but that was his mindset." Trump had a point, he added. "Grosvenor Square is the heart of London, and just so much history there," he said. "So that was the reason, I think."

"Bad deal," Trump posted on Twitter. "Wanted me to cut ribbon-NO!" The prospect of demonstrations and the absence of a formal state visit may have been factors, too. The former leader of the Labour Party, Ed Miliband, retweeted Trump an hour and a half later and added a comment of his own. "Nope it's because nobody wanted you to come," he wrote. "And you got the message."

For the British, there were worries about what Trump might say during a visit, what protests he might provoke. He had already been in a Twitter war with the mayor of London and a social-media skirmish with the prime minister.

As time passed, though, there were also concerns about the repercussions if Trump *didn't* visit, especially after being feted in France, Germany, Poland, and Italy. "The US is the biggest single investor in the UK—yet Khan & [Jeremy] Corbyn seem determined to put this crucial relationship at risk," Boris Johnson tweeted, referring to the mayor and the leader of the Labour Party. "We will not allow US-UK relations to be endangered by some puffed up pompous popinjay in City Hall."

Finally, the British embassy in Washington was given what Ambassador Darroch called "a flickering green light" to plan Trump's visit. "That is probably a very good example of her being used to achieve a diplomatic outcome," a senior British official said of Elizabeth. "The desire to be with the Queen and meet the Queen . . . did allow Britain to some degree to normalize relations with that first Trump presidency."

A face-saving arrangement was reached. A working visit to London would be scheduled in July 2018, sandwiched between Trump's trip to a NATO summit in Brussels and a summit with Putin in Helsinki. Those news-making events presumably would overshadow any unpleasantness in Great Britain. There would be no state dinner, not yet. On the other hand, Trump did score a presidential first with a dinner at Blenheim Palace, where Churchill had been born, an apt connection with the return of the Churchill bust. The events held in the countryside there and at Chequers also meant that any demonstrations would be kept at a distance. There was no chance Trump would see the protesters' helium-filled balloon effigy depicting him as a scowling orange baby dressed in a diaper and holding a smartphone, presumably at the ready for tweeting.

Most importantly, there would be tea with the Queen at Windsor Castle, though the full regalia of a state visit would not take place until a year later.

"I really look forward to meeting her," Trump said beforehand, calling her "a tremendous woman." "I think she represents her country so well. If you think of it, for so many years she's represented her country, she's never really made a mistake. You don't see, like, anything embarrassing."

SOMETHING EMBARRASSING WOULD ERUPT AS THEY WERE ABOUT TO meet—but not by the Queen. By the president.

On the eve of his visit, when he was in Brussels, Trump gave an interview to the *Sun* as a favor for Rupert Murdoch, the media mogul who owned the British tabloid, not to mention Fox News and *The Wall Street Journal* in the United States. In the interview, Trump blasted Prime Minister May and talked up Boris Johnson. The headline on the front page: "TRUMP'S BREXIT BLAST."

"I actually told Theresa May how to do it, but she didn't agree, she didn't listen to me," Trump had said, criticizing her effort to negotiate a "soft" Brexit strategy. She had proposed adopting common rules on goods and agricultural produce in an effort to keep customs borders open with the EU. "If they do that, their trade deal with the US will probably not be made," he warned. What's more, he said Khan had done a "terrible job" as mayor and opined that European leaders had destroyed the continent's culture and identity by permitting "millions of migrants" to move in. He also volunteered that Johnson would be a "great prime minister." He wasn't pitting May against Johnson, he insisted. "I'm just saying I think he would be a great prime minister."

"It made her look like a fool," John Bolton, then the White House national security adviser, said, recalling his alarm when he read the story. "It was pretty insulting." The remark also demonstrated Trump's undiplomatic penchant for chaos. Buckingham Palace, like everywhere else, took notice. The Queen, who had spent a lifetime keeping her personal views about foreign leaders out of the newspapers, could not have appreciated seeing an American president humiliate her prime minister in public, and while visiting her turf. At times, she also seemed especially sensitive to the patronizing treatment of women in top jobs; she knew what it could be like.

Trump realized he had blundered.

That morning, when his helicopter landed for a tour of the Royal Military Academy at Sandhurst, May was there to greet him. Bolton had flown on a second helicopter but managed to run up to hear the leaders greet each other. "Theresa, I'm so sorry about that interview," Trump said. It was one of the few times Bolton heard Trump apologize for anything. She replied, "Don't worry about it," and they moved on, at least for the moment.

The two leaders had lunch at Chequers. That night, there was a banquet in his honor at Blenheim Palace, the seat of the Duke of Marlborough. But everyone involved understood that wasn't what had drawn the president to Britain. "It was made very clear to us that the reason Donald Trump wanted to come was to meet the Queen," Foreign Secretary Jeremy Hunt said. "She was our greatest asset, and so we were told by the Americans, 'If you want him to come and it involves tea with the Queen, he'll come.'"

He wasn't the first president to feel that way. Trump's anticipation echoed Ronald Reagan's excitement about the prospect of riding horses with Elizabeth, the event he most prized during his initial European trip nearly four decades earlier. But for Trump, the imprimatur of the Queen seemed personally crucial in a way it hadn't for the self-contained Reagan. Trump had won the White House without carrying a majority of the popular vote, which grated on him. He had few friends among foreign leaders; even some allies regarded him with ill-disguised concern or even contempt. But the Queen could counter all that.

ON JULY 13, 2018, TRUMP AND FIRST LADY MELANIA TRUMP BOARDED *Marine One* at Winfield House for the hop to Windsor and made the short final leg of the trip in a gleaming British-built Range Rover. At the castle's entrance, the Queen was waiting to greet them, extending her white-gloved hand and a smile. The rows of Coldstream Guards in brilliant red coats and towering bearskin hats stood at attention on the lawn. The Trumps flanked the Queen as a military band played "The Star-Spangled Banner."

What was going through the president's mind when he finally met the Queen?

"I was thinking about my mother," he said.

What was the Queen thinking? Presumably, what she was always thinking: that she had a job to do.

But there was a stumble.

Elizabeth, by now ninety-two years old, led Trump across the lawn to review the Guard of Honor. It was the first time she had performed this ceremonial role, typically the task of the Duke of Edinburgh. But he had retired from public life a year earlier at age ninety-six, and he was not on the scene. (On this day, he had the excellent excuse of going to Hampshire to attend the baptism of a godchild, the grandson of the Earl Mountbatten.) The Queen stopped at the head of the line and gestured for Trump to stand beside her. But he didn't seem to see that, stepping ahead and then coming to an abrupt stop directly in front of her—a breach of royal protocol, which bars turning one's back on the sovereign. For an instant, the Queen was entirely blocked from camera view by the president's height and bulk. Then the top of her periwinkle hat could be glimpsed as she first tried to walk around him to his left, then instead to his right. She came up beside him as he was glancing the other way, in search of his partner.

He had been maladroit, but she may have contributed to their awkward dance. One of her royal equerries said afterward that she had initially moved to walk on his left side when protocol put her on his right. That may have added to the confusion.

Social media was merciless about the gaffe, putting full blame on Trump, but there was no sign that the Queen was offended. She was amused, biographer Gyles Brandreth said later. "That night when she saw herself on television, bobbing about behind him, she laughed out loud."

Everyone was wondering what Her Majesty really thought about this unexpected new president—and no one more so than Trump himself.

AT WINDSOR CASTLE, ELIZABETH LED THE TRUMPS TO THE OAK ROOM, A cozy space despite the grand candelabra hanging from the gilt ceiling. Decorated with family photos and knickknacks, the sitting room was a favorite spot for Elizabeth and for Queen Victoria before her. On this day, there was just the Queen and the Trumps. "Her Majesty had graciously poured us tea and offered us scones with jam, while her cherished corgis lounged at her feet," Melania would recall. The meeting "extended far beyond the scheduled time," she said.

"We were going to have a 15- or 20-minute meeting, and it ended up being for a long time, and everybody was going crazy," President Trump said. "But we just got along."

The National Security Council had prepared briefing papers beforehand, detailing the event and explaining the Queen's role as head of state, not head of government. The memoranda outlined what topics Elizabeth and others in the royal family were particularly interested in, subjects that might come up during their conversation. Bolton was never sure how carefully Trump read the papers beforehand, though, and afterward a private word from the British side indicated that Trump had done more of the talking than the Queen. Actually, that wouldn't be unusual. She had long followed the axiom that the best way to handle big personalities—foreign leaders, corporate titans, maybe men in general—was to let them be the star of their show. And despite his bombastic persona, Trump had the natural charm of a salesman when he wanted to impress someone. He wanted to impress Her Majesty the Queen most of all.

"We talked about everything," Trump said, relishing the memory of that day. "We just got along." The instant ease of his exchanges with the Queen, and the fact that their tea lasted twenty-two minutes past its scheduled twenty-five minutes, indicated to him the feeling was mutual. That is, that she enjoyed his company, too.

Afterward, in an interview with ITV's Piers Morgan, Trump disclosed that they had discussed Brexit. That was another breach of royal protocol. Leaders typically refrained from revealing anything about their conversations with the Queen, and Brexit was the most explosive topic of the day. She had carefully avoided taking a position on it, at least in public. "She said it's a very—and she's right—it's a very complex problem," Trump declared. "I think nobody had any idea how complex that was going to be." Then he seemed to have second thoughts about relaying that, though the comment sounded more common-sense than controversial. "I've heard very strongly from a lot of people, you just don't talk about that conversation with the Queen, right?" he said. "Let me tell you what I can talk about. . . . She is an incredible woman, she is so sharp, she is so beautiful, when I say beautiful—inside and out. That is a beautiful woman."

When he left for a weekend at Turnberry, his golf course in Scotland, Trump was expansive about the state of the "special relationship," protests and prime ministers aside. "I would give our relationship with the UK—and now, especially after these two days with your prime minister, I would say the highest level of special," he said at a joint news conference with May. "Am I allowed to go higher than that?"

THE QUEEN COULD HAVE HER OWN WAYS OF EXPRESSING HER VIEWS.
On the day Trump arrived in the United Kingdom, flying to Stansted Airport from Brussels, the Queen happened to be having an audience at Windsor Castle with the Archbishop of Canterbury and the Grand Imam of Al-Azhar, Egypt. In the official photo of the solemn trio, she was wearing a small vintage pin that depicted a green flower made from yellow gold, diamonds, and moss agate. It nearly disappeared against the background of her brightly patterned dress, but it proved to be impossible to miss.

It was the pin Michelle Obama had given her in 2011. The Queen had worn it in public only once before, at the reciprocal dinner the Obamas hosted for her during that visit. Wearing it on the day Trump arrived in Great Britain for the first time as president was unlikely to be coincidental, or to go unnoticed. A blog called *From Her Majesty's Jewel Vault* had been documenting every item of jewelry she had worn since 2012. "I thought this brooch would be a one-and-done thing, never to be seen after its original 'courtesy' appearance—only because it's not really Her Maj's style—so this was a big surprise!" the blog's author observed. "You'll note I'm pretty specifically NOT making a comment on why she may have chosen to wear this brooch today. That's because I like to keep politics away from here."

There would be speculation on social media about the Queen's other sartorial choices in Trump's presence, though the evidence for those arguments was thinner. For their tea, she wore a dress of blue and yellow, the colors of the European Union, and the Cartier brooch her mother had worn at the lying-in-state for her husband. Maybe she was in mourning for the EU, after the exit that Trump, among others, had touted? A year later, at the state dinner in Trump's honor, she wore a Burmese ruby tiara, seen by the Burmese as having protective properties guarding the wearer against illness and evil. Was she suggesting she needed protection from Trump? To be fair, the red of the rubies also meant she was dressed in the colors of both the British and the American flags, paired with her white dress and blue sash.

Another blog devoted to tracking the Queen's jewelry, the *Court Jeweller*, disputed the entire notion that the monarch would use jewelry as a subtle jab at a president. "She is the living embodiment of the state, and in that representative role, she remains studiously neutral," blogger Ella Kay insisted.

Still, it seems unlikely that Elizabeth accidentally wore the Obama brooch for the first time in seven years on the day of Trump's arrival. Kay suggested she might be wearing a gift from one American presidential family simply because she was about to meet with another. But surely that explanation seems naive for a queen who was one of the most experienced diplomats on the planet. She knew that these two particular presidents had the most contentious of relationships. Trump had accused Obama of lying about his birthplace, an allegation with racist overtones; Obama had accused Trump of endangering democracy itself.

The Queen had formed a personal bond with the Obamas; that was no secret. Her view of Trump was less clear, but her expectations were surely shaped by what she had seen and heard during the first years of his presidency. He had attacked her friends, the Bushes, faulting George W. Bush for the 9/11 attacks. Trump had publicly berated her prime minister. He had labeled the nations of Africa, a continent that included members of the British Commonwealth, as "shithole countries." That remark wouldn't sit well with a sovereign who had devoted her life to the protection of the Commonwealth she headed, and whose ties with African leaders were particularly close.

"There definitely had been a deliberate decision to wear that pin," a senior British official said flatly. "It was a silent act of resistance."

THE FORMAL INVITATION FOR THE FULL-FLEDGED STATE VISIT THAT Trump had wanted from the start finally arrived. He was exultant.

"This state visit will reaffirm the steadfast and special relationship between the United States and the United Kingdom," the White House announcement said. It would take place while Trump was scheduled to be in the neighborhood for commemorations marking the seventy-fifth anniversary of D-Day, on June 6, 2019.

"The level of pomp and circumstance in the UK was critical" to Trump, Fiona Hill said. "The West Wing staff was perpetually fearful that he was not getting the same treatment as previous American presidents or other world leaders when he traveled." The White House compiled charts to track what previous presidents had scored: Reagan riding horses with the Queen. Clinton addressing Parliament. Obama staying overnight in Buckingham Palace.

To Trump's disappointment, the palace's guest quarters were under reconstruction, part of a ten-year refurbishment to update the building's lead pipes and electrical wiring, though the state dinner would be held there. "The Americans pushed very hard on that," Hunt recalled, saying the Queen would have accommodated him if she could have. Trump didn't care about giving speeches and he expressed little interest in talking policy with the soon-to-exit Theresa May. "In our planning sessions, it was apparent that the main purpose of the state visit was to introduce one dynasty (his) to another (the Queen's family), not to celebrate US–UK ties," Hill said.

During the trip, that was the same conclusion reached by Stephanie Grisham, then the spokesperson for Melania Trump who a month later became the White House press secretary. "It didn't dawn on me at first, but over the course of the next few days, I finally figured out what was going on," she said. "Jared and Ivanka thought they were the royal family of the United States—on the same level as William and Kate in the United Kingdom. We didn't call [Ivanka] 'the Princess' for nothing, after all."

It was the only trip during Trump's first term that every adult child in his family signed up to join: Ivanka Trump and husband, Jared Kushner, Eric and wife, Lara Trump, Donald Trump Jr., and Tiffany Trump. Only Barron, then thirteen years old, stayed home. "Everyone began maneuvering almost immediately," Grisham reported, trying to get a seat on *Air Force One* and pushing for invitations to the state dinner for Don Jr.'s girlfriend and Tiffany's boyfriend. "We are going to look like the Beverly Hillbillies," warned Lindsay Reynolds, then Melania Trump's chief of staff, who would be dressed down by the president for her efforts at corralling his children.

The first lady backed her up, though, blocking Ivanka and Jared from joining the Queen's private welcome. "It is inappropriate," Melania ruled. "It should be just the president and I."

When they arrived at Buckingham Palace on June 3, 2019, rather than driving from Winfield House, the Trump White House wanted *Marine*

One to land on the grounds, offering more dramatic visuals. Even the pilots had gotten in the mood. At the center of the dashboard of the Osprey carrying the press pool was a six-inch-tall statue of the Queen, wearing a pink dress and white gloves and a double strand of tiny pearls, with a small black handbag draped over her left arm. Her right hand was raised—perhaps in greeting, perhaps in benediction. The tiny Queen was smiling. Prince Charles and Camilla walked out to escort Trump and Melania to Her Majesty. An eighty-two-gun salute thundered—forty-one shots to welcome the president, forty-one more to mark the sixty-sixth anniversary of the Queen's coronation, celebrated the previous day. As Melania stood on the palace steps, a gust of wind threatened to send her broad-brimmed Hervé Pierre hat sailing; she grabbed it in place to the amusement of the Queen and Camilla. Camilla, the future queen, was her own force in the family, perhaps because she had spent her life waiting to be part of it. She had little concern about what others thought and, like the Queen, could find mishaps in formal events amusing. "It was a lighthearted and spontaneous moment," Melania said. For now, the chaos that typically surrounded Trump seemed distant, including the protesters on the streets and an ongoing Twitter war. (Lately, the mayor of London had labeled the president a "global threat"; the president had replied that Khan was a "stone-cold loser.")

After lunch at the palace, the Queen showed the Trumps eight tables of artifacts from the royal collection that had been put on display in the Grand Hall for them to review, among them a British copy of the Declaration of Independence and a pewter horse that the Trumps had given her when they had visited the previous year. Trump didn't recognize the horse, but Melania did, rescuing her husband. Trump did recognize the yellow Clan MacLeod tartan, from his mother's family, displayed in a book from the Royal Collection. "That's my tweed!" he exclaimed.

At the white-tie banquet that night, on June 3, 2019, were eight Trumps and sixteen members of the royal family, spanning three generations—170 guests in all.

Jeremy Corbyn, leader of the opposition Labour Party, had declined his invitation, and Meghan Markle was missing, home with her month-old son, Archie. Given their history, both sides were undoubtedly relieved about her absence: She had called Trump "misogynistic" during the 2016 campaign; he had called her "nasty" in his interview with the *Sun*. The menu was appropriately regal: steamed halibut with watercress mousse to start, new-season Windsor lamb with herb stuffing as the main course, and strawberry sable with lemon verbena cream for dessert, accompanied by a procession of seven wines. The meal was served on George IV's Grand Service, gilded in silver and two centuries old; the napkins were embroidered with the Queen's monogram.

In the photograph taken as they entered, Trump is to the Queen's right and Melania to her left, with Prince Charles and Camilla next. The women are all dressed in glittering white gowns; the three royals have blue sashes; Elizabeth's enormous crown is festooned with rubies.

Trump, who often adopts a serious, even glowering mien in formal photographs, couldn't stop smiling as the two photographers in the press pool, one American and one British, snapped pictures. The president was bursting with delight. "Oh, there's Doug Mills, the Pulitzer Prize–winning photographer from *The New York Times*; there he is, right over there," he said to the Queen, gesturing to the journalist. She said politely to Mills, "Hello." "I was like, oh my gosh, I said, 'Hello, Your Majesty,'" Mills said later. "And with that, one of the British press aides grabbed me by the arm and said, 'We have to go now,'" earlier than was customary. "As I walked out, I was told I wasn't supposed to speak to the Queen," he said. "And I was like, 'I'm sorry, I didn't know.' If the President of the United States introduces you to somebody . . . you say 'hello.'" Even if it is a queen.

That was the start of an evening of lively conversation between Elizabeth and Trump. "I was in the groove," he told Woody Johnson the next morning. The ambassador, who had known Trump for decades, offered: "My own judgment is, after the first four years and maybe to this day, of all the people that he met, the Queen had the most special relationship, the most special impact on him."

Later, the president gave me a rundown on their conversation that night.

"I said, 'So could I ask you who was your favorite president?'"

The Queen replied, "Why? They were all so good."

"I know, but did you like Ronald Reagan the best?" Trump asked.

"Oh, yes, I liked him very much, but they were all good."

"Oh, well, what about Nixon?"

"Oh, he was excellent."

"So what do you mean you liked them all?" Trump pressed.

"I liked them all. I can't say anything bad about any of them. They were great."

"OK, let's go to prime ministers. Who was your favorite prime minister? It had to be Churchill, right?"

"No, no, no. He was wonderful, Winston. But they were all so good. They worked so hard. They were very different, but they worked so hard. They were all so good."

Trump was dazzled by her skill at charming deflection. "I said to myself, how genius is this?" he said. "I couldn't get her to say a bad thing about anybody. She was amazing, actually. And not for any reason other than I don't think she wanted to create controversy. It was unnecessary." She could not be baited into saying more. "I don't think she's ever let slip who was her favorite anything," biographer Robert Hardman said. "She wouldn't even let slip what her favorite food was, for fear that she'd always get served it thereafter."

For Trump, she prompted a rare moment of self-reflection. "I hate to say this because it's very disparaging to myself. She was sort of the opposite of me. She didn't mix it up." That discipline was at the foundation of her reputation and her role. "She was there for so many decades, and she literally never made a mistake," he said. "If you think about it. I mean, everyone was making mistakes around her, but she never made a mistake."

He mentioned her composure even when an intruder in 1982 managed to sneak into Buckingham Palace and confront her in her private quarters. ("He thinks so much of the Queen," the mother of the intruder explained later. "I can imagine him just wanting to simply talk and say hello and discuss his problems.") A scandalous breach of security, the incident prompted legal changes to make trespass at the palace a criminal offense. "Even when the vagrant went into her room, she sat him down," Trump said. "She gave him tea, she quietly pressed a button. They eventually came in. I would imagine the head of security wasn't so well-treated after that, but she was so cool."

Her composure—and her discretion—were unshakable with Trump as well.

She parried his queries about Prince Harry and Meghan, her wayward grandson and his problematic bride. The couple was catnip for the tabloids with leaked depictions of the royal court as cold, even racist to the biracial American actress. It was the messiest airing of family dysfunction since the split between Charles and Diana. Seven months after Trump's state dinner, Harry and Meghan announced they would step back from their duties as senior royals and in short order moved to Montecito, California. The seemingly endless controversies harkened back to the "annus horribilis" of 1992, when the failing marriages of Charles and Diana and later Andrew and Sarah Ferguson overshadowed the Queen's official duties. Once again it had become distressingly clear that Her Majesty was more successful at managing American presidents than her own family.

It was, perhaps, a touch of humanity that made Elizabeth seem less regal and more real. Her struggles with her children and grandchildren were heartaches that families everywhere could recognize.

That said, there were some distinctly royal aspects to their travails.

A senior royal aide said Harry's bitterness toward the palace staff and his own family stemmed in part from his resentment over being treated as a "lesser royal" than William—perhaps inevitable, given that his brother was the heir apparent. Harry complained that he was put in a bedroom "miles away" from William's posher surroundings, the aide said. Some staff openly speculated about whether Harry was in fact Charles's biological son—the unsubstantiated gossip that the red-haired royal was the product of an affair between Princess Diana and the red-haired Calvary officer James Hewitt. In his memoir, Harry said that even Prince Charles joked about his parentage. "Who knows if I'm even your real father," Charles would say, then "laugh and laugh." After all, Charles said, a patient at a nearby psychiatric hospital had insisted to him that *he* was the true Prince of Wales. The "remarkably unfunny joke" made him feel more isolated, Harry wrote. He was already emotionally vulnerable: He had been just twelve years old when his mother had been killed in a spectacular car crash, paparazzi in pursuit.

Meghan came in for rumors and critiques of her own, some similar to those made against Wallis Simpson in an earlier generation. Meghan was viewed as a stronger personality than her husband, and one with her own agenda and ambitions. William reportedly complained that she used tears and threats, and their children, to maintain "coercive control" of his brother. A senior aide to the Queen used the word "brainwashed" to describe Meghan's effect on her husband. It was just the sort of public family drama Elizabeth had long struggled to avoid. As with Charles and Diana, she had little patience for privileged relatives who didn't simply suck it up and do their duty. Her Majesty had become wary of Meghan as an opportunist—was "on to her from the start," the aide said—and one with public relations skills that left the palace's outdated press operation in the dust.

Despite the headlines that Harry and Meghan were generating—no one could possibly have missed them—Trump was almost certainly one of very few guests who raised that most personal of topics directly with the Queen. She responded with the most diplomatic of stonewalls.

"I asked her about it constantly," Trump told me. "I'd say, 'Come on, tell me.' 'No, no. It's very nice.' Everybody was nice. She liked everybody." But he was prepared to take offense on her behalf. "I couldn't get her to say it. I'm good at that, too," he said. She demurred. "She would always say, 'No, no, would be lovely, lovely.' But it wasn't lovely, and I think it hurt her. I really think it hurt her. It was tremendous dissension, and I just don't think they treated her with the respect that she should have, frankly."

He said he wouldn't have reacted to a similar affront in the same forgiving way. "I actually told her I couldn't do what she does, because she was very cool on the subject. She would talk about it but never said anything bad about either of them, and I think she loved Harry, really loved Harry. But Harry's been, I feel, led astray. I really do. I think he's been terribly led astray. It's just so disrespectful the way that happened, and she didn't deserve that. This is a woman that everybody respected so much. I think she was stunned by what was happening, actually. She couldn't believe it in real time."

The Queen never confided her private feelings on the matter to Trump. The monarch hoped and believed that Harry would eventually reconcile with his family, a senior palace aide said, if only arrangements for his children could be worked out.

(Trump later suggested he was ready to punish Harry with more than words, saying he could be deported from the United States for not revealing past drug use on his visa application. "If he lied they'll have to take appropriate action," he told Nigel Farage in an interview on Britain's GB News during the 2024 campaign, after the Queen's death. But soon after starting his second term, he said he was "not interested" in deporting Harry. "I'll leave him alone," he told the *New York Post*. "He's got enough problems with his wife. She's terrible.")

The grand banquet at Buckingham ended with a dozen bagpipers circling the room three times as they performed, a tradition Queen Victoria had begun. Trump's after-dinner tweet showed his enchantment. "Could not have been treated more warmly in the United Kingdom by the Royal Family or the people," he posted. "Our relationship has never been better, and I see a very big Trade Deal down the road."

That was precisely what the British had been hoping to hear, though the trade deal was never reached, not during Trump's first term. Liz Truss, then the trade minister and later, briefly, the prime minister, argued that the blame wasn't with him. "I think President Trump was very up for it," she said. "I think there was a deal to be done," but the "anti-Trump faction" in the government and the bureaucracy were against it, and the opportunity passed.

Trump would revive it during his second term, though. It took another six years, but at a crucial moment, a "very big Trade Deal" was finally delivered—thanks in part to the ameliorating assistance of the Crown.

THERE HAD BEEN A SMALL DISCORDANT NOTE AT THE STATE DINNER. Stephanie Grisham was seated next to Darroch, the British ambassador. "We bonded over wine and American football," the first lady's spokesperson recalled, "but I did get an odd vibe from him when he asked, 'How do you do it? Work for a man like your president?'"

Two days later, Darroch was among the dignitaries gathered at Southampton to say goodbye to Trump as he boarded *Air Force One*. "This was a wonderful visit, and UK-US relations are now in the best state ever," Trump told him, shaking his hand. A jubilant Darroch sent a diplomatic telegram with his "impressions and implications" of the state visit—a trip that the British had delayed as long as they could.

"With this unorthodox President, there were genuine risks," he wrote, but "the gamble paid handsomely." The highlight for Trump had been the "extensive personal engagement" with the Queen at their private lunch, at the glittering dinner, at the D-Day commemorations in Portsmouth. Trump's team had been "dazzled," he said. "We are basking in a big success, with doors open everywhere in Washington."

Three weeks later, the door would be opened for Darroch's forced exit. The problem: Trump found out what the ambassador really thought about him in leaked cables from 2017 that said the President "radiates insecurity" and led a dysfunctional administration.

Darroch didn't intend his candid views to be read by the White House or by anyone beyond an elite circle in London with the security clearance to see documents stamped "Official Sensitive." It was the sort of insider analysis that diplomats are supposed to write for their bosses, not to be released until decades later. By then, Trump and Darroch would likely be otherwise occupied or gone from the scene altogether.

But on July 7, 2019, his cables were leaked and splashed on the front page of Britain's *Mail on Sunday*.

The British government's first instinct was to stand behind him. "We had a fine diplomat who was just doing what he should have been doing—giving a frank assessment, a personal assessment of the political situation in the country that he was posted" to, Foreign Secretary Hunt said. He called it "absolutely essential that when our diplomats do their job all over the world . . . we defend them."

But the president was "absolutely livid," Bolton, the White House national security adviser, recalled. "He was saying, 'I want him out of here; get him out of here.' I tried to explain that when it's not our ambassador, we can't fire him." What the president could do, Bolton told him, was make it clear to the British that he wasn't happy. Bolton called Mark Sedwill, the national security adviser for May, to give him a heads-up. "I said, 'Look, this isn't going to end well,'" Bolton told him. "'You got to pull him back.'"

That Sunday afternoon, landing on the White House lawn after a weekend at Bedminster, his New Jersey club, the president told reporters, "The ambassador has not served the UK well, I can tell you. We are not big fans of that man." On Monday morning, he dialed up his rhetoric. "I do not know the Ambassador, but he is not liked or well thought of within the US," he posted on Twitter. "We will no longer deal with him." He then took a new slap at May on how she handled Brexit and made yet another endorsement of Boris Johnson. On Wednesday, the ambassador acknowledged the inevitable. "The current situation is making it impossible for me to carry out my role as I would like," he said in his resignation letter.

Behind the scenes, Queen Elizabeth reached out to calm troubled waters, as she had so often before, with so many presidents.

"She couldn't believe it; she thought he was terrible," Trump said, revealing a conversation not previously reported. "I think they fired him over that, didn't they? They fired him. She said, 'He doesn't speak for our government.' Oh, she was furious over that. He was a total lightweight. He was just a guy; he was trying to be a Mr. Tough Guy." Trump's evolving account of their conversation to me reflected the delicacy of the Queen's comments. "She apologized," Trump said at first. Then he qualified that statement, saying, "It wasn't an apology." She distanced herself and her government from Darroch's comments, but after Trump labeled the ambassador "a fool," he added, "She didn't call him a fool, but she basically indicated that he was a stupid person."

Whatever she said, it was enough. She had calmed his ire without actually apologizing. She had made it clear she disapproved of Darroch's comments without, perhaps, throwing the ambassador himself overboard. "She didn't have to apologize," Trump said. "She didn't apologize. She just said how terrible he was to do such a thing. So it wasn't an apology. She wasn't an apologist. But what she was—a great woman."

Trump, a creature of television, met with the Queen during an era when she became, begrudgingly, a television sensation of her own. Four days before his first election, *The Crown* debuted on Netflix. Though it has its share of historical inaccuracies, the series accurately depicted the Queen as a duty-bound, sharp, and emotionally distant figure, sometimes baffled by her needy and complicated family. While the palace said the Queen never watched the series—disputed by some tabloid reports—an insider said that Camilla did. So did Catherine, reportedly watching it whenever she was visiting her parents at their home.

Trump and the Queen would meet one more time, in December 2019.

Then, another controversy would flare. Trump, in London for the seventieth anniversary of the NATO alliance, had met happily enough with Prince Charles and the Duchess of Cornwall at Clarence House, where

Melania and Camilla exchanged chummy kisses on the cheek. That evening, the Queen hosted a reception at Buckingham Palace for the visiting leaders. But at their meetings that day French President Emmanuel Macron had challenged Trump, an exchange on live television that embarrassed Trump. Then a video clip from the reception that went viral showed Canadian Prime Minister Justin Trudeau mocking the president to a cluster that included Macron, Johnson, Dutch Prime Minister Mark Rutte, and Princess Anne.

An irate Trump canceled an expected news conference and abruptly headed home from Britain the next day.

IN 2024, BRITISH AUTHOR CRAIG BROWN GOT HEADLINES WHEN HE REported in his breezy, bestselling book, *A Voyage Around the Queen*, that Elizabeth had confided to an unnamed lunch guest that she had found Trump "very rude." He wrote that she particularly disliked the way he couldn't stop looking over her shoulder, as though in search of someone more interesting. "Totally false," Trump replied, calling the author "a sleaze bag."

Brown had more, this time on Melania: "She also believed President Trump 'must have some sort of arrangement' with his wife Melania, or else why would she have remained married to him?" There would be a separate report later that the Queen, a skilled mimic, had portrayed the president's private and elusive wife as the actress Greta Garbo, silent and remote. "I want to be alone," she was said to have mischievously muttered, quoting Garbo's signature line from 1932's *Grand Hotel*.

There was another secondhand report of Elizabeth's opinion of the president. Monty Roberts, a famed California horse trainer who had a long and close relationship with the Queen, said in the documentary *The Cowboy and the Queen* that she had told him she didn't like Trump. She didn't like bullies, he said, mentioning Putin as another example.

Whatever she thought of Trump, Elizabeth had a long history of welcoming rogues far more notorious than he was. It was part of her job description. During her reign, she had hosted formal dinners honoring despots and dictators—Bashar al-Assad of Syria, Mobutu Sese Soko of the Congo, Robert Mugabe of Zimbabwe, Idi Amin of Uganda. She toasted

Emperor Hirohito of Japan, the head of state of an Axis power that had waged World War II against Great Britain and the free world. Especially ruthless was Romanian dictator Nicolae Ceaușescu, who was a house guest at Buckingham Palace with his wife, Elena, during a state visit in 1978. When the Queen spied the infamous couple in the garden while she was walking her dogs, she hid behind a bush to avoid them.

"She's very streetwise," Trump said of the Queen, not a word typically used to describe her. "For a person that was never on the streets, she's very streetwise." In our interview, he veered into a discussion of the Queen's sister, Margaret, whom he had met on a few occasions and called "vivacious." "She had a mouth that was a little bit wild," the president noted, "and I said, 'Is your sister like you?'" Margaret told him, "She's even more."

The Queen could find mishaps entertaining and controversial characters intriguing. "She didn't mind rogues at all, no," Boris Johnson said. By the time she met Trump, she was in her nineties and had the broad perspective and bemusement that age can sometimes bring. Johnson, an ally of Trump who was a bit of a rogue himself, was careful not to reveal his private conversations with the Queen. But he disputed reports that she had been put off by Trump. "Seriously, I think she was amused by President Trump and liked him," the former prime minister said. "That was my impression."

That was Trump's impression, too. While she refused to answer the question when he posed it, he said he was given to understand that she had identified her favorite president to others.

It was him.

"We just got along," he said.

TO BE CLEAR, IT WASN'T A RANKING THAT HER MAJESTY REVEALED.

Even so, Woody Johnson thought Trump was right. "The President has a very keen sense of things like that," his ambassador said. "It was his perception that, yeah, she was fond of him." That wouldn't have surprised Johnson, given Trump's personality and drive. "I think she recognized that Trump is a different kind of person, that's putting it mildly, and so he's not going to play by the rules. He didn't go to How-to-Be-a-President School . . . and that's why he's effective."

She recognized his flaws and had been braced for the worst: Witness Michelle's brooch. Still, that was before the Queen and Trump had met. Whatever her concerns about his policy positions and personal behavior, she appreciated his energy and his exuberance in his Scottish roots, aides said later. "There was definitely a rapport," Hardman said, and their state dinner "was something that she looked back on fondly." She had hosted 113 state visits in all through her reign; Trump was the last one.

Even so, those who knew the Queen well were skeptical about the notion that Trump could have been her favorite president, whatever that meant. Several senior officials in the palace and the British government responded with startled laughter to the idea that her relationship with him could have matched the affection she felt for some of his predecessors. Dwight Eisenhower had been a hero and Ronald Reagan a friend. She had met with George W. Bush more often than any other president—the only president to have the honor of state visits in both Washington and London—and her clear fondness for Barack Obama had struck officials on both sides of the Atlantic.

Perhaps Her Majesty had the gift of some mothers—to convince each of her children, without ever saying so, that he or she was her favorite. She once confided that she made a point of laughing equally at all the acts at a Royal Variety Performance, even though she didn't find them equally funny, because she wanted "to be seen giving everybody the same amount of support." Part of her diplomatic deftness was her ability to persuade presidents that she particularly enjoyed their company. She never dissed any of them in public, not even the difficult ones, not the too-affectionate Jimmy Carter or the absent Lyndon Johnson. Presidents from Truman to Trump came away feeling that they had forged a personal bond with her. Even Nixon, whom she cultivated and then dodged. Even Joe Biden, whose Irish American mother had written poems about her hatred of the British.

When I asked former Prime Minister David Cameron about Trump's belief that he was the Queen's favorite president, he noted only that she was a "very good diplomat" who was "very discreet about those sorts of things." Others thought that assessment was more telling about Trump than about the Queen. "That's hysterical," Jill Biden said as Joe Biden shook his head. "Oh, that fits his character, for sure." Hillary Clinton responded, "Why am I not surprised by that?" She added, "I don't think there is any evidence to believe that could possibly be true." Bill Clinton was similarly dubious. He recalled a conversation he had with Obama and Biden in 2024. "We were all joking at Ethel Kennedy's funeral about how she tried to make every Democratic president feel like he was her favorite, and she was shrewd about that, Ethel was. And Queen Elizabeth was no dummy. She knew what she was doing. . . ."

He would be "shocked" if Elizabeth had ever identified a favorite, Clinton said. "I have no idea what she really thought of any of us. I just know . . . what I thought of her, and I thought she was really special."

Fifteen

Don't Tell His Mother

Sunday, June 13, 2021—Windsor Castle

Before Joe Biden met Her Majesty the first time, his mother gave him strict instructions about what to do—and what not to do, ever.

Jean Biden called her son just before he left for London for a meeting of the British-American Parliamentary Group in 1982. The itinerary included an audience with Queen Elizabeth. "Don't you bow down to her," his mother ordered her forty-one-year-old firstborn, then in his second term as a US senator. "Remember, Joey, you're a Biden. Nobody is better than you. You're not better than anybody else, but *nobody* is any better than you."

Joe Biden's wife, Jill, had her own reaction to the instructions US protocol officials gave the spouses who were on the trip. "They told us we had to wear white gloves," she said. "And they wanted us to curtsy. Well, I think the Senate wives didn't really want to curtsy so much." They decided instead on a respectful nod of the head.

When he was growing up, Joe Biden's family had always been sensitive to status, to the suggestion that someone outranked them by virtue of money or lineage or position—even within their own Catholic religion. When his mother heard he was going to meet Pope John Paul II, she gave similar instructions. "Don't you kiss his ring," she said.

Irish antipathy to the royal family was also part of it, built through centuries of resentment over British rule. As a descendent of the Blewitts of County Mayo and the Finnegans of County Louth, Catherine Eugenia Finnegan Biden bore considerable animus toward the English in general and Elizabeth in particular. When Biden was vice president, a British television writer, Georgia Pritchett, had visited him at his official residence. She was working on a surprise video for President Obama that involved actress Julia Louis-Dreyfus, the fictional vice president in the HBO series *Veep*. The actual vice president had just returned from Ukraine. Biden and Pritchett chatted about the trip. "Noticing I was English, he changed the subject to how much his mother hated the English," she said. Jean Biden "had written several poems about her hatred of the English. He went off to find them and returned with hundreds of poems describing how God must smite the English and rain blood on our heads."

There was more. "He also told me that when his mother visited the UK she had stayed in a hotel where the Queen had once stayed," Pritchett said. "She was so appalled that she slept on the floor all night, rather than risk sleeping on a bed that the Queen had slept on." That demonstration of principle over comfort, however peculiar, earned Pritchett's admiration. Her Majesty was well aware of Biden's Irish American perspective—detailed in the briefing papers prepared for his visit—if not the specifics of his mother's hotel preferences. By the age of ninety-five, sharp mentally but increasingly frail physically, Elizabeth would not have been thrown by that. She already had seen it all.

Biden's Irish roots were a key to his self-identity. His mother was thoroughly Irish, his father a combination of English, French, and Irish descent. Great-aunt Gertie Blewitt had reassured him as a child, "Now, honey, your father's not a bad man," a notion that had never occurred to him. "He's just English." Biden "would often tell the story about his mother telling him, 'You never bow or curtsy to the Queen of England—ever,'" said Kate Bedingfield, then his White House communications director. When his first presidential trip abroad was being planned in 2021, including tea with Elizabeth at Windsor Castle, he had focused on the protocol of their greeting "to ensure that this went off in a way that both stayed true to his misgivings about the monarchy without disrespecting her."

Afterward, he told reporters that Queen Elizabeth reminded him of his mother—all things considered, an extraordinary comparison, and proof of Her Majesty's charm. "I don't think she would be insulted, but she reminded me of my mother in terms of the look of her and just the generosity," he said. Both women had been strong matriarchal figures in their families. Still, perhaps it's fortunate that his own mother, who had passed away eleven years earlier, at age ninety-two, was no longer around to hear her Joey say those words.

BRITISH OFFICIALS AROUND THE QUEEN WERE NERVOUS ABOUT THE NEW president.

Biden promised a return to steadier leadership and a stronger commitment to traditional allies than President Trump had held over the previous four years. But he made clear that he didn't share his predecessor's awe for the royal family or emotional sentiment for the special relationship. On the day Biden won the White House in 2020, BBC reporter Nick Bryant reposted on social media an exchange from the campaign trail in Iowa, where the opening caucuses had been held. The candidate was walking from a crowded corridor into a meeting room as Bryant asked expectantly, "A quick word for the BBC?" Biden replied with a smile, "The BBC? I'm Irish"—and pointedly didn't stop to talk.

Decades earlier, he had been among the most prominent Democrats to support granting Gerry Adams of Sinn Féin a visa for the United States—an issue that dismayed the Queen, the Duke of Edinburgh, and others still mourning the IRA assassination of Lord Mountbatten. When Biden was the top Democrat on the Senate Judiciary Committee, he helped lead opposition to revisions to a treaty that would have made it harder for IRA members to avoid being extradited to Great Britain from the United States. (He eventually voted in favor of the new treaty, which was ratified in 1986.) "There was the [Reagan] administration's desire to go out and justify the treaty, saying the issue was terrorism," he said in an unusually candid interview with *Irish America* magazine in 1987. "It really wasn't about terrorism. They never made a case, in my view. I think that, more than anything else, it was a reflection on how we have never—I'm going to get myself in real trouble here—come to grips with our relationship with Great Britain."

Americans have "overwhelming admiration and awe for the British jurisprudential system, a phenomenal respect for British majesty and power," the senator said. But "in a sense that many Irish are ambivalent about the IRA, we have been ambivalent about Britain. We have fought them and we have loved them. As they are in the twilight of their position as a world power, we are reluctant to take issue with them. And this treaty is something that Margaret Thatcher wanted, so rather than challenge it, we shirked."

In the twilight of their position as a world power.

The interview was during Biden's first, brief bid for the Democratic presidential nomination. When he finally moved into the White House eight presidential elections later, in 2021, the British worried they saw that same ambivalence—and an early warning sign when the saga of the White House busts reignited. Winston Churchill was booted out of the Oval Office, again. In his place, Biden added five busts of notable Americans—civil rights heroes Cesar Chavez, Rosa Parks, and Martin Luther King Jr. as well as Robert F. Kennedy and Eleanor Roosevelt. The London tabloids took it personally. "CHURCHILL SNUB" was the headline in the *Sun*.

"My view of Trump is he's very pro-Britain, and he is prepared to overlook quite a lot," a top British official said. In contrast, "Biden just didn't like Britain—that was always the perception. There was the time when he came to visit and he spent more time in the Republic of Ireland than he did in Britain." In 2023, President Biden went to Belfast and Dublin on a three-day trip marking the twenty-fifth anniversary of the Good Friday Agreement, at one point posing for a smiling selfie with Gerry Adams. The Queen's stance on Adams had softened over the years, and she had made peace with President Clinton's efforts on Northern Ireland. In 2011, she became the first reigning British monarch to visit the Republic of Ireland in a century, since the time the entire island of Ireland had been part of the United Kingdom. But the strong feelings on both sides hadn't completely evaporated. Biden didn't make the brief detour to London on the trip, and they noticed. "He never came across as being desperately enthusiastic about Britain," Prime Minister Liz Truss told me dryly.

At his first full-scale news conference as president, Biden made an aside that showed historical grudges hadn't been forgotten. When a reporter asked about the flood of migrants from Central America trying to cross the southern US border, he responded by telling the story of James

Finnegan, who had left Ireland as a boy in 1850, in the middle of the Great Famine. The ships of Irish migrants were so crowded and disease-ridden that deaths were common during the journey. Their bodies were buried at sea. "When my great-grandfather got on a coffin ship in the Irish Sea, expectation was: Was he going to live long enough on that ship to get to the United States of America? But they left because of what the Brits had been doing."

A blight had devastated the potato crop in Ireland, creating starvation conditions. British economic and social policies had made things worse.

"They didn't want to leave," Biden said of his ancestors, "but they had no choice."

GREAT BRITAIN WAS THE FIRST STOP ON HIS FIRST FOREIGN TRIP AS PRESIdent, albeit by happenstance. The G7 Summit of the world's wealthiest democracies, its location rotating among the participants, was being held in the Cornish seaside resort of Carbis Bay. Her Majesty welcomed the visiting leaders. In his debut on the world stage, Biden declared that "America was back"—back as a reliable ally—although the question of whether Trump's distinctive brand of populism had been vanquished or simply interrupted would shadow Biden's presidency to its end.

There already had been a more personal issue when Prince Harry reached out to Jill Biden during the transition, after her husband had won the presidency in 2020. She and Harry had met before in support of Harry's charity for wounded warriors; in 2017 both Bidens had joined him in Toronto to celebrate the end of the third annual Invictus Games. Then, Joe Biden had been out of office. Now he was president—and the relationship between Harry and his family had headed toward a nadir. He was preparing to write a memoir that would bear his pain and anger over how the palace had treated him and Meghan Markle. In a few months, she would accuse the royals of racism in a sensational interview with Oprah Winfrey. For the royal family, livid and hurt, the allegations only buttressed the belief among some that Meghan had taken Harry off the rails. Her Majesty was in no mood to do her wayward grandson any favors—especially at a point before she and the incoming first lady had even talked. The British made it known that the palace didn't want Jill to take Harry's call. Putting US relationships with the British government over her friendship with the prince, she reluctantly agreed.

The Queen's government also had a top item on its agenda. In the aftermath of Great Britain's withdrawal from the European Union, London wanted a trade deal with Washington—a goal that Trump had endorsed but never completed. Now the White House had a new and less accommodating resident. Trump not only adored the Queen; he also had supported Brexit and embraced its biggest backer, Boris Johnson. But Biden had disparaged the prime minister as a "kind of a physical and emotional clone" of Trump. Biden's priority was different: to protect the hard-fought accord between Britain and the Irish. Ireland was still part of the European Union, and Northern Ireland had a special negotiated arrangement with the EU that it wanted to protect. "We can't allow the Good Friday Agreement that brought peace to Northern Ireland to become a casualty of Brexit," he had vowed during the campaign. "Any trade deal between the US and the UK must be contingent upon respect for the Agreement and preventing the return of a hard border. Period."

That was a source of friction. As the summit was about to open, *The Times* of London reported that Biden had issued a démarche—a formal diplomatic reprimand, rare between allies—to the British government. Talks on border transit arrangements were stalled, and the United States said the British government was "inflaming" tensions with Ireland and Northern Ireland.

The Queen hosted the summit's opening reception on June 11, 2021, at the Eden Project, a futuristic site where giant biospheres shelter the world's largest indoor rainforest. She was joined by Prince Charles and the Duchess of Cornwall as well as Prince William and the Duchess of Cambridge—the royal family's first major public event together since the funeral in April of the Duke of Edinburgh. Philip had been a skeptic of Irish intentions and never forgave the assassination of Mountbatten, his uncle and surrogate father. When the prince died at age ninety-nine, the statement of sympathy by the Bidens was factual and relatively brief, citing the details of his life and the charities he supported. Trump's statement was more effusive. An "irreplaceable loss for Great Britain, and for all who hold dear our civilization," it read.

At the economic summit, the Queen seemed relaxed and upbeat, wearing a cheerful green-and-pink floral dress and short white gloves, a small black handbag looped over her arm. She took her place at the center of the careful arrangement on a blue dais for the official photo, the silver biospheres looming behind them and the leaders spaced at a distance because of the COVID-19 pandemic. "Are you supposed to be looking as if you're enjoying yourself?" she asked to laughter after the group had posed, all with serious expressions on their faces.

"Yes," Boris Johnson replied. "We have been enjoying ourselves in spite of appearances."

That prompted the photographer to take a second version that showed them more at ease.

Two days later, on June 13, 2021, the Queen's first private meeting with a foreign head of state since Philip's death was a tea with the Bidens. It happened to fall three days after what would have been the prince's hundredth birthday. Earlier that day, Jill Biden and Catherine, Duchess of Cambridge visited a school to spotlight an early childhood development program. "Joe and I are looking forward to meeting the Queen," the first lady told reporters. "That's an exciting part of the visit for us. We've looked forward to this for weeks and now it's finally here. It's a beautiful beginning."

Under a cloudless sky and a blazing sun, the Queen stood on the steps of Windsor Castle to greet President and Dr. Biden as the *Marine One* helicopter landed on the lawn and they took the brief ride to the quadrangle in the back seat of a black Land Rover. For the record, the greeting was friendly and respectful, but there was no bow from Joe Biden, no curtsy from Jill. The military band, which had already played "God Save the Queen," now performed "The Star-Spangled Banner." Biden reviewed a row of the Guard of Honor, in their distinctive scarlet uniforms and towering bearskin caps.

Then they went inside the castle.

Jill Biden was struck by how unpretentious a host the Queen was during a visit that lasted nearly an hour. Her Majesty insisted on serving the tea herself. When President Biden offered to help, she said, "No, no, sit down, please," as she poured. She was curious about what the president was hearing about the world. She wanted to know about the rest of his trip, to the NATO and EU summits in Belgium and then his meeting with Russian President Vladimir Putin in Geneva. She asked about his impressions of Putin and China's Xi Jinping. She had hosted both at state visits in London.

"All she wanted to do was pick Joe's brain," Jill Biden recalled. Joe Biden was surprised at the substance of their conversation, among other things about European unity and the transatlantic alliance.

There were both seasoned leaders of a certain age—Biden at seventy-eight years old, the Queen at ninety-five. The COVID pandemic had isolated her, though she had become proficient at using Zoom as a substitute for in-person meetings. A senior palace aide told me she sometimes seemed lonely, and those close to her became even more protective, though at their instructions the Bidens didn't wear face masks. "Remember her husband had just died two months previously, and the staff said to us, 'Whatever you do, don't talk about family. We don't want to get her upset,'" Jill Biden said.

"Then her first question to us: 'How's your family?' And Joe and I looked at each other, like, do we say? Do we talk about it? And we said, 'Well, how are you?' And of course we gave our condolences." Joe Biden mentioned the losses he had suffered in his family, of his first wife and his daughter, then of his older son. He told her, "I find you'll be somewhere where you remember, 'That's where I took her or him for this,' and you'll smile before you cry, and that's when you know . . . that you're going to make it."

She replied something like, "It's good; it's similar," Joe Biden recalled. "She seemed pretty stoic," Jill Biden said, a trait Elizabeth had displayed since the day she learned her father had died, making her the monarch. The conversation moved on to the joyful topic of grandchildren. She was awaiting the birth of her twelfth great-grandchild, the daughter of Princess Beatrice who would be born three months later. When one of her corgis nudged his way into the room, she took one of the tiny sandwiches from the tray and surreptitiously slipped it to him under the table.

The Queen presented them with her standard gift, a portrait of herself in a silver frame. As they were leaving, the Bidens also were given a basket of strawberries just picked from the royal garden, with a bundle of red Windsor Castle pencils that had tiny golden crowns rather than erasers at their ends.

Biden was the thirteenth and final sitting US president to meet with Elizabeth. "A seemingly timeless ritual," *The Times* in London wrote afterward, and one that seemed especially crucial at the moment. "At a time when trust in Boris Johnson's government, and therefore Britain itself, is being openly questioned by its closest allies, including the US, the continuity that the Queen brings to the country's international relationships has never been more vital. That she continues to do her duty with such diligence and dignity is a blessing for which we should all be grateful."

"When we left, we said, 'We hope you're going to be okay,'" Jill Biden said. "And she said, 'Oh, I have new puppies and they're going to help me get through all this.'"

THE FIRST US AMBASSADOR TO THE COURT OF ST. JAMES'S WAS JOHN ADAMS, presenting his credentials to King George III on June 1, 1785, after being appointed by George Washington, the first president of the newly independent United States of America. (Adams would become the second president.)

Two hundred and thirty-seven years later, on July 19, 2022, Jane D. Hartley, appointed by the forty-sixth president, arrived to present her credentials to George's great-great-great-great-granddaughter, Elizabeth II.

By then, Her Majesty was ninety-six years old and ailing. A few months earlier, she had suffered a bout of COVID. With increasing mobility problems, she was seen at Windsor Castle using her late husband's cane to get around. But she insisted on scheduling the diplomatic ceremony. She seemed especially determined not only because the new ambassador was from the United States but also because she was a woman, just the second to serve in the post since the days of Adams.

"Normally, a horse-drawn carriage picks you up at Winfield House and takes you through the streets of London to Buckingham Palace," Hartley said. Everything was arranged—until it turned out to be the hottest day in London's recorded history, reaching 40.2 degrees Celsius, or just over 104 degrees Fahrenheit. "They called me in the morning, Buckingham Palace . . . and said she was really worried about the horses, and she didn't think it was good to have them out in this heat."

She was worried about the horses. Of course.

Hartley assured them that she could make her own way to the palace. The United States embassy had cars. "'No, no, no,'" they told her. "The Queen is worried about the horses, but she wants to send her Rolls Royce to pick you up. She feels so bad about it." So the ambassador and her husband arrived at the palace in the back seat of Her Majesty's Rolls. The Queen wasn't feeling up to an in-person meeting, so the ceremony was conducted via Zoom. It was one more sign of the isolation of the pandemic, and of age. The palace posted a photo of it on the @RoyalFamily official Twitter account, Hartley smiling into a Zoom screen that showed the Queen, sitting in a chair, dressed and bejeweled.

"I hope we're treating you well in London," Elizabeth said to her. "I hear you're here alone." Hartley's husband, Ralph Schlosstein, was spending about half his time in London. "I said, 'Yes, everybody's treating me very well.' Then I told her I had a dog who was with me 100 percent of the time, and that brightened her up immediately."

It was the last time Elizabeth would accept diplomatic credentials from anyone.

After Boris Johnson resigned a few months later, Liz Truss became the fifteenth prime minister, and the last, to meet with Her Majesty for the ceremony known as "kissing hands," this time at Balmoral Castle. "There'd been a long interregnum that had been this leadership contest, so I got the sense she was keen to get things back on the road," Truss said. "There was absolutely no sense that this was her final meeting. No sense at all."

Two days later, on September 8, 2022, the Queen died.

Her memorial service drew the leaders of the world, from most of the biggest nations and many of the smallest ones. There was royalty: The Sultan of Brunei, the Emperor of Japan, the Emir of Kuwait, the King of Jordan, and the Queen of Denmark. And prime ministers, from Australia and New Zealand to the Bahamas and Tuvalu. And presidents, from India and South Africa and Singapore. Biden, then seventy-nine years old, hadn't been enthusiastic about making the trip, a standalone journey across the Atlantic for a ceremony in which he would play no significant role. "Was there a little moment of 'Do I really have to go?'" a senior Biden aide said. "And it was like, 'Yes, sir, you have to go.'" Fine, he said. "I think almost just out of a nod to his Irish roots more than anything, he was like,

'Am I really going to go to the Queen's funeral?' But he pretty much immediately agreed that, of course, he needed to go."

"I thought it was important [to go] because it was my way of expressing how much I appreciated her," Biden told me. She had "defined an era," he said. In Washington, he ordered American flags at the White House and other federal facilities flown at half-staff until her internment. In London, he paid his respects at her lying in state, joined a reception hosted by King Charles, and attended the state funeral at Westminster Abbey. Most of the world leaders arrived in a specially chartered bus, but for security reasons the Bidens were given special dispensation to arrive at the abbey in an armored presidential limousine. Still, protocol ruled once they arrived: They were seated on the aisle of the fourteenth row of the south transept. As it happens, in the world of the Crown, elected presidents and their ilk rank behind fellow members of royalty and leaders of the Commonwealth.

The president had shown up, doing his duty. As the Queen always had.

Sixteen

God Save the King

Thursday, February 27, 2025—The Oval Office

As reporters and photographers jumbled for position in the Oval Office, British Prime Minister Keir Starmer pulled a cream-colored envelope from his breast pocket, the red royal seal embossed on the flap, and handed it to President Trump with an expectant smile. With Starmer's encouragement, Trump took out the two-page letter and read it on the spot as TV cameras rolled, his face at first guarded and then solemn, even a bit stunned. "This is really special," the prime minister declared when Trump had finished, clamping his hand on the president's shoulder for emphasis. "This has never happened before. This is unprecedented."

In the letter, King Charles III had invited Trump to a state visit, another one. The presidents who had been honored with the most formal of palace dinners during their first terms—George W. Bush and Barack Obama—had been greeted with private luncheons at Windsor Castle when they visited during their second. Trump would be the first elected leader in modern times from any country to be offered two state visits in Britain. For someone who was enchanted by the royal family, and always eager for ways in which he could outshine his predecessors, it was both a prize and a surprise.

"I think that just symbolizes the strength of the relationship between us," Starmer said. "I think the last state visit was a tremendous success. His Majesty the King wants to make this even better than that. So this is, this is truly historic."

Never mind that Trump had complained to aides that Prince Charles bored him during their first meeting, in 2019. Afterward, Trump told Stephanie Grisham that the conversation had been terrible. "Nothing but climate change," Trump groused, rolling his eyes. Melania Trump confirmed that with a laugh. "Oh, yes, he was very bored," she said of her husband. Trump was not the first person to find Charles less engaging and more pretentious than his mother. Like the president, he had been given a head start in life by the circumstances of his birth. He also lived most of his life, in a maudlin sense, waiting for his mother to die. But Trump said he had had a change of heart about Charles since then. "He is a beautiful man, a wonderful man," Trump said of Charles, now the king. "I've gotten to know him very well, actually." Calling him a "great, great gentleman," the president held up the letter's second page so reporters could admire the "beautiful" signature, an oversized "Charles R," just as Trump routinely showed off his own bold signature after he signed executive orders. The first page of the letter, hanging down, was visible, too, enabling reporters to decipher it later from the photographs snapped.

His Majesty began by citing the "breadth of challenges across the world" and "the vital role" that their two countries had to play in promoting the values they shared. "I remember with great fondness your visits to the United Kingdom during your previous Presidency," he wrote. He noted that the G7 summit in 2020, planned for Dumfries House in Scotland, had been canceled because of the COVID-19 pandemic. "All bets—and flights!—were off," he recalled. He suggested planning another meeting at Dumfries House, an eighteenth-century mansion near Glasgow that a consortium headed by Charles had purchased in 2007. Or perhaps a visit to Balmoral, the royal family's Scottish retreat where Queen Elizabeth had once hosted a cookout for President Eisenhower. Charles had been there—a ten-year-old in a plaid kilt and knee socks, meeting his first US president. (He had encountered nine more in the decades since then: Richard Nixon, Jimmy Carter, Ronald Reagan, George H. W. Bush, Bill Clinton, the younger Bush, Obama, Trump, and Joe Biden.)

Both sites were convenient to Trump's Scottish golf resort at Turnberry—thirty miles from Dumfries, sixty miles from Balmoral. The meeting would be an opportunity to discuss a wide range of issues, the king said. "In so doing, working together, I know we will further enhance the special relationship between our two countries, of which we are both so proud."

"The answer is yes," Trump told Starmer, not needing a moment to consider or the counsel of others. "On behalf of our wonderful first lady Melania and myself, the answer is yes." (This time, unlike during Trump's first term, there would be no British second thoughts, no delay. The president and the first lady would arrive at Windsor Castle a little more than six months later, in September.)

The headline on the front page of the *Daily Mirror* called it "Keir's Trump Card." The subhead: "King's Invite Sets Tone as PM and President Bond."

A few weeks later, Trump announced his first framework for a deal to lower the stringent tariffs he had announced for the world, setting them at 10 percent for Great Britain and declaring that was likely to be the low-water mark for any country, anywhere. Negotiations on the specifics would stretch for months and more. But even as the European Union and such US allies as South Korea and Japan struggled to reach arrangements to avoid Trump's toughest tariffs, London was well ahead of them.

Did the diplomacy of Queen Elizabeth, and then King Charles, make a difference in that?

In global affairs, "the very big things were not going to be influenced" by the royals, said Lord Donoughue, an adviser to three British prime ministers during Elizabeth's reign. "But because she was so wonderful, people ended up probably being a bit more favorable to the U.K. than they might have been, or the U.K. deserved." Exhibit A: the Trump trade deal, a relatively favorable economic framework delivered with unexpected speed, one that the president had predicted during his first welcome at Windsor Castle by Elizabeth and finally delivered soon after an invitation to return by her son and heir.

Even two and a half years after her death, Her Majesty's hidden hand was shaping the moment.

NO PRESIDENT TESTED THE QUEEN'S "SOFT POWER" MORE THAN TRUMP. During his first term, she proved to be a royal salve even as he erupted at more than one prime minister, and at a time the British economy and its politics had been upended by Brexit. His encounters with the Queen—first tea at Windsor Castle and then a state dinner at Buckingham Palace—were highlights of his tenure that had helped keep relations between the United States and the United Kingdom on an even keel during a turbulent time.

Now, during Trump's second term, Charles faced a similar challenge. Not everyone thought he would be up to it.

Elizabeth was "truly a legendary figure," Trump said. "Time will go by, but it's not going to be easy to replace somebody like that." He mused briefly about the king—"Hopefully Charles will be able to have a chance to do that"—then turned to the next generation, the Prince and Princess of Wales. He called Catherine "a terrific person," "fantastic," and someone who, like her mother-in-law, rarely took a step wrong. "It's going to be very hard for William, I think," he said. "That's a very tough role, and the critics, like they are with me, the critics are nasty."

Some of the royal magic conveyed to the next generations. Trump met with Prince William in Paris after both attended the reopening of the Notre Dame cathedral in 2024. "Good man, this one," Trump said to news photographers as he arrived at the British ambassador's residence, gesturing toward the prince and patting him on the shoulder. Their meeting, scheduled for fifteen minutes, lasted more than forty. It went on for so long that French officials called the British to ask, politely, when Trump was planning to come to the Élysée Palace, where he was late for dinner.

King Charles's invitation to another state dinner was a deft diplomatic turn, and one that succeeded in warming Starmer's first meeting with Trump.

In their talks that day, the president endorsed a deal negotiated by the prime minister involving a necklace of islands in the Indian Ocean. Trump also gave Starmer credit for making Britain's case on tariffs. "He earned whatever the hell they pay him over there," Trump told reporters. But he dismissed Starmer's top priority, that the United States commit to providing a security "backstop" for any British and European peacekeeping troops in Ukraine. That issue would persist.

"I've always found about the British, they don't need much help," Trump said, not the message the United Kingdom and NATO wanted to hear. "They can take care of themselves very well." Still, he added offhandedly, "If they need help, I'll always be with the British, OK?"

CHARLES INHERITED THE WEALTH OF THE MONARCHY AND ITS STORIED history, the palaces and the castles and the jewels. The question: Did he inherit from his mother not only her crown but also her diplomatic heft?

Some of her personal assets—the gift of time and the circumstances of her day—weren't transferable. She had been on the scene from one century into the next, through critical decades as a new world order emerged. When she assumed the throne, some bomb craters in London from the Blitz hadn't yet been repaired; chocolate and sugar were still being rationed. Her reign continued through the decline of the British empire and the expansion of the Commonwealth. Through the peaceful end of the Cold War and the eruption of hot wars in Vietnam and Afghanistan and Iraq. Through the 9/11 attacks and the global financial meltdown and the pandemic. Through the invention of the Internet and the early rise of artificial intelligence. No other leader in modern times could claim a tenure that spanned so many momentous developments. No other leader in the history of the world had ever met, in person, so many other leaders of the world.

"She was front and center to so much of the historical events of the twentieth century," Hillary Clinton said. She had encountered Elizabeth both as first lady and later as secretary of state. "She was very knowledgeable. She was curious. She had opinions, which she would rarely, but occasionally, express." After the September 11 attacks in 2001, Prime Minister Tony Blair sought her perspective on the Arab world. "She's dealt with many of the ruling families over a long, long period of time," he said, "and she has a lot of real insight into how they work, how they operate, how they think, the best way of trying to make sure that we reach out to them."

Charles was destined to have a shorter tenure. He was seventy-three years old when he finally became monarch on September 8, 2022; a year and a half later he was diagnosed with cancer. He had been the heir apparent almost his entire life, and at a time of increasingly scathing scrutiny of public figures, even royal ones—perhaps especially royal ones. His disastrous marriage to Diana Spencer ended in divorce and was followed by her tragic death. Every detail of the drama of his relationship with Camilla Parker Bowles was chronicled in the British tabloids. He suffered a painful public estrangement from his younger son, Prince Harry. In 2025, as king, he took the stunning step of stripping his brother, Andrew, of his royal titles amid an outcry over allegations of sexual abuse and his relationship with Jeffrey Epstein.

"It's a terrible thing that's happened to the family," Trump told reporters. "That's been a tragic situation, and it's too bad."

During Trump's visit to Windsor weeks earlier, it had been hard to escape Epstein's shadow. Starmer had just fired Peter Mandelson, the British ambassador to the United States, for his ties to the disgraced financier, who committed suicide in jail in 2019. While the president was visiting, protesters projected images of him with Epstein on the castle walls.

In his toast to Charles on September 17, 2025, Trump began by noting, clearly delighted, that he was returning for a second state dinner. "That's the first and maybe that's going to be the last time; I hope it is actually," he quipped as Charles chuckled. "But this is truly one of the highest honors of my life." Earlier, the president and Melania had visited St. George's Chapel on the castle grounds, laying a wreath at the tomb of Queen Elizabeth II.

It is not criticism of Charles to say that he was a less unifying and less beloved figure than his mother—an inevitable reality, given her unique history and the increasing polarization of the world's politics. "I think the mission remains the same, and I've seen Charles since he became king, and he's trying very hard to make his contribution," Hillary Clinton said. "But it's a different time, and it's much less forgiving. Being in any public position in the time of social media is very, very hard, so much more challenging than whatever came before."

The monarch's role was made both more difficult and more crucial by Trump's disregard for the transatlantic alliance, on matters economic and security, that had been built since World War II. That modern-day turbulence underscored the contrast with the enduring resilience of the British monarchy. While some dismissed the Crown as a relic of another era, it provided stability and legitimacy at a time both were in short supply, on both sides of the Atlantic.

As political polarization sharpened and authoritarianism rose around the globe, there was the sovereign, still on the throne a thousand years later.

Epilogue

London's Bridge

For seven decades, she had been the promise and the prize who had charmed presidents, not to mention prime ministers and emperors and emirs and the occasional despot. Her travels to the United States and presidents' visits to the United Kingdom had proved to be the single most reliable way for London to preserve the "special relationship," the one her father had helped forge, when it seemed at risk.

The modern operations of the British government presumably could have proceeded just fine without a royal family—goodbye and thank you for your service—which was an idea a growing fraction of the nation's citizenry endorsed. After she died, a record 25 percent of Britons agreed either that the monarchy should be abolished or that it was "not at all important." Once a year, she was required to address the State Opening of Parliament and read the legislative agenda of whatever party happened to be in power, poker-faced whether she agreed or not. She couldn't order troops into battle or deny requests for their deployment, even though they were called Her Majesty's forces. It would have been seen as inappropriate if she had publicly weighed in on the fundamental questions of whether Great Britain should enter or, later, exit the European Union. She was generally constrained from expressing her views on almost any topic, beyond love of country and opposition to tyranny. After she met each week with the string of prime ministers during her reign, they were forbidden by tradition from revealing anything she had said.

That policy may well have made those conversations more candid and more influential. "She would in private to me as a serving member of the government, she said, 'Have you thought about that properly?'" said George Osborne, a former chancellor of the Exchequer. "And 'didn't the last government try something like that? And it didn't work.' So she'd ask probing questions without saying, 'I don't think you're doing the right thing.'"

"I felt there was nothing I could not tell her, and her genius—as I gave her my descriptions of government infighting or foreign chicanery—was to sound both understanding and sympathetic, and then, at just the right moment, to give the tiniest nudge of advice," Prime Minister Boris Johnson recalled. "Whatever crisis you laid before her—like one of her dogs finding something revolting on the moor and putting it on the carpet—she had seen worse."

She had seen worse.

When the coronavirus threatened to kill millions and upend the economy, she was the embodiment of "keep calm and carry on." The iconic slogan first appeared on a British motivational poster in 1939 as the country prepared for World War II, when she was a thirteen-year-old princess. "Oh well," the Queen said briskly in the face of this once-in-a-century challenge. "I suppose we will all just have to start again."

"Her power came from respect," Donald Trump said. "People with power like prime ministers and like Boris and like others—they had total respect and admiration for her. So she may not have had official (power)—that she's allowed to say what to do—but she had great influence over prime ministers, I can tell you that, and anybody else that she touched.... She was so calm, and yet you could see an inner toughness that was really amazing."

The glimpses that emerged here and there showed a sovereign engaging not only in social chitchat but also in substance, at times of the most serious sort.

She repaired the breach with Dwight Eisenhower after the Suez crisis. With an African trip that Winston Churchill warned was too dangerous to dare, she facilitated efforts by JFK and the British to keep Ghana from moving to the Soviets during the Cold War. She asserted herself to establish a relationship with Richard Nixon when her prime minister seemed determined to downgrade their nations' ties. She sealed Ronald Reagan's support in the Falklands war with a horseback ride. Again and again, she helped England maintain a global influence that its military and economic position no longer could necessarily command. Even as Britain's empire eroded on her watch, she was crucial in preserving its stature as a voice that should be heard.

The whole idea of a "special relationship" was "peculiarly impervious to abstract theories," mused Henry Kissinger, the leading foreign policy strategist of his generation. "It did not depend on foreign arrangements; it derived in part from the memory of Britain's heroic wartime effort; it reflected the common language and culture of the two sister peoples." The relationship was extraordinary "because it rested on no legal claim; it was formalized by no document." Instead, "Britain turned conciliation into a weapon by making it morally inconceivable that its views could be ignored."

Queen Elizabeth played no small part in that. "Wrongly stereotyped as rather stodgy," in Kissinger's judgment. That was the public monarch. In private, "she impressed me with her knowledge of world affairs and her insight into the personalities involved." As a girl, her mother urged her not to forget "the human element" of history. She had heeded the advice. "For more than seventy years, I have been lucky to meet and to know many of the world's great leaders," she said near the end of her life, in remarks at a summit on climate change. "And I have perhaps come to understand a little about what made them special."

Two days before Her Majesty died in 2022, Johnson visited Balmoral Castle to submit his resignation as prime minister. As they discussed the war in Ukraine, he mentioned how hard it had been to convince India to take a tougher line with Moscow in the wake of Russia's invasion. She recalled a meeting she had six decades earlier with Jawaharlal Nehru, India's first prime minister. "He told me that India will always side with Russia, and that some things will never change," she told Johnson. "They just are."

That same day, Liz Truss arrived at Balmoral to become prime minister in the final official act of the Queen's reign. "She was very wise," Truss told me. "And if she was influencing people, they didn't know she was influencing them, I would say."

WITHOUT HARD POWER—WITHOUT THE IMPRIMATUR OF ELECTION— what were the tools in her toolbox?

Her skill at listening and her discretion about talking, for starters. Her sharp judgment of leaders, grounded in having talked with them, hosted them as house guests, met with those who preceded and succeeded them in their office. She could be insightful about those she respected most—Nelson Mandela, for one—and those she did not, however subtly she expressed that. At a time when the British and French were in endless negotiations over Brexit, she observed that there was a wide age gap between French President Emmanuel Macron and his wife, Brigitte; he was twenty-four years younger than she was. "Yes, he married his teacher," Johnson said. The Queen replied, "Well, she didn't teach him much history."

History was a topic Elizabeth knew well, and from personal experience. Because of her time on the throne and the attention she paid, her knowledge of foreign affairs during her reign may well have been unequaled. "If you have seen it all before, if you've been there, done that, and got the tee-shirt—she must have a whole wardrobe of them by now—then there is a value," said Joe Haines, a British journalist and press secretary to Prime Minister Harold Wilson.

For Americans, she was the subject of fascination and affection. She could bedazzle; surely no one had a bigger collection of priceless tiaras for an endless procession of white-tie dinners. She could make small talk with anyone from a visiting sultan to a hospitalized child to an incoming ambassador who found himself suddenly tongue-tied in her presence. She could stand and wave from balconies on big national occasions, including the official celebration of her birthday, a stoic figure surrounded by family members who sometimes lacked her discipline in avoiding controversy and sidestepping scandal.

In one measure of relevance in popular culture, a movie plot that centered on efforts to foil her threatened assassination launched *The Naked Gun* series of comedic spoofs. She was repeatedly portrayed on NBC's *Saturday Night Live*, a clashing mix of caricatures featuring actors from Joan Cusack to Mike Myers. Fred Armisen, in drag, portrayed the Queen as a gangster-like figure behind closed doors, threatening singer Elton John, who was playing himself. Kate McKinnon channeled Elizabeth as a dizzy gram who found herself trapped beneath a towering pile of gifts for Meghan's baby shower.

The Queen harbored a belief in the supernatural. She didn't reject out of hand even the value of exorcism. Some of the staff at Sandringham had been uneasy about going into one of the rooms in the main house, the room where George VI had died. She arranged for a small religious service in the room "to bless it" and calm their fears.

Then there was the superstition that seeing a single magpie would bring bad luck. The myth dates to the crucifixion of Jesus, when the magpie was said to be the only bird that didn't comfort or mourn him. A British nursery rhyme from the eighteenth century detailed the omens of seeing a specific number of magpies: "One for sorrow / Two for mirth / Three for a funeral / Four for a birth." Elizabeth had developed a ritual to banish the curse of one—the sort of no-nonsense attitude forged during her long and consequential life. "If you see a single magpie, you just say, 'Good morning, Mr. Magpie. Today is Monday the 12th of March'—or whatever the date is," she advised. "That sorts it out."

SEEN BY SOME AS AN ICON AND NOTHING MORE, EVEN AN ARCHAIC ONE, she was often underestimated as a force—in the way history has discounted some women. The way "soft power" is underestimated in a world that respects hard power most of all.

"There are so many different kinds of leadership," Barack Obama said. "Obviously, she did not have the same impact in terms of day-to-day policy or how much money was allocated to the National Health Service or what have you. But I do think that that symbolic authority that she had earned by virtue of having done her duty, and remained steadfast, and been reliable and restrained—all those qualities that people would remark on about her—I do think had an impact on how people viewed not just Great Britain but also the West."

While rarely expressing an opinion, she could leave others convinced that she was in tune with them. "To the optimist, she seemed an optimist; to the pessimist, a pessimist," Craig Brown wrote. "To the insider, she appeared intimate, to the outsider, distant; to the cynic, prosaic, and to the awestruck, charismatic." Perhaps that's why so many presidents described her as reminding them of members of their families. Harry Truman saw in her echoes of his daughter. She reminded Jimmy Carter and Joe Biden of their mothers, never mind that Biden's mother harbored an Irish disdain for her. Obama recognized in her the qualities of the grandmother who helped raise him.

Trump could hardly find the words to describe his conversations with her. "She had a way of convincing people in the most non-controversial way," he said. That trait was "sort of the opposite of me," he added ruefully. "You would leave, and you wouldn't even know that she was in favor of something, and yet she would convince you that there was a certain way to go."

She was a bridge—London's bridge. (Indeed, the official plan for her funeral, first devised in the 1960s and repeatedly updated, was called Operation London Bridge, and "London Bridge is down" was the phrase scripted to inform the prime minister of her death.) "There was a sense of her symbolizing and embodying some aspect of the old Western order that was decent and had admirable qualities and other societies could relate to or admire, and I think that was important," Obama said. "I think it helped smooth out a lot of these transitions that were taking place during her reign. And I think that made a difference."

Acknowledgments

The secret to writing biographies, I think, is to find a person who had a big impact but whose story hasn't been fully told. There are many outstanding books about Queen Elizabeth II, but the story behind her dealings with thirteen sitting US presidents—not to mention a fourteenth before he moved into the White House and a fifteenth after he moved out—had not been seriously explored. What did Her Majesty do with that unprecedented access? Quite a lot, as it turned out. She proved to be more than an unflappable figure in a tiara. She was a deft diplomat and a shrewd judge of character and, by the way, a skilled mimic. She was also the single strongest force in maintaining Great Britain as a voice that would be heard even as its empire declined.

That is the story I wanted to tell. Let me start by acknowledging my debt to her for the extraordinary life she lived.

My agent, Matt Latimer, partner at Javelin with the inestimable Keith Urbahn, helped shape this book from conception to delivery. Matt is indefatigable, brilliant, and hilarious. My editor at HarperCollins, Sean Desmond, believed in this book before a word had been written. His enthusiasm, his skilled and sometimes ruthless editing, and his smart perspective on the British royal family made every passage better. I am fortunate that he has been the editor for three of the four books I have written.

At HarperCollins, I am also grateful to Kate D'Esmond, Jackie Quaranto, Tina Andreadis, Katie O'Callaghan, Jocelyn Larnick, and Laura Brady.

Journalist Lillianna Byington brought her meticulous research and steady presence to even the most impossible of requests, and at all hours, for the third book we have done together. Across an ocean, national security author Tom Griffin, working in Britain's National Archives, uncovered documents that had never before been brought to light. I am indebted to the archivists at the eight presidential libraries where I did on-site research—at the libraries of Harry Truman, Dwight Eisenhower, Lyndon B. Johnson, Richard Nixon, Ronald Reagan, George H. W. Bush, Bill Clinton, and George W. Bush. The George Washington University Gelman Library was an important resource, available to me courtesy of Peter Loge, and my local branch of the District of Columbia Public Library, at West End, was a haven.

Any errors are mine alone, of course.

My thanks to all those, in the United States and Great Britain, who agreed to be interviewed for this book. I am especially grateful for the opportunities to discuss their encounters with the Queen with Presidents Donald Trump, Joe Biden, Barack Obama, and Bill Clinton as well as first ladies Jill Biden, Michelle Obama, and Hillary Clinton, and with Prime Ministers Boris Johnson, Liz Truss, and David Cameron.

The flexibility and support of the bosses at my day job, as Washington Bureau chief of *USA Today*, have made it possible for me to also write books. I'm indebted to editor in chief Caren Bohan for her backing and to Mike Reed, Kristin Roberts, Monica Richardson, Toby Zakaria, Holly Rosenkrantz, and others.

Many people offered introductions, encouragement, and expert advice. They include early readers Dylan Colligan, Mimi Hall, and Lee Horwich. Established biographers of the royal family were generous with their knowledge, among them Sally Bedell Smith, Robert Hardman, Will Swift, and Hugo Vickers. My thanks for their help to Jeffrey Engel, Michael LaRosa, Heath Hardage Lee, Anita McBride, Luigi Parasmo, Frederick Ryan, Robin Sproul, and Mark Updegrove. I am grateful to Kim Hjelmgaard and Ben Quinn for their guidance in negotiating London, and to member of Parliament Adam Jogee for introducing me to the bars tucked away in the Palace of Westminster.

Finally and first, to my family. Carl Leubsdorf Jr. and Ben Leubsdorf provided technical support; Will Leubsdorf historical correction; Katie List knowledge about trains; and John Leubsdorf an explanation of the legal foundations of constitutional monarchy. Most of all, Carl Leubsdorf, my husband of more than four decades, served as accountant, fact-checker, trip adviser, sounding board, psychiatrist, memory bank, and more. Once again.

Thank you.

Notes

Introduction | Her Father's Daughter

xii *"A living flag":* Author interview with Joseph Nye, Jan. 17, 2024.

xiii *"What a woman!":* Diary, Joseph P. Kennedy, April 14, 1939. Kennedy Presidential Library, JPKPP-100–010.

xiii *The royal couple were honored:* Diary, Joseph P. Kennedy, May 23, 1939. Kennedy Presidential Library, JPKPP-100–010-p0030.

xiii *"A very extraordinary visit":* Unpublished interview with Eleanor Roosevelt.

xiv *"King and Queen End":* "King and Queen End US Visit After Eating Hot Dogs at Picnic," *Philadelphia Inquirer,* June 12, 1939, 1A.

xiv The Miami News: "Royalty's Visit Places Crown upon 'King Hot Dog,'" *Miami News,* June 11, 1939, 1A.

xiv *Each had been tested:* Diary, Joseph Kennedy, June 22, 1939. Kennedy Presidential Library, JPKPP-100–010-p0046.

xiv *When they left Hyde Park:* Associated Press, "Monarchs Leave for Canada with Grateful Hearts," Hastings (Neb.) *Daily Tribune,* June 12, 1939, 1A.

xiv *"Good luck to you!":* Sally Bedell Smith, *George VI,* 364.

xiv *The trip to America:* Diary, Joseph P. Kennedy, June 23, 1939. Kennedy Presidential Library, JPKPP-100–010-p0038. Kennedy and the king spoke at a luncheon at Guildhall London on their return.

xv *"Lilibet is my pride":* Hugo Vickers, *Elizabeth: The Queen Mother.* Arrow Books, 2005, 114, n.16. Source: William Tallon to author, London, Feb. 2005.

xv *from the start:* Letter, Winston Churchill to Queen Elizabeth, Nov. 25, 1954. Shawcross, *Queen Mother,* 696.

xv *"astonishing in an infant":* Mary Soames, ed., *Speaking for Themselves: The Personal Letters of Winston and Clementine Churchill.* Toronto: Doubleday, 1998, 328. Letter from Churchill to Clementine, writing from Balmoral Castle, Sept. 25, 1928.

xv *"She watched America":* Author interview with Lord David Owen, Nov. 19, 2024.

xvi *"This is now":* Public Papers of the Presidents of the United States: George H. W. Bush, *1991, Book I,* May 14, 1991, 510–12.

xvii *In the classic definition:* Walter Bagehot, *The English Constitution,* London: Chapman and Hall, 1867, 103.
xvii *"Her Majesty impressed me":* Bill Clinton, *Life,* 599.
xvii *"one of the world's great diplomats":* Author interview with David Cameron, May 8, 2025.
xvii *"Sometimes, one can help":* Aldrich, *Royals,* 350.
xviii *"She had opinions":* Author interview with James A. Baker III, July 9, 2024.
xviii *"You could get her":* Author interview with George Osborne, Feb. 24, 2025.
xviii *She once confided:* Author interview with Bernard Donoughue, May 11, 2025.
xviii *"Try and learn":* Sally Bedell Smith, *George VI,* 353.

Chapter One | "All Will Be Well"

1 *"I know she will be lovely":* "Mary Pickford Finds 6 Kennedy 'Diplomats.'" *New York Journal-American.* Kennedy Presidential Library, Kennedy Family Collection, Scrapbooks and Albums, Embassy Clippings, 1938–1939. KFC-064-001.
1 *"As I entered the Palace":* Eunice Kennedy, "My Court Presentation," 1939. Kennedy Presidential Library, NAID 192733. Eunice's developmentally disabled sister, Rosemary, then nineteen, was presented as a debutante at the palace as well, four years before a lobotomy would leave her incapacitated.
1 *In a conversation:* Diary, Joseph Kennedy, April 4, 1938. Kennedy Presidential Library, JPKPP 100-006.
2 *Rose Kennedy recalled:* Diary, Rose Kennedy, April 9–11, 1938. Kennedy Presidential Library, Rose Kennedy Papers.
2 *Tapping his Hollywood connections:* Amanda Smith, *Hostage,* 331 and 435. The thank-you note was dated May 22, 1940, from Windsor Castle.
3 *Kennedy found young Elizabeth:* Diary, Joseph P. Kennedy, April 9, 1938. Kennedy Presidential Library, JPKPP 100-006.
3 *"For Worst Ambassador":* Seitz, *Here,* 61.
4 *"Obviously an upstart":* Nasaw, *Patriarch,* 377–78.
4 *"Everyone thinks war inevitable":* Letter, Kennedy to LeMoyne Billings, March 23, 1939, Kirk LeMoyne Billings Papers, Kennedy Presidential Library.
4 *Princesses Elizabeth and Margaret:* United Press, "Birthday Presents Hidden from Princess Elizabeth," *Pittsburgh Press,* April 19, 1938, p. 2.
5 *"The first couple of times":* Diary, Edward Kennedy, April 20–21, 1939. Kennedy Presidential Library.
5 *"I made a great deal of time":* Letter, John F. Kennedy to LeMoyne Billings, March 23, 1939. Kirk LeMoyne Billings Papers, Kennedy Presidential Library.
5 *At a luncheon:* Diary, Joseph Kennedy, April 15, 1939. Kennedy Presidential Library, JPKPP 100-101.
5 *"What the American people fear":* Diplomatic Memoirs of Joseph P. Kennedy, Chapter V, 6B, Kennedy Presidential Library.
6 *On Sunday afternoon:* "King as Host to Premier & U.S. Ambassador," *Daily Telegraph and Morning Post* (London), April 17, 1939, 13.
6 *Eleven days after Britain declared war:* Nasaw, *Patriarch,* 410.

6 *He moved out of London:* The country house that Joseph Kennedy moved to would later be the site of the Legoland Windsor Theme Park. Libby Lubin, "Acres of Primary Colors in an English Legoland," *New York Times*, July 14, 1996, Section 5, 8.
6 *"I thought my daffodils":* The Papers of Randolph Churchill, University of Oxford. Quoted in Thomas Maier, *When Lions Roar: The Churchills and the Kennedys.* Crown, 2014.
6 *He had argued:* Sally Bedell Smith, George VI, 385. Sourced to Wheeler-Bennett, *George VI*, 419.
6 *There were only:* Sally Bedell Smith, *George VI*, 385.
7 *"I never want to see":* Beschloss, *Kennedy*, 229.
7 *In his diary:* Smith, *George VI*, 387.
7 *"Mr. Kennedy is a very foul specimen":* Nasaw, *Patriarch*, 430–31.
8 *Earlier, when government officials urged:* A. J. P. Taylor, *English History: 1914–45*, 1975 revised Pelican edition, reprinted 1985, 600, n.1.
8 *In the fall of 1940:* Pimlott, *Queen*, 58–60.
9 *In Washington,* The Evening Star: Associated Press, "'All Will Be Well' in End, Princess Elizabeth Broadcasts" *Evening Star* (Washington), Oct. 14, 1940, A3.
9 *The Atlanta Journal published:* "Princess Elizabeth's Radio Message," *The Atlanta Journal*, Oct. 18, 1940, 24.
9 *At one point:* Stewart, *Army*, 115.
10 *There hadn't been time:* Butcher, *Eisenhower*, 27.
10 *"Suddenly we heard":* Margaret Rhodes, *Curtsey*, 71–72.
11 *He described the two Americans:* Butcher, *Eisenhower*, 17.
11 *Eisenhower "was so staggered":* Quotes from unused footage shot for the 1969 documentary *The Royal Family* and stored at the British Film Institute. Source: Chris Hastings, "Day That the Queen and George VI Hid from Eisenhower Under a Table: The Bizarre Royal Conversations That Didn't Make It into Landmark Film," *Daily Mail*, Jan. 15, 2011.
11 *"Even if they weren't":* Butcher, *Eisenhower*, 550.
11 *When asked:* Philip Ziegler, *Mountbatten: A Biography*, 181. Alfred A. Knopf, 1985.
11 *On the day it was conferred:* Sydney Gruson, "Eisenhower Wins London's Acclaim and Highest Honor," *New York Times*, June 13, 1945, 1A.
12 *"You led the Allied Expeditionary":* Order of Merit, King George VI to Eisenhower, June 12, 1945. Eisenhower Presidential Library, DDE Pre-presidential/principal file, Box 46, George VI folder, 1945–1954.
12 *"My dear General":* Letter, Lascelles to Eisenhower, 1946, Eisenhower Presidential Library, Pre-presidential/principal file, Box 70, 1944–1946.
12 *"George and Ike":* "George and Ike . . . A Kansas Yankee at Court," *New York Daily News*, Oct. 10, 1946.
13 *John Eisenhower, twenty-four years old:* "Eisenhowers Attend Church with Royalty," *St. Louis Globe-Democrat,* Oct. 7, 1946, 7A.
13 *His father was "quite captivated":* Strober, *Elizabeth*, 38.
13 *When Elizabeth married Sir Philip Mountbatten:* Letter, Eisenhower to Elizabeth. Pre-presidential/principal file, Box 38, Elizabeth II folder.
14 *In July 1951:* Newsreel, "London Honours U.S. Heroes," Gaumont British News.

Chapter Two | Falling in Love

15 *On this trip with Prince Philip, a Washington society columnist reported:* Jeanne Rogers, "'Twas Kow and Tow as Liz's Flunkeys Met H. T. Retinue," *Washington Times Herald*, Nov. 1, 1951.

16 *"There are fears":* Associated Press, "Italian Physician Says King George Had Lung Cancer," Everett, Wash., *Daily Herald*, Oct. 24, 1951, 3B.

16 *the palace had announced:* Brandreth, *Elizabeth*, 312.

16 *So dire that during the weeks:* Pimlott, *Queen*, 170.

16 *"Wherever we went":* Strober, *Elizabeth*, 22.

17 *He told her "not to be uneasy":* Weber, *Talking*. The volume includes transcripts of interviews Truman recorded with literary agent William Hillman and former journalist and speechwriter David Noyes in preparation for Truman's book, *Mr. Citizen*, published in 1960. But the memoir incorporated little material from the interviews.

17 *The* Des Moines Register *reporter:* Fletcher Knebel, "Capital Cheers Royal Couple," *Des Moines Register*, Nov. 1, 1951, 1A.

17 *"When I was a little boy":* Welcoming remarks, President Truman, on the arrival of Princess Elizabeth and the Duke of Edinburgh. Harry S. Truman Library. SR60–96 NAID 331916413.

18 *"I was most happy to hear":* Remarks, President Truman on the arrival of Princess Elizabeth and the Duke of Edinburgh, Washington National Airport, Oct. 31, 1951. Truman Presidential Library.

18 *"My mother":* Author interview with Clifton Truman Daniel, June 5, 2024.

18 *"An endearing person":* Margaret Truman, *Souvenir*, 289.

19 *When she stepped to the bank of microphones:* "U.S. Greets Princess," *Liverpool (U.K.) Daily Post*, Nov. 1, 1951, 6. Note: The technology to transmit a live television feed coast-to-coast was in its infancy. A month earlier, on Sept. 4, 1951, a speech by Truman announcing the acceptance of a treaty that ended the US post–World War II occupation of Japan had been the first.

19 *"Free men everywhere":* Remarks, Princess Elizabeth on arrival at Washington National Airport, Oct. 31, 1951. Truman Presidential Library.

19 *In the* Daily Express: "Mr. President takes the Princess by the arm and says—I THANK YOU, DEAR." London *Daily Express*, Nov. 1, 1951, 1A.

19 *Sir Oliver Franks:* Pimlott, *Queen*, 171–2.

20 *She hoped to catch a glimpse:* There were two identical open cars used at times by Harry Truman during his presidency. One of them is on display at the Truman Presidential Library in Independence, Mo.

20 *Her first column:* "Inquiring Photographer," *Washington Times-Herald*, Nov. 2, 1951, 8C.

20 *"as pretty as her picture":* Anthony, *Girl*, 161–63.

20 *Earlier, she had worn:* Berton, *Family*, 157.

20 *British journalists told:* "Sidelights on Princess Elizabeth's Visit," Washington *Evening Star*, Nov. 1, 1951, A3.

20 *she had been taken:* Sally Bedell Smith, *Elizabeth*, 58.

20 *"Respectful but not overawed"*: Author interview with Clifton Truman Daniel, June 5, 2024.
21 *Elizabeth and Philip would traverse*: Boothroyd, *Philip*, 188.
21 *Truman demonstrated his trust*: Alden Hatch, *The Mountbattens*, 312. Random House, 1965.
21 *Harold Macmillan called it*: Horne, *Macmillan I*, 298.
22 *"I see reports"*: Letter, Attlee to Truman, June 16, 1945. No. 93 TNA PREM 4/10/3.
22 *"I shall keep the promise"*: Letter, Truman to the prime minister, personal and top secret, June 18, 1945. TNA PREM 4/10/3.
22 *"I am glad"*: Letter, King George VI to President Truman, June 28, 1945, TNA PREM 4/10/3.
23 *"forestalled by the French"*: Memo, A. R. K. Mackenzie, Foreign Office, June 19, 1950. TNA FO 371/81639.
23 *the king quickly signed off on the invitation*: Memo, Alan Lascelles to R. E. Barclay, July 10, 1950, TNA FO 371/81639.
23 *Finally, in January 1951*: Memo, Roderick Barclay, private secretary to the foreign secretary, to G. R. Downes, private secretary to the lord president of the Council, January 1951, TNA FO 371/81639.
23 *First Earl of Halifax, who had served*: Pimlott, *Queen*, 170.
24 *When the Canadian tour was announced*: Swanson, Frank, "Princess Elizabeth and Prince Philip to Tour Canada from Coast to Coast," *The Evening Citizen*, Ottawa, Canada, July 5, 1951, 1A.
24 *"Were no official United States invitation forthcoming"*: Cable, US embassy to the secretary of state, July 5, 1951. Quoted in Kelley, *Royals*, 93.
24 *"I have no knowledge"*: News conference, Harry Truman, July 5, 1951, Truman Presidential Library.
24 *His comments were immediately radioed*: Canadian Press (CP), "Elizabeth, Philip Will Wait Invitation by U.S." *Victoria (Canada) Daily Times*, July 5, 1951, 1A.
24 *"If she delivers"*: Letter, Lascelles to Sir F. Browning, Aug. 17, 1951. Royal Archives GVI 10135 (3), (8).
25 *Churchill, now a former prime minister, wrote*: Letter, Winston Churchill to Clement Attlee, Sept. 23, 1951, TNA PREM 8/1513.
25 *A plane it would be*: Memo, Cabinet Conclusions, Sept. 27, 1951. TNA PREM 8/1513.
25 *The trip had*: Alden Hatch, *The Mountbattens*, 436. Random House, 1965.
25 *In the upstairs bar of the aircraft*: Berton, *Family*, 188.
26 *When the royal party reached Victoria*: "Princess 'Tired, Nervous' as Victoria Salutes Her," *Windsor Daily Star*, Oct. 23, 1951, 7.
26 *she was "obviously a bit overwhelmed"*: How, Douglas (CP), "Princess So Awed She Forgets to Smile," *Vancouver Sun*, Oct. 11, 1951, 3.
26 *"Are you smiling enough?"*: Pierre Berton, "A Fairy Queen, or a Mother in Tweeds," *The (Toronto) Examiner*, Jan. 23, 1954, 11.
26 *She was "mindful"*: Brandreth, *Elizabeth*, 415.
26 *"My face is aching"*: Pimlott, *Queen*, 171. Attributed to author's interview with Lord Charteris.

26 *Philip, who had a rowdy streak, would try:* Pimlott, *Queen*, 171.
26 *"It was a long trip":* Brandreth, *Queen*, 259.
27 *"I suppose you haven't got":* Boothroyd, *Philip*, 188.
27 *"Princess!" "Liz!":* Berton, *Family*, 197.
28 *The next morning:* Weber, *Harry*, 295–96.
29 *"We have many distinguished visitors":* Remarks, Harry Truman, November 1951, Collection HST-PSF: President's Secretary's Files (Truman Administration). Series: Personal Files. File Unit: Elizabeth II, Queen. National Archives and Records Administration.
29 *During the ceremony:* Worker inscription from 1951 visit, George W. Bush Library, OA/NARA 9388/9295 7523.
29 *"Lilibet's Conquest":* Washington *Evening Star*, Nov. 2, 1951.
30 *confidential annexes:* Precedent Book, Part V, Relations with Buckingham Palace, TNA CAB 181/7. Denis Rickett, note for file, June 26, 1950, TNA PREM 8/1271.
30 *A month later:* Associated Press, "Newspaperwomen Select Reporter 'Woman of Year,'" Washington *Evening Star*, A32.
30 *They paused for a moment:* Associated Press, "Eisenhower, President Meet, Start Conferences," *Sacramento Bee*, Nov. 5, 1951, 1A.
31 *"The memory of our visit":* Letter, Princess Elizabeth to President Truman, Nov. 4, 1951. National Archives. NAID 210023709. Footnote.
31 *In a letter to his cousin:* Letter, Harry Truman to Mary Ethel Noland, Dec. 12, 1951. National Archives and Records Administration. HST-MEN: Mary Ethel Noland Papers. Correspondence Files, 1904–1970. File Unit: Truman, Harry S. to the Noland Family, 1951.
31 *"Much has happened":* Letter, King George to Truman, Dec. 22, 1951. Truman Presidential Library, NAID 210023729.
32 *In his private sessions:* Aldrich, *Hand*, 328–29.
33 *"May I in this hour":* Telegram, Truman to Elizabeth, Department of State, Office of the Historian.
33 *"He was a grand man":* Diary, Harry Truman, Feb. 6, 1952, Truman Presidential Library.

Chapter Three | The Favorite Uncle

34 *Her royal bloodline traced back:* Ben Johnson, "Kings and Queens of England & Britain," Historic UK.
34 *Still, she kept:* Monique Jessen, "The Moment Queen Elizabeth Broke Down in an Airplane Bathroom After Her Father's Death," *People*, Feb. 3, 2022.
34 *In a letter to General George Marshall:* Letter, Elizabeth to George Marshall, Feb. 28, 1952. The George C. Marshall Foundation.
35 *The former first lady felt:* Eleanor Roosevelt, "My Day," Feb. 12, 1952.
35 *On Coronation Day:* "The Queen's Coronation: All the Queen's Horses by Lionel Edwards," *Country Life*, May 28, 2013.
35 *"The Coronation has given":* Memo, US Embassy Great Britain to Department of State, Despatch 5746, June 3, 1953, file 741.11/6–353.

Notes

35 *After the film footage had been flown:* Ronald G. Shafer, "Queen Elizabeth II's Coronation Was Televised and Captivated the World," *Washington Post*, May 4, 2023.

35 *"For all practical purposes":* Jack Gould, "Coronation Marks Birth of World TV," *New York Times*, June 3, 1953, 46.

36 *"You know what they should call":* Jacqueline Bouvier, "Liner Heading to Coronation a Happy Ship," *Washington Times Herald*, 3.

36 *"Let's lunch at Claridge's":* Jacqueline Bouvier, "Crowds of Americans Fill 'Bright and Pretty' London," *Washington Times Herald*, June 2, 1953, 8A.

36 *The inquiring reporter investigated:* Sandford, *Union Jack*, 140–41.

36 *Standing on the sidewalk outside:* Jacqueline Bouvier, "The Question: Will There Be More Queens?" *Washington Times Herald*, June 4, 1953, 4.

36 *from a palace window:* Jacqueline Bouvier, "Crowds of Americans Fill 'Bright and Pretty' London," *Washington Times Herald*, June 2, 1953, 8.

37 *One of his earliest memories:* Trump, *Art*, 55.

37 *Years later, when he was president:* Stephen Castle, "When U.S. and U.K. Leaders Swap Gifts, Some Thoughts Count Less," *New York Times*, Aug. 1, 2025, A9.

37 *"she was absolutely great":* Author interview with Donald Trump, June 4, 2024.

37 *He "was very brick-and-mortar":* Michael Gove and Kai Diekmann, "Full transcript of interview with Donald Trump," Jan. 16, 2017. *The Times* (UK).

37 *"So she ended up":* Author interview with Donald Trump, June 4, 2024.

37 *He had fallen:* Philip Ziegler, "Churchill and the Monarchy," *History Today*, vol. 43, no. 3, March 1993, 7.

37 *Churchill's daughter agreed:* Emma Soames, "As Churchills We're Proud to Do Our Duty," *The Daily Telegraph*, June 2, 2012, W11.

38 *"It is natural":* Winston Churchill, ed., *Never Give In: The Best of Winston Churchill's Speeches*. New York: Hyperion, 2003, 479.

38 *"She did a lot more":* Author interview with Joseph Nye, Jan. 17, 2024. He died the following year, at age eighty-eight. He initially explored the concept of "soft power" in his 1990 book, *Bound to Lead: The Changing Nature of American Power*, published by Basic Books.

38 *Two months after:* Letter, Churchill to Eisenhower, Aug. 3, 1953. Boyle, *Correspondence*, 88.

38 *Eisenhower didn't bite:* Letter, Eisenhower to Churchill, Aug. 8, 1953, Boyle, *Correspondence*, 88–89.

38 *"When I had my last Audience":* Letter, Churchill to Eisenhower, Dec. 7, 1954. Boyle, *Correspondence*, 180.

38 *"I cannot see":* Letter, Eisenhower to Churchill, Dec. 14, 1954. Boyle, *Correspondence*, 182.

39 *"so profoundly grateful":* "Queen Elizabeth II and Winston Churchill's unlikely friendship," British Heritage, Dec. 18, 2024.

40 *"The United States was not":* Eisenhower, "Radio and Television Report to the American People on the Developments in Eastern Europe and the Middle East," Oct. 31, 1956. The American Presidency Project, UC Santa Barbara.

40 *On December 3:* "Suez Crisis, 1956," US State Department Archive.

40 *"Whatever the arguments":* Macmillan, *Riding*, 175–76.

40 *Eisenhower's reply:* Martin Gilbert and Larry P. Arnn, eds., *The Churchill Documents*, vol. 23, *Never Flinch, Never Weary, November 1951 to February 1965*. Hillsdale, Mich.: Hillsdale College Press, 2019, 2146–47.

41 *"We don't leak":* Margaret Rhodes, *Curtsey*, 165.

41 *But in the firestorm:* Ryan, *Queen*, 111.

42 *"Queen believed Eden":* Pimlott, *Queen*, 255.

42 *"dishonesty of the whole thing":* Peter Hennessy, "What the Queen Knew," *The Independent*, Dec. 21, 1994.

42 *She could "absolutely":* Strober, *Elizabeth*, 170.

42 *In almost a caricature:* Valentine Low, "The Queen's Relationship with Her Prime Ministers," *The Times* (UK), Sept. 9, 2022.

42 *The idea "had been mooted":* Letter, Harold Caccia to Sir Ivone Kirkpatrick, Foreign Office, Dec. 28, 1956, TNA FO 372/7428.

42 *"An invitation will be regarded":* Memo, H.A.A. Hankey, Foreign Office minutes, Jan. 3, 1957, TNA FO 372/7428.

42 *Eisenhower had privately:* Gilbert & Arnn, *Churchill Documents*, 2146–47.

43 *To Macmillan, "this relationship":* Brandon, *Relationships*, 136. Brandon's interview with Macmillan was on July 12, 1957.

43 *"The collapse of the military thrust":* "We Need Britain but Not a Bankrupt One," *Miami Herald*, Dec. 12, 1956, 6A.

43 *"tail of the US kite":* "Great Britain Is No Longer a Great Power in World," *Council Bluffs (Iowa) Nonpareil*, May 15, 1957.

43 *"stronger ties between us":* Sally Bedell Smith, *Elizabeth*, 116. Sourced to Martin Gilbert, *Winston S. Churchill*, Vol. 8, *"Never Despair," 1945–1964*. Boston: Houghton Mifflin, 1988.

43 *"Britain was fortunate":* Longford, *Queen*.

44 *The royal staff set out:* Memo, Nigel Bicknell, Foreign Office minutes, June 19, 1957. FO 372/7642.

44 *"program like theirs":* Eisenhower, *Peace*, 213.

44 *When Prince Philip was given:* Buchanan, *Carpet*, 123.

44 *"For a moment I thought":* Buchanan, *Carpet*, 121–22. Patrick Henry Airport is now named Newport News/Williamsburg International Airport.

44 *At a reception:* George Tucker, "A Queenly Presence Felt in Virginia 42 Years Ago," *The Virginian-Pilot*, Aug. 9, 1999. Reprinted Aug. 8, 2019.

45 *Now they were accompanied:* "List of Party," Martin Charteris, Buckingham Palace, to Denis Laskey, Foreign Office, July 10, 1957. TNA FO 372/7464.

45 *As usual, the royal couple brought their own water:* Buchanan, *Carpet*, 74.

45 *"Your Majesty, you are* most *welcome":* Buchanan, *Carpet*, 132.

46 *"I do hope our visit":* Pimlott, *Queen*, 283–84.

46 *Sputnik's impact:* Horne, *Macmillan II*, 55.

47 *"It was as if":* Queen to Eden, Nov. 10, 1957. Lacey, *Monarch*, 207.

47 *"The Queen was full of delight":* Pimlott, *Queen*, 284. Attributed to a "confidential source."

47 *Around his neck:* Buchanan, *Carpet*, 134.

48 *"[T]he respect we have":* Toast, Eisenhower to Queen Elizabeth, Oct. 17, 1957, Eisenhower Presidential Library.

48 *Beforehand, she walked on the field:* Buchanan, *Carpet,* 132.

48 *She asked Maryland Governor:* Associated Press, "No Injury! Elizabeth Is Amazed," *Charlotte Observer,* Oct. 20, 1957, 3A.

48 *Elizabeth's distant cousin:* Elizabeth was the seven times great-granddaughter of Queen Anne's second cousin. Source: Family tree, Royal Collection Trust.

49 *Called at home:* Buchanan, 141.

49 *By the time they left:* Sue Jeweler, "Remembering When Queen Elizabeth Passed By," Letters to the Editor, *Washington Post,* June 4, 2012.

49 *that Philip "was delighted":* Memo, Sir Caccia to Foreign Office, June 19, 1957, TNA FO 372/7462.

49 *"Please come back":* Associated Press, "Queen, Philip Say Goodbye and Thanks to Ike, Mamie," *San Bernardino Daily Sun,* Oct. 21, 1957, 1A.

50 *"If you have had a moment":* Letter, Eisenhower to Queen Elizabeth, Oct. 20, 1957. Eisenhower Presidential Library, POTUS/International Series, Box 17, 1957–61, Folder 4.

50 *Elizabeth and Philip took a special train:* Buchanan, *Carpet,* 152.

51 *"As we sped through Manhattan":* Buchanan, *Carpet,* 149–50.

51 *"Don't Put the Queen Behind Bars": Daily Herald* (London), Oct. 23, 1957, 1A.

52 *When Prince Charles was visiting:* Author interview with Alvin Feltzenberg.

52 *"A personal triumph":* Memo, Caccia to Foreign Office, Oct. 22, 1957. TNA CAB 21/3122.

52 *Their crisscrossed travel: Record* (Troy, N.Y.), Oct. 23, 1957. "Queen Returns Home In Triumph," by John D. Parry (UP), and "Ike, Dulles Prepare to Meet Macmillan," by William Galbraith (UP).

52 *An Associated Press story:* "Macmillan to See Ike on Mideast," *Hartford Courant,* Oct. 18, 1957, 1A.

53 *"The end of the McMahon Act":* Horne, *Macmillan II,* 56 and 59.

53 *when he had met Elizabeth:* Lee, *Mrs. Nixon,* 87. In a letter to a friend, Pat Nixon described Queen Elizabeth as "very pretty and most gracious" and Prince Philip as "smooth."

53 *He had hoped:* Buchanan, *Carpet,* 136.

53 *"Your Majesty":* Letter, Richard Nixon to Queen Elizabeth, Oct. 19, 1957, Nixon Presidential Library.

54 *nights in the future:* Nixon, *Memoirs,* 200. Among his depressing election nights were his defeats in the 1960 presidential race and his loss of the 1962 California gubernatorial race, which he then vowed would be his last campaign. It wasn't; he won the White House in 1968 and 1972, then resigned in 1974.

54 *"It is to commemorate":* Sally Bedell Smith, "The Royal Family's First American Thanksgiving," *Royals Extra,* Nov. 27, 2024.

55 *"I'll never let":* Associated Press, "Tux Cramps Nixon's Style," *Pittsburgh Post Gazette,* Nov. 28, 1958, 4.

55 *Punch magazine lampooned:* Julie Eisenhower, *Pat Nixon,* 268.

55 *"Nixon's Borrowed Tuxedo"*: AP, "Nixon's Borrowed Tuxedo Doesn't Fit," *Winston-Salem Journal*, Nov. 28, 1958, 1A.

55 *The Liverpool* Daily Post: "All were suited in the end," *Liverpool Post*, Nov. 28, 1958, 1A.

55 *"All the impeccably tailored"*: Draft toast, Chequers, Oct. 1970. Nixon Presidential Library, Series: President's Trip file; Document: US/UK Relations, Box 470.

55 *When Nixon explained:* Julie Eisenhower, *Pat Nixon*, 268.

55 *"It was the only time"*: Buchanan, *Carpet*, 177.

56 *"A delightful dinner party"*: Letter, Queen Elizabeth to Pat Nixon, Nov. 28, 1958, Nixon Library.

56 *"The Queen takes"*: UPI, "Nixon Discusses Berlin Crisis with British," *Indianapolis Star*, Nov. 28, 1958, 4.

56 *"project in hand"*: Remarks, Opening of the St. Lawrence Seaway, Dwight Eisenhower and Queen Elizabeth, June 26, 1959. American Presidency Project, UC Santa Barbara.

56 *"The royal yacht"*: Author interview with Tricia Nixon Cox, June 17, 2025.

57 *"You may be interested"*: Letter, Dwight Eisenhower to Queen Elizabeth, July 7, 1959. Eisenhower Presidential Library, DDE, International series Box 17, 1957–1961.

57 *"Marvelous chap"*: Sally Bedell Smith, *Elizabeth*, 145.

58 *"One quality of the Royal Family"*: Eisenhower, *Peace*, 420.

58 *"Seeing a picture"*: Letter, Elizabeth to Eisenhower, Jan. 24, 1960. Truman Presidential Library, NAID 5721366, Collection DDE-1260. The news photo she had seen showed Eisenhower at the hunting estate of a friend, W. Alton Jones, in Albany, Ga., during a shooting trip.

Chapter Four | The Ambassador's Son

60 *The president was:* Horne, *Macmillan Vol II*, 303. Macmillan letter to the Queen, Sept. 15, 1961.

60 *"I think had the Kennedys"*: Bradford, *Elizabeth*, 124.

61 *"Meet the Queen"*: "Meet the Queen of America," *Sunday Dispatch*, May 28, 1961, 7.

61 *The* Evening Standard *depicted her:* "The Londoner's Diary," *Evening Standard* (London), June 5, 1961, 6.

61 *"always lacked—Majesty"*: Jean Campbell, "Magic Majesty of Jackie," *Evening Standard* (London), Nov. 25, 1963, 15.

61 *Jackie confided in:* Buckle, *Self Portrait*, 341.

61 *Elizabeth had been:* Vidal, *Palimpsest*, 372.

63 *The outgoing US ambassador:* Horne, *Macmillan II*, 281–282. The outgoing US ambassador was John Hay (Jock) Whitney, a wealthy venture capitalist.

63 *"I am sure that the sooner"*: Macmillan to the Queen, Jan. 31, 1961, TNA PREM 11/3510.

63 *"affection for the President"*: Horne, *Macmillan II*, 280.

63 *But his tone brightened:* Horne, *Macmillan II*, 293. The meeting was on March 26, 1961.

63 *The president had surrounded himself:* Macmillan, *Pointing*, 352.

Notes

63 *"We seemed to be able":* Smith, *Elizabeth,* 157. Quoting from a letter from Harold Macmillan to Jacqueline Kennedy, Feb. 18, 1964, in the Macmillan Archive at Bodleian Library, Oxford University.

63 *"I talked to him":* Author interview with Bernard Donoughue, May 11, 2025.

64 *"I could really perform":* Louis et al., *Relationship,* 91.

64 *At one point:* "Great Britain: The Cavendishes & the Kennedys," *Time,* May 15, 1944.

64 *Kathleen, known as Kick:* Joseph M. Siracusa, *Encyclopedia of the Kennedys: The People and Events That Shaped America.* Bloomsbury Publishing USA, 423.

64 *Kennedy had suggested:* Smith, *Elizabeth,* 156.

65 *While prime minister, he would travel:* "British Prime Minister Harold Macmillan Talks of 'Interdependence' at DePauw's Nationally Televised 119th Commencement," June 8, 1958, DePauw University.

65 *"in the dark days":* Remarks, Kennedy, upon signing a proclamation conferring honorary citizenship on Sir Winston Churchill, Kennedy Presidential Library, April 9, 1963. Note: The printed text of his remarks said "when Britain stood alone," but the recording shows he used the word "England" instead. In addition, the written text of his remarks began "We meet to honor a man whose honor requires no meeting—for he is the most honored and honorable man to walk the stage of human history in the time in which we live." But a recording of the event shows Kennedy made an off-script introduction and didn't speak those words.

65 *"He likes letters":* Letter, Macmillan to the Queen, Dec. 24, 1961. TNA PREM 11/3510.

66 *"It was a great pleasure":* Letter, the Queen to Kennedy, May 14, 1962. Kennedy Presidential Library, OF-127–007-p0042.

66 *"I have always thought":* Letter, Macmillan to the Queen, Aug. 5, 1961. TNA PREM 11/3510.

67 *"I have risked":* Telephone conversation, Macmillan and Kennedy, Dec. 4, 1961. Bodleian Library, Archive of Harold Macmillan, MS. Macmillan dep. C. 951.

67 *The Queen was so concerned:* Brandreth, *Elizabeth,* 426.

67 *In September 1961:* Letter, Macmillan to Churchill, Oct. 19, 1961. Bodleian Library, Archive of Harold Macmillan, MS. Macmillan dep. c. 951.

68 *Indeed, Elizabeth was annoyed:* Horne, *Macmillan II,* 399.

68 *"She is grateful":* Macmillan, *Pointing,* 459–72.

68 *He wanted her to go:* Horne, *Macmillan II,* 398.

68 *"I remember being on the roadway":* Author interview with Lord Boateng, Oct. 11, 2024.

70 *The American investment:* Transcript, telephone conversation, Macmillan and Kennedy, Oct. 27, 1961. Bodleian Library, Archive of Harold Macmillan, MS. Macmillan dep. C. 951.

70 *"There does remain":* Letter, Kennedy to Macmillan, Oct. 19, 1961. Bodleian Library, Archive of Harold Macmillan, MS. Macmillan dept. C. 951.

70 *"We must not lose it":* Transcript, telephone conversation, Macmillan and Kennedy, Dec. 4, 1961. Bodleian Library, Archive of Harold Macmillan, MS. Macmillan dep. C. 951. Nikita Khrushchev was then the leader of the Soviet Union.

70 *"President Kennedy rang me up":* Letter, Macmillan to the Queen, Dec. 14, 1961. TNA PREM 11/3510.

70 *cited his assurances:* Letter, Kennedy to Nkrumah, Dec. 14, 1961. Department of State, AF/AFW Files: Lot 66 D 53.

70 *The United States loaned:* Associated Press, "Ghana Project Loans Okayed," Orangeburg (S.C.) *Times and Democrat,* Dec. 27, 1961, 5A.

71 *On behalf of the British government:* "World Leaders Voice Sympathy and Shock as Their Countries Mourn President," *New York Times,* Nov. 23, 1963, 8.

71 *was invited to the White House:* Scott Stump, "The Tender Story of How Prince Philip Comforted JFK Jr. After Father's Assassination," NBC Today, April 12, 2021.

72 *Macmillan, who had stepped down:* Remarks, Macmillan, Runnymede Memorial. Kennedy Presidential Library, JBKOPP ST075–007.

Chapter Five | Nadir

73 *"On this celebration":* Letter, President Johnson to Queen Elizabeth, June 9, 1966, Johnson Presidential Library.

74 *"I send to you":* Letter, Queen Elizabeth to President Johnson, June 14, 1966. Johnson Presidential Library.

75 *During the Cuban missile crisis:* Ginsberg, *Friends,* 264.

75 *Ike's official appointments diary:* Presidential Appointment Book-1957, Oct. 17, 1965, p. 5. Eisenhower Presidential Library.

75 *"Well, the only Democrat invited":* Jacqueline Cochran, oral history, March 28, 1968. Eisenhower Presidential Library.

76 *"An acute and ruthless 'politician'":* Home, *Macmillan II,* 282.

76 *"Predictably, the reticent Swedes":* P. M. Crosthwaite, British Ambassador to Sweden, to Foreign Secretary, Sept. 13, 1963. TNA FO 371/168478. Note: Johnson was distributing entry cards for the vice president's gallery in the Senate chamber of the Capitol.

76 *"Mr Lyndon Johnson arrived":* Memo, P. F. Hancock to Foreign Secretary, Sept. 16, 1963. TNA FO 371/168478.

77 *"Perhaps the worst lapse":* Memo, A. E. Lambert to Foreign Secretary, Sept. 18, 1963. FO 371/169405.

77 *"Having experienced two years ago":* Memo, Cosmo Stewart to Foreign Secretary, Sept. 19, 1963. TNA FO 371/169382.

78 *"The British prime minister":* Roundtable, Dean Rusk and other former Johnson administration officials, April 17, 1984. Johnson Presidential Library.

78 *Lady Bird Johnson was "a little starstruck":* Author interview with Luci Baines Johnson, April 11, 2024.

78 *"Going over temporary plans":* President's Daily Diary, Jan. 17, 1965, Johnson Presidential Library.

79 *Three thousand people:* Christopher Klein, "Winston Churchill's History-Making Funeral," Jan. 30, 2015, History Channel.

79 *After his inauguration:* Associated Press, "15,000 Marchers Salute Johnson," *Danville Register* (Va.), Jan. 21, 1965, 1A.

79 *The White House peppered:* Sally Bedell Smith, "How the Queen Orchestrated Churchill's Funeral Sixty Years Ago This Week," *Royals Extra*, Jan. 24, 2025.
80 *In his diary:* Sally Bedell Smith, "How the Queen Orchestrated Churchill's Funeral Sixty Years Ago This Week," *Royals Extra*, Jan. 24, 2025.
81 *As the prime minister's coffin:* Sally Bedell Smith, "How the Queen Orchestrated Churchill's Funeral Sixty Years Ago This Week," *Royals Extra*, Jan. 24, 2025.
81 *In 1967, when Johnson turned down:* Author interview with George Condon, author of an unpublished history of the White House Correspondents Association, Oct. 6, 2024.
81 *"Funeral Riddle":* "Funeral Riddle: President's Choice," *Daily Telegraph*, Jan. 29, 1965, 1A.
81 *The front page of the* Huddersfield Daily Examiner: "Johnson Made Churchill Funeral Blunder Worse," *Huddersfield Daily Examiner*, Feb. 6, 1963, 1A.
81 *"A shabby faux pas":* Ted Lewis, "Capitol Stuff," *New York Daily News*, Jan. 29, 1965, 4.
82 *"I hope you will":* Toast, Harold Wilson to Lyndon Johnson, the White House, Dec. 7, 1964. The American Presidency Project, UCSB.
82 *"Please let us know":* Memo, Oliver Wright to David Ormsby-Gore, Jan. 6, 1965. TNA PREM 13/1899. Note: Ormsby-Gore as of February 1964 became the 5th Baron Lord Harlech.
83 *"I am not quite sure":* Memo, Prime Minister's office to Prime Minister, Nov. 21, 1966. TNA PREM 13/1899.
83 *"The United Kingdom":* Memo, George Ball to President Johnson, July 22, 1966. State Department, *Foreign Relations of the United States, 1964–1968*, Vol. XII, Western Europe, Document 264.
84 *"[F]or someone as important":* Letter, P. H. Gore-Booth to Sir Patrick Dean, Dec. 19, 1966. TNA FO 372/8206.
84 *"come to Britain":* Memo, Prime Minister's Office to Prime Minister, Nov. 21, 1966. TNA PREM 13/1899.
85 *LBJ sarcastically complained:* Jonathan Colman, *A 'Special Relationship'? Harold Wilson, Lyndon B. Johnson and Anglo-American Relations 'at the Summit', 1964–68*. Manchester University Press, 2004.
85 *"A little creep":* Seitz, *Here*, 195.
85 *when the prime minister pressed for:* Memo, call by McGeorge Bundy, Feb. 10, 1965. Johnson Presidential Library, National Security File, Memos to the President, McGeorge Bundy, Vol VIII.
85 *An angry letter to Wilson:* Letter, Johnson to Wilson, Jan. 15, 1968. State Department, Office of the Historian, Foreign Relations of the US, 1964–1968, Vol. XII.
86 *In it, LBJ hadn't blamed:* Draft letter, Johnson to Wilson. Johnson Presidential Library, National Security files, Special Head of State Correspondence, United Kingdom, file 2 of 4.
86 *"Daddy, he thought":* Author interview with Lynda Bird Johnson Robb, March 4, 2024.
86 *"It saddened Daddy":* Author interview with Luci Baines Johnson, April 11, 2024.

87 *Netflix's* The Crown: *The Crown*, "Margaretology," Season 3, Episode 2, Netflix.
87 *"Outrageous" and "all made up":* Author conversation with Lloyd Hand, "White House History with Susan Page," White House Historical Society, Feb. 15, 2021.
87 *That said, reports of undiplomatic behavior:* Andrew Alderson and Peter Day, "Jet-Set Friends Got Princess Margaret 'Barred' from US," *The Sunday Telegraph,* Sept. 14, 2003.
87 *"I heard with great concern":* Letter, Queen Elizabeth to President Johnson, Oct. 8, 1965, Johnson Presidential Library.
87 *"I am told":* Toasts, the President and Princess Margaret, Nov. 17, 1965. The American Presidency Project, UCSB.
88 *intimate scene in the East Room:* Mark Kauffman, The LIFE Images Collection via Getty Images.
88 *A picture of them:* "Princess at the White House: The President's State Dinner for Margaret and Lord Snowdon is a Radiant Interlude in History," *Life,* Dec. 3, 1965, 32.
88 *"Daddy was just the biggest dancer":* Author interview with Lynda Bird Johnson Robb, March 4, 2024.
88 *The official White House diary:* President's Daily Diary, Nov. 17, 1965, Johnson Presidential Library.
88 *"My father was a beautiful dancer":* Author interview with Luci Baines Johnson, April 11, 2024.
89 *Humphrey's traveling plans appeared:* Memo, S. D. L. Morphet, FCO, to Miss I. A. Clarke, Government Hospitality Fund, March 21, 1967, TNA FCO 7/776.
89 *vice president later marveled:* Betty Beale, "Washington Letter," *Sacramento Bee,* April 30, 1967, W8.
89 *His request to meet:* Letter, Michael Palliser to Sir Patrick Dean, Jan. 21, 1967, TNA FCO 7/794.
90 *After the session with Humphrey:* Letter, David Gore Booth to Sir Patrick Dean, April 21, 1967. TNA FCO7/776.
90 *"I think LBJ":* Author interview with Bernard Donoughue, May 11, 2025.

Chapter Six | Lifeline

91 *Hannah Milhous Nixon:* Jonathan Aitken, *Nixon: A Life*. Washington, D.C.: Regnery, 1993, 11.
91 *"His mother was":* Author interview with Tricia Nixon Cox, June 17, 2025.
91 *She surely would have been amazed:* New England Historic Genealogical Society. Note: Hannah Milhous Nixon died on Sept. 30, 1967.
91 *Who was:* Gareth Russell, *The Palace: From the Tudors to the Windsors, 500 Years of British History at Hampton Court*, Atria Books, 363.
92 *believed them to be true:* Tom Mangold, *Cold Warrior: James Jesus Angleton: The CIA's Master Spy Hunter.* New York: Simon and Schuster, 1991, 280.
93 *British diplomat put it:* G. S. Littlejohn Cook, counsellor, British Embassy Thailand, to Foreign Office, Aug. 18, 1969. TNA FCO 15/798.

- 93 *A British briefing paper:* Memo, Tomkins to Foreign Office, Feb. 15, 1969. TNA DEFE 13/994.
- 93 *"[B]y the 1970s":* Schlesinger, *The Imperial Presidency.*
- 94 *The regal trappings:* "The Royal Family."
- 95 *Hugh Sidey:* Hugh Sidey, "A Lingering Love of the Royal," *Life,* July 31, 1970, 4.
- 95 *The US General Services Administration:* "The Press Was Not Impressed," *White House History,* No. 32, Fall 2012, White House Historical Association.
- 95 *"I was just saying":* "Royal Family," June 21, 1969.
- 96 *George H. W. Bush:* Bush, *Portrait,* 94.
- 96 *"America's little princess":* "People," *Time,* July 11, 1969.
- 96 *She sent an apologetic letter:* Letter, the Queen to Tricia Nixon, July 3, 1969.
- 96 *When reporters pressed:* Associated Press, "Tricia Would Like to Invite Prince Charles, Sister to US," *Sacramento Bee,* July 3, 1969, A15.
- 97 *Nixon was disgruntled:* Diary, H. R. Haldeman, Jan. 18, 1969–April 30, 1973, March 29, 1971. NARA 7787364.
- 97 *"Over and over again":* Memo, Chapin to Haldeman, "Prince Charles/Princess Anne-White House Entertainment," July 15, 1970, Nixon Library, Dwight Chapin Chronological File, Box 2.
- 98 *"We were told":* Author interview with Tricia Nixon Cox, June 17, 2025.
- 99 *"'We aren't going'":* Julie Eisenhower, *Special,* 93–94.
- 99 *"He was hardworking":* Julie Eisenhower, *Special,* 101.
- 99 *The president gave the prince:* Julie Eisenhower, *Special,* 114.
- 99 *"My visit to Washington":* Prince Charles to President Nixon, July 2, 1970.
- 100 *"I remember the first time":* Max Foster, "Spotlight: Charles and Camilla," CNN, March 14, 2015.
- 100 *In 2005, Charles:* Sally Bedell Smith, *Elizabeth,* 244.
- 100 *Tricia, by now seventy-nine:* Author interview with Tricia Nixon Cox, June 17, 2025.
- 100 *"May I offer":* Letter, Prince Charles to President Nixon, April 18, 1971. White House Special Files, President's Personal File, Box 14.
- 100 *In an undated letter:* Lee, *Mrs. Nixon,* 237.
- 101 *"The head must rule":* Julie Eisenhower, *Special,* 109.
- 101 *"We assume the Prime Minister":* Memo, "Johnny," presumably John Graham, to Peter Moon, the prime minister's private secretary on foreign affairs, Sept. 16, 1970, TNA PREM 15/714.
- 102 *"I'm afraid I have":* Memo, Robert Armstrong to Ian McCluney, Sept. 21, 1970. TNA PREM 15/714.
- 103 *one memo reported:* Memo, Peter Moon to Robert Armstrong, Sept. 23, 1970. TNA PREM 5/714.
- 103 *"It would mean exiling":* Memo, Robert Armstrong to the Prime Minister, Sept. 22, 1970, TNA PREM 15/714.
- 103 *At Health's request:* Memo, Robert Armstrong to Donald Maitland, Heath's press secretary, Sept. 22, 1970, TNA PREM 15/714.
- 103 *Indeed, a senior Labour member of Parliament:* Letter, Charles Morris, MP, House of Commons, to Sir Michael Adeane, Nov. 1970. TNA PREM 15/164.

103 *A White House official:* Memo, Robert Armstrong to I. McCluney, Sept. 21, 1970. TNA PREM 15/714.
103 *"The general atmosphere":* Memo, Michael Adeane to Edward Heath, Oct. 3, 1970. TNA PREM 15/714.
103 *In a letter to Nixon:* Letter, Edward Heath to Richard Nixon, Oct. 6, 1970, TNA PREM 15/714.
104 *Kissinger wrote Heath:* Letter, Henry Kissinger to Edward Heath, Oct. 10, 1970. TNA PREM 15/714.
104 *"The first thing":* Letter, Edward Heath to the Queen, Oct. 13, 1970. TNA PREM 15/714.
104 *Eventually, Kissinger:* Kissinger, *Years*, 603.
104 *a British biographer of Nixon:* Paul Nizinskyj, "Aitken: Nixon & Wilson Sang HMS Pinafore Together," *Parliament Street*, 2014.
104 *The relationship between:* Seitz, *Here*, 317.
105 *He had liked Nixon:* Philip Ziegler, *Mountbatten: A Biography*, 665.
106 *"He spent a lot of time":* Author interview with Bernard Donoughue, May 11, 2025.
106 *When Wilson saw Nixon:* "Note for the Record," April 19, 1974, TNA PREM 16/291.
106 *Thomas Brimelow:* Letter, Sir Peter Ramsbotham to Sir John Killick, FCO, April 16, 1974. TNA PREM 16/291.
107 *"Kissinger cannot afford":* Memo, Sir Peter Ramsbotham to Sir John Killick, FCO, April 16, 1974. TNA PREM 16/291.
107 *In July, Annenberg:* Report, A.A. Acland to Sir Martin Charteris, Buckingham Palace, July 12, 1974. TNA PREM 16/291.
108 *"I am sure Her Majesty":* Letter, Bill Heseltine to A.A. Acland, FCO, July 12, 1974. TNA FCO 82/447.
108 *Jonathan Aitken:* Paul Nizinskyj, "Aitken: Nixon & Wilson Sang HMS Pinafore Together," *Parliament Street*, 2014.
109 *"Old glories":* Paul Callan, "Old glories on the presidents roadshow," *Daily Express* (UK), Dec. 4, 1992, 52.
109 *"bag from time to time":* Stephen Bates, "The Queen Mother: Enigmatic and Elusive, She Lent a Mystique to Upper-Class Strengths and Failings," *The Guardian*, April 1, 2002, 20.

Chapter Seven | West Wing Meets The Crown

111 *"It may be argued":* Letter, Rowland Baring to Sir Denis Greenhill, FCO, Oct. 18, 1972. TNA FCO 82/486.
111 *present in his name:* Letter, R. T. Armstrong to Sir Martin Charteris, Feb. 6, 1973. TNA PREM 15/2091.
111 *Foreign Office memo noted:* Letter, Martin Charteris to Sir Thomas Brimelow, FCO, March 26, 1974, TNA FCO 82/486.
112 *"Planning for the Bicentennial":* Letter, Lord N. Gordon Lennox to Sir J. Killick, May 28, 1974. TNA 82/486.

112 *the Prince of Wales:* Letter, Rowland Baring [Lord Cromer] to Sir Denis Greenhill, Oct. 18, 1972. TNA FCO 82/486.

112 *"I do not believe":* Letter, Martin Charteris to Robert Armstrong, Feb. 7, 1973. TNA PREM 15/2091.

113 *"I am sure":* Letter, Peter Ramsbotham to Sir Thomas Brimelow, Oct. 18, 1974. TNA FCO 82/486.

113 *"In a little more than a year":* United Kingdom—Queen Elizabeth II, National Security Council Adviser's Presidential Correspondence with Foreign Leaders, Box 5, Gerald R. Ford Presidential Library. The draft was dated May 23, 1975, the letter May 27, 1975.

114 *"the Queen's visit":* Jack Marsh, oral history, Oct. 7, 2008, Ford Presidential Library.

114 *"July 4th was really pushing it":* Linda Charlton, "The British Embassy Has a Queen-Size Problem: Getting Set for Elizabeth's Bicentennial Visit to the U.S.," *New York Times*, June 13, 1976, 11.

114 *"Cupcakes," he recalled:* Harry, *Spare*, 275.

116 *one of the Axis powers:* Hardman, *Queen*, 206–7.

116 *A year earlier:* Lina Mann, "A Pool for the President," White House Historical Association, Feb. 21, 2023.

116 *When the doors of the elevator opened:* Author interview with Susan Ford Bales, April 22, 2025.

116 *"I wanted to die":* Maria Downs, oral history, Ford Presidential Library.

117 *"Well, you know the Queen":* Weidenfeld, *Lady*, 191.

118 *"A cute little song":* Donnie Radcliffe, "Being Dealt a Queen, a Jack and a Headache," *Washington Post*, March 5, 1983.

118 *Or, as the British ambassador:* Letter, Peter Ramsbotham to Anthony Crosland, July 30, 1976. TNA FCO 82/681.

118 *Ford, who typically masked:* James Crawford-Smith, "Gerald Ford Was 'Incandescent' After Queen Elizabeth Gaffe," *Newsweek*, Sept. 3, 2024.

118 *"become our best friend":* Mary McGrory, Washington Star Syndicate, "Queen a Perfect Bicentennial Guest," July 13, 1976, *News and Observer* (Raleigh, N.C.).

119 *The instructions the State Department:* "The State Visit of Her Majesty Queen Elizabeth II and His Royal Highness the Prince Philip, Duke of Edinburgh," Department of State, Office of the Chief of Protocol. Sheila Weidenfeld Files, "State Dinners," Box 34, Ford Presidential Library.

119 *"While the Watergate storm":* Letter, Peter Ramsbotham to Sir Thomas Brimelow, Oct. 17, 1974. TNA FCO 82/486.

120 *Ramsbotham declared the visit:* Letter, Peter Ramsbotham to Anthony Crosland, July 30, 1976. TNA FCO 82/681.

120 *a briefing paper from the Foreign Office:* Memo, D. Darling, North America Department, to Miss Westwood, Protocol and Conference Department, "Background Note: Anglo-American Relations," April 23, 1976. TNA FCO 82/679.

120 *"The Queen's visit":* Memo, Bob Mead, "Visit of Queen Elizabeth in July," March 18, 1976. Betty Ford White House Papers, 1973–77, Box 40, folder "Memoranda (East Wing)," Ford Presidential Library.

120 *It was a deal:* Barbara Gamarekian, "State Dinner for Elizabeth Will Be on PBS on July 7," *New York Times*, June 9, 1976, 56.
121 *"I was hustling":* Author interview with James A. Baker III, July 9, 2024.
121 *"I was furious":* Nancy Reagan, *Turn*, 192.
122 *Rockefeller "was given":* Letter, J. O. Morton to Sir Philip Moore, June 17, 1976. TNA FCO 82/680.
122 *"The President was squared":* Letter, Peter Ramsbotham to Anthony Crosland, July 30, 1976. TNA FCO 82/681.
122 *"How are you feeling?":* Bradford, *Elizabeth*, 185.
122 *Then there was the blind date:* People staff and Katie Labovitz, "Elizabeth Taylor's Dating History: From Conrad Hilton Jr. to Richard Burton," *People*, Oct. 6, 2023.
123 *"Ford could see":* Kate Nagle, "EXCLUSIVE: This RI Governor Dined Next to Queen Elizabeth II Aboard Royal Yacht," GoLocalProv.com, Sept. 9, 2022.

Chapter Eight | The Kiss(-Off)

124 *to gaze at Buckingham Palace:* Dewitt Rogers, "'The Charmer': This Time, Carter Is Allowed Inside Buckingham Palace," *Atlanta Constitution*, May 9, 1977, 1A.
125 *His absence would create:* Memo, A. E. Palmer to Mr. Melhuish, March 17, 1977. TNA FCO 82/764.
125 *"A bit wide eyed":* Charles Mohr, "Carter's Act Plays Well in London," *New York Times*, May 9, 1977, 65.
125 *called him "openly awed":* James O. Jackson, "Grits Puts on the Ritz with Queen," *Chicago Tribune*, May 8, 1977, 2A.
125 *Another reporter said:* Bill Neikirk, "Europe Expected a Hard-Nose, Found Jimmy a Soft Touch," *Chicago Tribune*, May 11, 1977, 5A.
125 *Afterward, the president stopped:* Jimmy Carter, exchange with reporters following a state dinner, 244115. The American Presidency Project, UCSB.
126 *he disclosed decades later:* Carter, *Life*, 147.
126 *"She could chat":* Mary McGrory, Washington Star Syndicate, "Queen a Perfect Bicentennial Guest," July 13, 1976, *News and Observer* (Raleigh, N.C.).
126 *The White House delegation:* Letter, Sue Darling to J. Davidson, May 18, 1977. TNA FCO 82/764.
126 *"One of the banes":* Shawcross, *Mother*, 900.
126 *"It was not his intention":* Author interview with Evan Dobelle, April 15, 2025.
127 *"We are in the embassy":* Royal Family documentary, quoted in Pimlott, *Queen*, 383–84.
127 *"Even the president":* Author interview with Adam Jogee, March 17, 2025.
127 *A London gossip columnist quoted:* Pendennis (pseudonym), "Lese-majeste," *The Observer*, Feb. 13, 1983. Quoted in Charter, 129.
127 *"He wasn't over-concerned":* Author interview with Evan Dobelle, April 15, 2025.
127 *Nicholas Henderson:* Henderson, *Mandarin*, 492. He attributed the turn of phrase to writer Arthur Koestler.
128 *A kiss he had once aimed:* Author interview with Evan Dobelle, April 15, 2025.

128 *"There were no blaring trumpets"*: Ed Hodges, "British Give Carter Simple Welcome," *Herald Sun* (Durham, N.C.), May 6, 1977, 1A.
128 *"Jim Callaghan asked"*: Author interview with Lord David Owen, Nov. 19, 2024.
129 *"The warmth of the reception"*: Letter, Sue Darling to J. Davidson, May 18, 1977. TNA RCO 82/764.
129 *"During these awkward middle years"*: Seitz, *Here*, 318.
129 *Callaghan was fond of Carter:* Author interview with Bernard Donoughue, May 11, 2025.
130 *"My mind had grown accustomed"*: Letter, Sue Darling to J. Davidson, May 18, 1977. TNA FCO 82/764.
130 *"I spoke twice"*: Letter, Peter Jay, Ambassador at Washington, to Foreign Secretary, Nov. 15, 1977. TNA FCO 160/192/9.
130 *after the state banquet:* Author interview with Evan Dobelle, April 15, 2025.
131 *"You're Chip Carter"*: Author interview with Chip Carter, April 17, 2025.
131 *The Queen's assistant private secretary:* Letter, Robert Fellowes to Jimmy Carter, June 9, 1977. Carter Library, Office of the Staff Secretary; Presidential Files; Folder 6/25/77, Container 28.
132 *"He wasn't big"*: Author interview with Evan Dobelle, April 15, 2025.
132 *Dobelle and his wife:* Kit Dobelle also served as a chief of protocol during Carter's presidency.
132 *A year earlier:* Memo, Protocol Chief Henry E. Catto Jr. to President and Mrs. Ford, June 9, 1976.
132 *"I was delighted"*: Telegram, Secretary of State to US embassy in London, Nov. 22, 1977. Carter Presidential Library. WHCF, Name file: James Quello, Box 2704.
132 *"They have to be born"*: Donnie Radcliffe, "Glimpses of a Gracious Princess Royal," *Washington Post*, June 16, 1977.
133 *Mountbatten had been warned:* Abbie Llewelyn, "Lord Mountbatten 'Ignored Warnings He Was IRA Target' to Holiday in Ireland," *Express* (London), Dec. 6, 2020.
133 *"[A] mixture of desperate emotions"*: Jonathan Dimbleby, *Prince of Wales: A Biography*. William Morrow & Co., 1994.
133 *"What makes it so bitter"*: Tom Cotterill, "Unearthed Letter Reveals Prince Philip Was 'So Bitter' After IRA Murdered His Uncle Lord Louis Mountbatten with Boat Bomb," *Daily Mail,* Jan. 16, 2025.
133 *She felt "bitter anger"*: Letter, Queen Elizabeth to Walter Annenberg, Sept. 25, 1979. Annenberg's goddaughter, India Hicks, posted a copy of the letter on Instagram after the Queen's death. Hicks was also Mountbatten's granddaughter. Source: Jessica Taylor, *Daily Mail*, Feb. 13, 2023.
134 *Prime Minister Margaret Thatcher:* Written statement on the murder of Lord Mountbatten, Aug. 27, 1979, Thatcher Archive.
134 *"It is with a profound"*: Letter, Thatcher to Carter. Margaret Thatcher archives, PREM 19–0013, 113.
134 *As chair:* Richard Hough, *Mountbatten: A Biography*, Random House, 1981, 264–65.
134 *Even Lyndon Johnson:* Lyndon B. Johnson, "Toasts of the President and Prime Minister Harold Wilson." The American Presidency Project, UCSB, 241388.

135 *In his thirtieth book:* Carter, *Life,* 147.
135 *"There is a deliberate conspiracy":* Memo, Robin Renwick to FCO, Jan. 21, 1992. CJ4/10795.
136 *one of the first messages:* Transcript, telephone conversation between the Prime Minister and Reagan, Jan. 21, 1981. Margaret Thatcher Foundation archives.

Chapter Nine | Horses and Hollywood

138 *On April 5, the same day:* Transcript, question-and-answer session with reporters, April 5, 1982. Reagan Presidential Library.
138 *"If the Argentines":* "The US & the Falklands War (1): the US 'Tilt' Towards Britain (30 Apr 1982)." The Margaret Thatcher Foundation.
138 *While the president's senior advisers:* Author interview with James A. Baker III, July 9, 2024.
138 *In Congress:* Senate Resolution 382—A resolution stating United States policy regarding the Falkland Islands, submitted and passed April 29, 1982, 97th Congress.
139 *on Haig's orders:* Message, Jeane Kirkpatrick to William Clark, June 5, 1982. US State Department, Office of the Historian, *Foreign Relations of the United States, 1981–1988, Vol. XIII,* Conflict in the South Atlantic, 1981–1984, document 323.
139 *The Argentines seemed:* Memo, James Rentschler to William Clark, "The Guns of April?" April 20, 1982. US State Department, Office of the Historian, *Foreign Relations of the United States 1981–1988, Vol. XIII,* Conflict in the South Atlantic, 1981–1984, document 155.
140 *"This is proper":* Author interview with Robert Hardman, May 21, 2025.
140 *Though his family roots:* Reagan, *Life,* 57.
140 *While attending the performance:* "Briefs for H. M. The Queen," biography of Ronald Reagan before her 1983 trip to the West Coast. TNA FCO 82/1396.
140 *Reagan would remember:* Reagan, *Life,* 119.
140 *"People around her":* Author interview with Frederick Ryan Jr., May 7, 2024.
140 *the Queen saw every film:* Lee Pfeiffer, "Queen Elizabeth: Movie Fan," *Cinema Retro,* Sept. 9, 2022.
141 *A photograph of the evening:* Jon Nordheimer, "Prince Charles's Palm Springs Visit: Film Stars, Caviar and Golf," *New York Times,* March 19, 1974, 33.
141 *dangerously deep décolleté:* Michelle Morgan, "The True Story of How Marilyn Monroe Met Queen Elizabeth," *Town and Country,* May 3, 2022.
141 *"I so enjoyed meeting":* Prince Charles' thank-you note was later displayed at Sunnylands when it was opened to the public as a historic site and retreat.
141 *"Mrs Reagan and the Prince":* Henderson, *Mandarin,* 396.
142 *"Saw 'Mommie' off":* Reagan, *Diaries.*
142 *When she arrived:* John Ezard, "Star Billing for Nancy—but No Publicity," *The Guardian,* July 25, 1982, 1A.
142 *He was the modern president:* Cannon, *Reagan.*
142 *Reagan, who had few confidants beyond his wife, was "like":* Henderson, *Mandarin,* 487.
142 *"With her interior world":* Brown, *Papers,* 19.
143 *"They both understood":* Author interview with Mark Weinberg, April 5, 2024.

143 *In a notorious episode:* "Queen Dismayed by 'Uncaring' Thatcher," *Sunday Times*, July 20, 1986, 1A.
144 *"The trip was coming up":* Author interview with James A. Baker III, July 9, 2024.
144 *"Reagan is just":* Aldous, *Reagan*, 112.
144 *He called it:* Reagan, *Diaries*, 88.
144 *one of his often-repeated aphorisms:* The quote is sometimes attributed to Winston Churchill, but the National Churchill Museum in Fulton, Missouri, says that isn't accurate. Perhaps the earliest attribution is to Lord Palmerston, mentioned in a 1906 book, *Social Silhouettes*, by George William Erskine Russell. Source: Leslie Potter, "Who Said That? Probably Not Winston Churchill," *Horse Illustrated*, Jan. 28, 2013.
145 *"The press is already predicting":* Letter, Henderson to Foreign Office, June 1, 1982, TNA FCO 82/1230.
145 *Despite tensions over the Falklands:* Letter, Lord Chamberlain to the prime minister's office, May 20, 1982. Margaret Thatcher Foundation archives.
145 *The prime minister's office:* Prime Minister's office to Lord Chamberlain, May 21, 1982. Margaret Thatcher Foundation archives.
146 *Deaver recalled:* Strober, *Elizabeth*, 106.
146 *"They just kind of hit it off":* Author interview with Mark Weinberg, April 5, 2024. Weinberg, an assistant press secretary and special assistant to the president in the White House, was also director of public affairs for Reagan after he left office.
146 *"She had an obvious rapport":* Author interview with Lord Boateng, Oct. 11, 2024.
146 *"I need hardly to say":* Letter, Henderson to FCO. TNA FCO 82/1217.
146 *There were disputes:* Royal aide Michael Fawcett said later that Reagan's aides said he "needed" a shower in his accommodations. Source: Smith, *Elizabeth*, 312.
146 *But there was never a question:* It wouldn't be the first time that Her Majesty's love of horses proved helpful politically. She had found it an easy way to bond with her first prime minister, Winston Churchill. "They spent a lot of the audience talking about horses," his daughter, Mary, recalled. She recounted her father's surprise when the Queen "asked me about my pig-sticking days on the North-West frontier," a reference to the sport of hunting boar on horseback. Elizabeth and Churchill would often discuss horse racing as well.
147 *The Queen did draw the line:* "Keeping a Rein on Fatigue, Reagan Rides with Queen," *Buffalo Evening News*, June 8, 1982, A4.
147 *National security adviser:* Henderson to Foreign Office, March 22, 1982, TNA FCO 82/1218.
147 *"Clearly, too, the Queen":* Henderson, *Mandarin*, 434–35.
148 *The Queen was "tidy":* David Hewson, "Two Styles of Horsemanship," *The Times* (UK), June 9, 1982.
148 *"Hollywood itself":* Charles Nevin, "President Rides Tall at Windsor," *Daily Telegraph*, June 9, 1982, 3.
148 *at his address in the Royal Gallery:* Michael Deaver had prematurely told the *Los Angeles Times* that Reagan would be the first president to address a joint session of Parliament in Westminster Hall, a rare honor. After the opposition Labour Party objected, Prime Minister Margaret Thatcher proposed the Royal Gallery. Deaver initially resisted the venue but eventually agreed.

148 *"On distant islands":* Ronald Reagan, Address to Members of the British Parliament, June 8, 1982. Ronald Reagan Presidential Library.

149 *At a white-tie banquet that night:* Some sources say King George V hosted a dinner at Windsor Castle in President Woodrow Wilson's honor in 1918. That dinner was actually held at Buckingham Palace; the visit marked the first meeting between a sitting US president and a reigning British monarch. Source: Woodrow Wilson, "Remarks at Buckingham Palace in London, England," Dec. 27, 1918. The American Presidency Project, UCSB.

149 *"I greatly enjoyed":* Toasts, Reagan and the Queen, Windsor Castle, June 8, 1982, Reagan Presidential Library.

150 *"The queen was dying to go riding":* Nancy Reagan, *Turn,* 261–62.

150 *When Henderson met:* Henderson, *Mandarin,* 273.

150 *"There was a gleam":* Henderson, *Mandarin,* 485.

150 *The briefing paper:* Memo, "Briefs for H. M. The Queen." TNA FCO 82/1396.

151 *"But she's never been on a bus":* Sally Bedell Smith, *Elizabeth,* 318.

151 *She and Prince Philip:* Sally Bedell Smith, *Elizabeth,* 318.

151 *"The Queen is in":* Dan Ehrlich, "A Jolly Time in California: The Queen 'Laughed Like A Schoolgirl,'" *San Francisco Examiner,* March 4, 1983, 3.

152 *"Here she was":* Hardman, *Queen,* 294–95.

152 *The lunch at the ranch:* Shawcross, "The Last Icon."

153 *On the sidelines:* Author interview with an informed source, speaking on condition of anonymity.

153 *"I spent that evening":* Nancy Reagan, *Turn,* 262.

153 *Elizabeth confided:* Sally Bedell Smith, *Elizabeth,* 320.

154 *"That caused me":* Strober, *Elizabeth,* 120.

154 *The engraved silver box:* Nancy Reagan, *Turn,* 262–63. In her memoir, Nancy Reagan complained that federal law mandates any gift from a foreign official worth more than $180 belonged to the government. "We had to buy it from the United States government," she complained in her memoir. "Yes, we had to buy our own anniversary gift!"

155 *For his gift to her:* "Who Gave Queen $24,000 Computer?" *Miami News,* March 14, 1983. It wasn't at taxpayers' expense. A Hewlett-Packard spokesman said the company, at the president's request, had given the computer to the White House, which then presented it to the Queen.

155 *"It was very early on":* Author interview with James Rosebush, Dec. 19, 2024.

155 *About a month before:* FBI, The Vault, Queen Elizabeth II Part 01 (Final).

155 *designed to cause only pain:* "List of People Killed by 'Rubber' and 'Plastic' Bullets," the Cain Archive, Ulster University.

155 *There was no sign:* The tight security couldn't prevent tragedy. Three Secret Service agents driving a few miles ahead of the royal motorcade on a winding road to Yosemite—Donald A. Bejcek, George P. Labarge, and Donald W. Robinson—were killed when a patrol car driven by a Mariposa County sheriff's deputy crashed headlong into their car. Source: Patt Morrison, "3 Guarding Queen Die in Car Crash," *Los Angeles Times,* March 6, 1983, 1A.

156 *Later in the trip:* Sally Vincent, "Is That It?" *The Guardian,* Feb. 23, 2002.

156 *After they arrived:* Author interviews with Selwa Roosevelt, May 29, 2024, and June 18 and 30, 2025.
156 *"Prince Philip was very irritated":* Michael Deaver, oral history, Strouber, *History*, 231.
156 *"has a bit of a temper":* Author interviews with Selwa Roosevelt, May 29, 2024, and June 18 and 30, 2025.
156 *After a small luncheon:* Author interview with Gyles Brandreth, Aug. 6, 2025.
156 *Reagan's affection for the Queen:* Author interviews with Selwa Roosevelt, May 29, 2024, and June 18, 2025.
157 *Even the dreadful weather:* Letter, Oliver Wright to Francis Pym, March 17, 1983. TNA FCO 82/1396.
158 *"It didn't upset my breakfast":* Francis X. Clines, "It Was a Rescue Mission, Reagan Says," Nov. 4, 1983, *New York Times*, A16.
158 *"She was livid":* McFarlane, *Trust*, 265.
158 *He was obligated:* Ryan, *Queen*, 154.
158 *Reagan listened:* McFarlane, *Trust*, 265.
158 *Reagan was "deeply disappointed":* Shultz, *Turmoil,* 340.
159 *"There were a lot of things":* Author interview with Raymond Seitz, Jan. 30, 2024.
159 *"I think the Queen":* United Press International, "Thatcher Defends U.S. Invasion; Furor Grows," *Los Angeles Times*, Oct. 27, 1983, 2.
159 *"I wouldn't get unduly fussed":* Robert Hardman, *Queen of Our Times*, 296.
159 *"It was a warm & pleasant visit":* Reagan, *Diaries*, June 5, 1984, 244.
159 *on the sidelines at his first summit:* Author interview with Kenneth Adelman, Jan. 26, 2024.
160 *She told him:* Memorandum of conversation, Reagan and Thatcher and aides, Camp David, Dec. 22, 1984. Margaret Thatcher Foundation archives, 109185.
160 *During an interview:* Transcript, Margaret Thatcher interview with CNN, Sept. 17, 1987. Margaret Thatcher Archive, THCR5/1/5/482.
161 *The two men rubbed each other the wrong way:* Mark Weinberg, "Reagan Was Also Annoyed with a Canadian PM Named Trudeau," CNN.com, June 11, 2018.
161 *"everybody at the table applauded":* Reagan, *Life,* 354. The phrase "pinched his poke" means she stole gold dust from the small bag he was carrying.
161 *cooperate with that goal:* Neil, *Disclosure,* 207.
162 *"Your Majesty," he began:* Letter, Ronald Reagan to Queen Elizabeth, July 9, 1990. Reagan Foundation.
162 *"Dear Mr. Reagan":* Letter, Queen Elizabeth to Ronald Reagan, July 15, 1990. Reagan Foundation.
163 *After the Reagan Presidential Library was opened:* Author's observation during a tour in 2024.

Chapter Ten | The Talking Hat

164 *"Absolutely," Bush said:* Popadiuk, *Leadership,* 23.
165 *A Washington Post story:* Michael Farquhar, "Lifestyles of the Rich and Unbelievably Naughty," *Washington Post,* May 12, 1991.
165 *"The tree speech":* Memo, President Bush to White House speechwriters, May 11, 1991. George H. W. Bush Presidential Library, Speech File/Draft Files 1989–1993.

165 *the draft of his toast:* "Mem, Jim Pinkerton to Chriss Winston from Jim Pinkerton," May 19, 1989. George H. W. Bush Presidential Library, Jim Pinkerton File, Speech File/Draft Files 1989–1993.

166 *"I objected":* Author interview with Jim Pinkerton, April 24, 2024.

166 *Bush's luncheon toast in 1989:* Memo for President Bush through Chriss Winston from Edward E. McNally, May 23, 1989. George H. W. Bush Presidential Library, NAID 323150507, ID 13489–011.

166 *An early version:* Draft, British embassy toast, May 16, 1991. George H. W. Bush Presidential Library, NAID 323151459, ID 13567–004.

167 *"The relationship between America and Great Britain":* Toasts, State Dinner for Queen Elizabeth, May 14, 1991, The American Presidency Project, UCSB.

168 *"Of course, one forgets":* Roxanne Roberts, "Jewel in the Crown: On PBS, A View of Britain's Model Monarch," *Washington Post*, Nov. 15, 1992. The exchange was quoted in a review of *Elizabeth R*, the BBC documentary airing on PBS.

168 *A Washington Post columnist:* Henry Allen, "Hail, and Thunder, to the Queen!" *Washington Post*, May 15, 1991.

169 *"I don't know":* Oral history, Bobbie Kilberg, University of Virginia Miller Center, Nov. 20, 2009. Her account was confirmed to the author by two senior Bush aides.

169 *"She was very understanding":* Popadiuk, *Leadership*, 24.

169 *"Her husband, the Duke of Edinburgh, however":* Author interview with Anna Perez, June 4, 2025.

169 *"How come you didn't":* George H. W. Bush, "Question-and-Answer Session with Reporters," May 15, 1991. The American Presidency Project, UCSB.

169 *He said he wanted:* Joan Mower, Associated Press, "Queen's Message to Congress: Can You See Me?" *West Central Tribune* (London), May 17, 1991, 1A.

169 *he had never seen:* Updegrove, *Republicans*, 231.

170 *"She had quite a sense":* Oral history, Bobbie Kilberg, University of Virginia Miller Center, Nov. 20, 2009.

170 *"Her Private Secretary and I":* Hardman, *World*, 251.

170 *"Whether to say that new first line":* Strober, *Elizabeth*, 234.

170 *Representative Joseph P. Kennedy II and some others:* Joan Mower, AP, "Queen's Message to Congress: Can You See Me?" May 17, 1991.

171 *"I asked her":* Barbara Bush, *Memoir*, 298.

171 *Thatcher had been a driving force:* Memo, account of phone conversation between Bush and Thatcher, Aug. 26, 1990. Margaret Thatcher Foundation.

171 *The Queen requested a series of briefings:* Pimlott, *Queen*, 538. Sourced to *The Guardian*, Feb. 12, 1992.

172 *"As a nation":* Speech, Queen Elizabeth. The Royal Channel, YouTube, Feb. 24, 1991.

172 *A rare video:* Rebecca Taylor, "Unearthed Clip Shows Queen Joking Around and Talking French with World Leaders," Yahoo! News, July 23, 2021.

172 *British broadcaster ITV later reported:* ITN. YouTube.

173 *The instructions were:* Author interview with Anna Perez, June 4, 2025.

173 *"They said I wasn't":* "'Dodge City' Hug for the Queen," *Daily Telegraph*, May 16, 1991, 1A.

173 *"She has her palace"*: Tim Larimer, "My Palace Is Your Palace," *USA Today*, May 15, 1991, 6.
173 *"All the Brits"*: Barbara Bush, *Memoir*, 416.
173 *"One didn't want"*: Hardman, *World*, 252–53.
173 *"In the US"*: Strober, *Elizabeth*, 232.
173 *The Queen also attended:* Roxanne Roberts, "Jewel in the Crown: On PBS, a View of Britain's Model Monarch," *Washington Post*, Nov. 15, 1992.
173 *"The Queen and The Duke"*: Sig Rogich file, Queen Elizabeth II Visit, loose sheets, 13756, George W. Bush Presidential Library.
173 *sizable block of seats:* FBI, The Vault. Queen Elizabeth II Part 01 (Final).
173 *"England Out of Ireland"*: ITN. YouTube.
174 *a standing ovation:* Associated Press, "No Peanuts or Boos for Queen at Game," *Arizona Daily Sun*, May 16, 1991, 1A.
174 *"She sometimes came down"*: Author interview with Benedicte Valentiner, March 18, 2025.
175 *British sovereign:* "No Sword and No Kneeling, Schwarzkopf Is Knighted," *New York Times*, May 21, 1991.
175 *"The boys were told"*: Sheldon Fox, "Queen Elizabeth II's Passing Sparks Memories of 1991 Florida Visit," Channel 7 News Miami, Sept. 8, 2022.
175 *"Too long"*: *Sunday Mirror*, May 19, 1991, 4.
175 *"Probably not"*: Peter McKay, "The Pathos of Being Queen," *Evening Standard*, May 20, 1991.
176 *the castle in the past:* Memo, C.D. Powell to Richard Gozney, Feb. 13, 1989. PREM 19–2868.
176 *In a flurry:* Memo, Program for Gorbachev visit, Feb. 17, 1989. PREM 19–2868.
177 *"It would be wrong"*: Letter, Anthony Acland to Douglas Hurd, June 4, 1991. TNA FCO 160/297.
178 *As his marriage was:* Diana Pearl, "Prince Charles Called His Marriage to Princess Diana a 'Greek Tragedy' in Letter to Nancy Reagan," *People*, June 8, 2017. The letter was dated June 21, 1992.
178 *"Nineteen ninety-two"*: Speech, Queen Elizabeth, Nov. 24, 1992, Official Website of the British Monarchy.
179 *"extremely cautious"*: Letter, J. N. Powell to David Brooker, Oct. 2, 1992. TNA CJ4/10795.
179 *"[I]t is extremely irritating"*: Letter, J. N. Powell to Jonathan Margetts, SIL Division, Northern Ireland Office (London), Oct. 23, 1992. TNA CJ4/10795.
179 *"Obviously we're rooting"*: Memorandum of telephone conversation, George H. W. Bush and John Major, March 6, 1992. Bush Presidential Library, 2012–2388-MR.
179 *"If you think"*: Letter, Prime Minister to Secretary Baker, Aug. 19, 1992, TNA FCO 82/2357.
179 *the Bush campaign invited:* Peter Goldman, Thomas M. DeFrank, Mark Miller, Andrew Murr, Tom Mathews, *Quest for the Presidency 1992*. College Station, Texas: Texas A&M University Press, 1994.
180 *Their actions, when exposed, would prompt:* Walter Pincus, "Independent Counsel Calls '92 Clinton Passport Search 'Stupid' but Not Illegal," *Washington Post*, Nov. 30, 1995.

180 *Major had sent the new president:* Letter, Prime Minister to President-Elect Clinton, Jan. 19, 1992, TNA FCO 82/2468.

180 *The letter Major sent Bush:* Letter, Prime Minister to President Bush, Jan. 19, 1993. TNA FCO 82/2468.

Chapter Eleven | Hard Feelings

181 *The timing was "not ideal":* Memo, R. J. Sawers to Mr. Pellew NAD, July 26, 1993. TNA FCO 2533.

182 *"Other members":* Memo, J. S. Smith to Roderic Lyne, Nov. 29, 1993. TNA FCO 82/2533.

182 *"We will need to be braced":* Memo, Peter Westmacott to Susan Avent, Oct. 22, 1993. TNA FCO 82/2533.

183 *"Billy has regretted":* Email, Andrew D. Sens to Brenda Hilliar, March 23, 1995. QA/ID 341, Clinton Presidential Library.

183 *"I was actually happy":* Author interview with Bill Clinton, April 30, 2025.

183 *Clinton's briefing paper beforehand:* Memo, "Sample questions and answers before news conference," OA/ID20, Clinton Presidential Library.

184 *Then he joked:* Video, "U.S.-Great Britain Joint News Conference," Feb. 24, 1993, C-SPAN, 159671.

184 *"John Major had literally rifled":* Author interview with Hillary Clinton, March 4, 2025.

184 *She had been inviting:* Memo, Douglas Hurd to British Embassy, Jan. 18, 1993. TNA FCO 82/2468.

184 *But Clinton told British Ambassador Robin Renwick:* Memo, Mark Pellew to FCO, July 9, 1993. TNA FCO 82/2532.

185 *"Clinton spent the year":* Memo, Jonathan Powell, Dec. 31, 1993. TNA FCO 82/2643.

186 *Raymond Seitz, then the US ambassador:* Author interview with Raymond Seitz, Jan. 30, 2024.

186 *"thought I was wrong":* Author interview with Bill Clinton, April 30, 2025.

186 *In a letter:* Steven Greenhouse, "Clinton in Bind Over Visa for I.R.A. Wing Leader," *New York Times,* Jan. 27, 1994, A7.

186 *Delaware Senator Joe Biden:* Patrick Sawer, "Joe Biden Angered British Government over US Visa for Gerry Adams," *Sunday Telegraph,* Nov. 7, 2020.

186 *Real estate developer Donald Trump:* Sheila Langan, "That Time When Donald Trump Attended a Sinn Fein Fundraiser with Gerry Adams," IrishCentral, Aug. 20, 2015.

186 *He posed this question:* Transcript, Bill Clinton exchange with reporters aboard *Air Force One,* Dec. 14, 2000. American Presidency Project, University of California at Santa Barbara.

186 *"Clinton wanted to do things":* Author interview with Leon Panetta, Jan. 27, 2025.

187 *In his drive:* Author interview with a senior national security official, speaking on condition of anonymity.

187 *"A good gamble":* Transcript, Bill Clinton exchange with reporters aboard *Air Force One,* Dec. 14, 2000. American Presidency Project, UCSB.

187 The Sunday Times *in London:* "Adams and the Alliance—Clinton's Foreign Policy," *Sunday Times,* Feb. 6, 1994.
187 *The decision was "naive":* Seitz, *Here,* 280, 292.
187 *Major was so furious:* Westmacott, *Diplomacy,* 95.
187 *For a time, the British:* Seitz, *Here,* 291.
187 *"What the I.R.A. did":* "Northern Ireland: It Is Clearly a War Situation," *Time,* Nov. 19, 1979.
187 *An official IRA statement:* "Statement by I.R.A.," *New York Times,* Aug. 31, 1979, A6.
188 *"Well, that looked like":* Author interview with Hillary Clinton, March 4, 2025.
188 *"The Queen had been placed":* Hardman, *Her Majesty,* 38.
189 *"They had an amazing":* Author interview with Hillary Clinton, March 4, 2025.
189 *"She wasn't just":* Author interview with Bill Clinton, April 30, 2025.
190 *"Bill's major role":* Author interview with Hillary Clinton, March 4, 2025.
190 *Clinton presumably would want:* Memo, L. V. Appleyard to Mr. Hope, Oct. 19, 1993. TNA FCO 82/2532.
190 *In December, Renwick queried:* Memo, Robin Renwick to FCO, Dec. 6, 1993. TNA FCO 82/2532.
190 *Yes, the answer quickly came back:* Memo, Douglas Hurd to Washington embassy, Dec. 9, 1993. TNA FCO 82/2532.
190 *The next day, Renwick:* Memo, Robin Renwick to Alex Allan, Dec. 10, 1993. TNA FCO 82/2532.
190 *"Pres. Clinton will now stay":* Memo, Janice Sweid to Mr. Pellew, Feb. 7, 1994. FCO 82/2683.
190 *"The Americans are leaning":* Memo, Mark Pellew to P. J. Westmacott, March 8, 1994. TNA FCO 82/2683.
190 *Finally, six weeks before:* Memo, P. J. Westmacott to Private Secretary, FCO, April 25, 1994. TNA FCO 82/2683.
190 *In the morning:* Hardman, *World,* 256–57.
191 *"We were in close quarters":* Anders Hagstrom, "Hillary Clinton Compares Nancy Pelosi to Queen Elizabeth II, Calls Her 'Gutsiest Woman in Politics,'" Fox News, Sept. 12, 2022.
191 *"It was comfortable":* William Shawcross, "The Last Icon," *Vanity Fair,* June 2002.
192 *"The Americans said":* Memo, Philip Barton to Dominick Chilcott, May 21, 1997. TNA PREM 49/185.
193 *In a story allegedly told:* Tim Shipman, "She Was a PM's Best Confidante, but What Did the Queen Really Think of Them?" (London) *Sunday Times,* Sept. 11, 2022.
193 *"She had been":* Warren Buffett on "Squawk Box," CNBC, Dec. 2, 2012.
193 *"For myself, I will always":* "USA-President Clinton on Diana's Death," AP Newsroom, June 16, 2008.
193 *Later, in a private telephone call:* Tim Sculthorpe and Steph Cockroft, "'Like a Star Falling': Extraordinary Exchanges Between Tony Blair and Bill Clinton After Prince Diana's Death Are Revealed in Private Call Transcripts," *Daily Mail,* Jan. 7, 2016.
194 *The next day, she gave:* Sally Bedell Smith, *Elizabeth,* 404–405.
194 *Hillary Clinton attended:* Email, Glyn Davies to Kristen Cicio et al., National Security Council, Sept. 4, 1997, OA/Box 620000. Clinton Presidential Library.

195 *"We will always remember":* CNN/Time All Politics, "Clintons Mourn Diana's Death," Aug. 31, 1997.
195 *On Howard Stern's radio show:* Tierney McAfee, "Donald Trump Once Boasted He Could Have 'Nailed' Princess Diana—but Only If She Passed an HIV Test," *People*, May 18, 2018.
195 *Actually, Trump so aggressively:* Simon Perry, "Donald Trump Hoped Princess Diana Would Be His 'Trophy Wife,' Says British TV Anchor," *People*, Aug. 17, 2015.
195 *Queen Elizabeth didn't make:* President Reagan didn't have what was officially labeled a state dinner, but he had their functional equivalents in both Britain and California.
195 *Hillary Clinton told friends:* Author interview with a senior official in the Clinton White House, speaking on condition of anonymity.
195 *"The president ends the week":* Memo, Meyer to FCO, Jan. 31, 1998. TNA PREM 49/569.
196 *"Bill, I am pleased":* Toasts at the White House dinner, Feb. 5, 1998, C-SPAN.
196 *"Your prime minister":* Memo, Meyer to FCO, Jan. 31, 1998. TNA PREM 49/570.
196 *The Clinton administration appreciated:* Memo, Christopher Meyer to John Holmes, March 19, 1998. TNA PREM 49/571.
196 *"We decided to go slow":* Memo, John Kerr to Mr. Astley, April 20, 1998. TNA PREM 49/571.
197 *"dig up something really damning":* Memo, Sir Christopher Meyer to Sir John Kerr, April 22, 1998. TNA FCO PREM 49/571.
197 *"The Queen is very relaxed":* Memo, Dominick Chilcott to Philip Barton, May 14, 1998. TNA PREM 49/571.
197 *"She was not prudish":* Author interview with a senior British official, speaking on condition of anonymity.
197 *"I do not see":* Memo, Christopher Meyer to Philip Astley Esq LVO, Dec. 8, 1998, TNA PREM 49/1132.
197 *Now the White House told London:* Memo, Tim Barrow to John Sawers, "Possible Visit to the UK by President Clinton," July 27, 1999. TNA PREM 49/1134.
197 *"We had previously thought":* Memo, John Sawyers to Christopher Meyer, Oct. 25, 1999. TNA PREM 49/1683.
198 *a Foreign Office memo advised:* Memo, Christopher Meyer to John Sawers, Sept. 20, 1998, TNA PREM 49/1134.
198 *"So there are no free rides":* Author interview with Bill Clinton, April 30, 2025.
198 *"Early on, there was":* Author interview with Sir David Manning, June 12, 2025.
199 *"She's very careful":* Transcript, Bill Clinton exchange with reporters aboard *Air Force One*, Dec. 14, 2000. American Presidency Project, UCSB.

Chapter Twelve | A Wink and a Nod

201 *"Mother said":* Barbara Bush, *Memoir*, 414. Sally Bedell Smith, *Elizabeth*, 537.
202 *At that first meeting:* Interview of President Bush by RDF, White House transcript, May 4, 2007. George W. Bush Library, OA/NARA 9388/9295 7523.
202 *"My mother and I":* Ben Macintyre, "Bush Vows to Bury 'Obsolete' Missile Treaty," *The Times* (UK), July 18, 2001.

203 *"In public, she's very demure"*: Hardman, *Times*, 454.
203 *"She thought Mother"*: Hardman, *Times*, 325.
204 *A thirty-one-year-old PETA activist:* Adam Kovac, "WL Native Streaks for His Beliefs," Lafayette, Ind., *Journal and Courier*, July 20, 2001, A8.
206 *She landed in Adelaide:* Patrick Barkham, "Queen Triumphs Through Scandal and Dust," *Guardian*, Feb. 28, 2002.
206 *An Australian security agent:* Anthony Manning, "Sitting Outside Important Meetings," Antman blog, Aug. 18, 2024.
207 *Prince Philip "was free":* Author interview with Bill Clinton, April 30, 2025.
207 *"INTRUDER" was stamped:* Jane Kerr and Ryan Parry, "Buckingham Palace's Extraordinary Secrets Revealed by Fake Footman," *Daily Mirror*, Nov. 30, 2018.
208 *The president reported:* Ryan, *Queen*, 172.
208 *That was a storyline:* When *The Audience* was staged on Broadway in 2015, starring Helen Mirren, it portrayed the Queen pleading with Tony Blair to call off the planned 2003 invasion of Iraq.
208 *"No," a senior palace adviser:* Author interview with senior palace adviser, on condition of anonymity.
209 *That was the concern:* "Prince Charles's private letters published," BBC, May 13, 2015.
209 *In 2005, the* Daily Express: Richard Palmer and Mark Reynolds, "Queen's Fury at Snub to War Heroes," Jan. 20, 2005, 1A.
209 *In 1999, when the Clinton administration:* Robert Booth, "Secret Papers Show Extent of Senior Royals' Veto Over Bills," *The Guardian*, Jan. 14, 2013. The court-ordered release of papers in 2013 showed the Queen had vetoed the Military Actions Against Iraq Bill in 1999.
209 *In June 2003, Vladimir Putin:* "Putin, queen reach out on Iraq," June 25, 2008, CNN International.
209 *"Dogs have interesting instincts":* Jessica Wang, "Inside Queen Elizabeth II's Complex Relationship with Russian President Vladimir Putin," News.com.au, Sept. 12, 2022.
210 *"It was pointed out":* Transcript, George W. Bush toast at Whitehall Palace in London, Nov. 19, 2003, American Presidency Project, UCSB.
210 *"Like all special friends":* Transcript, toasts by George W. Bush and Queen Elizabeth at Buckingham Palace in London, Nov. 19, 2003. State Department Archives, 26432.
210 *"Our places were set":* Bush, *Decision*, 285.
211 *"I'm fond of her":* Hardman, *Times*, 439.
211 *"Now, if you've got two-thirds":* Hannah Parry, "The Next Generation Are Going to Have a Very Hard Time," *Daily Mail*, Dec. 12, 2017.
212 *They had exchanged letters:* Letter, Queen Elizabeth to Ronald Reagan, Feb. 13, 1994. Reagan Foundation.
212 *"I shall remember":* Letter, Queen Elizabeth to Nancy Reagan, June 10, 2004. Reagan Foundation, Stack LG Row 59 Compartment 1 Shelf 6.
213 *visit in 1957:* Author interview with Sir David Manning, June 12, 2025.
213 *"At the start of 2007":* Laura Bush, *Spoken*, 389.

213 *"I've seen her":* Author interview with Sir David Manning, June 12, 2025.
214 *She greeted the Queen:* Charter, *Audience,* 209.
214 *In the late afternoon:* Sally Bedell Smith, *Elizabeth,* 472.
216 *"I wanted to put":* Hardman, *Queen,* 454–5.
216 *The purpose of the stop:* Memo, "Social Visit with Her Majesty Queen Elizabeth II and His Royal Highness The Prince Philip, Duke of Edinburgh," June 15, 2008, Folder title 761301, Bush Presidential Library.
217 *"We are happy":* Associated Press, "Queen Elizabeth Pays Tribute to U.S. Soldiers," May 8, 2007.

Chapter Thirteen | Good Vibes

218 *Quite the opposite:* Obama, *Dreams,* 417–18.
219 *Files in Britain's National Archives:* Memo, E. W. Griffith-Jones to P. D. Webber, Colonial Office, Aug. 22, 1959, FCO141–6703.
219 *"You wouldn't necessarily think":* Author interview with David Cameron, May 8, 2025.
219 *The White House was also aware:* Author interview with Ben Rhodes, March 10, 2025.
219 *Still in place:* Dan Pfeiffer, "Fact Check: The Bust of Winston Churchill," July 27, 2012, The White House, President Barack Obama.
220 *"Some said it was":* Boris Johnson, "UK and America Can Be Better Friends Than Ever Mr. Obama . . . if We LEAVE the EU," *Sun,* April 22, 2016.
220 *"Everything was such":* Author written interview with Michelle Obama, May 30, 2025.
220 *"We're still trying":* "President Obama at Buckingham Palace," C-SPAN, April 1, 2009.
221 *"The unthinkable":* Ali Ahmad, "Michelle Obama's G20 Faux Pas Brings Out Queen's Touchy-Feely Side," *Guardian,* April 2, 2009.
222 *"No-one—including":* Jimmy Orr, "Michelle Obama Hugs Queen—Breaks Royal Protocol," *Christian Science Monitor,* April 2, 2009. *Daily Mail.*
222 *Michelle worried:* Michelle Obama, *Becoming,* 318.
222 *The controversy gained:* Valentine Low, "Queen and Michelle Obama, the Story Behind a Touching Moment," *The Times* (UK), April 2, 2009.
222 *Gyles Brandreth saw:* Author interview with Gyles Brandreth, Aug. 7, 2025.
222 *"My suspicion is that":* Author interview with Barack Obama, June 5, 2025.
222 *"keep in touch":* Andrew Alderson, "Queen's Secret Palace Tour for Mrs Obama," *Sunday Telegraph,* June 14, 2009, 1A.
224 *Prince William visited:* Dan Roberts, "Cameras Clatter as Obama Hosts Prince William at the White House," *Guardian,* Dec. 8, 2014.
224 *"I think it's fair":* Transcript, Oval Office visit by the Prince of Wales and Duchess of Cornwall, March 19, 2015, Obama White House archives.
225 *"Remember, she was in Kenya":* Author interview with Hillary Clinton, March 4, 2025.
226 *"The five contingents' allegiance":* Susan Rice, "The Commonwealth Initiative in Zimbabwe, 1979–80: Implications for International Peacekeeping," Michaelmas Term 1990, Oxford University.

226 *"I think without her hand":* Author interview with Susan Rice, Sept. 9, 2024.
228 *"She and I shared":* Author written interview with Michelle Obama, May 30, 2025.
228 *"The Queen came up to me":* Author interview with George Osborne, Feb. 24, 2025.
229 *"Did you see the bling":* Ben Rhodes, *World,* 149.
229 *He had asked her:* Author interview with Ben Rhodes, March 10, 2025.
229 *"She had this wonderful":* Author interview with Barack Obama, June 5, 2025.
229 *"Courteous," he recalled:* Rhodes, *World,* 149.
229 *"I am told":* Transcript, Barack Obama speech to Parliament in London, May 25, 2011, American Presidency Project, UCSB.
230 *"I think it's fair":* Author interview with Barack Obama, June 5, 2025.
231 *Matthew Barzun, the US ambassador:* Author interview with Matthew Barzun, July 18, 2025.
233 *"Roosevelt never did this":* Cameron, *Record,* 341.
234 *The British royal couple:* Peter Allen, "Kate and William Awarded £92,000 in Damages over Topless Photos in Magazine," *Standard,* Sept. 5, 2017.
234 *"Kate Middleton":* Tweet, @realDonaldTrump, Twitter, Sept. 17, 2012, 2:03 p.m.
234 *There was "so much":* Author interview with Mathew Barzun, July 18, 2025.
234 *As a documentary crew:* Roxanne Roberts, "Jewel in the Crown: On PBS, a View of Britain's Model Monarch," *Washington Post,* Nov. 15, 1992.
235 *"I sometimes imagined":* Author interview with Barack Obama, June 5, 2025.
235 *"They're similar people":* Author interview with Susan Rice, Sept. 9, 2024.
235 *"I just got her":* Author interview with Barack Obama, June 5, 2025.
235 *"I was given":* Author written interview with Michelle Obama, May 30, 2025.
236 *"QUEEN BACKS BREXIT":* Tom Newton Dunn, "Revealed: Queen Backs Brexit as Alleged EU Bust-Up with Ex-Deputy PM Emerges," *The Sun,* March 8, 2016.
236 *A 2025 book:* Valentine Low, "The Queen Was a Remainer: Her Secret Views on Brexit Revealed," *The Times* (UK), Aug. 29, 2025. The article was drawn from Low's book, *Power and the Palace: the Inside Story of the Monarchy and 10 Downing Street,* Headline Press.
236 *It was the only time:* Author interview with Barack Obama, June 5, 2025.
237 *During the campaign:* Author interview with a knowledgeable British official, speaking on condition of anonymity.
238 *"She told me":* Brandreth, *Elizabeth,* 483–4.
238 *"each of them":* Author interview with Barack Obama, June 5, 2025.
238 *In his speech:* Transcript, Barack Obama's eulogy for Shimon Peres, Sept. 30, 2016. American Presidency Project, UCSB.
239 *"It was all very pleasant":* Harry, *Spare,* 292.

Chapter Fourteen | The Favourite?

240 *"It ruined the garden":* Author interview with a senior palace aide, speaking on condition of anonymity.
240 *she reportedly complained:* "Did Donald Trump's Helicopter Ruin Queen Elizabeth's Lawn at Buckingham Palace?" *South China Morning Post,* SCMP, Aug. 28, 2019.

240 *"made it in life"*: Hill, *Nothing,* 212–3.
241 *"ultimately get to know her well"*: Author interview with Donald Trump, June 4, 2024.
242 *"No fuss, no hassle"*: Darroch, *Damage,* 141.
242 *"Why isn't Boris Johnson"*: Haberman, *Confidence,* 276.
242 It *"took Theresa"*: Peter Beaumont, "How Donald Trump's Hand-Holding Led to Panicky Call Home by Theresa May," *The Guardian,* Feb. 7, 2021. The story discusses a three-part BBC documentary, "Trump Takes on the World," that included the comment by Fiona McLeod Hill, May's former joint chief of staff.
242 *"The special relationship"*: Transcript, White House news conference with Donald Trump and Theresa May, Jan. 27, 2017, American Presidency Project, UCSB.
243 *[H]aving secured the first"*: Darroch, *Damage,* 146.
243 *"According to one"*: Hardman, *World,* 270–71.
243 *The Liberal Democratic leader:* Darroch, *Damage,* 146.
243 *"Donald Trump's well documented"*: "President Trump: State Visit," UK Parliament, Vol. 621, Feb. 20, 2017.
244 *"I was a celebrity"*: Author interview with Donald Trump, June 4, 2024.
244 *"We played polo"*: Georgia Dullea, "For the Princess of Wales, a Night at the Opera, a Day at a Settlement House," *New York Times,* Feb. 3, 1989, B2.
245 *"I only have one regret"*: Trump, *Comeback.*
245 *"Charles and Di join"*: Associated Press, "Charles and Di Join, but Separately," *Daily Courier* (Arizona), Dec. 28, 1994, 6A.
245 *"Complete nonsense"*: Associated Press, *Pittsburgh Post-Gazette,* Dec. 30, 1994.
245 *"bells and whistles"*: Fiona Hill, *There Is Nothing for You Here: Finding Opportunity in the 21st Century.* Mariner, 2021, 212.
246 *"He liked Grosvenor Square"*: Author interview with Woody Johnson,
246 *"Bad deal"*: Tweet, @realDonaldTrump, Twitter, Jan. 11, 2018, 11:57 p.m.
246 *"Nope it's because"*: Tweet, @Ed_ Miliband, Twitter, Jan. 12, 2018, 1:36 a.m.
247 *Finally, the British embassy:* Darroch, *Damage,* 250.
247 *"That is probably"*: Author interview with a senior British official, speaking on condition of anonymity.
247 *"I really look forward"*: Tom Newton Dunn, "Trump's Brexit Blast / Donald Trump Told Theresa May How to Do Brexit 'but She Wrecked It'—and Says the US Trade Deal Is Off," *Sun,* July 13, 2018, 1A.
248 *"It made her look"*: Author interview with John Bolton, Oct. 10, 2024.
249 *"It was made very clear"*: Hardman, *Queen,* 542–3.
249 *"I was thinking"*: Piers Morgan, "Up close and VERY personal with The Donald on Air Force One," *Mail on Sunday,* July 14, 2018.
250 *He had been maladroit:* Author interview with Gyles Brandreth, Aug. 6, 2025.
250 *no sign that the Queen was offended:* Brandreth, *Elizabeth,* 484.
250 *"Her Majesty had"*: Melania Trump, *Melania,* 133.
250 *"We were going to have"*: Author interview with Donald Trump, June 4, 2024.
250 *The National Security Council:* Author interview with John Bolton, Oct. 10, 2024.
251 *"We talked about everything"*: Author interview with Donald Trump, June 4, 2024.
251 *"it's a very complex problem"*: Piers Morgan, "Up close and VERY personal with

The Donald on Air Force One,' *Mail on Sunday*, July 14, 2018. Hardman, *World*, 271–72.

251 *"I would give our relationship"*: Transcript, White House news conference by Donald Trump and Theresa May, July 13, 2018. American Presidency Project, UCSB.
252 *"She is the living"*: "Much Ado About the Queen's Brooches," *The Court Jeweller*, July 19, 2018.
253 *"There definitely had been"*: Author interview with a senior British official, speaking on condition of anonymity.
254 *"The Americans pushed"*: Hardman, *Queen*, 543.
254 *"Everyone began maneuvering"*: Grisham, *Questions*, 169.
255 *At the center:* Author interview with Doug Mills, Aug. 12, 2025.
255 *"It was a lighthearted"*: Melania Trump, *Melania*, 134.
255 *Lately, the mayor:* Hardman, *Queen*, 543–44.
255 *Trump didn't recognize:* Terri-Ann Williams, "Melania to the Rescue!" *Daily Mail*, June 3, 2019.
256 *"Oh, there's Doug Mills"*: Author interview with Doug Mills, Aug. 12, 2025.
256 *"I was in the groove"*: Author interview with Woody Johnson, Aug. 20, 2025.
257 *"I don't think she's ever"*: Podcast, "REVEALED: What the Queen REALLY Thought of President Trump," *Palace Confidential*, Daily Mail Royals, Aug. 25, 2025.
257 *"He thinks so much"*: Spencer Davidson, "Britain: God Save the Queen, Fast," *Time*, July 26, 1982.
258 *Harry's bitterness:* Author interview with a knowledgeable source conducted on condition of anonymity.
259 *"should have, frankly"*: Author interview with Donald Trump, June 4, 2024.
259 *"If he lied"*: Oliver Trapnell, "Donald Trump Warns Prince Harry He Could Be KICKED OUT of America in Stunning WORLD EXCLUSIVE Interview," March 18, 2024, GBnews.com.
260 *But soon after starting:* Miranda Devine, "Trump Rules Out Deporting Prince Harry: 'He's Got Enough Problems with His Wife,'" *New York Post*, Feb. 8, 2025.
260 *"Trade Deal down the road"*: Tweet, @realDonaldTrump, June 5, 2019, 8:02 p.m. American Presidency Project, UCSB.
260 *"I think President Trump"*: Author interview with Liz Truss, Jan. 14, 2025.
260 *"We bonded over wine"*: Grisham, *Questions*, 176–7.
261 *Trump's team had been:* Isabel Oakeshott, "Britain's Man in the US Says Trump Is 'Inept,'" *Mail on Sunday*, July 7, 2019, 1A.
261 *the president was "absolutely livid"*: Author interview with John Bolton, Oct. 10, 2024.
262 *"She couldn't believe it"*: Author interview with Donald Trump, June 4, 2024.
262 *the palace said:* Author interview with knowledgeable source speaking on condition of anonymity.
263 *In 2024, British author Craig Brown:* Craig Brown, *Voyage*, 370–1.
263 *"Totally false"*: Clip of interview, *Daily Mail*, posted on Twitter, @DailyMail, Aug. 22, 2024, 7:04 a.m.
263 *Brown had more:* Ephraim Hardcastle, "Did the Queen feel Sorry for the Latest Mrs Trump?" *Daily Mail*, March 11, 2025. The story quoted an unnamed source "who was present" for the portrayal.

263 *There was another:* Simon Perry, "Queen Elizabeth 'Didn't Like' Donald Trump, Friend Monty Roberts Claims in New Documentary," *People*, Sept. 5, 2024.

264 *When the Queen spied:* Hardman, *Times*, 262.

264 *"Seriously, I think":* Author interview with Boris Johnson, Oct. 31, 2024.

264 *"The President has":* Author interview with Woody Johnson, Aug. 20, 2025.

265 *"There was definitely":* Podcast, "REVEALED: What the Queen REALLY Thought of President Trump," *Palace Confidential*, Daily Mail Royals, Aug. 25, 2025.

265 *She once confided:* Brandreth, *Elizabeth*, 460–61.

265 *When I asked former Prime Minister David Cameron:* Author interview with David Cameron, May 8, 2025.

265 *"That's hysterical":* Author interview with Jill and Joe Biden, Sept. 10, 2025.

266 *Hillary Clinton responded:* Author interview with Hillary Clinton, March 4, 2025.

266 *He would be "shocked":* Author interview with Bill Clinton, April 30, 2025.

Chapter Fifteen | Don't Tell His Mother

267 *"Don't you bow down":* Biden, *Promises*, 11.

267 *Joe Biden's wife, Jill, had her own:* Author interview with Jill Biden, Sept. 10, 2025.

268 *"Noticing I was English":* Prichett, *Mess*, 270.

268 *"He's just English":* Biden, *Promises*, 17.

268 *"without disrespecting her":* Author interview with Kate Bedingfield, April 4, 2024.

268 *"I don't think she":* "Biden on Meeting with the Queen," *Guardian News*, June 13, 2021.

269 *"A quick word":* @NickBryantNY, Twitter, Nov. 7, 2020.

269 *"There was the [Reagan] administration's desire":* Niall O'Dowd, "Fiery Joe Biden—the First Ever Irish Interview from 1987," IrishCentral, Oct. 12, 2020.

270 *"CHURCHILL SNUB":* Jessica Kwong and Imogen Braddick, "CHURCHILL SNUB: Joe Biden removes bust of Winston Churchill from Oval Office and replaces it with union leader Cesar Chavez," *Sun*, Jan. 21, 2021.

270 *"My view of Trump":* Author interview with a senior British official, speaking on condition of anonymity.

270 *In 2023, President Biden went to Belfast:* Harriet Alexander, "Joe Biden Poses for a Selfie with Alleged IRA Member And Former Sinn Fein Leader Gerry Adams—After His Advisor Scrambled to Insist He Was NOT Anti-British," *Daily Mail*, April 13, 2023.

270 *"He never came across":* Author interview with Liz Truss, Jan. 14, 2025.

271 *"When my great-grandfather":* Transcript, White House news conference, March 25, 2021, National Archives.

272 *the palace didn't want:* Author interview with a knowledgeable source, speaking on condition of anonymity.

272 *But Biden had disparaged:* Quint Forgey, "Biden Warns That Boris Johnson's Victory Shows Dangers of Parties Leaning Too Far Left," *Politico*, Dec. 13, 2019.

272 *As the summit was about to open:* Patrick Maguire and Oliver Wright, "G7 summit 2021: Joe Biden Accuses Boris Johnson of 'Inflaming' Irish Tensions," *The Times*, June 10, 2021.

272 *the statement of sympathy by the Bidens:* Joe Biden, Statement on the Death of Prince Philip, April 9, 2021. American Presidency Project, UCSB.
272 *Trump's statement:* Gustaf Kilander, "Trump Pays Tribute to Prince Philip Calling His Death 'Irreplaceable Loss' for 'All Who Hold Our Civilization Dear,'" *The Independent*, April 9, 2021.
273 *At the economic summit:* Video, "The Queen meets G7 leaders at summit reception," *The Telegraph*, June 11, 2021, YouTube.
273 *"Are you supposed":* "Queen Elizabeth hosted G7 and EU leaders at a reception," The National, YouTube.com.
273 *"Joe and I are looking":* Anita Kumar, "The Queen Meets Her 13th U.S. President: Joe from Scranton," *Politico*, June 13, 2021.
274 *"All she wanted":* Author interview with Joe and Jill Biden, Sept. 10, 2025.
275 *"A seemingly timeless ritual":* "The Times view on the Queen's meeting with Joe Biden: Royal Diplomat," *The Times*, June 14, 2021.
275 *"When we left":* Author interview with Jill Biden, Sept. 10, 2025.
275 *"Normally, a horse-drawn carriage":* Author interview with Jane Hartley, July 31, 2025.
276 *"There'd been a long":* Author interview with Liz Truss, Jan. 14, 2025.
276 *"Was there a little moment":* Author interview with a senior Biden aide, speaking on condition of anonymity.
277 *"I thought it was":* Author interview with Joe Biden, Sept. 10, 2025.
277 *He said she had:* Joe Biden, "A Proclamation on the Death of Queen Elizabeth II," Sept. 8, 2022, National Archives.

Chapter Sixteen | God Save the King

279 *Never mind that:* Grisham, *Questions*, 173.
279 *His Majesty began:* Amarachi Orie, "What Did King Charles Say in His Letter to Donald Trump?" CNN, Feb. 28, 2025.
280 *The headline on the front page:* Lizzy Buchan, "Keir's Trump Card," *Daily Mirror*, Feb. 28, 2025.
280 *In global affairs:* Author interview with Bernard Donoughue, May 11, 2025.
281 *Elizabeth was "truly":* Author interview with Donald Trump, June 4, 2024.
281 *"He earned whatever":* Transcript, White House news conference with Donald Trump and Keir Starmer, Feb. 27, 2025. American Presidency Project, UCSB.
282 *"She was front and center":* Author interview with Hillary Clinton, March 4, 2025.
282 *"She's dealt with many":* Shawcross, "The Last Icon."
283 *"I think the mission":* Author interview with Hillary Clinton, March 4, 2025.

Epilogue | London's Bridge

284 *which was an idea:* "British Social Attitudes: Support for Monarchy Falls to New Low," National Centre for Social Research, April 29, 2024.
285 *"Oh well":* Johnson, *Unleashed*, 725–26.

286 *a "special relationship":* Kissinger, *White House Years,* 89–90.
286 *"Wrongly stereotyped":* Kissinger, *White House Years,* 94–95.
286 *"For more than seventy years":* Queen Elizabeth at COP26 reception, Nov. 1, 2021.
286 *"He told me that India":* Johnson, *Unleashed,* 727.
286 *"them, I would say":* Author interview with Liz Truss, Jan. 14, 2025.
287 *"Yes, he married his teacher":* Johnson, *Unleashed,* 574.
287 *Minister Harold Wilson:* Joe Haines, oral history. Strobel, *Elizabeth,* 175.
287 *In one measure:* Leah Williams, "Queen Elizabeth's 'Saturday Night Live' Portrayals, Ranked," *TVInsider,* Sept. 9, 2022.
288 *calm their fears:* Brandreth, *Elizabeth,* 459–60.
288 *"If you see":* Johnson, *Unleashed,* 727.
288 *"To the optimist":* Brown, *Voyage,* 19.
289 *"You would leave":* Author interview with Donald Trump, June 4, 2024.
289 *Indeed, the official plan:* Lauren Hubbard, "Operation London Bridge: The True Story of the Plan for Queen Elizabeth's Funeral," *Town and Country,* Dec. 21, 2023.
289 *"There was a sense":* Author interview with Barack Obama, June 5, 2025.

Selected Bibliography

Aldous, Richard. *Reagan and Thatcher: The Difficult Relationship.* W. W. Norton & Co., 2012.

Aldrich, Richard J., and Rory Cormac. *The Secret Royals: Spying and the Crown, from Victoria to Diana.* Atlantic Books, 2021.

Anthony, Carl Sferrazza. *Camera Girl: The Coming of Age of Jackie Bouvier Kennedy.* Gallery Books, 2023.

Arbiter, Dickie. *On Duty with the Queen: My Time as a Buckingham Palace Press Secretary.* Blink Publishing, 2014.

Arnold, Guy. *America and Britain: Was There Ever a Special Relationship?* Hurst and Company, 2014.

Baker, James A., III, with Thomas M. DeFrank. *The Politics of Diplomacy: Revolution, War, and Peace, 1989–1992.* G. P. Putnam's Sons, 1995.

Baker, Peter, and Susan Glasser. *The Man Who Ran Washington: The Life and Times of James A. Baker III.* Doubleday, 2020.

Berton, Pierre. *The Royal Family: The Story of the British Monarchy from Victoria to Elizabeth.* Alfred A. Knopf, 1954.

Beschloss, Michael R. *Kennedy and Roosevelt: The Uneasy Alliance.* W. W. Norton and Co., 1980.

Biden, Joe. *Promises to Keep: On Life and Politics.* Random House, 2007.

Boothroyd, Basil. *Prince Philip: An Informal Biography.* McCall, 1971.

Boot, Max. *Reagan: His Life and Legend.* Liveright, 2024.

Boyle, Peter G., ed. *The Churchill-Eisenhower Correspondence, 1953–1955.* University of North Carolina Press, 1990.

Bradford, Sarah. *Queen Elizabeth II: Her Life in Our Times.* Viking, 2012.

Brandon, Henry. *Special Relationships: A Foreign Correspondent's Memoirs from Roosevelt to Reagan.* Atheneum, 1988.

Brandreth, Gyles. *Elizabeth: An Intimate Portrait.* Penguin Michael Joseph, 2022.

Selected Bibliography

Brandreth, Gyles. *Philip: The Final Portrait*. Hodder and Stoughton, 2004.

Brinkley, Douglas, ed. *The Reagan Diaries*. HarperCollins, 2007.

Brown, Craig. *A Voyage Around the Queen*. Farrar, Straus and Giroux, 2024.

Brown, Tina. *The Palace Papers: Inside the House of Windsor—the Truth and the Turmoil*. Crown, 2022.

Buchanan, Wiley T., Jr. *Red Carpet at the White House: Four years as Chief of Protocol in the Eisenhower Administration*. E. P. Dutton and Co., 1964.

Buckle, Richard, ed. *Self Portrait with Friends; The Selected Diaries of Cecil Beaton 1926–1974*. Times Books, 1979.

Bush, Barbara. *Barbara Bush: A Memoir*. Lisa Drew Books, 1994.

Bush, George W. *Decision Points*. Crown, 2010.

Bush, George W. *A Portrait of My Father*. Crown, 2014.

Bush, Laura. *Spoken from the Heart*. Scribner, 2010.

Butcher, Harry C. *My Three Years with Eisenhower: The Personal Diary of Captain Harry C. Butcher, USNR, Naval Aide to General Eisenhower, 1942–1945*. Simon and Schuster, 1946.

Cameron, David. *For the Record*. Harper, 2019.

Cannon, Lou. *President Reagan: The Role of a Lifetime*. Simon and Schuster, 1991.

Carter, Jimmy. *A Full Life: Reflections at Ninety*. Simon and Schuster, 2016.

Carter, Miranda. *Anthony Blunt: His Lives*. Farrah, Straus and Giroux, 2001.

Charter, David. *Royal Audience: 70 Years, 13 Presidents—One Queen's Special Relationship with America*. G. P. Putnam's Sons, 2024.

Clinton, Bill. *My Life*. Alfred A. Knopf, 2004.

Clinton, Hillary Rodham. *Hard Choices*. Simon and Schuster, 2014.

Clinton, Hillary Rodham. *Living History*. Simon and Schuster, 2003.

Clinton, Hillary Rodham. *What Happened*. Simon and Schuster, 2017.

Colman, Jonathan. *A "Special Relationship"? Harold Wilson, Lyndon B. Johnson, and Anglo-American Relations "at the Summit," 1964–68*. Manchester University Press, 2004.

Crosland, Susan. *Tony Crosland*. Coronet Books, 1983.

Darroch, Kim. *Collateral Damage: Britain, America, and Europe in the Age of Trump*. PublicAffairs, 2020.

Donoughue, Bernard. *The Heat of the Kitchen: An Autobiography*. Politico's Publishing, 2003.

Eisenhower, Dwight D. *Waging Peace: The White House Years.* Doubleday and Company, Inc., 1965.

Eisenhower, Julie Nixon. *Pat Nixon: The Untold Story.* Zebra Books, 1986.

Eisenhower, Julie Nixon. *Special People.* Simon and Schuster, 1977.

Flesch, Rudolf. *The Art of Readable Writing.* Harper and Brothers, 1949.

Ginsberg, Gary. *First Friends: The Powerful, Unsung (And Unelected) People Who Shaped Our Presidents.* Twelve, 2021.

Goodwin, Doris Kearns. *The Fitzgeralds and The Kennedys.* Simon and Schuster, 1987.

Grisham, Stephanie. *I'll Take Your Questions Now: What I Saw at the Trump White House.* Harper, 2021.

Haberman, Maggie. *Confidence Man: The Making of Donald Trump and the Breaking of America.* Penguin Press, 2022.

Haig, Alexander M., Jr. *Caveat: Realism, Reagan, and Foreign Policy.* Scribner, 1984.

Hardman, Robert. *Her Majesty: Queen Elizabeth II and Her Court.* Pegasus, 2012.

Hardman, Robert. *Queen of Our Times: The Life of Elizabeth II, 1926–2022.* Macmillan, 2022.

Hardman, Robert. *Queen of the World.* Pegasus, 2019.

Harry, Duke of Sussex. *Spare.* Random House, 2023.

Henderson, Nicholas. *Mandarin: The Diaries of An Ambassador 1969–1982.* Weidenfeld and Nicolson Ltd., 1994.

Hill, Fiona. *There Is Nothing for You Here: Finding Opportunity in the 21st Century.* Mariner, 2021.

Horne, Alistair. *Macmillan: Volume I, 1894–1956.* Macmillan, 1988.

Horne, Alistair. *Macmillan: Volume II, 1957–1986.* Macmillan, 1989.

Judge, Edward H., and John W. Langdon. *The Cold War Through Documents: A Global History.* Rowman and Littlefield, 2018.

Kelley, Kitty. *Jackie Oh!* Lyle Stuart, 1978.

Kelley, Kitty. *Nancy Reagan: The Unauthorized Biography.* Simon and Schuster, 1991.

Kelley, Kitty. *The Royals.* Warner Books, 1997.

Kissinger, Henry. *Diplomacy.* Touchstone, 1994.

Kissinger, Henry. *White House Years.* Little, Brown and Company, 1979.

Kissinger, Henry. *Years of Renewal.* Simon and Schuster, 1999.

Lacey, Robert. *Monarch: The Life and Reign of Elizabeth II*. Free Press, 2002.

Lee, Heath Hardage. *The Mysterious Mrs. Nixon: The Life and Times of Washington's Most Private First Lady*. St. Martin's Press, 2024.

Leibovitz, Annie. *Annie Leibovitz at Work*. Phaidon Press Limited, 2018.

Leventhal, Fred M., and Roland Quinault. *Anglo-American Attitudes: From Revolution to Partnership*. Ashgate, 2000.

Longford, Elizabeth. *The Queen: The Life of Elizabeth II*. Ballantine Books, 1984.

Louis, William Roger, and Hedley Bull. *The "Special Relationship": Anglo-American Relations Since 1945*. Clarendon Press, 1986.

Macmillan, Harold. *Pointing the Way: 1959–1961*. Macmillan, 1972.

Macmillan, Harold. *Riding the Storm 1956–1959*. Harper and Row, 1968.

Marr, Andrew. *The Real Elizabeth: An Intimate Portrait of Queen Elizabeth II*. Henry Holt and Company, 2012.

Mastromonaco, Alyssa, with Lauren Oyler. *Who Thought This Was a Good Idea?* Twelve, 2017.

McDowell, Marta. *All the Presidents' Gardens: How the White House Grounds Have Grown with America*. Timber Press, 2016.

McFarlane, Robert C., with Zofia Smardz. *Special Trust*. Cadell and Davies, 1994.

Morton, Andrew. *The Queen: Her Life*. Grand Central, 2022.

Muzzey, David Saville. *History of the American People*. Ginn and Company, 1927.

Nasaw, David. *The Patriarch: The Remarkable Life and Turbulent Times of Joseph P. Kennedy*. Penguin Press, 2012.

Neil, Andrew. *Full Disclosure*. Macmillan, 1996.

Newton, Jim. *Eisenhower: The White House Years*. Doubleday, 2011.

Nixon, Richard. *The Memoirs of Richard Nixon*. Grosset and Dunlap, 1978.

Obama, Barack. *Dreams from My Father: A Story of Race and Inheritance*. Crown, 2004.

Obama, Barack. *A Promised Land*. Crown, 2020.

Owen, James, ed. *The Times: Queen Elizabeth II: A Portrait of Her 70-Year Reign*. HarperCollins, 2021.

Pimlott, Ben. *The Queen: A Biography of Elizabeth II*. John Wiley and Sons, 1996.

Poen, Monte M., ed. *Letters Home by Harry Truman*. University of Missouri, 2003.

Popadiuk, Roman. *The Leadership of George Bush: An Insider's View of the Forty-first President*. Texas A&M University Press, 2009.

Pritchett, Georgia. *My Mess Is a Bit of a Life: Adventures in Anxiety*. Faber and Faber Limited, 2021.

Prochaska, Frank. *The Eagle and the Crown: Americans and the British Monarchy*. Yale University Press, 2008.

Reagan, Nancy, with William Novak. *My Turn: The Memoirs of Nancy Reagan*. Random House, 1989.

Reagan, Ronald. *An American Life*. Simon and Schuster, 1990.

Renwick, Robin. *Fighting with Allies: America and Britain in Peace and War*. Times Books, 1996.

Rhodes, Ben. *The World as It Is: A Memoir of the Obama White House*. Random House, 2018.

Rhodes, Margaret. *The Final Curtsey: A Royal Memoir by the Queen's Cousin*. Umbria Press, 2012.

Richardson, Louise. *When Allies Differ: Anglo-American Relations During the Suez and Falklands Crises*. St. Martin's Press, 1996.

Robb, Thomas K. *Jimmy Carter and the Anglo-American "Special Relationship."* Edinburgh University Press, 2017.

Ronald, Susan. *The Ambassador: Joseph P. Kennedy at the Court of St. James's, 1938–1940*. St. Martin's Press, 2021.

Ryan, Catherine. *The Queen: The Life and Times of Elizabeth II*. Chartwell, 2022.

Sanders, Sarah Huckabee. *Speaking for Myself*. St. Martin's Griffin, 2020.

Sandford, Christopher. *Union Jack: John F. Kennedy's Special Relationship with Great Britain*. ForeEdge, 2017.

Seitz, Raymond. *Over Here*. Weidenfeld and Nicolson, 1998.

Shawcross, William. *The Queen Mother: The Official Biography*. Alfred A. Knopf, 2009.

Shultz, George P. *Turmoil and Triumph: My Years as Secretary of State*. Charles Scribner's Sons, 1993.

Skinner, Kiron K., Annalise Anderson, and Martin Anderson, eds. *Reagan: A Life in Letters*. Free Press, 2003.

Slevin, Peter. *Michelle Obama: A Life*. Alfred A. Knopf, 2015.

Smith, Amanda, ed. *Hostage to Fortune: The Letters of Joseph P. Kennedy*. Viking, 2001.

Smith, Sally Bedell. *Diana: In Search of Herself*. Random House, 1999.

Smith, Sally Bedell. *Elizabeth The Queen: The Life of a Modern Monarch*. Random House, 2012.

Stewart, Andrew. *The King's Private Army: Protecting the British Royal Family During the Second World War*. Helion and Company, 2015.

Strober, Deborah Hart, and Gerald S. Strober. *Queen Elizabeth: An Oral History*. Pegasus Books, 2022.

Swift, Will. *The Kennedys Amidst the Gathering Storm: A Thousand Days in London, 1938–1940*. Collins, 2008.

Swift, Will. *The Roosevelts and the Royals: Franklin and Eleanor, the King and Queen of England, and the Friendship That Changed History*. John Wiley and Sons, Inc., 2004.

Truman, Margaret, with Margaret Cousins. *Souvenir: Margaret Truman's Own Story*. McGraw-Hill, 1956.

Trump, Melania. *Melania*. Skyhorse, 2024.

Tumulty, Karen. *The Triumph of Nancy Reagan*. Simon and Schuster, 2021.

Updegrove, Mark K. *Indomitable Will: LBJ in the Presidency*. Crown, 2012.

Updegrove, Mark K. *The Last Republicans: Inside the Extraordinary Relationship Between George H. W. Bush and George W. Bush*. Harper, 2017.

Valentiner, Benedicte. *Bedtime and Other Stories from the President's Guest House*. Chregon Press, 2011.

Vidal, Gore. *Palimpsest: A Memoir*. Random House, 1995.

Weber, Ralph E., ed. *Talking with Harry: Candid Conversations with President Harry S. Truman*. Scholarly Resources, 2001.

Weidenfeld, Sheila Rabb. *First Lady's Lady: With the Fords at the White House*. G. P. Putnam's Sons, 1979.

Westmacott, Peter. *They Call It Diplomacy: Forty Years of Representing Britain Abroad*. Apollo, 2021.

Wilson, Harold. *A Personal Record: The Labour Government 1964–1970*. Little, Brown and Company, 1971.

Ziegler, Philip. *Edward Heath: The Authorised Biography*. Harper Press, 2010.

Index

Abell, Bess, 86
Accession Declaration, 16
Acland, Antony, 170, 173, 177
Adams, Gerry, 185–87, 190, 196, 269–70
Adams, John, 89, 115–16, 275
Adeane, Michael, 103
Adelman, Kenneth, 159–60
Adenauer, Konrad, 84
Ahern, Bertie, 198
Aitken, Jonathan, 104, 108
Albert, *see* George VI
Aldrich, Winthrop, 38
Alexander VI, 137
Alexandra, 47
Ali, Muhammad, 122
An American Life (Reagan), 140
American Revolution, 111, 116, 120, 123, 224, 225, 227
Amin, Idi, 127, 263
Anderson, Francis F., 29
Andrew, 57, 67, 102, 137, 177, 199, 204, 205, 244, 258, 283
Angleton, James Jesus, 92
Anne, 15, 48, 57, 89, 95, 96–101, 123, 132–33, 146, 177, 214, 216, 244, 263
Annenberg, Walter, 96–98, 106, 107–8, 127, 134, 141, 150, 151
anti-toasts, 127
Armstrong, Neil, xviii
Armstrong, Robert, 102, 112
Armstrong-Jones, Antony, 86, 88
Arpels, Louis, 36
Art of Readable Writing, The (Flesch), 53–54
Art of the Comeback, The (Trump), 245

al-Asad, Hafez, 130
al-Assad, Bashar, 263
Asō, Tarō, 220
Atomic Energy Act (1946), 22, 32, 53
Attlee, Clement, 18, 22, 25, 27
Auchincloss, Hugh, 62
Audience, The (play), 208
Auxiliary Territorial Service, xvi

Bagehot, Walter, xvii
Baker, James A., III, xviii, 121, 138, 172, 179
Bales, Susan Ford, 117, 118
Ball, Dave, 54
Ball, George, 83–84
balloon barrages, 6
Balmoral Castle, 12–13, 57–58, 276, 279
Baring, Rowland, 111, 116
Barton, Philip, 192
Barzun, Brooke Brown, 231–32
Barzun, Matthew, 231–32, 234
Bassett, James, 55
Bay of Pigs, 64
BBC, 8, 94, 269
Beaton, Cecil, 61
Beatrice, 274
Bedingfield, Kate, 268
Benn, Tony, 127, 144
Berger, Sandy, 186, 197
Berlin Wall, 60
Berlusconi, Silvio, 188
Biden, Catherine Eugenia Finnegan, 268
Biden, Jean, 267, 268
Biden, Jill, 265, 267, 271–72, 273–74

Index

Biden, Joe, 35, 186, 224
   Elizabeth and, xvi, xvii, 265, 267, 268–69, 273–75, 276–77, 289
   Falklands crisis, 138
   foreign trips, 267, 270, 271–75
   Irish roots, 267–68, 270–71
   on Philip's death, 272
   presidency, 269–71
   vice presidency, 268
Billings, Lem, 4
Blaine, David, 210
Blair, Cherie, 192
Blair, Tony, 180, 185, 191–94, 195–97, 198, 203, 205–6, 208–10, 219, 282
Blewitt, Gertie, 268
Blunkett, David, 209
Boateng, Paul Yaw, 68–69, 146
Bolton, John, 248, 251, 261
Borel, Calvin, 215
Bouvier, Jack, 20
Bouvier, Jacqueline. *See* Onassis, Jacqueline Bouvier Kennedy
Bouvier, Janet Lee, 61–62
Bowles, Camilla Parker, 101, 131, 224, 241, 255–56, 262–63, 282
Brabourne, John, 94
Bradley, Omar, 35
Brandon, Henry, 43
Brandreth, Gyles, 156, 209, 222, 238, 250
Brexit, 236–37, 248, 251, 272
Brimelow, Thomas, 106–7
Britannia, 56–57, 114–15, 122–23, 150–55, 164, 174, 190–91, 193, 211
British Commonwealth, 67–68, 70, 158, 225, 253
British Overseas Airways Corporation, 25
brooches, 47–48, 230–31, 252–53, 265
Brown, Craig, 142, 263, 288
Brown, Gordon, 220, 232
Bruce, David K. E., 65, 79–81
Bryan, John, 177
Bryant, Nick, 269
Brzezinski, Zbigniew, 130
Buchanan, Wiley, 44, 50, 51, 55
Buckingham Palace, 1, 8, 18, 59, 94–95, 159, 171, 194, 204–6, 207–8, 257
Buffett, Warren, 193
Burke, Edmund, 115
Burns, George, 152

Burton, Richard, 122
Bush, Barbara, 168, 171, 173, 201, 203
Bush, George H. W., xviii
   Clinton and, 182
   on Diana's death, 195
   election campaign, 179–80, 182
   Elizabeth and, xvi–xvii, 164–77, 181–82, 201, 202, 216
   funeral, 135
   Gulf War, 171–72, 181
   health issues, 169
   honors and awards, 181
   Iraq War, 219
   Major and, 178–80
   matchmaking hopes, 96
   military career, 170
   physical appearance, 167
   presidency, 121, 129, 177
   talking hat incident, 167–70
   tree speech, 165
Bush, George W.
   Charles and, 100
   Clinton and, 182
   date with Tricia Nixon, 96
   Elizabeth and, xvii, 171, 195, 201–6, 210–11, 214–17, 265
   foreign trips, 204, 227
   Iraq War, 203, 207–10
   presidency, 199, 206, 242
   September 11 terror attacks, 203, 204–6, 253
   on talking hat incident, 169
Bush, Jeb, 182
Bush, Laura, 202, 204–6, 213, 215–16, 227

Cable, Vince, 243
Caccia, Harold, 42–43, 52
Callaghan, James, 107–8, 128–29, 136
Cameron, David, xvii, 219, 232–33, 236–37, 265
Captain & Tennille, 118
Carter, Caron, 131
Carter, Chip, 131
Carter, Jimmy
   Charles and, 130
   condolences for Lord Mountbatten, 134–35
   death, 135
   election campaign, 120

Elizabeth and, 121–22, 124–32, 135–36, 219, 265, 289
Ford and, 121–22
foreign trips, 124–30
funeral, 135
Iran hostage crisis, 129
kissing propensity, 126–28
Philip and, 125
presidency, 124, 129–30, 132, 136
Queen Mother kiss, 126–27, 135
Carter, Rosalynn, 132
Catherine of Braganza, 37
Cavendish, William, 64
Ceaușescu, Nicolae, 264
Chamberlain, Anne, 2
Chamberlain, Neville, 2, 3, 5
Chapin, Dwight, 97–98
Charles I, 210
Charles II, 37
Charles III, 15, 89, 125, 160, 172, 203, 224, 255–56, 277
  ascension to throne, 101
  birth, 140
  Bush's funeral, 135
  Camilla and, 101, 131, 224, 282
  Carter and, 130
  Clinton and, 185
  Diana and, 101, 131, 142, 153–54, 177–78, 195, 244, 258, 282
  Elizabeth's Coronation Day, 36
  familiarity with American pop culture, 52
  health issues, 282
  Iraq War concerns, 209
  Lord Mountbatten's assassination, 133–34
  personality, 112
  Reagan and, 141
  Reagan's funeral, 135, 212
  reign, 282–83
  Trump and, 244–45, 262, 278–81, 283
  White House visit with Anne, 95–101
Charlotte, 115
Charteris, Martin, 26, 30, 41–42, 67, 102, 112
Chavez, Cesar, 270
Cheney, Dick, 117
Chequers, 55, 101–4, 188, 198, 247, 249
"Children in Wartime" (BBC program), 8–9

Christopher, Warren, 186
Churchill, Clementine, xv
Churchill, Randolph, 6
Churchill, Winston
  bust of, 219–20, 242, 247, 270
  death, 78
  diplomacy, xii, 14
  Eisenhower and, 38–39, 40–41, 42
  election to prime minister, 27
  Elizabeth and, xv–xvi, 25, 37–38, 39, 43, 78–79, 92, 285
  funeral, 78–81
  honorary US citizenship, 65
  on Kennedy's death, 71
  Macmillan and, 67–68
  Potsdam Conference, 18, 21
  retirement, 39
  Roosevelt and, 62, 216
  trip to America, 31–32
Church of England, 60
Cinderella (film), 28
Civilian Conservation Corps, xiii
Clarence House, 109, 127
Clark, Mark, 10, 11
Clark, William, 147
Clinton, Bill
  Blair and, 191–94, 195–97
  Bush and, 182
  Charles and, 185
  Diana and, 193
  election campaign, 177, 179–80, 182–84
  Elizabeth and, xvii, 184–85, 188–93, 195, 198–200, 205, 206–7, 219, 266
  foreign trips, 184, 188–93
  Good Friday Agreement, 187, 198, 270
  impeachment, 197
  inauguration, 180
  Lewinsky scandal, 195–98, 246
  Major and, 182–84, 187
  personality, 185
  Philip and, 207
  presidency, 129, 181, 185–86
  Rhodes Scholar, 180, 184
  "Slick Willie" nickname, 185
Clinton, Chelsea, 199
Clinton, Hillary, 184, 188, 189, 190–96, 225, 235, 265–66, 282–83
Cochran, Jacqueline, 75–76

Index

Cold War, 60, 67, 73, 83, 149, 152, 175, 285
Colville, Jock, 37
Colville, Richard, 49
Como, Perry, 152
constitutional monarchs, xvii, 38, 69, 92, 284
Corbyn, Jeremy, 247, 255
Cornwallis, Charles, xi
coronations, 35–37, 45
Court Jeweller (blog), 252–53
COVID-19 pandemic, 273, 274, 275, 279, 285
Cowboy and the Queen, The (documentary), 263
Cox, Edward, 100
Crathie Kirk, 13
Cronk, Hiram, xi
Cronkite, Walter, 36
Crosthwaite, Moore, 76
Crowe, William J., 186
Crown, The (TV show), 60–61, 87, 94, 262
Cuban missile crisis, 60, 75

Daley, Richard, 57
Daniel, Clifton Truman, 18
Danks, Clayton, 117
Darroch, Kim, 240–43, 247, 260–62
Davis, Patti, 153
Dean, Patrick, 89–90
Deaver, Carolyn, 146
Deaver, Michael, 144–47, 154
Declaration of Independence, xii, 28, 111–12, 255
Diana, 101, 102, 131, 153–54, 161–62, 172, 177–78, 180, 193–95, 232, 244–45, 258, 282
Disney, Walt, 2
divorce rule, 60
Dobelle, Evan, 126, 130, 132, 135
Dobelle, Kit, 132
Donoughue, Bernard, xviii, 63–64, 90, 106, 280
Douglas, Kirk, 87
Douglas, Sharman, 86
Douglas-Home, Alec, 71
Downing Street Declaration, 186
Downs, Maria, 117
Duchin, Peter, 88

Dunham, Ann, 219
Dunham, Madelyn Payne, 229

Eden, Anthony, 39–40, 41–42, 43
Edward, 71, 82, 89, 135
Edward III, 91
Edward VIII, xii–xiii, 2, 5, 33, 36, 227
Ehrlichman, John, 105
Eisenhower, David, 95, 98
Eisenhower, Dwight
  Churchill and, 38–39, 40–41, 42
  Churchill's funeral, 80–81
  Elizabeth and, xvi, 11, 13–14, 38–39, 41, 45–48, 49–50, 56–58, 61, 75, 202, 216, 265
  European tour, 12–13
  George VI and, 11–14
  health issues, 47
  honors and awards, 11–12, 47
  inauguration, 35
  lemon airlift, 12
  military career, xv, 10–14
  NATO, 14, 30
  presidency, 30, 40
  Suez crisis, 40–42, 285
  Truman and, 30–31
  Windsor visit, 10–11
Eisenhower, John, 12–13
Eisenhower, Mamie, 12, 45, 61, 75
Elizabeth, xiii, xviii–xix, 2, 5–6, 16, 125, 126, 135, 159, 160–61, 212, 224
Elizabeth II
  "All Will Be Well" address, 8–9
  American Bicentennial trip, 110–20, 125, 164
  assassination threats, 155–56
  children, 15, 57, 67, 71, 74, 82, 89, 140, 170
  clothing and accessories, 18, 47–48, 55, 61, 118, 125, 141, 147, 152, 154, 167, 173, 189, 213, 217, 220, 222, 230–31, 232, 250, 252–53, 255, 273
  corgis, 146, 206, 232, 274, 275
  Coronation Day, 35–37, 161
  death, xviii, 75, 276, 284, 286
  Diamond Jubilee, 223
  diaries, xviii
  diplomacy, xvii–xviii, 4–5, 30, 43, 92, 116, 199–200, 263–65
  education, xv, xix, 3

Index

film appreciation, 140–41
funeral, 276–77, 289
on George VI's trip to America, xiii
Ghana trip, 67–70, 285
Golden Jubilee, 206
Hitler's kidnapping plot, 9–10
honors and awards, 17
horseback riding, 139, 144–45, 146–48, 162–63, 167, 212, 286
Lilibet nickname, xv, 9
media coverage, 8–9, 17, 19–20, 26, 29–30, 44, 49, 51, 68, 118, 147–48, 151, 165, 168, 175, 221–22, 236
military service, xvi
North American tour, 15–21, 23–33, 62
personality, 20, 28, 34, 52, 66, 93, 112, 117, 142–43, 189, 194, 229, 238, 257, 287
Philip and, xvi, 7, 13, 15, 25, 26, 105–6, 133–34, 154, 235–36
physical appearance, 15, 20, 167, 220
portrayals of in popular culture, 287–88
pregnancies, 57, 67, 71, 82, 140
reign, xii, xvi, xvii–xix, 34, 282
relationship with parents, xi, 9, 26
royal bloodline, 34
Ruby Jubilee, 178
Silver Jubilee, 119, 129, 131, 147
state visits, 42–53, 56–58, 74, 131, 150, 164, 172–75, 203, 213–17
superstitious beliefs, 288
titles, 60
West Coast trip, 150–57, 164
Elizabeth R (documentary), 211–12
Elliot, Dominic, 57
Elphinstone, Lady, 3
Empress of Britain, RMS, xiv
Epstein, Jeffrey, 199, 244, 283
Evans, Harold, 69

Falklands crisis, 137–40, 148–49, 286
Fall, Brian, 152
Farage, Nigel, 260
Farish, Sarah, 171, 214
Farish, William, 171, 205, 214
Favreau, Jon, 228
Fellowes, Robert, 131, 170
Ferguson, Sarah, 177, 204, 239, 244, 258

Finnegan, James, 270–71
Fitzgerald, Ella, 117
Flesch, Rudolf, 53–54
football, 48
Ford, Betty, 116–18
Ford, Gerald
    Bicentennial celebration, 110–21
    Carter and, 121–22
    election campaign, 120–21
    Elizabeth and, xvi, 113–20, 122–23, 152, 174, 211, 216
    foreign trips, 119–20
    personality, 112
    presidency, 110, 124
Ford, Jack, 116
Fournier, Ron, 183–84
Frank, Anne, 9
Franks, Oliver, 19, 23
Frazier, Alice, 172–73, 175, 222
From Her Majesty's Jewel Vault (blog), 252
Funk, Lisa, 215

Gallun, Marjorie, 217
Galtieri, Leopoldo, 137
Garfield, James, 133
Gaulle, Charles de, 61
Geidt, Christopher, 228
George, Duke of Kent, 1, 7
George, Prince, 237
George II, 130
George III, xii, 111, 115–16, 168, 224, 227, 275
George V, 59
George VI
    consort, xiii
    coronation, 35, 36, 165
    death, xiv, 32–33, 34–35, 288
    disabilities, xiv
    early years, xii
    Eisenhower and, 11–14
    health issues, 13, 15–16, 25
    hiding during Eisenhower's Windsor tour, 10–11
    Kennedys and, 1–2, 5–7
    media coverage, xiv
    reign, xii, xiv
    trip to America, xi–xiv, 123
    Truman and, 18, 22–23, 31–32
    World War II, 6–12

Gergen, David, 190
Ghana, 67–70, 285
Gibbs, Humphrey, 225–26
Giscard d'Estaing, Valery, 120, 125
Goldfinger, Uriah, 175
Goldwater, Barry, 82
Gorbachev, Mikhail, 151, 159, 164, 175–76
Gorbachev, Raisa, 176
Gore, Al, 199
Gore, Nina, 61
Gore-Booth, Paul, 84, 90
Grace of Monaco, 142
Graham, Katharine, 193
Grant, Cary, 117, 141
Great Britain
  "Bloody Sunday," 105
  Falklands crisis, 137–40, 148–49
  financial crisis, 87, 113, 128–29
  Iraq War opposition, 209–10
  September 11 terror attacks, 204–6, 216
  Suez crisis, 39–42
  The Troubles, 135, 155, 187–88
  United States and, xi–xii, 21–24, 29, 83–84
  World War II, xii, xiv–xv, 6–12
Great Depression, xiii
Greenhill, Denis, 103
Grenada intervention, 157–59
Grisham, Stephanie, 254, 260, 279
Gulf War, 171–72, 181

Haig, Alexander, 137, 139
Haines, Joe, 287
Haldeman, H. R., 97–98, 105
Hancock, Patrick F., 76
Hand, Lloyd, 77–78, 80, 81, 87
Hardman, Robert, 140, 152, 243, 257, 265
Harriman, Averell, 50
Harry, 114, 153, 161, 193–94, 223, 237, 239, 258–60, 271–72, 283
Hartley, Jane D., 275–76
Hasty Heart, The (film), 140
hats, 18, 167, 173, 213, 222, 250, 255
Healey, Denis, 159
Heath, Edward, 92, 101–5, 111, 172
Heinz, Henry, II, 117

Henderson, Mary, 147
Henderson, Nicholas, 127, 141, 142, 146–47, 150
Henson, Josiah, 225
Hepburn, Audrey, 141
Heseltine, William, 94, 159
Hewitt, James, 258
Higgins, Marguerite, 30
Hill, Fiona, 240, 245, 253
Hirohito, 116, 264
Hitchens, Christopher, 165
Hitler, Adolf, xii, xiv, 3, 6, 9
Hollande, François, 223
Hollingworth, Peter, 206
Holmes, John, 196
Holt, Harold, 84
Homer, Winslow, 131
Hoover, Herbert, xvi, 50
Hope, Bob, 118, 141, 152
Humphrey, Hubert, 79, 81, 88–90, 120
Humphrey, Muriel, 89
Hunt, Jeremy, 249, 254, 261
Hurd, Douglas, 190
Hussein, Saddam, 209

Inoki, Antonio, 122
International Monetary Fund, 87, 113, 128
Invictus Games, 223, 271
IRA. *See* Provisional Irish Republican Army
Iran hostage crisis, 129, 136
Iraq War, 171–72, 181, 203, 207–10, 219
ITV, 94

Jack Daniel's, 231
Jackson, Henry, 120
Jackson, Harry, 117
Jamestown, 44, 213, 214
Jay, Peter, 108, 130
Jogee, Adam, 127
John, 71–72
John Paul II, 139, 188, 267
Johnson, Boris, 219–20, 242, 247, 248, 262, 263, 264, 272, 273, 276, 285, 286
Johnson, Lady Bird, 78, 80, 87, 88, 174
Johnson, Luci Baines, 78, 86, 174
Johnson, Lyndon

British diplomats' opinions of, 76–78
Churchill's funeral, 78–81
Cuban missile crisis, 75
election campaigns, 82
Elizabeth and, xvi, 71, 73–76, 78, 82, 90, 91, 174, 219, 265
foreign trips, 82–83, 84
Great Society legislation, 82
health issues, 79, 87
inauguration, 78–79
JFK and, 74–75
presidency, 74, 76, 82–83
Princess Margaret and, 86–88
Johnson, Woody, 246, 256, 264
Journey's End (Sherriff), 140

Kaine, Tim, 213–14
Kay, Ella, 253
Kelly, Grace, xviii
Kennan, George, 4
Kennedy, Bobby, 6
Kennedy, Caroline, 72
Kennedy, David, 101
Kennedy, Edward, 4–5, 6, 72, 136, 186
Kennedy, Ethel, 266
Kennedy, Eunice, 1, 6
Kennedy, Jackie. *See* Onassis, Jacqueline Bouvier Kennedy
Kennedy, Joe, Jr., 4, 6, 64, 72
Kennedy, John F., 6
 African leaders and, 67
 assassination, 71
 Cuban missile crisis, 75
 election campaign, 63–64
 Elizabeth and, xvi, 5, 59–62, 65–67, 73, 219, 285
 European travels, 3–5
 foreign trips, 70–71
 funeral, 135
 Jackie and, 36
 Johnson and, 74–75
 Khrushchev meeting, 59–60
 Macmillan and, 59–60, 62, 63–70, 146
 presidency, 62
 Runnymede memorial, 71–72
 Why England Slept, 4, 65
Kennedy, John F., Jr., 71, 72
Kennedy, Joseph P., II, 170
Kennedy, Joseph P., Sr., xiii, xiv, 1–7, 63

Kennedy, Kathleen, 6, 64, 71
Kennedy, Robert F., 72, 89–90, 98, 270
Kennedy, Rose, 1, 2–3, 6
Kentucky Derby, 213, 214, 215
Kenya, 218, 225–26
Kenyatta, Jomo, 225
Kenyatta, Uhuru, 225
Kerry, John, 186, 197
Khan, Ayub, 66
Khan, Sadiq, 243, 247, 248
Khrushchev, Nikita, 57, 59, 70, 176
Kilberg, Bobbie, 169
Kimmel, Jimmy, 220
King, Martin Luther, Jr., 242, 270
Kirkpatrick, Jeane, 137–38
Kissinger, Henry, 93, 103–5, 107, 113, 123, 286
Knatchbull, Nicholas, 133
Knatchbull, Patricia, 133
Knebel, Fletcher, 17
Kushner, Jared, 254

Lake, Anthony, 186
Lambart, Elizabeth, 10–11
Lambert, Anthony, 76–77
Lascelles, Alan, 6, 12, 24
Lawford, Patricia Kennedy, 6, 72
Lee, Heath Hardage, 100
Lewinsky, Monica, 195, 197, 246
Lincoln, Abraham, 224–25
Lloyd, Christopher, 199
Longford, Elizabeth, 43
Louis-Dreyfus, Julia, 268
Low, Valentine, 236–37
Luers, William H., 20

MacArthur, Douglas, 80
MacDonald, Margaret "Bobo," 102
Mackenzie, A. R. K., 23
Macmillan, Harold, 21
 Churchill and, 67–68
 Eisenhower and, 43–44, 52–53, 57, 58
 Elizabeth and, 63, 65
 JFK and, 59–60, 62, 63–70, 146
 Johnson and, 76
 prime minister tenure, 46–47
 resignation, 102
Macron, Brigitte, 287
Macron, Emmanuel, 246, 263, 287

Madison, James, 89, 116
Magna Carta, 71–72
Major, John, 171, 178–80, 182–84, 186–87, 188–89
Major, Norma, 172
Mandela, Nelson, 226, 238, 287
Mandelson, Peter, 283
Manning, Anthony, 206–7, 213
Manning, David, 198
Maples, Marla, 245
Margaret, xv, 4–5, 8, 13, 62, 86–88, 125, 131, 176, 264
Marina, 62
Markle, Meghan, 114, 239, 255–56, 258–59, 271
Marriott, J. Willard, 117
Marsh, Jack, 114, 119
Marshall, George, 34, 35
Marten, Henry, xix
Mary, 5, 48, 217
Mature, Victor, 141
Maxwell, Paul, 133
May, Theresa, 241–43, 245, 248–49, 251, 254, 262
McCormack, John, 99
McFarlane, Robert (Bud), 158
McGrory, Mary, 118
McKeldin, Theodore, 48
McMahon Act. *See* Atomic Energy Act (1946)
Mead, Bob, 120
media coverage
  "All Will Be Well" address, 8–9
  Bicentennial celebration, 118, 120–21
  Brexit, 236, 248
  Bush's London trip, 207, 209–10
  Carter's London trip, 125, 128
  Charles in America, 141
  Churchill bust, 270
  Churchill's America trip, 32
  Churchill's funeral, 81
  Coronation Day, 35–37
  Eisenhower's Balmoral Castle visit, 12–13
  Falklands crisis, 138
  George VI's America trip, xiv
  Ghana trip, 68
  horseback riding with Reagan, 147–48
  Jackie Kennedy's London trip, 61
  Margaret and LBJ, 88
  Nancy Reagan at Royal Wedding, 142
  Nixon's London trip, 55
  North American tour, 20, 26, 29–30
  Obama's visit, 221–22
  state visits, 44, 49, 51, 165, 175
  talking hat incident, 168, 169
  Thatcher and Elizabeth, 143
  Truman and Elizabeth, 17, 19
  West Coast trip, 151
Mellon, Paul, 65
Merkel, Angela, 242
Meyer, Christopher, 195–98, 205
Middleton, Catherine, 227, 233–34, 237, 262, 273, 281
Miklaszewski, Jim, 167
Miliband, Ed, 246
Miller, John, 147
Mills, Doug, 167, 256
Mitterrand, François, 172, 188–89
Mobutu Sese Soko, 263
Monroe, James, 116
Monroe, Marilyn, 141
Morgan, Piers, 251
Morrah Dermot, 25–26
Morrison, Scott, 240
Mountbatten, Louis, 7, 133–34, 187–88
Mountbatten, Philip, *see* Philip
Moynihan, Daniel Patrick, 101, 186
Mugabe, Robert, 263
Mulroney, Brian, 151
Murdoch, Rupert, 248
"Muskrat Love" (song), 118
Mussolini, Benito, xiv

Nantz, Jim, 216
Nasser, Gamal Abdel, 39–41
National Children's Week, 8
Nehru, Jawaharlal, 286
Netanyahu, Benjamin, 229
New Deal, xiii
Newman, Paul, xviii, 87
Nixon, Hannah Milhous, 91
Nixon, Julie, 55, 95, 97–101
Nixon, Pat, 55, 56, 97–98, 101–4
Nixon, Richard
  Charles and Anne's White House visit, 96–101
  election campaigns, 74

Elizabeth and, xvi, 53–56, 82, 91–95, 96–97, 102–6, 108–9, 111, 132, 265, 285
exile, 113
foreign trips, 93–95, 101–5
impeachment, 107–8
inauguration, 92
matchmaking hopes, 95–97, 100–101
name origins, 91
personality, 92–93
presidency, 55, 92, 95, 111, 124
resignation, 111, 119
Thanksgiving trip, 54–57
vice presidency, 53–54
Watergate scandal, 105, 107, 111, 196, 197, 245–46
Nixon, Tricia, 56–57, 91, 95–101
Nkrumah, Kwame, 67–70, 229
Noel, Philip, 123
Noland, Mary Ethel, 31
North Atlantic Treaty Organization (NATO), 14, 30, 85, 106, 124, 134, 246, 247, 262, 281
nuclear weapons, 21–22, 32, 52–53
Nugent, Patrick, 88
Nye, Joseph, 38, 63–63

Obama, Barack
    Cameron and, 232–33
    Elizabeth and, 189, 195, 218, 220–31, 234–38, 241, 253, 265, 288
    foreign trips, 218, 220–22, 224–31, 234
    personality, 238
    Philip and, 227
    presidency, 188, 219–20, 225, 231–33, 242
    Trump and, 223, 253
Obama, Barack, Sr., 218–19
Obama, Malia, 223
Obama, Michelle, 220–24, 228, 235–36, 252–53, 265
Obama, Sasha, 223
Oberon, Merle, 117
Ogilvie, Frederick, 8
Onassis, Jacqueline Bouvier Kennedy, 20, 36, 59–62, 66, 127
Operation Desert Storm, 171–72
Organization of African Unity, 67

Organization of Eastern Caribbean States, 157
Ormsby-Gore, David, 59, 62, 64, 72, 75, 82
Osborne, George, xviii, 228, 285
Owen, David, xv–xvi, 128, 130, 136

Palliser, Michael, 147
Palmer, Arnold, 216
Pan-Africanism, 67
Panetta, Leon, 186
Parker, Michael, 16
Parks, Rosa, 270
Parry, Ryan, 207–8
Paul VI, 84, 101
Payne, Berkeley, 20
Peace Corps, 67
Pearl Harbor attack, xv, xvi
Penn, William, 115
Peres, Shimon, 238
Perez, Anna, 173
Perlman, Itzhak, 216
Perot, H. Ross, 177
Philip
    Carter and, 125
    Clinton and, 207
    death, 272, 274
    Eisenhower and, 11, 14
    Elizabeth and, xvi, 7, 13, 25, 26, 62, 105–6, 133–34, 154, 235–36
    funeral, 272
    Kennedy's funeral, 71, 135
    lineage, 45
    Lord Mountbatten's assassination, 133–34, 187–88, 272
    military career, 170
    Nixon and, 94, 95
    North American tour, 15–21
    Obama and, 227
    Reagan and, 145, 156
    retirement from public life, 249
    state visits, 44–53, 131
    Truman and, 21
    Trump and, 244
Phillips, Mark, 132, 177
Phillips, Peter, 216
Phillips, Zara, 214
Pickford, Mary, 1
Pimlott, Ben, 47

Pinkerton, James, 166
Pinocchio (film), 2–3
Pius XII, 4
Popadiuk, Roman, 169
Porcester, Henry, 69
Potsdam Conference, 18, 21
Powell, Charles David, 176
Powell, Colin, 167
Powell, Jonathan, 179, 185
Price, Leontyne, 87
Pritchett, Georgia, 268
Provisional Irish Republican Army (IRA), 133–35, 155, 186–87, 189, 269–70
Putin, Vladimir, 209, 242, 247, 263, 274
Pym, Francis, 157

Quayle, Anthony, 141
Quayle, Dan, 167
Queen Mother. *See* Elizabeth

Radziwill, Anna Christina, 59
Radziwill, Lee, 59, 60
Radziwill, Stanislaw Albrecht, 60
Ramsbotham, Peter, 106–7, 113, 119, 121
Rayburn, Sam, 53
Reagan, Maureen, 153
Reagan, Michael, 153
Reagan, Nancy, 121, 141–42, 144, 147, 150, 152–53, 160, 162, 178, 194–95, 212, 216
Reagan, Ronald, xviii
   acting career, 140–41
   An American Life, 140
   assassination attempt, 141
   Charles and, 141
   death, 211
   Diana and, 161–62
   election campaign, 120–21
   Elizabeth and, xvi, 82, 109, 136, 139, 140–41, 142–57, 159–60, 162–63, 171, 174, 189, 202, 211–12, 223, 249, 265, 286
   Falklands crisis, 137–40, 148–49
   foreign trips, 139–40, 143–46
   funeral, 135
   honors and awards, 181, 211
   inauguration, 136
   Iran hostage crisis, 136
   Nancy and, 141–42, 153
   Nixon and, 108–9
   Operation Urgent Fury, 157–59
   personality, 142–43
   Philip and, 156
   presidency, 121, 175
   Queen Mother and, 160–61
   Rancho del Cielo, 150–51, 152
   Thatcher and, 145–46, 151, 158, 160
Reagan, Ron, Jr., 153
Reed, Clarke, 121
Reed, Joseph Verner, 164, 168–69
Reedy, George, 79
Rentschler, James, 139
Renwick, Robin, 135, 184, 190
Reynolds, Albert, 186
Reynolds, Lindsay, 254
Rhodes, Ben, 219, 220, 223, 228–29, 238
Rhodes, Margaret, 10–11, 41
Rhodesia, 225–26
Rice, Condoleezza, 216
Rice, Susan, 235
Richards, Ann, 166, 174
Richard the Lionheart, 91
Ripley, S. Dillon, 133
Robb, Lynda Bird Johnson, 86, 88, 174
Roberts, John, 216
Roberts, Monty, 263
Robinson, Marian, 223
Rockefeller, Nelson, 121–22
Rogers, William, 103
Rogich, Sig, 167–68, 173
Roosevelt, Eleanor, xi–xiii, 7, 30, 34, 50, 152
Roosevelt, Franklin D., 35, 270
   Churchill and, 62, 216
   death, 21, 22
   disabilities, xiv
   Eleanor and, xi
   election campaigns, 3, 7
   George VI and, xi–xiv, 165, 211
   Hyde Park, 152, 224
   Hyde Park home, xiii–xiv
   Kennedy appointment, 1, 3, 7
   New Deal, xiii
   presidency, 175
Roosevelt, Selwa "Lucky," 151, 156–57
Rose, Kenneth, 226
Rosebush, James, 155
Royal Family (documentary), 94

Rusk, Dean, 78, 80–81
Rutte, Mark, 263
Ryan, Frederick, Jr., 140

Savalas, Telly, 117
Sawers, John, 197–98
Schlesinger, Arthur, Jr., 93
Schlosstein, Ralph, 276
Schmidt, Helmut, 120
Schwarzkopf, Norman, 174–75
scone recipe, 58
Scoon, Paul, 159
Sedwill, Mark, 261
Seitz, Raymond, 129, 159, 170, 173, 186–87
Selleck, Tom, 52
Sens, Andrew D., 183
September 11 terror attacks, 203, 204–6, 216, 253, 282
Service, Robert W., 161
Shawcross, William, 153
Shea, Michael, 151
Sherriff, R. C., 140
"Shooting of Dan McGrew, The" (Service), 161
Shultz, George, 158
Sidey, Hugh, 95
Simpson, Wallis, xii–xiii, 1, 5, 258
Sinatra, Frank, 141, 152
Sinn Féin, 186, 187, 269
Smith, Jean Kennedy, 1, 5, 6, 72
Smith, Sally Bedell, 7, 57
Smuts, Jan, 68
Snow White (film), 2, 5, 28
Soderberg, Nancy, 186
soft power, 38, 46, 69, 73, 164, 176, 280, 287
South Africa, 25, 68, 143, 225–26
Soviet Union, 18, 22, 30, 38, 39–42, 46–47, 60, 67, 107, 144, 152, 175–76
Spare (Prince Harry), 239
"special relationship" between US and Britain, xii, 29, 41, 50, 65, 83–84, 99, 104, 134, 144, 167, 183, 219, 227–28, 242–43, 251, 280, 284–86
Spencer, Diana. *See* Diana
Spencer, Sarah, 131
Sputnik, 46–47
Stalin, Joseph, xiv, 18, 30

Starmer, Keir, 185, 278, 280, 281
Stedman, Phyliss, 128
Steinberg, James, 196, 198
Stern, Howard, 195
Stewart, Andrew, 9
Stewart, Cosmo, 77
St. Lawrence Seaway, 56
Stock, Victor, 109
Stuart, Constance, 97–98
Suez crisis, 39–42, 43, 46, 285
supermarkets, 48–49
Swain, David, 214

Taylor, Elizabeth, 122
Thanksgiving, 54–56
Thatcher, Margaret, 136, 226
  Elizabeth and, 143, 145
  Falklands crisis, 137–39
  IRA denunciation, 134–35
  "Iron Lady" nickname, 175
  Operation Desert Storm, 171
  Reagan and, 145–46, 151, 158, 160
Travolta, John, 162
Trend, Burke, 103
The Troubles, 135, 155, 187–88
Trudeau, Justin, 263
Trudeau, Pierre, 120, 161
Truman, Bess, 17, 61
Truman, Harry, xvi
  assassination attempt, 27
  Eisenhower and, 30–31
  Elizabeth and, xvi, 15–21, 23–24, 27–33, 61, 62, 216–17, 238–39
  European tour, 18–19
  George VI and, 18, 22–23, 31–32
  presidency, 15, 17–24, 32, 175
  vice presidency, 17
Truman, Margaret, 17–19, 23, 28, 33
Trump, Barron, 254
Trump, Donald
  Art of the Comeback, The, 245
  on Catherine Middleton, 233–34
  Charles and, 244–45, 262, 278–81, 283
  criticism of "special relationship," 160
  Diana and, 195, 244–45
  election campaign, 235, 236
  Elizabeth and, 37, 82, 195, 240–41, 243, 247, 249–60, 262–66, 272, 280–81, 285, 289

Trump, Donald (*cont.*)
  foreign trips, 227, 240, 246–49
  inauguration, 240, 241
  Obama and, 223, 253
  personality, 257
  Philip and, 244
  on Philip's death, 272
  presidency, 240–43, 245, 269
  Sinn Féin fundraiser, 186
Trump, Donald, Jr., 254
Trump, Eric, 254
Trump, Fred, 37
Trump, Ivana, 244
Trump, Ivanka, 254
Trump, Lara, 254
Trump, Mary Anne MacLeod, 37
Trump, Melania, 249, 250, 254–56, 263, 279, 280
Trump, Tiffany, 254
Truss, Liz, 260, 270, 276, 286
Two Champs (sculpture), 117

United States
  American Revolution, 111, 116, 120, 123, 224, 227
  Bicentennial celebration, 110–21, 125
  Falklands crisis, 137–40, 148–49
  Great Britain and, xi–xii, 21–24, 29, 83–84
  Operation Urgent Fury, 157–59
  Suez crisis, 39–42
  World War II, xiv–xv, 14
United States, SS, 36

Valdoni, Pietro, 16
Valenti, Jack, 80
Valentiner, Benedicte, 174
Van Dyck, Anthony, 62
Vansittart, Robert, 7
Victoria, 7, 13, 25, 133, 160, 225, 230, 260
Vidal, Gore, 61–62
Vietnam War, 74, 82–83, 85–86, 93, 99–100

Virginia Tech shooting, 214
Volta Dam, 69–70
Voyage Around the Queen, A (Brown), 263

Wagner, Robert, 50
Waldrop, Frank C., 20
Walker, David, 114
Wallace, Madge Gates, 27
Warner, John, 122
War of 1812, xi, 116
Warren, Earl, 81
Warwick, Dionne, 152
Washington, George, xi, 28, 89, 98, 224
Watergate scandal, 105, 107, 111, 119, 196
Weidenfeld, Sheila, 117
Weinberg, Mark, 143, 146
Westmacott, Peter, 180, 182, 190
Why England Slept (Kennedy), 4, 65
Wigram, Clive, 10
William, 153, 193–94, 224, 227, 237, 258, 281
Wilson, Harold, xviii, 74, 78, 82, 83, 85, 92, 93, 106, 108, 287
Wilson, Woodrow, 22, 59, 142, 145
Winchester, Lucy, 98
Windsor Castle, 2, 8, 10–11, 139, 149, 176, 178, 247, 250, 280
Winfrey, Oprah, 271
Winthrop, John, 231
Wood, Edward, 23–24
Woodard, Robert, 174, 191
World War I, xi, 59
World War II, xii, xiv–xv, xvi, 5–12, 14, 54, 116, 215, 217
Wright, Oliver, 82, 157
Wyman, Jane, 153

Xi Jinping, 274

Yeltsin, Boris, 191

Zantzinger, Amy, 215

About the Author

Susan Page is the award-winning Washington bureau chief of *USA Today*, where she writes about politics and the White House. Susan has covered eight White House administrations and twelve presidential elections. She has interviewed the past ten presidents and reported from six continents and dozens of foreign countries. Her previous bestselling books are *The Matriarch: Barbara Bush and the Making of an American Dynasty*; *Madam Speaker: Nancy Pelosi and the Lessons of Power*; and *The Rulebreaker: The Life and Times of Barbara Walters*. She lives in Washington, DC, with her husband, Carl Leubsdorf.